BAPTIST HISTORY.

J. M. CRAMP
1796-1881

BAPTIST HISTORY:

FROM THE

FOUNDATION OF THE CHRISTIAN CHURCH TO THE CLOSE OF THE EIGHTEENTH CENTURY.

BY

J. M. CRAMP, D.D.,

AUTHOR OF
"A TEXT-BOOK OF POPERY," "THE REFORMATION IN EUROPE," ETC., ETC.

PHILADELPHIA:
AMERICAN BAPTIST PUBLICATION SOCIETY,
1420 CHESTNUT STREET.
1869

he Baptist Standard Bearer, Inc.
NUMBER ONE IRON OAKS DRIVE • PARIS, ARKANSAS 72855

Thou hast given a *standard* to them that fear thee;
that it may be displayed because of the truth.
-- *Psalm 60:4*

*Reprinted
by*

THE BAPTIST STANDARD BEARER, INC.
No. 1 Iron Oaks Drive
Paris, Arkansas 72855
(501) 963-3831

THE WALDENSIAN EMBLEM
lux lucet in tenebris
"The Light Shineth in the Darkness"

ISBN #1-57978-907-2

Sicut lilium inter spinas sic amica mea inter filias

On The Cover: We use the symbol of the "lily among the thorns" from Song of Solomon 2:2 to represent the Baptist History Series. The Latin, *Sicut lilium inter spinas sic amica mea inter filias*, translates, "As the lily among thorns, so is my love among the daughters."

CONTENTS.

THE PRIMITIVE PERIOD.

CHAP.   PAGE

I. Introductory Remarks—Pædobaptist Concessions 13

II. The Apostolic Fathers—Justin Martyr—Irenæus 19

III. Tertullian—Baptism of Children in Africa—Origen—First Appearance of Infant Baptism—The Clinics—Christianity in England... 26

THE TRANSITION PERIOD.

I. The Catechumens—Progress of Infant Baptism—Delay of Baptism—Gregory Nazianzen—Chrysostom—Basil—Ephrem of Edessa—The Emperor Constantine—Immersion still the Mode... 41

II. Christian Intolerance—Justin's Law, enjoining Infant Baptism —The Novatians—The Donatists—Pelagianism........... 51

THE OBSCURE PERIOD.

I. The Manichæans—Cautions to the Student—All Opponents of Infant Baptism not Baptists—Account of the Paulicians— Their Views of Baptism............................... 67

II. Religious Reform in Europe—The Canons of Orleans—Arras —Berengarius—Miscellaneous Anecdotes................ 82

CONTENTS.

THE REVIVAL PERIOD.

CHAP.   PAGE

I. State of Affairs in Europe during this Period—The Crusades—Other Important Events—The Scholastic Divines and Philosophers—Universities—Printing.................... 91

II. Paulicians in France and Italy—General View of the Reform Movement—Various Names given to the Reformers—Sentiments held by them—False Charge of Manichæism—Their Activity—Reinerus Saccho's Account.................... 97

III. Success of the Reforming Parties—Consternation at Rome—Anathemas—The Dominican and Franciscan Orders—Sanguinary Persecution—Crusade against the Albigenses—The Inquisition Movement in England—John de Wycliffe—The Lollards—Bohemia 110

IV. Various Opinions respecting Baptism—Berengar—Peter of Bruys—Henry of Lausanne—Arnold of Brescia—Cologne—England—Lombers—Pope Lucius III.................... 123

V. Heretics of the Fourteenth and Fifteenth Centuries—Wycliffe's Sentiments on Baptism—The Bohemians—Baptism among the Waldenses—Church Government—Immersion......... 141

THE REFORMATION PERIOD.

I. Rise of the Reformation—Opinions held by the Baptists—Misrepresented by the Reformers—Their Wonderful Increase—Support under Sufferings..... 151

II. German Baptists—Thomas Munzer—The Peasant War—Michael Satler — Hans Schaffler — Salzburg — Wolfgang Brand-Huebert—The Burggraf of Alzey—Imperial Edicts.. 160

III. Persecuting Tenets of the Reformers—German Diets—The Congregation at Steinborn—Leonard Bernkop—The Crown of Straw—Johannes Bair—Hans Pichner—Hans Breal—Baptists in Italy... 169

CONTENTS.

CHAP. **PAGE**

IV. Baptists in Switzerland—Zuingli—Concessions of Bullinger and Meshovius—Disputations—Drownings—Felix Mantz—Balthazar Hubmeyer—Louis Hetzer—Emigration to Moravia—Jacob Hutter.................................. 178

V. The Netherlands—Sicke Snyder—Furious Edict—The Inquisition—Severities of Philip II.—Torture—Lysken—Gerrit Hase-poot—Joris Wippe—Private Executions—Horrid Rackings...................................... 195

VI. Biography of Menno Simon—Account of his Publications—Church Government among the Baptists—Missionary Excursions 212

VII. Baptists in England—Proclamation of Henry VIII.—Latimer's Sermon before Edward VI.—Baptists excepted from "Acts of Pardon"—Royal Commissions against them—Ridley—Cranmer—Joan Boucher—Rogers—Philpot—Bishop Hooper's Scruples—George Van Pare—Protestant Persecutions Inexcusable—Congregations in Essex and Kent—Bonner—Gardiner—Disputations in Jail—Queen Elizabeth's Proclamation against Baptists—Bishop Jewel—Archbishop Parker—Dutch Baptists.................. 231

VIII. Enormities Perpetrated at Munster and other places—Injustice of Ascribing them to Baptist Sentiments............. 249

THE TROUBLOUS PERIOD.

I. Baptists Persecuted by all other Sects—Liberal Policy of William, Prince of Orange—The "Union of Utrecht"—Differences of Opinion—Persecution in Moravia and in Switzerland.. 261

II. Dutch Baptists Persecuted in England—Account of Hendrick Terwoort and Jan Pieters—Their Martyrdom—Their Religious Sentiments—Whitgift's Invectives against the Baptists. 270

III. Severity of Elizabeth's Government—Bigotry of James I.—The Hampton Court Conference—Emigration—John

CONTENTS.

CHAP.   PAGE

Smyth's Church—Their Confessions—Bartholomew Legate—Extracts from Baptist Publications on Liberty of Conscience—The King's distress at their Increase....... 283

IV. Character of Charles I.—Sufferings during his Reign—First Particular Baptist Church—Samuel Howe—Dr. Featley's Book—Baptist Confessions of Faith—Toleration hated by the Presbyterians—Their attempts to put down the Baptists—Milton's Lines—The Assembly of Divines—Outcry against Immersion—Parliamentary Declaration in favor of the Baptists—Fearful "Ordinance" against them—Their Activity during the Commonwealth and the Protectorate—Cromwell's Baptist Officers—The "Triers"—Baptists in Ireland... 301

V. Character of Charles II. and James II.—Commencement of Persecution—Venner's Rebellion—Disclaimer by Baptists—Severe Sufferings—John James—Act of Uniformity—The Aylesbury Baptists—Benjamin Keach Pilloried—Conventicle Act—Five-Mile Act—Their Effects............. 322

VI. History of the Broadmead Church, Bristol................ 345

VII. Declaration of Indulgence—Confession of Faith—Fierce Persecution — Thomas Delaune — The Duke of Monmouth's Rebellion—Account of the Hewlings—Mrs. Gaunt—The Dark Time—Another Declaration of Indulgence—William Kiffin—The Glorious Revolution....... 357

VIII. Principles and Practices of the Denomination—Human Tradition Renounced—Freedom of Conscience Demanded—Personal Piety requisite to Church Fellowship—Purity of Discipline—Cases cited—Mode of Public Worship—Plurality of Elders—Communion—Singing—Laying on of Hands—The Sabbath.................................. 379

IX. Biographical Notices—John Smyth, Thomas Helwys, and John Spilsbury—Henry Derne—Francis Cornwell, A.M.—Christopher Blackwood—Major-General Harrison—Col. Hutchinson........ 391

CONTENTS.

CHAP. | PAGE

X. Biographical Notices Continued—Henry Jessey, A.M.—John Canne—Vavasor Powell—Abraham Cheare........ 406

XI. Biographical Notices Continued—John Toombes, B.D.—Francis Bampfield, A.M.—Henry D'Anvers—Edward Terrill—Dr. Du Veil—John Bunyan...................... 421

XII. Biographical Notices Continued—Thomas Grantham—Hanserd Knollys—Benjamin Keach—William Kiffin—Anecdotes... 434

XIII. Baptists in North America—Church at Providence—Baptists in Massachusetts—Persecuting Enactment against them—The Whipping of Obadiah Holmes—First Church at Holmes—First Church at Boston—Newport—Swansea —Other Churches—Roger Williams—Gregory Dexter— Obadiah Holmes—John Miles—Elias Keach............ 460

THE QUIET PERIOD.

I. General Character of the Period—Baptist General Assembly in London—Questions—Particular Baptist Fund—Baptist Board—The Deputies—The Widows' Fund—The Book Society—Bristol College—Dr. John Ward—Toleration Act—Schism Bill—Dissenters excluded from Office—Restrictions—Relief—Decline of the General Baptists—Communion Controversy—Effects of High Calvinism on the Particular Baptists—Commencement of Revival—Fuller and Sutcliffe—State of the Denomination in England— Foreign and Home Missions......................... 483

II. Biographical Notices—Dr. John Gale—John Skepp—John Brine—Dr. Gill—John Macgowan—Robert Robinson— Robert Hall, Sen.—John Ryland—The Stennetts—Benjamin Beddome—Samuel Pearce—John Piggott—The Wallins--Dr. Andrew Gifford--Mordecai Abbott, Esq.— Thomas and John Hollis—Miss Steele—Mrs. Seward.... 504

III. Progress of the Denomination in North America—Sufferings in New England—Mrs. Elizabeth Backus—Mrs.

CONTENTS.

CHAP. PAGE

Kimball—Virginia—Whitefield's Preaching—The "New Lights"—First Churches in Different States—Philadelphia Association—Other Associations—Correspondence with London Ministers—Great Revivals—Brown University—Nova Scotia—New Brunswick—Canada.................. 527

IV. Biographical Notices—Shubael Stearns—Daniel Marshall—Samuel Harris—John Gano—Lewis Lunsford—John Waller—Isaac Backus, A.M.—Morgan Edwards—David Thomas—Ebenezer Kinnersley—Oliver Hart—Drs. Mercer, Smith, Manning, Foster, and Stillman............. 553

STATISTICS AND REFLECTIONS.

I. Effects of the Mission Enterprise—Revivals—Extension of the Denomination—Statistical Table—Societies—Diversity and Adaptation of Talent—Baptist Agency now employed—Peculiarities of the Present Period—Duties of Baptists. 575

THE PRIMITIVE PERIOD.

CHRONOLOGICAL NOTES.

FROM A. D. 31 TO A. D. 254.

31. The Christian Church founded.
34. Martyrdom of Stephen.
36. Conversion of the Apostle Paul.
41. Admission of the Gentiles to the church.
44. Martyrdom of the Apostle James.
50. So-called Council at Jerusalem, Acts xv.
60. Paul's voyage to Rome.
63. Paul released from imprisonment.
64. Persecution at Rome under Nero.
68. Martyrdom of Paul and Peter.
70. Destruction of Jerusalem.
100. Death of the Apostle John.
166. Justin Martyr put to Death.
201. Persecution under Severus.
218. Death of Clement of Alexandria.
220. Death of Tertullian.
249. The Decian Persecution.
250. Commencement of Monachism.
254. Death of Origen.

BAPTIST HISTORY.

CHAPTER I.

Introductory Remarks—Pædobaptist Concessions.

BAPTISTS are often asked for information respecting the history of their distinctive opinions and practices. Inquirers say that statements various and even contradictory are made in their hearing, and they are very desirous of being put on the right track, so that they may be able to correct the erroneous and expose the false. The writer will endeavor to meet their wishes.

Let us begin with the New Testament. Who can read that blessed book with serious attention without coming to the conclusion that the religion of which it treats is personal and voluntary, and that none are worthy to be called Christians but those who "worship God in the Spirit, rejoice in Christ Jesus and have no confidence in the flesh?" (Phil. iii. 3.) When Moses addressed the Israelites and exhorted them to obedience, he included their children in his exhortations, because the children were in the covenant. Judaism, with all its privileges and responsibilities, was hereditary. The rights and duties of the parents became the rights and duties of their offspring, *as such*. It is not so under the New Dispensation. Men are not *born* Christians, but they *become* Christians when they repent and believe. "As many as received him, to them gave he power to become the sons of God, even to them that believe on his name; which were born, not of blood, nor of the will of the flesh, nor of the will of man, but of God" (John i. 12, 13). Judaism was a national institute: Christianity is an individual blessing. The Jews were a nation, dealt with as such, and separated from other nations; Christians are believers, taken out of all nations, and in Christianity "there is neither Greek nor Jew, circumcision nor uncircumcision, barbarian, Scythian, bond nor free, but Christ is all and in all" (Col. iii. 11). Hence, when the apostles wrote to Christian churches, their mode of address was altogether different from that adopted by Moses. They did not say, "you and your children," or represent the children as in covenant with God, and therefore entitled to certain rights and bound to the performance of certain duties. The churches to which they sent their epistles were spiritual societies—that is, associations of individuals professing "repentance toward God and faith toward our Lord Jesus Christ," to whom they had surrendered themselves, as their Prophet, Priest, and King. If those individuals were parents, they were taught to bring up their children "in the nurture and admonition of the Lord;" but their children were not *classed with them*, as the children of the Jews were, nor could they be, till they themselves also repented and believed. It is an obvious inference that no modern society deserves to be called a Christian church which is not founded on such principles as have been now explained.

If you were to place a New Testament in the hands of an intelligent, impartial person, who had never heard of our divisions and denominations, what idea would he be likely to form of the spirit and design of Christianity, or of a Christian church? Would he not see, in every part of the book, appeals to men's understandings and emotions, and such requisitions as could only be addressed to those who were capable of thinking and acting for themselves? Would he not conclude that Christianity has to do with *mind*—that a Christian must be a man of faith, and that a church is a voluntary society, formed of such men?

We come to the question of baptism. What is baptism? It is "the answer of a good conscience toward God" (1 Pet. iii. 21). It is "putting on Christ" (Gal. iii. 27). It is the voluntary act of a believer, an act of obedience and self-dedication. Such is the uniform tenor of the history. So the multitudes went out to John, "even all the land of Judæa, and they of Jerusalem, and were all baptized of him in the river of Jordan" (Mark i. 5). So the Samaritans, "when they believed Philip preaching the things concerning the kingdom of God, and the name of Jesus Christ, were baptized, both men and women" (Acts viii. 12). Mark it well—"men and women"—no children! So, in later times, the baptized were reminded of their obligations; "we are buried with him by baptism into death, that like as Christ was raised up from the dead by the glory of the Father, even so we also should walk in newness of life" (Rom. vi. 4).

The New Testament tells of the baptism of believers, and of churches composed of believers. We read of no other baptism, no other churches. It will not do to say in reply that all who were baptized were not believers and that all the members of apostolic churches were not sincere. There were, doubtless, hypocrites then, as there are hypocrites now. Even the apostles were sometimes deceived. But this does not affect the case. All who were baptized professed to be believers in Christ, and were baptized as such. The profession of faith was held to be essential to baptism and to church fellowship. None could profess faith who were incapable of exercising it. The act of profession implied understanding, conviction, approbation, choice.

This, then, is the starting-point. Here is the beginning of the history of baptism. With the New Testament only before us, we find baptism connected with the profession of faith. It is a personal, voluntary act; and such an act only is befitting Christianity.

But in the Christianity of the nineteenth century, or what is called such, there is a service of another kind. It is sprinkling—not immersion; and the subjects are infants—not believers. How is this? In what manner was it introduced? How and when did it originate?

These questions will be answered hereafter. This chapter will be closed by placing before the reader a few extracts from Pædobaptist writers of the nineteenth century, showing how the learned men of these times regard the subject, in an historical point of view.

NORTH BRITISH REVIEW, *Presbyterian* (ascribed to the Rev. Dr. Hanna). "Scripture knows nothing of the baptism of infants. There is absolutely not a single trace of it to be found in the New Testament."[1]

PROFESSOR JACOBI, University of Berlin, *Reformed Church*. "Infant baptism was established neither by

[1] August, 1852.

Christ nor the apostles. In all places where we find the necessity of baptism notified, either in a dogmatic or historical point of view, it is evident that it was only meant for those who were capable of comprehending the word preached, and of being converted to Christ by an act of their own will."[1]

Dr. HAGENBACH, Basle, *Reformed Church*. "The passages from Scripture which are thought to intimate that infant baptism had come into use in the primitive church, are doubtful, and prove nothing."[2]

NEANDER, *the Church Historian*. "Baptism was administered at first only to adults, as men were accustomed to conceive baptism and faith as strictly connected. We have all reason for not deriving infant baptism from apostolic institution; and the recognition of it which followed somewhat later, as an apostolical tradition, serves to confirm this hypothesis." . . . "In respect to the form of baptism, it was, in conformity with the original institution and the original import of the symbol, performed by immersion, as a sign of entire baptism into the Holy Spirit, of being entirely penetrated by the same."[3]

PROFESSOR STUART, late of Andover, *Congregationalist*. "There are no commands, or plain and certain examples, in the New Testament, relative to infant baptism."[4]

REV. DR. HODGE, of Princeton, New Jersey, *Presbyterian*. "In no part of the New Testament is any other condition of membership in the church prescribed than

---

[1] Kitto's *Cyclopædia of Biblical Literature*. Art. "Baptism."
[2] *History of Doctrines*, i. 193.
[3] *History of the Church*, i. 310, 311.
[4] Haynes' *Baptist Denomination*, p. 31.

that contained in the answer of Philip to the eunuch who desired baptism. The church, therefore, is in its essential nature a company of believers."[1]

Rev. Dr. Woods, *Congregationalist*. "We have no express precept or example for infant baptism in all our holy writings."[2]

Dr. Chalmers, *Presbyterian*. "The original meaning of the word baptism is immersion; and though we regard it as a point of indifference whether the ordinance so named be performed in this way or by sprinkling, yet we doubt not that the prevalent style of the administrations in the apostles' days was of an actual submersion of the whole body under water."[3]

Dr. Bloomfield, *Episcopalian*. "There is here (Rom. vi. 4) plainly a reference to the ancient mode of baptism by immersion; and I agree with Koppe and Rosenmüller (two German commentators), that there is reason to regret it should have been abandoned in most Christian churches, especially as it has so evidently a reference to the mystic sense of baptism."[4]

Rev. W. J. Conybeare, M.A., *Episcopalian*. 'This passage (Rom. vi. 4) cannot be understood unless it be borne in mind that the primitive baptism was by immersion."[5]

Many more quotations might be given, but these will be sufficient. It will be observed that none of these writers are Baptists. But they do not venture to affirm that infant sprinkling is derived from the New Testament. Learned Pædobaptists generally admit that believers only were baptized in apostolic times.

---

[1] Haynes' *Baptist Denomination*, p. 31. [2] *Ibid.*
[3] *Lectures on Romans*, ch. vi. 4. [4] *Critical Digest*, in loc.
[5] *Life and Writings of St. Paul*, ii. American Edition.

CHAPTER II.

The Apostolic Fathers—Justin Martyr—Irenæus.

THIS, then, is our starting-point. The baptism of the New Testament is the baptism of believers. Our next inquiry will be, How the post-apostolic church thought and acted on this subject.

Christian baptism, as instituted by the Saviour, and practiced by the apostles, was the immersion of believers in water, "in the name of the Father, and of the Son, and of the Holy Ghost." It was the declaration of their adhesion to Christ, and the symbol of their death to sin. It was in every case the act of a free agent, and thus it harmonized with the spiritual nature of Christianity. All this is now generally admitted.

The next inquiry is, Did the usages of the period immediately succeeding the apostolic accord with these views? Or did they indicate any change or any departure from them?

Here it is necessary to interpose a caution. Apostolic example has the force of authority. It is the inspired exposition of the law. Not so the example of the primitive churches as they are called, that is, as they existed after the apostolic age. The plainness of the Christian ceremonial offended those who were fond of pomp and show, and the equality of the Christian brotherhood offended those who loved power. Hence corruptions crept in. They were anticipated and foretold by the apostles. And hence the necessity of distinguishing between divine law and human tradition. We have no power to change the law, or to make any addition to it. The assumption of such power in primitive times was a fatal error, the evil consequences of which are felt to this day. Instead of adhering strictly to the Scripture rule, men dealt with Christianity as they dealt with systems of philosophy. They treated it as if it were susceptible of improvement, and might be accommodated to circumstances. They took the liberty to engraft on it certain peculiarities of Judaism, and even of Paganism. They multiplied forms to the sore detriment of the spirit and the life.

It has been customary to appeal to the opinions and practices of the churches of the first three centuries after the apostles. In the controversy with the Church of Rome it is an available argument to this extent, that it takes from that church the plea of antiquity, since it proves that Romanism, as such, did not exist in the above-mentioned period. Yet it cannot be denied that the first steps toward Romanism were taken. Professing Christians soon abandoned the high ground of Scripture, and took pleasure in "vain deceit" and "will-worship." In this they are not examples for our imitation. We must go farther back—to the Book itself—to the recorded enactments of the Divine Lawgiver; and our object will be to ascertain how far, and by whom, the Saviour's will has been regarded.

This can only be accomplished by consulting the writers of the times now under consideration. "Apostolic Fathers" first claim attention. They are: Barnabas, Hermas, Clement of Rome, Ignatius, and Polycarp. To these some add Papias, a few fragments only of whose writings have been preserved by Eusebius, the ecclesiastical historian. They contain no reference to the subject now before us.

The writings ascribed to Barnabas and Hermas were probably composed in the second century by some weakminded Christians, who fathered their own poor effusions on the coadjutor of the Apostle Paul and the brother mentioned by him in his epistle to the Romans (ch. xvi. 14). But though they are not genuine books, they may be regarded as witnesses to the religious views entertained by the Christians of those times. In the work ascribed to Barnabas we find the following passage: "We descend into the water laden with sins and corruption, and ascend bearing fruit, having in the heart the fear [toward God], and in the spirit the hope toward Jesus."[1] There are several references to baptism in the writings bearing the name of Hermas, some of them exceedingly fanciful, but there is not the slightest allusion to infant baptism; he speaks repeatedly of descending into the water, and ascending out of it, evidently adverting to immersion.

Let us pass on to Clement of Rome. He was bishop, or pastor, of the Church of Rome, and died about the year 100. His epistle to the Corinthians is a precious gem. Baptism is not mentioned in it. A second epistle to the Corinthians is attributed to him, but without sufficient grounds. There is one sentence referring to baptism. It is as follows: "If we do not keep the baptism pure and undefiled, with what confidence shall we enter the kingdom of God?"[2]

[1] Ch. ii. [2] Sect. 6.

Ignatius comes next. He was pastor at Antioch in Syria, and suffered martyrdom by exposure to wild beasts at Rome, A.D. 116. Several letters were written by him, which have come down to us in an interpolated state. There are a few allusions to baptism. He refers twice to the baptism of our Saviour by John. He tells the Smyrneans that the ordinance should not be administered without the bishop.[1] In writing to Polycarp he uses this military phraseology: "Let your baptism continue as a shield, faith as a helmet, love as a spear."[2] This is all.

Polycarp suffered martyrdom by fire at Smyrna, A.D. 167. An epistle to the Philippians is attributed to him. It does not allude either to baptism or the Lord's supper.

Justin Martyr was a philosophic Christian. He was put to death at Rome, A.D. 166. In his first "Apology," addressed to the Emperor Marcus Aurelius, he gives the following account of baptism as practiced in his days: "As many as are persuaded and believe that what we teach is true, and undertake to conform their lives to our doctrine, are instructed to fast and pray, and entreat from God the remission of their past sins, we fasting and praying together with them. They are then conducted by us to a place where there is water, and are regenerated in the same manner in which we were ourselves regenerated. For they are then washed in the name of God the Father and Lord of the Universe, and of our Saviour Jesus Christ, and of the Holy Spirit."[3] Observe the manner in which he speaks of baptism. The candidates are those who are "persuaded" and "believe," and the ordinance is administered, not by sprinkling, but by the washing of immersion. Semisch, the learned biographer of

---

[1] Sect. 8.   [2] Sect. 6.   [3] Sect. 79.

Justin, says, "Whenever Justin refers to baptism, adults appear as the objects to whom the sacred rite is administered. Of infant baptism he knows nothing."

Irenæus became bishop of Lyons, in France, A. D. 177, and died A. D. 202. He mentions baptism several times, and seemingly connects it with regeneration, as Justin had done before him, in the passage just cited; but I am strongly inclined to think that neither Justin nor Irenæus thought that men were regenerated in or by baptism. Their object was to show that as the convert came under new obligations and entered into new relationships at his baptism, it was equivalent to the assumption of a new life: he was in this profession "born again unto God," and publicly entered into the spiritual family. I am confirmed in this view of the subject by another representation given of baptism by Justin in the course of his narrative. He says: "This washing is called '*illumination*,' because those who learn these things are enlightened in their minds."[1] Baptism is not "illumination," but it is so called because it is connected with an enlightened state of mind: in like manner, baptism is called "Regeneration," not because it regenerates, but because it is connected with a regenerate state and a new life, profession of which is then made.

Two passages used to be quoted by Pædobaptist writers, as testimonies in favor of infant baptism. One is from Justin Martyr: he writes thus: "Many men and many women, sixty and seventy years old, who from children have been disciples of Christ, preserve their continence."[2] The other is from Irenæus. These are his words: "He came to save all persons by himself; all, I say, who are

---

[1] Sect. 80.   [2] *Apol.* i. sect. 18.

regenerated by him unto God—infants, and children, and boys, and young men, and old men." But baptism is not mentioned in either of these passages, and modern critics have confessed that they afford no support to the Pædobaptist cause. All that Justin means is, that he knew many persons who had been disciples of Christ from early life; and he expressly connects "choice" and "knowledge" with baptism, of which infants are incapable. The language used by Irenæus " merely expresses," says Hagenbach (a German Pædobaptist), " the beautiful idea that Jesus was Redeemer *in* every stage of life, and *for* every stage of life; but it does not say that he became Redeemer for children by water baptism."[1]

We are now brought to the close of the second century. But few Christian authors had as yet appeared. Is it not remarkable, however, that in none of their writings which have been preserved is there any mention of infant baptism? If it existed, it must have been a prominent thing in the church transactions of the period. But these Christians knew nothing of it. Neither Clement of Rome, nor Ignatius, nor Justin, nor any other author wrote a word which would lead us to suppose that infants were baptized. There is a singular difference in this respect between the statements of these Christian Fathers and the correspondence of modern Pædobaptist missionaries. Read the letters of missionaries in the reports of missionary societies. How careful they are to give us full information respecting the number of children that have been baptized, and how numerous are the references

---

[1] *History of Doctrines,* i 193 Dr. Ira Chase has examined all the passages in Irenæus in which the phrase "regenerated unto God" occurs. See *Bibliotheca Sacra,* November, 1849.

to them! With what solicitude are arrangements framed, and their operation watched over, with a view to the religious instruction and training of baptized children! We search the Christian writings of the first two centuries in vain for anything of this kind. That the Christians of those times gave their children the benefit of religious teaching and example is not to be doubted; but they did not baptize them till they could answer for themselves, and voluntarily assume the obligations of the Christian profession.

We have now advanced two hundred years, and have not yet found infant baptism. It will come in sight soon along with other corruptions and inventions.

CHAPTER III.

Tertullian—Baptism of Children in Africa—Origen—First Appearance of Infant Baptism—The Clinics—Christianity in England.

WE are now approaching the development of those corrupting influences which had been at work from the apostolic age, silently sapping the foundations of personal piety. In adverting to the language employed by Justin Martyr and Irenæus, I endeavored to clear those authors from the imputation of unevangelical sentiments, and so interpret their expressions in a sound and safe sense. But though it may be possible to hold *them* guiltless, I fear that many of their contemporaries were fairly open to the charge of holding unscriptural opinions. A notion had grown up that baptism actually accomplished what was professed in it. As the miraculous gifts of the Spirit were often bestowed upon believers immediately after their baptism, men began to think that it was then first that the Spirit wrought on the soul. And as the act of obed.ence to the Saviour in the ordinance was commonly associated with spiritual enjoyments and manifestations, and happy converts, like the eunuch, "went on their way rejoicing," there were some who came to the conclusion that what was *connected* with baptism was *produced* by it. If the convictions that led the candidate to the baptismal water, and impelled him to the act of dedication to the Saviour's service, were greatly strengthened at his baptism, so that he then experienced a more intensely satisfying consciousness of pardon and union with Christ, *results* were confounded with *causes*, and the new believer was taught to ascribe to baptism the blessings which he had in fact enjoyed before, but which he realized more vividly when he obeyed the Lord.

This step taken, the transition to yet more perilous errors and evils was easy. When baptism was thus invested with a kind of supernatural power, the outward act was soon substituted for the spiritual qualification. Instead of directing inquiries to the atonement, and encouraging them to seek by prayer for the teaching and aid of the Holy Spirit, the religious instructions of that age expatiated on the vast powers of baptism. Tertullian, for instance, a Christian writer who flourished at the close of the second and the commencement of the third century, " declares the following spiritual blessings to be consequent upon baptism: remission from sins, deliverance from death, regeneration, and participation in the Holy Spirit. He calls it the 'sacrament of washing,' the 'blessed sacrament of water,' the 'laver of regeneration.'"[1]

When such opinions as these were entertained, is it not evident that the door was open to manifold abuses, and that those who had so far departed from Christian truth would be likely enough to interfere with Christian worship and obedience?

Tertullian was a native of Carthage in Africa, and spent most of his life in that city. It is supposed that he

[1] Bishop Kaye's *Tertullian*, p. 432.

died about the year 220. His tract, "*De Baptismo*," was probably written twenty years before his death. From that tract and from other writings of his, we learn that at the beginning of the third century there were some strange additions to the ordinance of baptism. The new convert was placed among the catechumens, that he might be fully instructed in the faith. After a sufficient probation he was admitted to baptism. The following account of the manner in which it was administered is taken from the "Ecclesiastical History of the Second and Third Centuries, illustrated from the Writings of Tertullian," by the late Bishop of Bristol:

"The candidate, having been prepared for its due reception by frequent prayers, fasts, and vigils, professed in the presence of the congregation and under the hand of the president, that he renounced the devil, his pomp, and angels. He was then plunged into the water three times, in allusion to the Three Persons of the Holy Trinity, making certain responses which, like the other forms here mentioned, were not prescribed in Scripture, but rested on custom and tradition. He then tasted a mixture of milk and honey—was anointed with oil, in allusion to the practice under the Mosaic Dispensation, of anointing those who were appointed to the priesthood, since all Christians are, in a certain sense, supposed to be priests—and was signed with the sign of the cross. Lastly, followed the imposition of hands, the origin of which ceremony is referred by our author to the benediction pronounced by Jacob upon the sons of Joseph."[1]

The administration of baptism was at that early period encumbered by ceremonies of merely human inven-

[1] P. 434.

tion; in fact, Tertullian complains in another work that "various forms and observances had been introduced into the Christian worship, of which some bore too close a resemblance to the customs and practices of the Gentiles." The signing with the sign of the cross was a superstition early practiced among the Christians. They crossed themselves perpetually. Whatever they undertook or engaged in—when they went out—when they returned home—when they dressed themselves, or put on their shoes, or sat down to a meal, or went to the bath or to bed—the sign of the cross was associated with everything. We need not wonder that the heathen suspected it to savor of magic.

I have mentioned these particulars for the purpose of showing that at the beginning of the third century religious declension had considerably advanced. No one will now be surprised at hearing that an attempt was made to extend the administration of baptism, in an unwarrantable manner. It is referred to by Tertullian in his tract, "*De Baptismo*," in terms of strong disapproval. Some persons had introduced children (not *infants*) to baptism, or advocated the administration of the ordinance to them. Tertullian indignantly reproves the practice. "Let them come," he says, "when they are taught to whom they may come; let them become Christians when they are able to know Christ. Why should this innocent age hasten to the remission of sins?"[1] Now, is it not obvious that Tertullian was entirely unacquainted with *infant* baptism, and that this *children's* baptism, which then first began to be talked of, was regarded by him as an unauthorized innovation? The sign of the

---
[1] *De Baptismo*, ch. xviii.

cross, the giving of milk and honey, and similar ceremonies, were comparatively small matters, trifling circumstances; they were uncalled-for additions to the ordinance, and were so far mischievous, but they did not change it. It was still connected with knowledge, and repentance, and faith. But the admission of children, if they were not old enough to repent and believe, would change the ordinance. It would dissever it from those religious prerequisites with which it had been hitherto uniformly associated. The Gentile or Jewish rites which had been added to it, tended to make it more imposing, and so attracted the notice of the weak-minded; but to allow children to be baptized, who were not subjects of repentance and faith, would be, in Tertullian's opinion, to revolutionize the ordinance altogether. We act more wisely, he remarked, in temporal matters; surely we should not admit to baptism those whom we consider unfit to manage temporal affairs. So he argued.

The case is quite clear. Children (not *infants*, but probably children from six to ten years old) are first mentioned in connection with the ordinance at the beginning of the third century, and then with disapprobation. "Tertullian's opposition," the learned Baron Bunsen remarks, "is to the baptism of young, growing children; he does not say a word about new-born infants."[1]

Some writers have laboured hard to prove that Origen referred to infant baptism in his writings, as a fact existing in his times, and that he assigned to it an apostolic original. Origen was the most learned Christian of that age. He flourished from A.D. 203 to A.D. 254, and at-

[1] *Christianity and Mankind*, ii. 115.

tained high repute, both as a teacher in the catechetical school of Alexandria, and as an author. But his references are to *child* baptism, not to *infant* baptism, and the difference between him and Tertullian is that the latter decidedly objected to the practice, while Origen spoke of it with approbation. How far, however, did that approbation extend? Only to the baptism of such children as were capable of instruction, and gave indications of personal piety; for he uniformly taught that "the benefit of baptism depended on the deliberate purpose of the baptized." His reply to an objection of Celsus expresses his views. That heathen writer, having stated that "intelligent and respectable persons" were invited to initiation in the heathen mysteries, proceeds thus: "And now let us hear what persons the Christians invite. Whoever, they say, is a sinner, whoever is unintelligent, whoever is a mere child, and, in short, whoever is a miserable and contemptible creature, the kingdom of God shall receive him." Origen answers him in the following manner: "In reply to these accusations we say, it is one thing to invite those who are diseased in the soul to a healing, and it is another to invite the healthy to a knowledge and discernment of things more divine. And we, knowing the difference, first call men to be healed. We exhort sinners to come to the instruction that teaches them not to sin, and the unintelligent to come to that which produces in them understanding, *and the little children to rise in elevation of thought to the man*, and the miserable to come to a more fortunate state, or—what is more proper to say—a state of happiness. But when those of the exhorted that make progress show that they have been cleansed by the word, and, as much as possible, have lived a better life, THEN we invite them to be initiated amongst us."[1]

Such children as Origen here describes would be "initiated," that is, baptized, by any Baptists in these days. If they have been "cleansed by the word," what more can we require? Tertullian's objection seems to have arisen from the undue eagerness of some persons to hurry children to the baptismal water before they could fully understand and receive the truth. But neither of these Fathers refers to infants. They ascribe to baptism influences which are nowhere mentioned in the New Testament. They used language implying that an outward ceremony produced an inward, spiritual effect. They taught the necessity of baptism in order to pardon and salvation. And yet they also maintained the necessity of repentance and faith; and therefore they demanded, that if young children were baptized, they should not be admitted to the ordinance till they were "able to know Christ," and were "cleansed by the word."

We have at length arrived at the origin of Infant Baptism. Its birth-place was a district of Northern Africa, one of the least enlightened portions of the earth in that age; the time, the middle of the third century; the occasion, certain unscriptural notions which had gradually gained prevalence respecting the design and efficacy of the baptismal rite. Having adverted to those extravagances in a former chapter, it is unnecessary to adduce further proof. But the reader can easily trace the progress of error. When believers, newly baptized, rejoiced in the forgiveness of sin, and exhibited satisfactory evi-

---

[1] See *Christian Review*, April, 1854, containing an article by Mr. Ira Chase on the "Opinions of Origen respecting Baptism."

dence of a regenerated state, men soon began to regard pardon and regeneration as the effects of baptism. Hence sprung the opinion of its necessity to salvation. That being admitted, the question of time came next under consideration. Was it not desirable to obtain pardon and regeneration at the earliest possible period? And besides, were not infants circumcised under the Jewish Law? These questions were in the mind of Fidus, a bishop of some place in Northern Africa. We can have no doubt as to his duty under such circumstances. He ought to have searched the New Testament, if he had one—we cannot be sure of it, for books were scarce and dear in those days—and inquired into the differences between the Old and the New Dispensations, the carnal and the spiritual Israel. If he had carried on the inquiry fairly, his difficulties would have been removed without further reference. But he either did not or would not conduct the requisite investigation. Cyprian was at that time bishop of Carthage, and was reverenced as a great authority in all church affairs. Fidus wrote to Cyprian. Certain persons, he said, had advised the baptism of infants immediately after birth; but he could not agree with them, and particularly for this reason, that whereas it was customary to receive the baptized with a brotherly kiss, a newly-born infant could not be so received, being treated as unclean for several days after its coming into the world. He thought it best, therefore, to wait till the eighth day, and to baptize the infant at the same time at which, under the law, it would have been circumcised. But he asked advice of Cyprian, who laid the case before a council which had assembled at Carthage, in the year 252, for the settlement of various ecclesiastical matters.

Sixty-six bishops met on that occasion. The answer s given in a letter written by Cyprian, from which the following extract is taken:

"None of us could agree to your opinion. On the contrary, it is the opinion of us all, that the mercy and grace of God must be refused to no human being, so soon as he is born; for since our Lord says in his gospel, 'The Son of man is not come to destroy men's souls, but to save them,' so everything that lies in our power must be done that no soul may be lost. As God has no respect of persons, so too he has no respect of age, offering himself as a Father with equal freeness to all, that they may be enabled to obtain the heavenly grace. As to what you say, that the child in its first days of its birth is not *clean* to the touch, and that each of us would shrink from kissing such an object, even this, in our opinion, ought to present no obstacles to the bestowment of heavenly grace; for it is written, 'To the pure all things are pure;' and none of us ought to revolt at that which God has condescended to create. Although the child be but just born, yet it is no such object that any one ought to demur at kissing it to impart the divine grace and the salutation of peace, since each of us must be led, by his own religious sensibility, to think upon the creative hands of God, fresh from the completion of their work, which we kiss in the newly-formed man when we take in our arms what God has made. As to the rest, if anything could prove a hindrance to men in the attainment of grace, much rather might those be hindered whose maturer years have involved them in heavy sins. But if even the chief of sinners, who have been exceedingly guilty before God, receive the forgiveness of sin on coming to the faith, and no one is precluded from baptism and from grace, how much less should the child be kept back, which, as it is but just born, cannot have sinned, but has only brought with it, by its descent from Adam, the infection of the old death; and which may the more easily obtain the remission of sins, because the sins which are forgiven it are not its own, but those of another?"[1]

This is a very misty theology. In fact, the religion of great numbers in the third century was a compound of Judaism and Paganism, with a slight seasoning of Christianity. Gaudy ceremonials were delighted in, and the strange power which had been ascribed to magical influences was transferred to the ordinances of the gospel. The immersion in water, the eating of the bread, and the drinking of the wine were associated in their minds, as producing causes, with spiritual transformations and blessings. The bodily act was substituted for the mental, and "faith was made void." I do not affirm that every professing Christian was enveloped in this darkness, but it is too evident that the views of the majority were confused, and that, under the leadership of such men as Cyprian, the churches were fast drifting into dangerous notions.

Nevertheless, they were consistent in some things. They did not separate baptism from the Lord's supper, as is done by all Pædobaptists in these times. They held that those who were entitled to the one had an equal right to the other. When the infant had been plunged into the baptismal water, it was considered a member of

[1] Labbe and Cossart, *Concil.* i., 742-744. Cypriani Opera, Pars I., p. 168-171. Ed. Goldhorn, Leipsic, 1838.

the church, and received the Lord's supper. If it was too young to eat the bread, they poured the wine down its throat. This, too, originated in Northern Africa, and there only we find it in the period now under our notice.[1]

Another innovation is traced to the third century. I allude to *clinic* baptism, that is, the baptism of sick persons confined to their beds. It was not baptism, properly so called, as they were only sprinkled with water, or had water poured on them. The reason alleged for this departure from apostolic practice was the necessity of baptism to the salvation of the soul, and the consequent danger of deferring it, lest the sickness should terminate in death. Thus one error led to another. If those clinics recovered, they were not baptized afterward; but they were not admitted to the ministry. Novatian, however, was an exception to this rule. He had been sprinkled or received a pouring on his bed, when his dissolution was hourly expected. After his recovery, his eminent qualifications for the ministry induced the churches to deviate from the established custom, and he was ordained. Subsequently, he took a high stand as a reformer.

We are now brought to the year 254, the date of Origen's death. The downward tendency is before us. Baptism, at first the voluntary act of a believer in Christ, has become, in numerous instances, the performance of a ceremony upon an unconscious infant. In all these cases the design of the Christian profession is subverted. Members are introduced into the churches who are necessarily destitute of the spiritual qualifications enumerated in the

[1] Bingham's *Christian Antiquities*, book xii., chap. i., sect. 3, and book xv., chap. iv., sect. 7.

New Testament. It does not require the gift of prophecy to foretell the disastrous consequences. Religious declension was both the cause and the effect of the introduction of infant baptism. The cause, inasmuch as so great a change could not have taken place if the Christian mind had not previously lost a due sense of the spiritual nature of religion: the effect, since the unholy mixture arising from the new arrangement could not but prove injurious to the interests of piety. "What communion hath light with darkness?"

It may be expected that some account of the introduction of Christianity into England should be given. It is highly probable that the gospel reached the country at an early period, by means of merchants of Gaul in the first instance, and of missionaries afterward. But dates and details are wanting. The statements of Tertullian and others are rather rhetorical flourishes than truthful records. That Joseph of Arimathea went to England, with several companions, and built a church "made of rods, wattled or interwoven," in which they "watched, prayed, fasted, preached, having *high* meditations under a *low* roof, and *large* hearts betwixt *narrow* walls,"[1] is now generally acknowledged to be a fable. That the Apostle Paul visited Britain when he traveled "to the extreme bounds of the West," as Clemens Romanus expressed it, is easier said than proved. That "Claudia," mentioned by Paul in 2 Tim. iv. 21, was of British origin, is a conjecture, and nothing more The story of King Lucius, as Dean Milman observes, " is a legend."[2] We must be content to remain in ignorance of the special instrument employed

---

[1] Fuller's *Church History*, cent. i., sect. 13.
[2] *History of Latin Christianity*, book iv., chap. iii.

for the enlightenment of England, and can only remark that the Christian church, when planted there, harmonized, in its doctrines and services, with the churches of Gaul, from which country missionary expeditions naturally took their westward course

THE TRANSITION PERIOD.

CHRONOLOGICAL NOTES.

FROM A. D. 254 TO A. D. 604.

258. Martyrdom of Cyprian.
303. General persecution.
306. Accession of Constantine.
311. Rise of Donatism.
312. Constantine's alleged vision of the cross.
318. Rise of Arianism.
325. Council of Nice—the First *General* Council.
337. Baptism and Death of Constantine.
373. Death of Athanasius.
381. Second General Council, at Constantinople.
406. Rise of Pelagianism.
420. Death of Jerome.
428. Rise of Nestorianism.
430. Death of Augustine.
431. Third General Council, at Ephesus.
451. Fourth General Council, at Chalcedon.
476. Dissolution of the Western Empire.
529. The Benedictine Rule established.
553. Fifth General Council, at Constantinople.
596. The Mission of Augustine, the monk, to England.
604. Death of Gregory the Great.

CHAPTER I.

The Catechumens—Progress of Infant Baptism—Delay of Baptism—Gregory Nazianzen—Chrysostom—Basil—Ephrem of Edessa—The Emperor Constantine—Immersion still the Mode.

THE statements made in former chapters are abundantly confirmed by impartial divines and historians. One of the most learned men of the present day, the Baron Bunsen, formerly Prussian ambassador in England, writes thus in his work entitled, "Christianity and Mankind:"

"The apostolical church made the school the connecting link between herself and the world. The object of this education was admission into the free society and brotherhood of the Christian community. The church adhered rigidly to the principle as constituting the true purport of the baptism ordained by Christ, that no one can be a member of the communion of saints but by *his own* free act and deed, his own solemn vow made in presence of the church. It was with this understanding that the candidate for baptism was immersed in water, and admitted as a brother upon his confession of the Father, the Son, and the Holy Ghost. It is understood, therefore, in the exact sense (1 Pet. iii. 21), not as being a mere bodily purification, but as a vow made to God with a good conscience through faith in Jesus Christ. This vow was preceded by a confession of Christian faith made in the face of the church, in which the catechumen expressed that faith in Christ, and in the sufficiency of the salvation offered by him. It was a vow to live for the time to come to God and for his neighbor, not to the world and for self; a vow of faith in his becoming a child of God, through the communion of his only begotten Son, in the Holy Ghost; a vow of the most solemn kind, for life and for death. The keeping of this pledge was the condition of continuance in the church; its infringement entailed repentance or excommunication. All church discipline was based upon this voluntary pledge, and the responsibility thereby self-imposed. But how could such a vow be received without examination? How could such examination be passed without instruction and observation?

"As a general rule, the ancient church fixed three years for this preparation, supposing the candidate, whether heathen or Jew, to be competent to receive it. With Christian children the condition was the same, except that the term of probation was curtailed according to circumstances. Pædobaptism in the more modern sense, meaning thereby the baptism of new-born infants with the vicarious promises of parents and other sponsors, *was utterly unknown to the early church, not only down to the end of the second, but indeed to the middle of the third century.*" [1]

The catechumen institution may be traced back to an early period—as far as the second century. At first, as we gather from the New Testament, converts were bap-

[1] II. pp. 105, 106.

tized as soon as they acknowledged Christ. Afterward, it was judged expedient to prepare them for baptism by a course of instruction, generally extending, as Baron Bunsen states in the above-cited passage, to three years. In the first ages they *experienced* Christianity, and then professed it. In after-times they *learned* Christianity, and that, in too many instances, was all; conversion and experience were unknown. But this catechumenical system was adapted to those only who were able to learn, and therefore excluded infants. Its very existence was incompatible with infant baptism, and the consequence was that when the latter became general the former disappeared, or dwindled down to an unmeaning form. But in the period which is now before us the catechumens were a distinct order. Certain persons, called catechists, were appointed to instruct them. They occupied a separate place in Christian assemblies, and were required to withdraw before the celebration of the Lord's supper, which they were not permitted to witness. From the Latin phrase used in dismissing the assembly, the whole service was called "*Missa*," from which the English word "mass" is derived. There was the *Missa Catechumenorum*, or service of the catechumens, and the *Missa Fidelium*, or service of the faithful; the former comprising the reading of the Scriptures and the sermon; the latter, the Lord's supper and the devotional exercises which preceded and accompanied it, denoting the fellowship of believers, to which class the catechumens did not belong till after their baptism.

It is a very noticeable fact, that the baptismal service, as prescribed in the earliest liturgies, was prepared for catechumens only There was no provision for infants

Had infant baptism been then in existence, the ecclesiastical arrangements would have recognized it, and there would have been a twofold service, as there is now in the Church of England—one for infants and the other for "those of riper years."

I have called the period from A. D. 254 to A. D. 604 the "Transition Period," because, as far as baptism was concerned, and, indeed, in many other particulars which might be adduced, if needful, the ecclesiastical system was in a formative state. It was neither one thing nor the other, but a mixture of incongruities. The catechumenical arrangement was founded on the theory of baptism on a personal confession of faith, and so far accorded with the New Testament. But infant baptism had sprung up in Northern Africa, and was gradually extending itself through the powerful influence of Augustine, bishop of Hippo, who wrote largely on the subject. His sheet-anchor in the argument was the supposed efficacy of baptism in removing the defilement of original sin. These two theories were in opposition to each other, for if all candidates for baptism were to become catechumens and receive preparatory instruction, infant baptism had no place. Yet there it was, daily gaining ground. Augustine's authority gave it the advantage in the West; but in the East the baptism of children from three to ten years of age, who could in some sort answer for themselves, lingered much longer. And great numbers followed the example of the Emperor Constantine, who deferred his baptism till the latest possible period, that all his sins might be washed away at once, as he, poor man, vainly imagined they would be, by the administration of the ordinance. Thus we find a great diversity of practice. There was infant baptism spreading from North Africa—child baptism prevalent in the East—catechumen baptism, properly so called, the ordinary mode of admitting converts—and procrastinated baptism, including such cases as Constantine's. It will be seen, then, that this period is rightly termed the "Transition Period."

Neander says, "It was still very far from being the case, especially in the Greek Church, that infant baptism, although acknowledged to be necessary, was generally introduced into practice. Partly, the same mistaken notions which arose from confounding the thing represented by baptism with the outward rite, and which afterward led to the over-valuation of infant baptism, and partly, the frivolous tone of thinking, the indifference to all higher concerns, which characterized so many who had only exchanged the Pagan for a Christian outside—all this together contributed to bring it about, that among the Christians of the East, infant baptism, though acknowledged in theory to be necessary, yet entered *so rarely and with so much difficulty* into the church-life during the first half of this period." [1]

"The baptism of infants," Gieseler observes, "did not become universal till after the death of Augustine." [2]

Had infant baptism been universally regarded as a divine ordinance, it would have been everywhere observed, and Christian parents would have been scrupulously heedful of their duty toward their children in this matter. But it was not so. Some of the best men of the time were children of pious parents, but were not baptized till they attained maturity. I say again, this could not have taken place if infant baptism had been from the beginning

---

[1] *History of the Church*, ii. 319.   [2] *Ecclesiastical History*, ii. 47.

regarded as an apostolic institution. A few instances may be given.

Gregory Nazianzen, archbishop of Constantinople who died in the year 389, and whose father was bishop of Nazianzen, was not baptized till he was nearly thirty years old. He expressly intimated his disapproval of infant baptism, in one of his public discourses, and advised that children should not be baptized till they were three years old or more, at which time they might be able to answer the questions proposed to candidates.[1]

Chrysostom, the golden-mouthed preacher, also arch bishop of Constantinople, and born of Christian parents, received baptism at the age of twenty-eight. He died in the year 407.

Basil of Cæsarea, though he could boast of Christian ancestry for several generations, was not baptized till he was twenty-seven years old. Addressing catechumens, he says (A. D. 350), " Do you demur, and loiter, and put it off, when you have been *from a child* catechised in the word? Are you not acquainted with the truth? *Having been always learning* it, are you not yet come to the knowledge of it? A seeker all your life long, a considerer till you are old? When will you become one of us?" Observe—"*from a child* catechised"—but baptism still delayed.[2]

Ephrem of Edessa, a learned writer of the Syriac Church (died A. D. 378), was born of parents who, as Alban Butler remarks, " were ennobled by the blood of martyrs in their family, and had themselves both con-

[1] Ullman's *Gregory of Nazianzen*, p. 27.
[2] " Oratio exhortatoria ad baptis.," quoted in Wall's *History of Infant Baptism*, chap. xii.

fessed Christ before the persecutors, under Diocletian or his successors. They consecrated Ephrem to God from his cradle, like another Samuel, but he was eighteen years old when he was baptized."[1] They would be called good Baptists in these times. They "consecrated" their child, that is, prayed for him, and trained him "in the nurture and admonition of the Lord;" but they did not think of his being baptized till he was a believer, which was not till he was "eighteen years old." Would they have acted thus if infant baptism had been the universal and binding practice of the church?

Speaking of the Emperor Constantine, the infidel historian Gibbon says, "The example and reputation of Constantine seemed to countenance the delay of baptism. Future tyrants were encouraged to believe, that the innocent blood which they might shed in a long reign would instantly be washed away in the waters of regeneration; and the abuse of religion dangerously undermined the foundation of moral virtue."[2] The truth of the last observation is undeniable. All ecclesiastical history illustrates it. And there is no more melancholy confirmation than that which is afforded by the records of baptism. The figment of baptismal regeneration, one of the earliest corruptions of Christianity, was an outrage on morals and religion. It encouraged men in sin, and bolstered them up with a false hope, substituting the outward form for repentance, faith, and a changed heart and life Infant baptism, also, soon unfolded its injurious tendencies and effects. They will present themselves at every step of our future progress. It seems astonishing that so gross

[1] *Lives of the Saints.* Art. "St. Ephrem."
[2] *Decline and Fall*, chap. xx.

a perversion of Christianity should have acquired such a firm hold of men's minds. But it is among the things that are doomed, and the day is not far off.

With the sole exception of the clinics, already referred to, baptism still consisted in the immersion of the candidate, who was ordinarily divested of clothing. The same method was adopted for children as for adults. And the immersion was still commonly performed thrice.

The following passages are taken from Bingham's "Antiquities" (book xi., ch. xi.):

"Cyril of Jerusalem" (died A. D. 386) "makes it an emblem of the Holy Ghost's effusion upon the apostles; for as he that goes down into the water and is baptized, is surrounded on all sides by the water, so the apostles were baptized all over by the Spirit; the water surrounds the body externally, but the Spirit incomprehensibly baptizes the interior soul."

"So St. Ambrose" (died A. D. 396) "explains it: Thou wast asked, Dost thou believe in God the Father Almighty? And thou didst answer, I believe; and then thou wast immerged in water, that is, buried.'"

"St. Chrysostom" (died A. D. 407) "proves the resurrection from this practice: 'For,' says he, 'our being baptized and immerged into the water, and our rising again out of it, is a symbol of our descending into hell or the grave, and of our returning from thence:'"

"St. Jerome" (died A. D. 410) "makes this ceremony to be a symbol of the Unity as well as the Trinity. 'For,' says he, 'we are thrice dipped in the water, that the mystery of the Trinity may appear to be but one; we are not baptized in the names of Father, Son, and Holy Ghost, but in one name, which is God.'"

"St. Augustine" (died A. D. 430) " tells us there was a twofold mystery signified in this way of baptizing. The trine immersion was both a symbol of the Holy Trinity, in whose name we are baptized, and also a type of the Lord's burial, and of his resurrection on the third day from the dead. For we are buried with Christ by baptism, and rise again with him by faith."

Leo the Great (died A. D. 461) says, "The trine immersion is an imitation of the three days' burial; and the rising again out of the water is an image of Christ rising from the grave."

Gregory the Great (died A. D. 604) wrote thus to Leander, bishop of Seville: "Concerning the three immersions in baptism, you have judged very truly already, that different rites and customs do not prejudice the holy church, whilst the unity of faith remains entire. The reason why we use three immersions at Rome is to signify the mystery of Christ's three days' burial, that whilst an infant is thrice lifted up out of the water the resurrection on the third day may be expressed thereby. But if any one thinks this is rather done in regard to the Holy Trinity, a single immersion in baptism does no way prejudice that; for so long as the unity of substance is preserved in three persons, it is no harm whether a child be baptized with one immersion or three; because three immersions may represent the Trinity of Persons, and one immersion the Unity of the Godhead."

At first, baptism was administered in rivers, pools, baths, wherever a sufficient quantity of water could be conveniently obtained. In the fourth century, baptisteries began to be erected. These were large buildings, contiguous to the churches. There was usually but one in a city, attached to the bishop's or cathedral church. The baptistery proper, or font, was in the centre of the building, and at the sides were numerous apartments for the accommodation of the candidates. Several of these baptisteries yet remain, and have been frequently described by travelers. The baptisteries at Rome (in the church of St. John Lateran), Ravenna, Florence, Pisa, and Parma may be particularly mentioned. The fonts in these baptisteries are from three to four feet deep, and of proportionate size. Of course they were intended for immersion.

CHAPTER II.

Christian Intolerance—Justinian's Law, enjoining Infant Baptism—The Novatians—The Donatists—Pelagianism.

THE period now under consideration was marked by one "transition" which can never be sufficiently deplored. Hitherto, Christians had endured afflictions for the Lord's sake, and had willingly suffered the loss of all things rather than renounce the faith. But a change had taken place, involving a temptation which proved too powerful for many of them. When Constantine the Great declared for Christianity, he expected to stand in the same position toward that religion as he had before occupied with regard to Paganism. The emperors were the high priests of Paganism, and the civil government had from time immemorial directed and controlled the religion of the country. Was not the same policy to be observed? Had Constantine examined the New Testament, the question would have been soon answered. But he was very imperfectly acquainted with that book; and, besides, the exclusive authority of God's word in matters of religion had been long given up, The profession of Christianity in those times was a very different thing from what it had been in the first and purest ages. Scripture was smothered by tradition. The simplicity of apostolic form had given place to complicated ceremonies. Expediency had supplanted right. The inquiry was not, What has Christ commanded? but rather, How may influence, and power, and patronage, and wealth be obtained? How may the gospel become popular? Such being the views of the leaders, it is not surprising that the people groveled in worldliness, or that rulers determined to use Christianity as a State machine, as they had used Paganism. Constantine led the way, and his successors naturally trod in his steps. He began by enjoining external compliance with Christian institutions. The observance of the Lord's Day was enforced by imperial law. Interference in Christian controversies followed. The bishops were too ready to invoke the exercise of his authority, and there was not religious intelligence enough among the people to discern and resist the usurpation. The State set up the idol, uniformity, and they bowed down and worshiped it. The views entertained by the majority were called "Catholic," because they were said to be held by *all*. and "Orthodox," because they were assumed to be *right*. Those who differed from the majority were termed *heretics*. The words "orthodoxy" and "heresy" were not always employed, however, in the same acceptations. As each man deemed himself right and his opponent wrong, every man was orthodox in his own eyes; and as successive emperors patronized one or another form of belief, he who was orthodox in one reign was liable to be stigmatized as a heretic in the next. Patronage, power, and persecution are closely allied. When imperial intervention was called for to settle Christian disputes or to suppress a rising sect, there was no way of exercising it but by means of penalties, for law must of necessity be powerless unless offences against it are punished. Hence arose the monstrous anomaly of Christian persecution. If orthodoxy was in the ascendant, the Catholic emperor pulled down Arian churches, and fined the people for attending Arian worship; the same measure was meted out to other sects. If an Arian sat on the throne, the Catholics were subject to the same indignities. It was unchristian on both sides. Pagans and Jews were hardened in their unbelief. When Christianity was forced into an alliance with the State, the form—though even that was disguised—remained, but the spirit had departed.

Were I writing an ecclesiastical history, I should enlarge here. I should expatiate on the sin of legislation in the church, whose duty it is to obey Christ's laws, not to make new ones—on the pomp and pride of bishops—the tyranny of kings—the arrogance of councils—and especially on the evils which have resulted from the worldly admixture connected with the introduction of infant baptism. But just now I must confine myself to the influence of the State on religion, and particularly in relation to the subject before us.

The Emperor Justinian, who reigned from A.D. 527 to A. D. 565, was a thorough despot. He would acknowledge no will but his own. The rights of conscience were altogether ignored by him. He claimed absolute mastery over his subjects, and required them to renounce Paganism and embrace Christianity, because he willed it, without reference to other considerations. A notable edict of his illustrates these remarks. It enacted, "that such parents as were yet unbaptized should present themselves, with their wives and children, and all that appertained to them, in the church; and there they should cause their little ones immediately to be baptized, and the rest as soon as they were taught the Scriptures according to the canons. But if any persons, for the sake of a public office or dignity, or to get an estate, received a fallacious baptism themselves, but in the mean time left their wives, or children, or servants, or any that were retainers or near relations to them, in their ancient error, their goods in that case are ordered to be confiscated, and their persons punished by a competent judge, and excluded from bearing any office in the commonwealth." [1]

Thus the fabric of infant baptism rested on two pillars —delusion and force: delusion, inasmuch as the ceremony was supposed to be invested with regenerating and saving power—force, as employed by the State, in the interest of the Church. It is true, they called it an "apostolic institution;" but that was an afterthought. Exorcism, unction, the sign of the cross, holy water, infant communion, and many other childishnesses, were also called "apostolic institutions"—not at first, but long after they were invented, to conceal their real origin, and prevent men from discovering the trickery.

Unquestionably the progress of religion in the community, which was emphatically designated "The Church," was altogether downward during the "Transition Period." It is an interesting inquiry, How far the spirit of the gospel was preserved, and its essential truths maintained, by those whom ecclesiastical historians have denominated "heretics" and "schismatics." I shall pursue this inquiry in succeeding chapters. In order to find the true church, we must look *out* of the "Church" commonly so called.

[1] Bingham, book xi., chap. iv.

The Novatians and Donatists were the two leading sects of the period now under consideration. There were many other sects so called, for it was the fashion to designate as a "heretic" every individual who thought differently from the majority, and to consider those who agreed with him as constituting a party, usually bearing his name. If we were to do so now, the multiplication of sects would be indefinite.

Novatian lived at Rome. He had embraced Christianity, but his baptism had been deferred, and it has been already stated that in a sickness which threatened to be fatal he had been sprinkled or poured on as he lay on his bed, since it was impossible to immerse him. This is the first recorded instance of *clinic* baptism. It was in fact no baptism at all, though it differed from infant sprinkling. In the latter, both the subject and the act are wrong. In Novatian's case, there was a proper subject, but the ceremony performed was not baptism, though it was the best substitute they could think of. It shows us, by the way, how error was creeping in. Novatian ought to have waited for his recovery, when he would have been in a fit state to receive the ordinance. Had it pleased God that his sickness should be fatal, he would have died without baptism, and he would have been in David's position, who desired to build the temple, but was not permitted. The desire was approved, though the purpose was not accomplished. He " did well that it was in his heart." Already, however, the pernicious notion of the necessity of baptism to salvation had become prevalent, and consequently Novatian was sprinkled or received a pouring.

Novatian possessed such talent and zeal that he became

a popular teacher. On the death of Fabian, bishop of Rome, in the year 250, there was a strong desire that Novatian should succeed him, and he would have done so, had it not been for his known sentiments on one point. Lax habits of discipline, as he believed, had grown up, and were very mischievous in their tendencies. In the Decian persecution great numbers had apostatized, who on the return of tranquillity sought readmission into the churches. Novatian differed from his brethren on this subject. He held that apostasy was a sin which wholly disqualified an individual for restoration to Christian fellowship, and that it would be destructive to the purity of the church to readmit those who had so grossly fallen. God might pardon them. They might find a place in heaven. But the church must not be defiled, for it is a congregation of saints. Now, whatever opinion we may form respecting Novatian's particular theory, it is undeniable that the principle on which it rested was derived from the New Testament. Yet it was too spiritual for the times. A majority declared in favor of Cornelius, who was duly installed bishop of Rome. Nevertheless, the minority would not yield. The time had come—so they argued—for a decided stand. The holiness of the church was in danger, and must be maintained at all hazards. Separation was better than corruption. They withdrew, formed a separate church, and invited Novatian to become their pastor. Others imitated their example in various parts of the empire, and Novatian churches sprang up in great abundance. They continued in existence more than three centuries. In all the principal towns and cities, these dissenting communities might be found. They were the "Puritans" of those days, and were so designated. There was a wholesome rivalry for some time between them and the "Orthodox" or "Catholic" body, each operating as a stimulus and a check to the other.

Carrying out their governing principle in all its details, they baptized all who joined their churches, even though they had been already baptized by ministers of the orthodox body, deeming the baptism of a corrupt church invalid. They were therefore the first "Anabaptists," in the strict and proper sense of that word. They were also genuine reformers. Dr. Waddington, an Episcopalian historian, observes that Novatian "considered the genuine church of Christ to be a society where virtue and innocence reigned universally, and refused any longer to acknowledge those as its members who had even once degenerated into unrighteousness. His followers were called *Cathari* or Puritans, and they comprehended many austere and independent Christians, in the East no less than in the West. But this endeavor to revive the spotless moral purity of the Primitive faith was found inconsistent with the corruptions even of that early age. it was regarded with suspicion by the leading prelates, as a vain and visionary scheme; and those rigid principles which had characterized and sanctified the church in the first century were abandoned to the profession of schismatic sectaries in the third."[1]

There is no evidence that at the time of Novatian's separation from the Roman Church infant baptism had found its way to Italy. The probability is all on the other side, since one hundred and sixty years after that event we find Boniface, bishop of Rome, propounding

[1] *History of the Church*, i. 166 (Second Edition).

doubts and questions to Augustine which indicated that infant baptism was looked on by him quite distrustfully. Those difficulties would not have existed if he had believed that the rite had a divine origin. The incongruity between the ceremonial employed and the reality struck him forcibly. The ceremonial had been originally prepared for catechumens, and was then a reasonable service. When infants were substituted for catechumens, the same forms were observed, but they were strangely out of place. In answer to the usual question, the sponsor replied on behalf of the infant, "I believe," whereas, as Boniface remarked, not only was the child unable to believe, but no one could tell whether he would believe in after-life or not. No wonder the good man was puzzled.[1] It reminds me of an incident that occurred in England some years ago. A lad, the child of Baptist parents, was sent to a school where the Church of England catechism was taught. Abraham—that was his name—was compelled to stand up with the other boys. It happened one day that it came to his turn to answer this question: "Why then are infants baptized, when by reason of their tender age they cannot perform them"—that is, the conditions of repentance and faith? Abraham looked full in his master's face, and said, "Why, indeed, sir?" He was not asked to recite any more.[2]

Novatianism and infant baptism were diametrically opposed to each other. It was impossible to preserve the purity for which the Novatians contended in any church

[1] See his letter in *Augustin. Opera*, xxxix. 235–244, (Ed. Caillau).
[2] The lad was a son of the Rev. Abraham Austin, many years pastor of the Baptist Church, meeting in Elim Chapel, Fetter Lane, London, who died in 1816. See *Baptist Magazine*, vol. viii., pp. 397, 441.

which had admitted the novel institution. Those who had been baptized in infancy might evince, when they reached maturity, an utter destitution of vital godliness, and consequent unfitness for union with a Christian body; but being already members by virtue of their baptism, they could not be expelled unless they fell into gross vice, and so their influence and example might operate most injuriously on the religious character of the church. This could not escape the observation of Novatian Christians. It would prove a salutary caution. We may safely infer that they abstained from compliance with the innovation, and that the Novatian churches were what are now called Baptist churches, adhering to the apostolic and primitive practice. Had the writings of Novatian authors been preserved, we should have had more explicit information; but it was the ancient policy to destroy all books written by alleged heretics. Novatian published a work on the Trinity, which has not been involved in the common destruction. A copy of it is now before the writer. It is generally commended for its clearness and orthodoxy, but there is no allusion to the baptismal controversy.

The Donatists first appeared in the early part of the fourth century. A dispute about an election to a bishopric was the occasion of their separation from the catholic church. Cæcilan was chosen bishop of Carthage in a somewhat irregular manner and hastily ordained. Among those who officiated at his ordination was Felix, bishop of Aptunga. This man was said to be a *traditor*, that is, one who had delivered up copies of the Scriptures to the civil authorities during the Diocletian persecution. His concurrence in the ordination was thought by some to vitiate the service. They refused to regard Cæcilian as a regularly-appointed bishop. A secession took place, which spread rapidly and extensively, so that in a short time the Donatist churches in Africa were nearly equal in number to those of the hitherto dominant party.

As in the case of the Novatians, the discussion of the general question of church purity arose out of the circumstances that originated the division. The Donatists pleaded for purity. They maintained that Christian churches should consist of godly persons and no others, and that in all the arrangements made for their management that important principle should be kept in view. They followed the example of the Novatians in rebaptizing those who joined them from other churches. They baptized new converts on a profession of faith, as a matter of course, for that was the practice of all churches. Whether they went farther than this is open to dispute. Their principles would undoubtedly lead them to the rejection of infant baptism. Some authors affirm that they did reject it. For my own part, I am inclined to think that they were divided in opinion, and that some of them admitted infant baptism, though the admission was inconsistent with their acknowledged principles. The majority, I am willing to believe, adhered to the New Testament practice.

At one of the African councils, held about the year 397, it was agreed to consult their "brethren and fellow-priests," Siricius, bishop of Rome, and Simplician, bishop of Milan, respecting those who had been baptized in infancy among the Donatists, and who, when they reached mature age, desired to join the church which assumed the title "Catholic."[1] It was subsequently decided that they should not be rebaptized. This proves that infant baptism was practiced in that sect; whether universally or not, is another question. Augustine never charges them, as a body, with heresy on that point; nor does Optatus, a celebrated writer against the Donatists.

There is another circumstance proper to be mentioned. The difference between the Donatists and their opponents had been submitted several times to imperial decision. In the first instance the Donatists, it appears, consented to the reference; but they soon discovered the impropriety. "What has the emperor to do with the church? What have Christians to do with kings, or bishops at court?" they asked. Were they not right? Have not the Baptists been distinguished in all ages by the maintenance of these views? Have they not ever held that civil government has nothing to do with religion, that Christianity asks for no support from the State, and that the union of Church and State has been productive of some of the worst evils that have defiled the Christian profession? Have they not always repudiated the use of carnal weapons in the defence and propagation of the truth, and demanded, for themselves and for all men, entire freedom of thought and action in all religious concerns? This is their glory, and no man can take it from them.

Both the Novatians and the Donatists suffered severely for their dissent—especially the latter. The celebrated

[1] Labbe and Cossart, ii. 1071. Bingham's *Antiquities*, book iv., chap. iii., sect. 12.

Augustine taught the unchristian doctrine that heresy should be suppressed by the civil magistrate, and invoked the imperial sword against the Donatists. Their property was confiscated, the prisons were crammed with them, and great numbers lost their lives by the hands of the executioner. A sanguinary law was enacted, that the rebaptizer and the rebaptized should be put to death. That so atrocious an enactment should excite tumults in a country where the separatists constituted one half of the Christian population cannot be considered surprising. Other persons, not connected with them, took advantage of it, and great disorders ensued. But Augustine and his party were the aggressors.

Pelagianism troubled the church in the fifth century. As Pelagius taught that infants derive no moral taint from Adam's transgression, it has been inferred that he was of necessity an opposer of infant baptism, since it had then become a generally admitted notion that baptism cleanses from original sin. Pelagius, however, did not deny the propriety of baptizing infants, who obtained, he said, the kingdom of heaven by their baptism, which "kingdom of heaven" he distinguished from eternal life, and represented as a kind of intermediate state. I need not dwell on such follies, and therefore pass on to observe, that as many in that age stoutly denied the right of infants to baptism, refusing to acknowledge the power of the church to add to the ordinances of Christ, the council of Milevi, held A. D. 416, passed a decree in the following terms: "Whosoever denies that newly-born infants are to be baptized, or affirms that they are indeed baptized for the remission of sins, but that they derive no original sin from Adam, . . . let him be accursed."[1] Such are the supports of infant baptism—the frail buttresses of the building—Justinian's mandate and this anathematizing decree of Milevi. But what has the Saviour said? "Every plant which my heavenly Father hath not planted shall be rooted up" (Matt. xv. 13).

Much has been said respecting the contest of Augustine, the monk, with the British Christians on the subject of baptism. It has been supposed that infant baptism was then unknown in England, and that Augustine endeavored to force it on the people as an integral part of Romish policy. Neither assertion is correct. There is no good reason to suppose that infant baptism, which had been gaining prevalence all over Europe by the zealous labors and powerful influence of Augustine of Hippo, had been kept out of England. We have just seen that Pelagius, who was a Welshman, did not oppose it. Augustine's object was to procure uniformity of ceremonies, and to induce the Britons to adopt the observances grafted by the Romish Church on the simple baptismal service of the New Testament. Nothing was said about children. *Their* baptism was, no doubt, gradually introduced into England, as in other parts, and ultimately superseded, as it did elsewhere, the primitive ordinance. At any rate, we find traces of it in Wales in the sixth century.[2] Whether compliance was refused by any parties, and in what numbers, cannot

---

[1] Labbe and Cossart, ii. 1538.
[2] See the *Liber Landavensis*. Llandovery, 1840.

now be ascertained. Here, as in many other respects, there is a lack of information. God's witnesses lay hid for ages.[1]

[1] Bede's *Ecclesiastical History* is the only authority for the account of Augustine's interview with the British clergy. The monk required of them, among other things, that they should "administer baptism, by which we are born to God, according to the custom of the holy Roman Apostolic Church" (Dr. Giles' Translation). The word used by Bede was "*compleatis*," and his meaning was that they should render the administration complete or perfect, by the addition of Romish ceremonies. In some editions of Fabian's *Chronicle*, Augustine is represented as saying, "that ye give Christendom to children." Fabian, it may be supposed, knew of no baptism but that of infants, and translated, or rather paraphrased, accordingly. He died A. D. 1513.

THE OBSCURE PERIOD

CHRONOLOGICAL NOTES.

FROM A. D. 604 TO A. D. 1073.

609. Commencement of Mohammedanism.
625. Rise of the Monothelite Controversy.
632. Death of Mohammed.
650. Rise of the Paulicians.
680. Sixth General Council, at Constantinople.
735. Death of Venerable Bede.
756. Temporal Power assumed by the Pope.
787. Seventh General Council, at Nice.
814. Death of Charlemagne.
831. Transubstantiation taught by Paschasius Radbert.
840. Death of Claude of Turin.
870. Eighth General Council, at Constantinople.
970. The Paulicians removed to Philippopolis, in Thrace.
993. First instance of Papal Canonization.
1054. Final Separation of the Eastern and Western Churches.
1073. Accession of Pope Gregory VII.

CHAPTER I.

The Manichæans—Cautions to the Student—All Opponents of Infant Baptism not Baptists—Account of the Paulicians—Their Views of Baptism.

SOME may wonder I have as yet said nothing about the Manichæans, a sect which first came into notice about the latter part of the third century, and continued in existence, if historians are to be believed, a thousand years or more. They were charged with denying infant baptism. But I wish it to be understood, that I consider those only as Baptists, in the New Testament sense of that term, who hold baptism as an ordinance binding on all believers, and refuse it to all other persons. Now, Manichæism was a compound of Oriental philosophy and Christianity. The fanciful and wild speculations in which Manes indulged were as ill-founded in reason as in Scripture, and justly entitled their author to the appellation "fanatic." He incorporated sundry portions of Christianity into his incongruous system, and therefore the party has been ranked among the heretics, though, as I think, with little propriety. The heretics, as they are called, were seceders from the established, or Catholic Church. Manes originated an independent body, on entirely original principles, and ought to be placed on the same list as Mohammed and other founders of systems. It is said that he admitted baptism and the Lord's supper among the services enjoined on his followers; but the supper was celebrated with water instead of wine, and baptism was optional; those only who wished it were baptized; those who did not desire it were not debarred from membership on that account, and infants were excluded from participation in the rite. After these explanations it will not be deemed strange that I have refrained from classing the Manichæans with the revivers of primitive religion.[1]

We are now entering on the period which I have denominated "obscure." It is so called because the information is generally scanty, and sometimes of very doubtful character. I may begin by remarking that the student of ecclesiastical history must beware lest he be led astray by the misrepresentations of bigoted historians. Manichæism was soon looked on as a concentration of all that was outrageous and bad in religious opinion, and it became the fashion to call all heretics "Manichæans." Hence many excellent men have been so stigmatized, whose views and practices accorded with the word of God. It is necessary to repair to the original sources of history, and even then to scan very closely the statements handed down to us, that they may be disentangled, as far as possible, from mistake or misrepresentation.

Further: it is not safe or proper to report all opponents of infant baptism as Baptists, in our sense of the

---

[1] Manes was a Persian. He was put to death by order of Varanes I., king of Persia, in the year 278. See Beausobre's *Histoire Critique de Manichée et du Manichéisme*, and Mosheim's *De Rebus Christianis*, etc., p. 728–903.

word. Throughout the Middle Ages there were many dissenters from the catholic faith, as it was called, who rejected baptism altogether, holding sentiments respecting that ordinance which much resemble those of the Quakers in these times. Possibly they were driven to those extreme views by contemplating the absurd ceremonies connected with baptism, and the superstitious notions entertained by the majority. It seemed to them better to have no baptism at all than to countenance such follies. Doubtless they were wrong, although much might be offered in excuse for them. But when these parties are adduced as opponents of infant baptism, an unfairness is sometimes committed. Their opposition was against all baptism, and not against infant baptism only. I am not disposed to regard any persons as primitive Baptists unless they practiced the baptism of believers; their rejection of infant baptism will not warrant the imposition of that worthy name on them. Mr. Orchard's "History of Foreign Baptists," and other works of a similar kind, have now and then fallen into this error.[1]

At the same time it must be confessed that there is

---

[1] It is not pleasant to be compelled to make any statements calculated to throw discredit on other writers; but the interests of truth are paramount to all other considerations, and Baptists ought to be especially careful in this matter.

Gibbon writes thus: "In the practice, or at least in the theory, of the sacraments, the Paulicians were inclined to abolish all visible objects of worship, and the words of the gospel were, in their judgment, the baptism and communion of the faithful."—*Decline and Fall*, chap. liv.

Jones, referring to Gibbon as his authority, says: "The sacraments of baptism and the Lord's supper they held to be peculiar to 'the communion of the faithful,' that is, ought to be restricted to believers." *Lectures on Ecclesiastical History*, ii. 181. It will be observed that this often the utmost difficulty in forming a satisfactory judgment in regard to the opinions held by the reformers of the Middle Ages. We know nothing of them but by the

is not by any means a correct representation of Gibbon. It is quoted by Orchard as an independent testimony.

Mr. Orchard (*History of the Baptists*, p. 130) gives the following as a quotation from Mosheim : " It is evident they [the Paulicians] rejected the baptism of infants. They were not charged with any error concerning baptism." I am sorry to say that the first part of this alleged quotation is not to be found in Mosheim. The second part is a mutilation. The words of the historian, which occur in a note, are here copied: "The Greeks do not charge the Paulicians with any error in respect to the doctrine of baptism. Yet there is no doubt that they construed into *allegory* what the New Testament states concerning this ordinance. And Photius (*Contra Manich.* lib. i. p. 29) expressly says, that they held only to a fictitious baptism, and understood by baptism, *i. e.*, by the water of baptism—the *gospel*."—*Ecclesiastical History*, cent. ix. part 2. chap. v. sect. 6.

Mr. Orchard gives also the following, as a quotation from Dr. Allix: " They, with the Manichæans, were Anabaptists, and were consequently often reproached with that term." I have looked in vain for this quotation. Dr. Allix, speaking of the Manichees, says : " In those barbarous and cruel ages, a small conformity of opinion with the Manichees was a sufficient ground to accuse them of Manichæism who opposed any doctrines received by the Church of Rome. Thus would they have taken the Anabaptists for downright Manichees, because they condemned the baptism of infants."—*Remarks upon the Ancient Church of Piedmont*, chap. xv.

Mr. Orchard says (p. 300), *Ecbertus Schonaugiensis*, who wrote against this people, declares, "They say that baptism does no good to infants; therefore, such as come over to their sect they baptize in a private way, that is, without the pomp and public parade of the Catholics."—*Wall's History*, part 2, p. 228.

This seems to be clear and explicit testimony. According to the statement, as here presented, the *Cathari* not only rejected infant baptism, but also baptized adults, " in a private way."

The reader will be astonished to learn that the very opposite was the reports of their adversaries, who were predisposed against them, and who, for want of religious sympathy, were unable to appreciate or even to understand their peculiar views. The same words were sometimes used by opposing parties in different senses, and truths were seen in different aspects. Hence the confusion and contradictoriness which are too often apparent.

These observations apply to the case of the Paulicians. They first appeared about the middle of the seventh century in Armenia, and soon spread wonderfully, till they were numbered by hundreds of thousands. Their enemies accused them of Manichæism, which accusation they indignantly repelled. The only ancient authorities whence we can derive a knowledge of their sentiments are Photius and Petrus Siculus, who wrote against them with great bitterness, and on that account can scarcely be

---

fact. These people, according to Eckbert, as very fairly quoted by Wall, rejected baptism altogether. Here is the entire passage, copied from Wall. He is speaking of Eckbert, or, as he calls him, *Ecbertus Schonaugiensis*:

He says, Sermon I.: "They are also divided among themselves; for several things that are maintained by some of them are denied by others." And of baptism particularly he says, "Of baptism they speak variously; that baptism does no good to infants, because they cannot of themselves desire it, and because they cannot profess any faith. But there is another thing which they more generally hold concerning that point, though more secretly—namely, that no water baptism at all does any good for salvation. And therefore such as come over to their sect they rebaptize by a private way, which they call baptism with the Holy Spirit and with fire." This was the "*consolamentum*." It is described in the next period.

Mr. Benedict copies Orchard, and thus unwittingly propagates the mistake; *History of the Baptists*, p. 67, edit. 1848. The original passage, translated by Wall, is in *Biblioth. Maxim. Lugdun.* xxiii. 601.

considered as worthy of entire credence. Photius was archbishop of Constantinople, and died A.D. 890; Petrus Siculus, a learned nobleman, died a few years later. He was sent by the Emperor Basil to Tibrica, a Paulician town, in the year 870, to negotiate an exchange of prisoners. He remained there seven months, and availed himself of the opportunity of learning the opinions and practices of the Paulicians, both by disputing with them and by instituting inquiries among the Catholics in the neighborhood. It is unfortunate that there is no better authority to consult, for Petrus Siculus was so bitterly prejudiced against the people that his statements cannot be received without doubt and distrust. The only safe course is to endeavor to disentangle facts from opinions, insinuations, and invectives, and thus to ascertain the truth. Yet even then it is impossible to furnish a complete picture. Petrus Siculus deals chiefly in negatives. He tells you what the Paulicians denied, and rails at them for presuming to differ from the Catholic party, but he leaves you to guess what they really believed in many important particulars. I mention these things that the reader may perceive the difficulty which lies in the way of an impartial narrator.

About the year 653, during the reign of the Emperor Constans II., a young man named Constantine resident at Mananalis, in Armenia, rendered hospitable attentions to a stranger whom misfortune had brought under his roof. The stranger proved to be a deacon of a Christian church, and he had in his possession a precious treasure, which he gave to Constantine on his departure, in return for the kindness shown him. It was a copy of the Gospels and of the Epistles of Paul. Constantine read, believed, and obeyed. Manichæism, by which he had been deluded, was immediately renounced. His Manichæan books were thrown aside, and the sacred writings were exclusively studied. Shortly afterward he removed to Cibossa, where he lived and laboured for twenty-seven years. He was a diligent and successful preacher. Great numbers received the truth. In what manner he proceeded to form them into societies or churches, and how they were governed, we have not the means of knowing. We may conjecture and infer, but inference is not history. If the report of Petrus Siculus be correct, they lay under considerable disadvantage in not having the book of the Acts in their hands, from which they would have gathered the practices of the apostolic churches, and perhaps this circumstance exerted an unfavorable influence on their arrangements. But we must not affirm positively on this subject.

Constantine died the death of a martyr. The Emperor Constantine Pogonatus sent Simeon, one of his officers, to Cibossa, with a military detachment. He apprehended Constantine, compelled the congregation to present themselves before him, and ordered them to stone their minister. They stood in silence for a while, no one lifting up his hand in obedience to so cruel a command. At length a man named Justus stepped forward, and the murderous deed was done. Simeon then undertook the work of conversion. He disputed with the followers of Constantine, and labored hard to restore them to the Catholic Church. But he labored in vain. Not only so; the arguments used on the other side were too powerful for him. He yielded to the force of truth, and returned to Constantinople a Paulician in heart. At first he did not avow the change that had taken place, but at length he found it impossible to conceal it, and consequently he left the imperial service, retired to Cibossa, joined the persecuted sect, and became the successor of the very man whom he had murdered by the hand of Justus. After several years of usefulness, Justus, who had professed repentance and had been restored to the church, quarreled with him and betrayed him to a neighboring bishop, by whose means all the members of the church then resident in Cibossa were seized and burned alive in one vast pile. Paulus only escaped. He fled to Episparis. His two sons, Genesius and Theodotus, became Paulician ministers. Genesius was on one occasion apprehended as a heretic and taken to Constantinople, where he underwent an examination before the patriarch. It is thus reported by Petrus Siculus:

Patriarch.—" Why hast thou derided the orthodox faith ?"

Genesius.—" Anathema to him who denies the orthodox faith"—meaning thereby his own heresy, which he boasted of as the true " orthodox faith."

Patriarch.—" Wherefore dost thou not believe in and adore the venerable cross?"

Genesius.—" Anathema to him who does not adore and worship the venerable and life-giving cross"—meaning Christ himself, whose outstretched arms present the figure of the cross.

Patriarch.—" Why dost thou not worship and adore the holy mother of God ?"

Genesius.—" Anathema to him who does not adore the most holy mother of God, the common mother of us all, into whom our Lord Jesus Christ entered"—meaning the heavenly Jerusalem, into which Christ has entered as our Forerunner.

Patriarch.—" Why dost thou not partake of the immaculate body and precious blood of our Lord Jesus Christ, but dost rather despise the same?"

Genesius.—" Anathema to him who despises the body and blood of Jesus Christ"—meaning thereby the *words* "body and blood," and nothing more.

" In like manner," says Petrus Siculus, " he spake of baptism, saying that Jesus Christ himself is baptism, and that there is no other, because he said, 'I am the living water.' And thus perverting everything by his own false interpretations, he was acquitted and honorably dismissed."

After this, Mananalis was again the headquarters of the Paulicians. Genesius lived there thirty years, and died in peace. Various troubles and disasters followed. Joseph, who seems to have succeeded Genesius, withdrew to Episparis, and afterward to Antioch, in Pisidia, where he labored thirty years. He was succeeded by Bahanes. But there must have been many more engaged in the work beside these, for the imperfect notices that are left indicate an extensive series of operations, embracing a large number of churches and a powerful body of adherents.

About the year 810 the Paulicians were joined by Sergius, who became one of the most eminent men of their community. The account of his conversion is exceedingly interesting. He was an intelligent, well-educated young man, and much esteemed for his many excellent qualities; but he was profoundly ignorant of religion. One day a Christian woman, evidently a Paulician, met with him and entered into conversation. "Why," said she, "do you not read the holy Gospels?" "Because," he replied, "it is not lawful for us laymen, but only for the priests." "You are altogether mistaken," she rejoined, "for there is no respect of persons with God; he will have all men to be saved." She then proceeded to expose the priestly tyranny of the age and the gross superstitions by which the people were deluded, urging the young man to examine the matter for himself. He did so. He read, and thought, and prayed, and became a Christian "in deed and in truth." The genuineness of his conversion was proved by his eminently holy life and incessant zeal. He traversed a large part of Western Asia, preaching everywhere, and calling on the people to abandon the follies of a corrupted Christianity, and "worship God in the spirit." Thirty-four years were thus spent, and marvelous results accompanied his efforts. Multitudes were converted. So general was the defection from the established church, that the Greek emperor was greatly alarmed, and adopted the severest measures for the suppression of the reformation. The Paulicians had endured persecution from the beginning, and had "increased and multiplied" under it. But the storm raged with such terrific fierceness during the first half of the ninth century that utter extermination seemed inevitable. It is affirmed that under the auspices of the Empress Theodora, who held the regency during the minority of her son Michael, from A. D. 832 to A. D. 846, no fewer than one hundred thousand Paulicians were put to death "by the sword, the gibbet, or the flames." Sergius was one of the victims. He and his brethren went to join those of whom it is said that they constantly cry, "How lng, O Lord, holy and true, dost thou not judge and avenge our blood on those that dwell on the earth?" (Rev. vi. 10).

"Oppression maketh a wise man mad."

Imperial cruelty at length provoked retaliation and revenge. The Paulicians took up arms in defence of their families and their homes. The transition from self-defence to active rebellion is easy, and the provinces of the East were convulsed with civil war, for all the miseries of which the persecutors were responsible. It continued many years. The co-operation of the Saracens was sought, and many provinces of the empire were desolated. But I will not pursue the history any farther. It is difficult to trace the progress of religion when carnal weapons have been taken up. I will only observe that the Paulician revival had early extended to Thrace, now the Turkish province of Roumelia; and in the tenth century a large number of Paulicians were removed to Philippopolis in that country, and also to Bulgaria, the adjoining province; and that in the following age they began to migrate into Italy, France, and other parts of Europe.[1]

When Petrus Siculus sat down to write his history, he was predetermined to blacken the Paulicians to the utmost. Consequently, he maintained that they were Manichæans, notwithstanding the disclaimer of Constantine, their founder; and having taken that position, he was re-

[1] The "Historia" of Petrus Siculus is printed in the sixteenth volume of the *Biblioth. Maxim. Lugdunens.* Gieseler has given an abstract of the statements of Photius in his *Ecclesiastical History*, ii. 209-212.

solved to hold it. I shall not think it worth while to discuss the question. There may have been some among them who still retained a regard to the philosophic speculations with which they were familiar before conversion, and which had for many ages proved very injurious to spiritual Christianity; and that unworthy persons sometimes crept in among them may be readily admitted. That is the fate of all parties. But here was their distinction: they withdrew from the Greek Church because that church had abandoned the high ground of gospel truth and spiritual worship. They asserted the right and duty of searching the Scriptures, and would admit no other rule. They abhorred saint-worship. They would not adore the cross, nor bow down before images. They abjured the ecclesiastical hierarchy. In a word, they appear to have been Protestants before the Reformation, and even before those who have been commonly reckoned as its precursors. The meagre accounts of them which remain, tinged as they are with obstinate prejudice, fail to give us satisfaction. Had we the letters of Sergius, which Petrus Siculus tells us his followers valued highly, we should be able to obtain full and accurate information. This, however, is certain, that a religious movement springing from God's word, and so firmly maintained against opposition that two hundred years after its rise the astonishing number of one hundred thousand of its adherents were cut off without destroying the body, must have possessed a mighty influence. I agree with Joseph Milner, the ecclesiastical historian, who observes that in this case we have "one of those extraordinary effusions of the Divine Spirit by which the knowledge of Christ and the practice of godliness is kept alive in the world."[1]

But I cannot agree with that writer in the statement that the Paulicians " were simply scriptural in the use of the sacraments." Neander says, more truly, that "they combated the inclination to rely on the magical effects of external forms, particularly the sacraments: indeed, they went so far on this side as wholly to reject the outward celebration of the sacraments."[2]

On the question of baptism, Photius writes to this effect: that though the Paulicians despise "saving baptism," they pretend that they have received it, inasmuch as they received the gospel, wherein Christ declares that he is the "living water;"[3] and he adds, that they are willing that the priests should baptize their children, notwithstanding their disbelief in any saving benefit accompanying the rite. Admitting the correctness of this account, the Paulicians rejected water baptism, teaching that the knowledge of Christ, which is spiritual baptism, is sufficient. If they allowed the priests to baptize their children, as Photius states, it was probably to save themselves from annoyance, perhaps from persecution; and as, in their opinion, the baptism did the children neither good nor harm, it was looked on as a matter of indifference. I do not justify or commend them. Whatever *their* views were, the priests judged that they had saved the children by baptizing them, and there should not have been any opportunity given for cherishing that antichristian notion. Still, it is to be remembered that we are by no means certain of the truth of the statement, as the

---

[1] *History of the Church*, cent. ix. chap. ii.
[2] *History of the Church*, iii. 263. [3] *Ibid.*, i. 9.

writer was a virulent opposer of the Paulicians, and aimed to excite hatred against them. The same remark will apply to Petrus Siculus, who, as Gibbon very properly says, wrote "with much prejudice and passion."

Some maintain that the Paulicians did not reject either baptism or the Lord's supper—which also they are said to have held in a spiritual sense only—but the unauthorized additions that had been made to the ordinances, and the current opinions respecting their design and efficacy. In other words, they rejected baptismal regeneration and transubstantiation. The progress of perversion, it is truly affirmed, had brought men to this point, that baptism was no longer regarded as a profession of Christ, nor the Lord's supper as a memorial of his love; the former was held to be the instrument of regeneration, and in the latter there was said to be an actual reception of the Saviour's body and blood. Whoever refused to acquiesce in these representations was reproached as a denier of the ordinances, whereas his opposition was confined to corruptions and abuses. This is not an improbable supposition, but we have not the means of verifying it, for want of historic materials.

It is, however, to be considered, that the Paulicians were not altogether agreed among themselves. There were divisions and parties. It may possibly be that Photius and Petrus Siculus designedly referred to those of them whose opinions were, in their judgment, the farthest removed from catholic verity, and that while some wandered into errors and excesses, the remainder pursued a scriptural course. Photius himself states that some of them observed the Lord's supper, though, as he affects to believe, they did it to "deceive the simple."

This indicates the existence of two parties. Those who observed one ordinance were not likely to neglect the other. I am therefore not indisposed to believe that there were among the Paulicians many who preserved the truths and worship of Christianity, as derived from the New Testament.

CHAPTER II.

Religious Reform in Europe—The Canons of Orleans—Arras—Berengarius—Miscellaneous Anecdotes.

ALTHOUGH certain scattered notices in historical writings render it probable that during the "Obscure Period" religious reformers were silently working their way in different parts of Europe, the expressions used are so general and vague that we cannot fully gather from them the opinions supposed to be held by the said reformers. Whatever their various sentiments were, we find them indiscriminately libeled as "Manichæans," which was as much as to say that they were children of the devil, and should be left to their fate. It is a curious fact that Italy was the fountain-head of these heresies. Powerful and cunning as the popes were, they could not preserve their own territories from the spiritual infection.

Now and then the hidden seed sprouted up and showed itself above ground. An instance occurred at Orleans, in France, in 1022. Ten canons of the church were discovered to be imbued with heretical notions, which they were said to have received from Italy, by means of a lady of that land. The discoveries excited great horror. Forthwith the king and queen, attended by a large retinue of prelates, hastened to the spot to make inquisition. One Arefastus, who had pretended to be an inquirer into the new opinions, and by that means had won the confidence of the leaders, became a witness against them. They were charged, among other things, with holding that there is *no washing away of sins in baptism*, that in the Lord's supper the bread and wine are not changed into the body and blood of the Saviour, and that it is unlawful to pray to the saints. These were unpardonable sins. The accused were men of learning and piety, whose unimpeachable characters and holy lives were well known, and by whose benevolence many poor were daily relieved; but they did not believe in baptismal regeneration, transubstantiation, and saint-worship, and therefore they must be burned alive; and burned they were on the very day of their trial. First, however, they were solemnly degraded from the priestly office, the queen standing guard at the church door while the ceremony of degradation was performed, lest the populace should push in and anticipate the execution by murdering them. Her majesty gave a striking manifestation of her zeal for orthodoxy, immediately afterward, by knocking out the eye of one of the sufferers, who had been her own confessor, and against whom, therefore, she was especially enraged. They were then taken outside the city walls and committed to the flames. One author states that three or four other persons, who had embraced the same opinions, and were of very respectable standing in society, suffered with them.[1]

Three years afterward another band of heretics made their appearance at Arras in Flanders. They were ap-

[1] Labbe and Cossart, ix. 836-842.

prehended and brought before a council convened on the occasion, when they gave this account of themselves:

"Our law and discipline," said they, "which we have received from the Master, will not appear to be contrary to gospel decrees and apostolic sanctions, if any one will diligently consider the same. For it is this: to relinquish the world, to restrain the flesh from concupiscence, to provide for our support by the labor of our own hands, to seek the hurt of none, to show charity to all. This righteousness being preserved, there is no need of baptism; if this be turned from, baptism cannot save. This is the sum of our justification, to which the use of baptism can add nothing, for it comprises the entire purpose of all apostolic and evangelical instruction. But if any say that some sacrament lies hid in baptism, the force of that is taken away by these three considerations: First, the reprobate life of the ministers can afford no saving remedy to the persons to be baptized; secondly, whatever sins are renounced at the font are afterward taken up again in life and practice; thirdly, another's will, another's faith, and another's confession do not seem to belong to, or to be of any advantage to, a little child, who neither wills nor runs, who knows nothing of faith, and is altogether ignorant of his own good and salvation, and from whom no confession of faith can be expected."[1]

These men, up to a certain point, were scripturally orthodox. They saw clearly that religious service must be a personal, voluntary act, flowing from faith, and that therefore infant baptism could have no foundation in the word of God, since infants were unable to believe. They rejected it, and in doing so they rejected baptism alto-

[1] *Act. Synod. Attrebatenses*, Gieseler, ii. 496.

gether, for at that time infant baptism was *the* baptism of the Catholic Church. See here an illustration of our Lord's statement to the Jews, "Ye have made the word of God of none effect by your traditions." According to the tradition, regeneration and grace were bestowed in infant baptism, and hence that ceremony, being generally adopted, superseded the baptism of believers. Hence, too, the effect produced on inquiring minds. "This baptism," said they—and they argued conclusively from the premises—"is manifestly a vain and useless thing. It cannot accomplish the promised results. It never did. If we are already pious, baptism is needless; if we are not, baptism cannot make us so." Thus a Christian ordinance was suppressed. The men of Arras were "not far from the kingdom of God," but it is evident that they were imperfect Christians. They discerned error, but they did not perceive the whole truth, for the error eclipsed it. This was the position of a large number of the reformers of the Middle Ages. They held Baptist principles as we now hold them, so far as regarded the rejection of infant baptism. Whether they practiced the baptism of believers, historians do not say, though I would not build an argument on that silence. Those of them who were priests of the Catholic Church, as the canons of Orleans, must have been accustomed to administer infant baptism. How they reconciled that practice with their convictions, I know not.

It is a remarkable fact that the decrees of councils contain no references whatever to heretics for several centuries previous to the eleventh. There are enactments in abundance touching the honors and privileges of the clergy, anathemas in rich profusion against breaches of ecclesiastical law, and threatenings of punishment for gross and unnamable violations of chastity. But heresy is not mentioned, except in two or three individual cases. It is clear that there was no disturbing movement. The operations of the Paulicians were confined to the East till nearly the close of the "Obscure Period," when they entered Europe. There were men in the West who "sighed and cried for all the abominations that were done," but they mourned in secret, and they were not numerous enough to attract attention or excite opposition.

Certain miscellaneous matters will be now adverted to in conclusion.

A.D. 692. Ina, king of the West Saxons, enacted a law by which it was enjoined that all infants should be baptized within thirty days after birth, under a penalty of thirty shillings. If the child died without baptism the father's entire estate was to be confiscated.[1]

A.D. 741. Pope Zachary, writing to Boniface, a German bishop, affirmed that immersion in the name of the Trinity was essential to baptism, but that the moral character of the administrator was not essential. The pope's meaning was, that a bad man might be a good priest. Certainly the pope was a poor theologian.

The same pope, writing to the same bishop, referred to a priest, who, being ignorant of Latin, the only language then used in church services, in trying to repeat the form, said, "Baptizo te in nomine *Patria, et Filia. et Spiritu Sancta.*" You see what nonsense he made of it. Nevertheless, said the pope, as the priest was not heretical, but only ignorant, and as he intended to baptize in the name of the Trinity, though he blundered over

[1] Labbe and Cossart, vi. 1325.

it, there was no need to rebaptize the child. It must be considered all right.¹

In another letter the same pope mentioned one Samson, a Scotch priest, who held that a person might be made " a catholic Christian" by the imposition of the bishop's hands without baptism, and, as far as appears, without repentance or faith. Verily, there were singular people in those days!²

A.D. 754. Pope Stephen II. declared that if an infant was baptized in wine, there being no water to be had, the baptism was valid. And if, the infant being very sick, the baptism was performed *with* water, not *in* it, the water being poured from a shell or by the hand, and the proper words used, *that* baptism was valid. The pope might have spared himself the trouble of giving these decisions. There was no validity in either case.³

Immersion was the ordinary mode of celebrating baptism during all this period. The case mentioned above was one of the exceptions that were sometimes allowed when children were supposed to be in danger of death. Yet even in such circumstances the Anglo-Saxon priests were warned to abide by the ritual. At a Synod held at Calcuith, England, in 816, it was ordained that the priests should not pour water on the heads of the infants, but immerse them, according to the example of the Son of God, who was thrice immersed (so the Synod declared) in the water of Jordan.⁴ With this agrees Dr. Lingard's account. He states that "the regular way of administering it was by immersion." In the case of an adult, he " descends into the font, the priest depressed his head

---

¹ Labbe and Cossart, 1505.   ² *Ibid.* p. 1520.
³ *Ibid.* p. 1652.   ⁴ *Ibid.* vii. 1489.

three times below the surface, saying, 'I baptize thee, etc." In the case of an infant, "the priest himself descends into the water, which reached to his knees. Each child was successively delivered undressed into his hands, and he plunged it thrice into the water."[1]

A.D. 787. By a canon of the Second Council of Nice, all persons were forbidden to conceal heretical books. Bishops, priests, or deacons, disobeying the canon, were to be deposed; monks or laymen, excommunicated.[2] No wonder we are often so much at a loss respecting the opinions held by those who were called heretics, many of whom were not properly heretics, but genuine religious reformers. Their books were carefully gathered and burned, and it was made a crime to conceal them. You may write it thus:

"*Infallible recipe for the suppression of heresy.*

"If it is propagated by preaching, silence the preacher; if he *will* preach, put him out of the way. If it is propagated by writing, burn the books; should the author still persist, burn *him* too. *Probatum est.*"

A.D. 797. A capitulary of Charlemagne contains the following enactments:

All infants must be baptized within a year of their birth. Penalties for neglect—a nobleman 120 shillings; a gentleman 60 shillings; other persons 30 shillings.[3] These were heavy fines, for at that time the price of a good sheep was a shilling. A fine of one hundred and twenty sheep for neglecting the baptism of a child! Is it not monstrous?

[1] *History and Antiquities of the Anglo-Saxon Church*, i. 317–320.
[2] Labbe and Cossart, vii. 603.   [3] Labbe and Cossart, 1152.

THE REVIVAL PERIOD

CHRONOLOGICAL NOTES.

FROM A. D. 1073 TO A. D. 1517.

1077. Submission of the Emperor Henry IV. to the Pope.
1086. Plenary Indulgences first granted.
1095. Commencement of the Crusades to the Holy Land.
1099. Jerusalem taken by the Crusaders.
1123. Ninth General Council, at Rome.   Lateran 1.
1124. Peter of Bruys put to death.
1139. Tenth General Council, at Rome.   Lateran 2.
1153. Death of Bernard.
1155. Arnold of Brescia burned.
1170. Murder of Becket, December 29th.
1179. Eleventh General Council, at Rome.   Lateran 3.
1197. Death of Peter Waldo.
1209. Crusade against the Albigenses.
1215. Twelfth General Council, at Rome.   Lateran 4.
1216. The Dominican Order established.
1223. The Franciscan Order established.
1229. Rise of the Inquisition.
1245. Thirteenth General Council, at Lyons.
1249. University of Oxford founded.
1257. University of Cambridge founded.
1274. Fourteenth General Council, Lyons 2.
1300. The First Jubilee.
1308. The Papal See removed to Avignon.
1311. Fifteenth General Council, at Vienne.
1378. Commencement of the Great Western Schism.
1384. Death of John de Wycliffe, December 31st.
1409. Sixteenth General Council, at Pisa.
1414. Seventeenth General Council, at Constance.
1415. Martyrdom of John Huss, July 6th.
1416. Martyrdom of Jerome of Prague, May 30th.
1417. Martyrdom of Sir John Oldcastle.
1429. End of the Great Western Schism.
1431. Eighteenth General Council, at Basle.
1438. Invention of Printing.
1483. Birth of Luther, November 10th.
1484. Birth of Zuingli, January 1st.
1489. Birth of Cranmer, July 2d.
1497. Birth of Melanchthon, February 16th.
1498. Savonarola burnt at Florence.
1505. Birth of Knox.
1516. The Greek Testament published by Erasmus.
1517. Commencement of the Reformation.

CHAPTER I.

State of Affairs in Europe during this Period—The Crusades—Other important events—The Scholastic Divines and Philosophers—Universities—Printing.

I HAVE termed the period we are now entering on the "Revival Period," not on religious grounds only, but also because throughout the whole time a new and powerful impulse was acting on the human mind. In some sense it might be said that the darkness had passed away. That expression, however, must be taken in a very modified acceptation. What I mean is this: before the days of Hildebrand the darkness became denser and denser; but after those days light gradually forced itself in, and the commingling led to fierce conflicts. The Church of Rome continued as dark as ever; in some respects and in certain districts, it was an infernal blackness. Nevertheless, there were gleamings here and there, growing brighter and brighter, and tending to permanence; so that many men began to see where they were, which was a great point gained. It was as in Egypt of old. While the masses slumbered amid a darkness "which might be felt," there was a goodly number of God's people in the land, the true "children of Israel," and they "had light in their dwellings."

Significant and momentous events characterized the period. All Europe was in a ferment. First came the struggles between the popes and the emperors, in which many gallant warriors bit the dust, and flourishing kingdoms were laid waste. Then the Crusades—the veriest triumphs of ignorance, folly, superstition, and savageness that the world had ever seen—which more than decimated the nobility of Europe, exalted crowns at the expense of coronets, and stuffed the maw of the Church of Rome, already pretty well gorged with ill-gotten wealth. And yet some good came out of the evil. The tyrants of the world, whether despots or republicans—France has furnished types of both—"do not think so, or mean it in their hearts;" but the "King of kings" is on his throne, "judging right," and they work out his will, unwittingly, it may be, yet surely. So it was with the Crusades. At first the popes seemed to have it all their own way. They had hit upon a grand expedient to lull the European population to sleep in the arms of the church. Those who went to the holy wars traveled blindfold as priests guided them; and those who remained at home handed out gold, and silver, and precious things at the holy father's bidding. Rome drove a profitable trade in those days! But loss was at hand. The Crusades aroused and expanded men's minds. Commerce found additional avenues. Municipal institutions were established. The learning and the arts of the East became known. Intercourse with foreign nations was extended. Curiosity was awakened and inquiry stimulated. The literary treasures which had long been hidden in Eastern monasteries were brought to light and circulated, and "forgotten tongues" were learned again. All this was adverse to antichristian interests, and showed how the wise were once more "taken in their own craftiness." I am referring here to the great events of the period now before us. A simple enumeration must suffice. Think of Magna Charta, and the establishment of the English House of Commons—the invention of the mariners' compass, of gunpowder, of linen paper, and of the printing press—the battles of Crecy, Poictiers, and Agincourt, with their consequences—the great Western schism—the Council of Constance—the Wars of the Roses—the discovery of America and of the passage to the East Indies round the Cape of Good Hope. Were they not times of activity and progress?

Do not suppose that this has no connection with "Baptist History." It has. We found the records of the last period scant and fragmentary. Why? The world was asleep—intellectually and morally asleep. Rome had administered an opiate, and Europe lay slumbering in her lap. It is not surprising that under such circumstances it is difficult to spell out the annals of thought and freedom. Baptist sentiments can hardly be understood, much less appreciated, in such dozing days as those. They require for their full development a time of mental stir. They rejoice in those collisions which produce sparks and flames, and thus illuminate the nations. They have a tendency to produce them.

Let me proceed, then, to show how enlightenment sprang up and brought forth fruit in the "Revival Period."

It began with the Scholastic Philosophers and Divines. "The scholastic theology," says Mr. Hallam, "was, in its general principle, an alliance between faith and reason, an endeavor to arrange the orthodox system of the church, such as authority had made it, according to the rules and methods of the Aristotelian dialectics, and sometimes upon premises supplied by metaphysical reasoning." The scholastic philosophy, according to the same author, " seems chiefly to be distinguished from the theology by a larger infusion of metaphysical reasoning, or by its occasional inquiries into subjects not immediately related to revealed articles of faith."[1] These philosophers and divines are often described as learned triflers, who wasted their time and their energies in speculations, inquiries, and disputes which might have been as well or better let alone; and their ponderous folios, scarcely ever read, but mouldering away in public libraries, are pointed at as monuments of laborious folly. But this is a partial, perhaps a prejudiced, verdict. It is true that these men did perplex their brains with questions which they could not answer, and sometimes, like the angels Milton speaks of, "found no end in wandering mazes lost." It is also true that their theological investigations were conducted in a preposterous manner, since they strove to *reason out* their theology by the aid of the Aristotelian philosophy, instead of deriving it from the pure fountain of Holy Writ. And it must be granted that in their philosophical disquisitions they generalized and distinguished in a very dark manner, and that the student of their works is constantly thrown into inextricable doubt and difficulty by their twisted reasonings, the cloudy verboseness of their style, and the barbarous, unintelligible epithets they were in the habit of employing. Yet, with all these deductions, it cannot be denied that

[1] *State of Europe during the Middle Ages,* chap. ix. part ii. See also Bishop Hampden's *Bampton Lectures* on "The Scholastic Philosophy."

the school-men rendered great service in their day. There are bright gems in their writings, though hidden beneath much rubbish. If one sometimes meets with the uncouth, the ridiculous, or the hopelessly obscure, there are also vestiges of the profound and glimpses of the sublime. Their powerful intellects—for some of them were literary giants—were devoted, for the most part, to the upholding of Popery, and on that account we may not be sorry for the oblivion into which they have fallen. But they taught men to think, although their methods were as rude as were the mechanical tools of the times in which they lived; and the process of learning consequently slow. Their influence gradually extended, till at length it reached those who were more desirous of applying to practice the knowledge already acquired than of striking out new paths, which might, after all, lead into a wilderness. There was an imperceptible and general sharpening of the human mind. The number of independent inquirers continually increased, and the circle of 'nformation was widened. Then improved methods of mental training were devised. The establishment of numerous schools and universities was the result.

The following is a list of the principal school-men with the curious and whimsical titles given them:

	DIED A.D.
Peter Lombard, Master of Sentences	1164
Alexander of Hales, Irrefragable Doctor	1245
Thomas Aquinas, Angelic Doctor	1274
Bonaventura, Seraphic Doctor	1274
Alan of Lille, Universal Doctor	1294
Roger Bacon, Wonderful Doctor	1294
Richard Middleton, Solid and Copious Doctor	1304
Duns Scotus, Subtle Doctor	1308
William Occam, Singular and Invincible Doctor	1347

	DIED A.D.
Archbishop Bradwardine, Profound Doctor	1349
John Tauler, Sublime and Enlightened Doctor	1361
Durand of St. Pourcain, Most Resolute Doctor	1383
Peter de Alliaco, the Eagle of France, and the Maul of Errorists	1425
John Gerson, Most Christian Doctor	1429

Universities have been mentioned. The University of Paris was founded A.D. 1206. Eight others in different parts of Europe, including Oxford and Cambridge, were founded in that century. The next century was the age of Dante, Petrarch, Boccaccio, and the English Wycliffe and Chaucer; sixteen universities were founded in that century. Between the commencement of the fifteenth century and the close of the "Revival Period," twenty-nine more were added to the list. Great numbers of students attended those institutions. Many of them did not learn much, and in all cases the course of study was very limited. But assuredly the poet's affirmation—"A little learning is a dangerous thing"—is not to be regarded as an oracle. The students of the fourteenth and fifteenth centuries were undoubtedly inferior to those of the present age; but was it not better to get "a little learning" than to remain in ignorance? And may it not be fairly inferred that the universities and schools of the times now under consideration—for schools also increased and extended in every direction—exerted a highly beneficial influence on society at large?

Printing was invented about the middle of the fifteenth century; and the study of classical literature, which had been revived more than a hundred years previously, received a powerful impetus after the fall of Constantinople, when educated Greeks emigrated into Italy and France, and the love of learning was everywhere diffused.

CHAPTER II.

Paulicians in France and Italy—General View of the Reform Movement—Various Names given to the Reformers—Sentiments held by them—False Charge of Manichæism—Their Activity—Reinerus Saccho's Account.

WE have glanced at the Paulicians—their labors— their sufferings—and their various dispersions. Many of them sought a home in Italy and France about the close of the tenth and the beginning of the eleventh century. There they met with congenial spirits. Right-minded men in those countries had protested from time to time, though unavailingly, against Romish encroachments. The coming of the Paulicians inspired them with fresh courage, and from the middle of the eleventh century we read of a succession of valorous attacks upon those errors, superstitions, and vices, which not only abounded in less enlightened parts, but disgraced even the metropolis of Christendom.

These dissidents formed a numerous and compact body in Italy, where the Papal yoke chafed the necks of the people and made them restive. Had it not been for the support derived from the imperial power, Italy would have been Protestant before the Reformation. The success of Arnold of Brescia was an impressive warn'ng.

In the year 1143 he established a new form of government in Rome, which wrested the civil power out of the hands of the popes, and compelled them to content themselves with the management of ecclesiastical affairs. That the attempt was ill-advised, because society was not sufficiently prepared for it, seems evident; but the continuance of the new order of things for eleven years, and the alacrity with which the people adopted an anti-Papal policy, were remarkable signs of the times.

Peter of Bruys began his career as a reformer in the year 1104, and labored twenty years in the good work, chiefly in the south of France. He was followed by Henry of Lausanne, who preached the word of God with great success in the same district.

In the year 1170, Peter Waldo, a merchant of Lyons, renounced his secular engagements, and devoted himself to the revival of religion. He procured a translation of the New Testament into the French language, and spent his life in toilsome journeys among the people, during which he circulated portions of the Scriptures, preached, and by other methods sought to promote true godliness. Being joined by a number of like-minded men, their united efforts produced an extensive reformation. The "Poor Men of Lyons," as they were called, because they sacrificed worldly prospects and lived in poverty, became a numerous and formidable body. But persecution scattered them. Waldo himself escaped to Bohemia, and died there. Many of his followers settled in the same country.

Almost everybody has heard and read of the Waldenses. I will not enter into any account of the disputes respecting their origin. Some trace them to Peter Waldo, or some other person of a similar name. Others maintain that their name is derived from the Latin word " *Vallis*,' whence *Vallensis*, and by a slight corruption, *Valdensis*, in the plural, *Valdenses*, and then, *Waldenses*. The valleys of Piedmont, and other Alpine districts secluded from general observation, had given shelter for several ages to numbers of protesters against Romish corruptions. There they studied the Scriptures, cultivated practical piety, and served God according to the dictates of their consciences. There is no doubt that they sympathized heartily with the religious movements which were going on in other parts of Europe. In persecuting times their valleys were welcome places of refuge.

I have said that the south of France was the scene of the efforts of Peter of Bruys and Henry. Other reformers rose up in the same district. Toulouse and Albi were the towns about which they chiefly clustered. From the latter was derived the term " Albigenses."

Many other appellations were used to designate the reforming sects of the twelfth and thirteenth centuries. An inquirer is apt to be misled by them. He wonders at their divisions, and he asks, What were the diversities of opinion or practice by which they were distinguished from one another? But he asks in vain. The fact is, that the numerous names and descriptions found in imperial edicts and decrees of councils refer to parties who held substantially the same views. The occupations in which many of them were engaged, the places where they lived, or some peculiarity in their manners, furnished the distinctive titles which appear in ecclesiastical histories. Thus, they were called *Cathari*, or *pure*, because they pleaded for personal holiness and a pure church ; or

Humiliati, because of their modest deportment. The *Arnaldistæ* were the followers of Arnold ; the *Speronistæ*, of Speron. The *Garatenses, Albanenses, Bagnoroli, Roncaroli*, and *Concorrezenses* were inhabitants of the towns from which those appellations were derived. To the *Inzabatati* that name was given because so many of them belonged to the lower classes, who wore *sabots*, or wooden shoes ; or, as others suppose, because they refused to observe saints' days, holding that the Christian Sabbath is the only feast-day of the church, whence they were called *Inzabatati*, or *Sabbath-men*. Those who lived in southern France were often called *Texerants*, weavers, a large number of them gaining their livelihood by that trade. But all these names, and many more, were given to persons in Italy, France, Germany, Spain, and Flanders—for they were found in all those countries—whose religious views and practices were substantially the same. I say "substantially," because it is not to be supposed that they agreed with each other in every minute particular. The freedom which they claimed in separating from the Roman Church was still farther indulged among themselves. They would "call no man master." But the diversities of opinion which might prevail among them were perfectly consistent with unity in regard to the essential truths of the gospel.

However they might differ from one another on matters of small moment, they were " of one heart and one soul' in opposing the abominations of the Papacy.

They held the Pope to be Antichrist, and they regarded the Church of Rome as the mystical " Babylon" spoken of in the book of Revelation ; " the mother of harlots and abominations of the earth.' They maintained that the true church consisted only of believers. They pleaded for the translation of the Scriptures into all modern languages, that men might read "in their own tongues the wonderful works of God." They derided the ceremonies of Roman worship—the holy water, the incense, the bowing and kneeling, the ringing of bells, etc., etc., and taught that God is to be worshiped with "pious affections." They read and studied the divine word continually, so that many of them could repeat large portions of it from memory, and all were skillful in illustrating and defending their sentiments by appropriate quotations from Holy Writ. They denied the authority of bishops, the validity of the numerous distinctions of rank among the clergy, and the lawfulness of ecclesiastical titles. They denounced tithes. They declaimed against donations and legacies to churches or monasteries. They rejected councils. They abhorred image-worship and the reverence paid to relics. They did not believe in transubstantiation. They would not confess to the priests, saying that confession was to be made to God only. They laughed at dedications, consecrations, exorcisms, blessing of salt, spices, and candles, and other superstitious rites, regarding them as fitter themes for ridicule than reasoning. They would not pray to any saints. They held purgatory to be a fable, and they knew that it was a profitable one to the priesthood. They mocked at penances, indulgences, and all such trumpery. In a word, they acknowledged no authority in the church but that of the Lord Jesus Christ; and they refused to obey any laws relating to religion which were not to be found in the New Testament.

The ecclesiastical historians charge many of them with

Manichæism. But we ought to be careful how we entertain that charge. The evidence on which it is founded is derived from the writings of their enemies—their own books have been industriously destroyed—or from statements made by renegades, who saw that the more monstrous the picture which they drew of their former associates, the more acceptable would it be to the priesthood. It is well known that most of them were distinguished by such peculiarities as refusing to take oaths or to bear arms. It may also be admitted that some of them indulged in foolish, perhaps injurious speculations, mainly derived from the old Gnostic notions, "intruding into things which they had not seen." But the errors of a few ought not to be imputed to all; and it deserves to be considered, that when the church had substituted trash for truth and form for power, there was a strong temptation to get to the farthest possible remove from her. It might be innocently enough believed, that whatever was denounced and opposed by Rome was *therefore* worthy of regard; and in that twilight period it was difficult to see all things clearly.

Another thought or two may be added. Even if it be granted that Manichæan speculations prevailed among some of these sects, it is not to be supposed that they were understood by the mass of their adherents, who were unquestionably incompetent to engage in controversies of that kind. They knew something of faith in the Lord Jesus; they could trust, and love, and obey; and they could exemplify all gospel brotherly kindness; but as for discussions respecting the "two principles," the nature of souls, and such like matters, they were altogether out of their reach. Nor is it to be imagined that their teachers enlarged on such topics in their public ministrations, for that would have spoiled their usefulness. It is further to be considered, that the same writers who brought forward the charge of Manichæanism do also accuse the Cathari of horrible and not-to-be-mentioned crimes, which were said to be perpetrated by them in their religious assemblies—just as the heathen, in the first ages of the church, propagated similar calumnies against the Christians. The accusations were equally baseless in both cases, and were met by indignant denial. But if one accusation is manifestly outrageous and unfounded, may not the other be? Are we not entitled to the inference that there was, at the least, gross exaggeration, if not malicious libel? And finally, is it credible that those who avowed and manifested unlimited deference to the word of God were led astray by the fantasies of the Manichæan theory?

My readers may be surprised that I am saying nothing about the Baptists. Let them be patient. I am working my way toward them. In fact, many of those of whom I have just been writing advocated Baptist sentiments, and will have to be mentioned again before the account of this period is closed. But I think it preferable to give first a general outline of the history of all the dissenting parties.

The old writers bitterly complain of the activity of those who were called heretics. They could not understand it. The priests celebrated mass, heard confessions, attended to their various parochial duties, and were satisfied. As for the monks, if they fasted, meditated, prayed punished themselves, or said they did, that was sufficient The authors I am speaking of had no sympathy with the yearnings of Christian compassion for souls, and thought such efforts as the sectarians employed extremely irregular and troublesome. Human nature is the same everywhere and at all times. "They do exceedingly trouble our city," said the men of Philippi. The Jews of Thessalonica inflamed the mob by telling them that the men who "had turned the world upside down" had come to their city. Sleeping sinners wished not to be roused. False teachers, administering opiates to souls, look upon truth-tellers as intruders and foes, and raise the hue and cry against them.

Our Lord and his apostles experienced such treatment. The faithful in succeeding ages shared like sufferings. But they quailed not, nor did they desist. They delivered the message entrusted to them, whether men would hear or whether they would forbear.

This is attested by all the records. The Cathari in Germany, France, and Italy in the early part of the twelfth century, and the Lollards of England in the fifteenth, were equally guilty of the unpardonable crime —in Rome's eyes—of endeavoring to save their fellowmen from sin and hell, by directing them to the only Saviour. They saw them "perishing for lack of knowledge." They saw the pretended spiritual father giving his children a stone for bread, a serpent for a fish, and a scorpion instead of an egg, so that the people were dying for want of food. God had given *them* the "bread from heaven," and they were under orders to distribute it to the starving, "without money and without price." They spent their lives in obeying the command. In the exercise of their pious zeal they sometimes exposed themselves to great dangers. Reinerus Saccho, who will be mentioned presently, tells of one of the Cathari who swam over a piece of water in the depth of winter for the purpose of conveying a knowledge of the truth, as he understood and believed, to a person who lived on the opposite side.

Their zeal was guided by judgment. Preaching occupied the first place in their esteem. Whenever they could gain the public ear they gathered congregations and proclaimed " the glorious gospel of the blessed God," striving to convince men of the vanity of their hopes, and to lead the sinner from self and the creature to the finished work of Jesus. As it was in the days of our Lord himself, many thousands of the " common people" heard them gladly. Like their Master, they " went about doing good." While some itinerated from place to place, preaching as they could find opportunity, others visited houses and entered into familiar conversation with the inmates. To do this more effectually they carried with them packs of merchandise, like the peddlers of these times, and thus frequently contrived, during the disposal of their wares, to excite in the minds of their hearers an earnest desire to obtain that wisdom which is " better than rubies." Nor was this all. They established schools in many places, in which religious instruction was freely given; and it is said that not unfrequently they sent their own youths to the University of Paris, where they received the best education the world at that time afforded, and returned to their friends well qualified to meet Romish disputants and fight them with their own weapons. Another method adopted by them was the preparation of books. Those among them who were able composed treatises, which were copied—for printing was not invented till the middle of the fifteenth century—and circulated as widely as the means they possessed would allow. Thus great good was accomplished. Several of their books have been preserved. Among these is "The Noble Lesson," a precious Waldensian treatise, which is ascribed to the twelfth century, and forcibly exposes the follies and frauds of Rome. But the larger portion of the works of these early reformers have been destroyed. Such was the policy of the false church, to stifle thought, prevent discussion, and exact blind, uninquiring obedience.

Reinerus Saccho wrote a book against the Waldenses, under which title he evidently referred to the several bodies of alleged heretics then existing. This was about the year 1250. He said that he had belonged to the Waldenses about seventeen years, but had rejoined the dominant church. He received an appointment as inquisitor, doubtless because his knowledge of the sentiments and practices of his former associates eminently qualified him for that hateful office. In one part of his work he gives the following account of the manner in which the peddlers introduced religious topics among the families they visited:

"The heretics employ very cunning methods, by which to insinuate themselves into the society of the noble and great. They do it in this way. One of them takes with him some suitable articles of merchandise, such as rings or dresses, and offers them for sale. When they have bought what they choose, and ask the man if he has anything else to sell, he answers, 'I have more precious jewels than these; I would give them to you, if you would promise not to betray me to the clergy.' The promise being given, he proceeds: 'I have a gem so brilliant, that a man may know God by it. I have another, whose glow lights up the love of God in the heart of him who possesses it,' and so forth, speaking of the gems figuratively. Then he recites some chapter of the New Testament, such as the first of Luke—'In the sixth month the angel Gabriel was sent from God,' etc., or the Saviour's discourse in the thirteenth of John. When he observes that his hearers are beginning to be pleased, he quotes a passage from Matthew—' The Scribes and Pharisees sit in Moses' seat,' etc.—' Woe unto you, for ye shut up the kingdom of heaven,' etc., or that of Mark—' Woe unto you, for ye devour widows' houses,' etc. If he is asked to whom those threatenings apply, he answers, ' To the clergy and the monks.'

"Then he compares the state of the Roman Church with their own, saying, ' The teachers of the Roman Church are proud and pompous; they love the uppermost rooms at feasts, and to be called of men, Rabbi, Rabbi; but we desire no such rabbis. As for them, they are incontinent; but all our teachers are married, and live chastely with their wives. They are rich and covetous, as it is said, " Woe unto you that are rich, for ye have received your consolation;" but we, having sufficient food and clothing for our support, are therewith content. They themselves fight, and they excite others to war, and they give orders to kill and burn Christ's people, to whom it was said, " All they that take the sword shall perish with the sword;" but we suffer persecution for righteousness' sake. They eat the bread of idleness, "working not at all;" but we work with our own hands. They pretend to be the only teachers, as it is said, " Woe unto you, for ye have taken away the key of knowledge," etc.; but among us the women as well as the men teach, and he who has been a disciple but seven days can instruct another. Among them there is scarcely a teacher to be found who can recite three successive chapters of the New Testament; but almost every man and woman among us can recite the whole of it; and because we hold Christ's true faith, and teach a holy life and doctrine, they persecute us to death, as the Scribes and Pharisees persecuted Christ.

" 'Moreover, they say and do not, and they bind heavy burdens on men's shoulders, but will not touch them themselves with one of their fingers; but we do all that we teach. They compel men to observe human tradition rather than God's commands—such as fasts, feasts, and many other things, which are human institutes; but we teach that the doctrine of Christ and his apostles is to be kept, and that only.'

"Having talked in this way, the heretic adds—'Consider, now, which is the better state and the better faith,—ours, or that of the Roman Church—and make your choice.' And thus many a one is turned aside from the Catholic faith, takes the heretic into his house, conceals him there month after month, and is confirmed in his perversion."[1]

In this passage Saccho represents the Waldensian as doing all in his power to inflame the hatred of the people against the priesthood, and would have us believe that *that* was the main object in view. I have no doubt that much *was* said on those occasions that was calculated to induce distrust and avoidance of the Romish clergy. But the pious peddler did not stop there. No! His aim was

[1] *Biblioth. Maxima,* xxv. 273.

to guide souls to Christ, and numbers were led by those conversational sermons to renounce fleshly confidence and seek peace through the blood of the cross. With that necessary addition to the statement, Saccho's narration may be taken as trustworthy. It is pleasing to reflect that many of our Baptist ancestors were so honorably and usefully employed. The same spirit animated their successors several centuries afterward. Gretser, the Jesuit—he died A. D. 1636—who edited Saccho's book, placed this note in the margin of the account which has been now quoted: "A true picture of the heretics of our age, *especially of the Anabaptists.*"

CHAPTER III.

Success of the Reforming Parties—Consternation at Rome—Anathemas—The Dominican and Franciscan Orders—Sanguinary Persecutions—Crusade against the Albigenses—The Inquisition—Movement in England—John de Wycliffe—The Lollards—Bohemia.

ALL the authorities agree in testifying to the astonishing success of the Reformers of the twelfth and thirteenth centuries. The fact was, that they found "a people prepared for the Lord." Disgusted with the absurdities which were palmed on them in the name of religion, and shocked at the frauds and crimes which were daily perpetrated, they panted for something better than Rome proffered. The gospel of Christ, as preached by the persecuted sects, satisfied their souls. Great numbers of them believed and rejoiced in God. And the converts lived so well that they won universal respect. The barons of Southern France encouraged and protected them. It was to their interest to do so, for they were an honest, industrious tenantry, cheerfully paying rents and taxes, and thus contributing materially to the improvement of the estates on which they were located. Peace, prosperity, and good order prevailed wherever their communities were established. How could it be otherwise? They were all brethren, and they were "taught of God to love one another." They trained their children in principles of truth and uprightness. They abjured litigation and violence. Accounting one day is good as another, they lost no time by observing the holidays of the church. They never left their farms and merchandise to wander about on pilgrimages. They spent no money in the purchase of indulgences. They thought it wrong to build and endow monasteries. In short, they were quiet, thrifty people, and the land was the better for them. So their landlords judged and felt, and they shielded them against Papal fury at the hazard of their own safety. This kindness cost some of them dear; they were involved in the general ruin which the crusading fiends brought upon the country.

Rome looked on and trembled. Her subjects were fast leaving her. Her dominion was crumbling away. What was to be done to secure the remainder, and recover lost ground?

Cursing was first thought of, because it was easy, and their church was expert at it. So the bishops met in council year after year, and in all places where the Reformers appeared. Right heartily did they curse them. As our Lord had foretold, they "said all manner of evil against them falsely," hurled plenty of anathemas at their heads, and called upon the people to "hate them with a perfect hatred." A long list of those councils is before me. The bishops must have been very busy in those days. A large portion of their time must have been spent in attending the meetings.

A more reasonable plan was next invented. The reforming sects owed much of their success to preaching. Addressing the people in their own language, and in strains of rough but forcible eloquence, in which Scripture phrases were largely interwoven, they acquired an influence which the clergy sought in vain to snatch from them. An unpreaching priesthood was powerless in such a conflict. Feeling this disadvantage, ecclesiastical ingenuity hit upon a new scheme. In the early part of the thirteenth century the Dominican and Franciscan orders were founded. In their establishment special regard was had to the great necessity of the times. From among the monks of those orders men were chosen whose talents pointed them out as best fitted for the work, and they were sent out, after proper training, as public preachers. The churches being open to them, they were placed at once on vantage-ground, which they occupied with much zeal and skill. They cultivated the arts of pleasing, and soon learned to adapt themselves to the popular taste. And whereas the greedy propensities of the resident clergy had long exposed them to the shafts of ridicule and sarcasm, the new orders professed absolute poverty, receiving alms from the people for their daily support, and abjuring all right to hold property. That self-denying habit did not last long, but reputation had been secured by it, and the Dominicans and Franciscans stood high in public favor.

We must not, however, look for uniform and unswerving adhesion to peaceable measures. It was not in the nature of Rome to restrict herself in this matter. She always had a keen scent for blood. Persuasion was very well when there was no power to force obedience; but what could be so effective as the dungeon, the sword, and the fire? All the various modes of persecution were brought into active operation. The German emperors, instigated by the popes, issued sanguinary edicts, threatening the severest punishments to heretics of every name. The popes themselves acted with characteristic ferocity, and all the councils breathed the same spirit. The general council held at Rome in the year 1179, called the third of Lateran, led the way. If any of the heretics held public offices, they were to be turned out of them as soon as they were detected. All intercourse with them was forbidden; there was to be no buying or selling. Contracts with them were declared null and void. Houses in which they were found were to be destroyed; and if any person allowed them to settle on his lands, those lands were to be confiscated. Noblemen were commanded not to offer them protection. In every parish two or three inhabitants were to be appointed to make diligent and constant search for heretics, and to denounce them, whenever found, to the authorities. No advocate was to be permitted to plead for them when they were placed on trial. On conviction they were to be delivered over to the secular power to be burned. And all magistrates and judges were warned that if they did not faithfully execute these decrees, they would be excommunicated.[1]

Fearful scenes were enacted. The human bloodhounds were at work in all directions. "This year," says one of the writers of the times, speaking of the year 1233, "innumerable heretics were burned in every part of Germany."

Still they were unsubdued. Some evaded the search and lived in concealment. Some withdrew to more friendly lands. In Southern France the barons were slow

[1] Labbe and Cossart, x. 1503-1535.

to deprive themselves of the advantages which they derived from the residence of industrious, orderly men on their estates, and the exterminating process seemed likely to fall into abeyance.

This was too much for popes to bear. All the bigotry and brutality by which the holders of that office have ever been signalized, appeared to be concentrated in Innocent III. Enraged at the failure of the measures hitherto employed, he gave commissions to extraordinary legates, authorizing them to require the co-operation of the civil powers in hunting down and extirpating heretics. They prosecuted the murderous enterprise with unremitting ardor. But they were baffled in France. Innocent then proclaimed a crusade. Full pardon of sins was promised to all who would engage in the unholy war, with whatever plunder they might obtain, and even the territories of such princes and nobles as should resist. A large army was quickly gathered. The narrative of their proceedings occupies some of the darkest pages of the world's history. I have not space for the horrid details, and must therefore refer the reader to the ordinary sources of information. When they read the narratives which contemporary historians transmitted to posterity—how the crusaders attacked town after town, and indiscriminately butchered the inhabitants—how, on one occasion, when it appeared that the population of the place was partly Roman Catholic and partly heretical, the monk who controlled the movements of the army said, "Kill all; God knows who are his own"—how terms of capitulation were granted, and afterward basely violated—how, at Carcassone, fifty were hanged and four hundred burned —how, at Lavaur, the lady of the castle was thrown into a well, and stones heaped over her, and "the numberless heretics that were in the fortress were burned alive with great joy"—how, in short, the whole country of Languedoc, one of the finest portions of France, was reduced to a desert, tens of thousands of its inhabitants slaughtered, and all property destroyed;—I say, when they read these accounts and mark the fiendish barbarity of the men who proclaimed themselves defenders of the faith, and note that they were taught to expect pardon and heaven for their diabolical outrages, the readers will be prepared to admit that the system which sanctioned such villainous proceedings could have no other origin than the pit of darkness. It has been well observed by a modern writer that Popery is "the masterpiece of Satan."[1]

To the crusaders succeeded the Inquisition. The germ of that institution appeared in the directions for parochial visitation which have been already mentioned, and in the appointment of legates to various districts armed with special power to punish heretics. In the pontificate of Gregory IX., about the year 1233, the tribunal of the Inquisition was established; that is, the work of punishing and suppressing heresy was taken out of the hands of the bishops, and committed to inquisitors. The first court was stationed at Toulouse. Afterward the arrangement was extended to Spain and other countries, wherever the pope could gain admittance for it. Dominic had shown so much zeal in forwarding the object, and the members of his order, after his death, evinced such alacrity in the cause, that it was, at length, judged advisable to entrust

---

[1] Sismondi's *History of the Crusades against the Albigenses.* Jones *History of the Waldenses,* chap v. sect. 6. Michaud's *History of the Crusades.* Rev. R. Cecil's *Works,* iii. 416. Edition 1816.

the Inquisition wholly to the Dominicans. They have managed the tribunal in the most effective manner for the interests of Rome, while they have covered themselves with deserved infamy. The ecclesiastical historians will fully gratify curiosity in this respect. Those who wish to enter on an extended inquiry may be advised to procure Limborch's "History of the Inquisition," or Llorente's "History of the Inquisition in Spain." The secresy of its processes, the withholding of evidence from the accused, the refusal to confront him with the witnesses, the employment of spies, the use of torture in every horrible form that malignant ingenuity could devise, and the unmercifulness and hardheartedness of the whole procedure, have fixed a stigma on the Inquisition which can never be effaced. It has accomplished the bloody work of Popery with terrible faithfulness. In doing so it has taught the world that Rome is the relentless enemy of truth, right, and freedom.

These tremendous demonstrations produced, to a great extent, the desired effect. In France, the Albigenses, though not altogether exterminated, were silenced for a time. Numbers escaped from the murderers and fled the country. Such as remained were compelled to abstain from public acts of worship and to cease from all attempts to spread their opinions. After the plans of the Inquisition had been brought into regular operation, the church in France was but little troubled with heretics for the next two hundred years. The suppression was not so complete in Italy and Germany, and other parts of Europe, whence there was freer access to regions beyond the reach of the Inquisition.

At a synod held in London in the year 1286, Archbishop Peckham condemned certain metaphysical speculations which had been recently introduced, and which indicated that those who held them were opposed to transubstantiation. The seventh article furnishes a key to the whole. It condemns those who affirm that in such matters they ought not to be bound by the authority of Augustine, or Gregory, or the popes, but only by "Scripture and necessary reason."[1] These men, whoever they were, had imbibed right principles. One cannot help thinking that they must have been Baptists, so entirely does the position they maintained harmonize with our own. All honor to those, of every age and of every land, who will not bow, in matters of religion, to any other authority than "Scripture and necessary reason!"

There were tens of thousands of such men in Europe in the fourteenth and fifteenth centuries. The seed sown by Peter of Bruys, Henry, Peter Waldo, and others, had produced a plentiful harvest. In vain did inquisitors rage, and plot, and torture, and burn. They were neither omniscient nor omnipresent; mighty as they were, they were not omnipotent. If they cursed heresy *here*, it sprung up *there*, and when hard pressed, found shelter in many an inaccessible mountain or secluded valley. It was only in France that the exterminating policy succeeded, or seemed to succeed. In other parts of the Continent, the Reformers, though "cast down," were not "destroyed." They labored on noiselessly, with good success, and prayed and waited for better times. They abounded in every part of the German empire, and were found as far east as Constantinople. The Pope could not suppress them in Northern Italy. So numerous were they that a

---

[1] Labbe and Cossart, xii. 1262.

member of any of their churches might travel from Cologne to Milan and lodge every night in a brother's house.

A quickening impulse was given in the fifteenth century, which may be traced to England. The absorbing propensities of the ecclesiastics had excited general disgust, which often ripened into hatred. By operating on the fears of ignorant or seriously disposed persons, they had procured, in return for promised masses and other imaginary benefits, gifts and legacies of property to an immense amount. It was even affirmed that one half of the freehold estates of the country was in their possession. Profligacy was connected with wealth, and it was generally believed that none led more licentious lives than those who had taken the vow of celibacy. Besides this, the Mendicant Orders were daily increasing in numbers and strength, and as their popularity grew they became formidable rivals of the parish clergy, whose revenues were proportionably diminished. Hence arose contentions fierce and long. Each party strove to blacken the other, and from the revelations made on both sides, the people gained information which would have been otherwise hidden from them; for when rogues fall out, knavery is disclosed. These circumstances concurred to create much bitter feeling against the clerical orders. Dislike of their characters and deeds led to doubts respecting their teachings. Who could hope to hear good words from foul mouths? Opinions which had been long current in the church began to be regarded with suspicion, and customs which had become venerable for their antiquity were neglected, or submitted to with reluctance, perhaps sneered at.

John de Wycliffe's influence greatly contributed to these results. The insolence and rapacity of the Mendicant Orders first moved his indignation. He lectured against them at Oxford so powerfully that a determination to withstand their encroachments became general among thinking men, who were encouraged in their opposition by a considerable number of the nobility and gentry. Pursuing his inquiries, Wycliffe went farther than he originally intended, and propounded opinions which were extremely unpalatable to the staunch supporters of Popery. Rome upheld and protected the Mendicants, and stirred up persecution against all who opposed them. Wycliffe himself was in great danger, and would have fallen a victim to Papal vengeance, but for the patronage of the Duke of Lancaster and other men of high rank. He was compelled to leave Oxford however, and to retire to his rectory of Lutterworth, Leicestershire, where he died in peace, December 31st, 1384. For many years before his death he had continued to follow the leadings of truth and to yield to conviction. The injustice of the popes in regard to the Mendicant controversy, and their steadfast resolve to uphold all abuses and resist all reforms, filled him with disgust. What was the character of the system which cherished such enormities? In answering that question, he was led to compare the professed Christianity of the fourteenth century with the New Testament. The contrast shocked him. He saw that the religion of Christ and his apostles had long been practically abjured. The cunning, crooked policy of the Church of Rome in withholding the Scriptures from the people, and thus placing them in a state of abject dependence on the priesthood, was contemplated with abhorrence. He devoted himself to the enlightenment of his countrymen. By the publication of short tracts and carefully-written treatises, he set before them, in plain, nervous style, the evils in which they had been involved, and the truths which claimed their faith. He exhorted them to think and judge for themselves. He spent the latter years of his life in translating the Scriptures into the English language, and happily accomplished his purpose. For the first time the people of England had the opportunity of reading the word of God in their own tongue. A more precious gift than the English Bible could not have been bestowed upon them.

When the pope condemned Wycliffe's sentiments, he ordered the government of England to deal with him as a heretic; but the Reformer's friends were so numerous and influential that the Papal shaft fell harmless. The subject was taken up by the Council of Constance, which met in the year 1415, and a sentence of condemnation was issued. Wycliffe was out of their reach, but his books were widely circulated, and his bones were in his grave at Lutterworth. Books and bones were deemed fit objects of revenge, and orders were given to burn them. The sentence was not executed on his bones till the year 1428, when, by command of Pope Martin V., the tomb was violated. After a repose of upward of forty years, the remains of the good man were disinterred. The fire reduced them to ashes, and the ashes were cast into the Swift, a small stream that runs through Lutterworth. Thomas Fuller, the quaint church historian, says: "This brook has conveyed his ashes into Avon, Avon into Severn, Severn into the narrow seas, they into the main ocean. And thus the ashes of Wycliffe are the emblem of his doctrine, which now is dispersed all the world over."¹

After Wycliffe's death, the work was carried on by the Lollards, as those who embraced his opinions were called. The origin of that appellation is hid in obscurity. Some derive it from the name of one of their traders, Walter Lollard. Others, with Mosheim, regard it as "a term of reproach, brought from Belgium into England."² So great was their success that a Romish writer of those times affirms that one-half of the people had become disaffected to the church. This was an exaggeration; but it is evident, from the strenuous endeavors of the ecclesiastics to procure the adoption of violent measures, that the reforming party had assumed a formidable appearance. The Lollards traveled from place to place, preaching and teaching, as the Waldenses and others did on the Continent. Sometimes they obtained the churches; for many of them belonged to the clergy, and kept their places as Wycliffe had done before them. Sometimes they preached in the churchyards; they went to the fairs and markets, where the people congregated in great numbers, and often addressed immense assemblies, who heard them with much sympathy and respect. They circulated portions of the Scriptures as they had opportunity, and thus there grew up a strong attachment to the word of God. Men would sit up all night to read it or to hear it read by others. Some "would give a load of hay for a few chapters of St. James or St. Paul in English," as John Foxe testifies. The bishops stormed and

---

¹ *Church History of Britain*, book iv. cent. 15, sect. 52-54. See De Vaughan's *Life and Opinions of John de Wycliffe*.

² *Ecclesiastical History*, cent. xiv. part 2, chap. ii. sect 20.

raved. In the year 1400 they procured the enactment of the statute *de hæretico comburendo*, and burned as many so-called heretics as they could lay their hands on. In some instances even children were compelled to set fire to the pile in which their parents were to be consumed. Others "had trial of cruel mockings and scourgings." Yet the light of the gospel was not extinguished. When the Reformation broke out, there were many thousands in England who were already prepared to side with the friends of truth against the pope and his abettors.

From England the movement spread eastward as far as Bohemia. To what extent the influence of Wycliffe's writings was felt in the intervening countries I am not able to say, but that they were very popular in Bohemia is matter of history. Anne of Bohemia, queen of Richard II., befriended the Reformer, and probably transmitted copies of his works to her own country. John Huss possessed them and studied them attentively. Many others, some of them persons of high rank, were eager to obtain the Englishman's books. When the Council of Constance ordered them to be burned, upward of two hundred volumes, most of them richly bound and adorned, were thrown into the flames. But many more, we may be sure, were retained by their owners. Wycliffe, though dead, continued to speak and instruct. Peter of Bruys and other godly men lived in their successors. At the close of this period there were vast numbers in every part of Europe who "worshiped God in the spirit, rejoiced in Christ Jesus, and had no confidence in the flesh." Councils had thundered forth their curses, popes had issued their bulls, and inquisitors had exhausted their ingenuity —but it was all in vain. The Church of God still lived.

CHAPTER IV.

Various Opinions respecting Baptism—Berengar—Peter of Bruys—Henry of Lausanne—Arnold of Brescia—Cologne—England—Lombers—Pope Lucius III.

THE Reformers of whom I have given a brief account, although they differed from one another on some minor points, agreed in these three things: The sole authority of Scripture in matters of religion, in opposition to the burdens of tradition which had been laid upon men's shoulders; the spiritual nature of Christianity, and the consequent necessity of personal faith and regeneration by the Holy Spirit, in opposition to dead forms and reliance on the priesthood; and the right of every one to think and act for himself in these all-important affairs, in opposition to the tyrannical assumptions of the Romish clergy, sustained by the secular power. They sought Bible truth, spiritual life, soul freedom. This threefold cord will guide us in the labyrinthine darkness of the Middle-Ages. Whenever we can lay our hands on it we find the grace and power of God.

I come now again to the consideration of baptism. On this subject there were differences of opinion. Some retained the doctrine and practice of the dominant church, others rejected both baptism and the Lord's supper; for the former they substituted a ceremony which they called "consolamentum," or the "baptism by fire," in allusion to the words of John the Baptist. "They assembled in a room dark and closed in on all sides, but illuminated by a large number of lights affixed to the walls. Then the new ca didate was placed in the centre, where the presiding officer of the sect laid a book, probably the Gospel of John, on his head, and gave him the imposition of hands, at the same time reciting the Lord's prayer."[1] In arguing against infant baptism they adopted the same course of reasoning as has been employed by the Baptists in all ages. They uniformly exposed the absurdity of baptizing those who could not believe. A third party propounded scriptural truth, but evidence is wanting as to how far their views were developed. It may be inferred that they abstained from baptizing children, as in all consistency they were bound to do. The fourth class consisted of those who not only taught Baptist sentiments, but openly reduced them to practice. I will furnish such information as I have gathered respecting them, derived from the original sources. There will be no hazarding of conjectures or surmises.

Many of the councils of this period refer in general terms to the heretics of the times, condemning them in the lump, without enumerating the various sects, and sometimes without any specification of their opinions. In some instances, however, there is such reference. Those who rejected "baptism of children" were condemned by the following councils, viz.: Toulouse, A.D. 1119; Lateran II., A.D. 1139; Lateran III., A.D. 1179; London, A.D. 1391. I do not affirm that all the parties condemned

[1] Eckbert cont. Catharos, in *Biblioth. Maxima*, xxiii. 615.

were Baptists, because probably some of them rejected both baptism and the Lord's supper; but I wish to direct particular attention to the fact that their denial of infant baptism was uniformly justified by them on the ground of the non-existence of faith in the child. They saw clearly that in the New Testament faith was always represented as the prerequisite to baptism, and hence they naturally enough said, " These children cannot believe— why do you baptize them ?"

Berengar of Tours was an excellent man. He was principal of the cathedral school in that city, and afterward archdeacon of Angers. His fame as a teacher induced young men in different parts of France to repair to him for instruction. Neander says, " He was constantly deviating from the beaten track—striking out his own path, in matters both of secular and ecclesiastical science —a proof of the independence and freedom of judgment with which he pursued all his inquiries. Thus, for example, he studied to make improvements in grammar, and endeavored to introduce a new pronunciation of Latin."[1] This freedom and independence eminently characterized his theological researches. The controversy on transubstantiation attracted his attention, and he was quickly repelled by the absurdities propounded on that subject. He saw that Christian ordinances required faith in those who observed them, without which the observance was altogether useless; and in regard to the Lord's supper, in particular, he abjured the commonly received opinion, and taught the spiritual presence of the Saviour, in connection with the believing apprehension, on the part of the communicant, of the truths embodied in the

---

[1] *History of the Church*, iii. 533.

institution. For this he was severely persecuted, condemned, and compelled, through fear of death, to renounce his alleged heresies. But he reasserted them, and they were embraced by great numbers of his former pupils, and by many other persons in France and Germany.

In the following extract from one of Berengar's writings, we may see in what light he viewed baptism and the Lord's supper: "Our Lord Christ requires of thee no more than this. Thou believest that out of his great compassion for the human race he poured out his blood for them; and that thou, by virtue of this faith, wilt be cleansed by his blood from all sin. He requires of thee, that, constantly mindful of this blood of Christ, thou shouldst use it to sustain the life of thy inner man in this earthly pilgrimage, as thou sustainest the life of thy outward man by meat and drink. He also requires of thee that, in the faith that God so loved the world as to give his only begotten Son as a propitiation for our sins, thou shouldst submit to outward baptism, to represent how thou oughtest to follow Christ in his death and in his resurrection. The bodily eating and drinking of bread and wine—says he—should remind thee of the spiritual eating and drinking of the body and blood of Christ, that whilst thou art refreshed in the inner man by the contemplation of his incarnation and of his passion, thou mayest follow him in humility and patience."[1] A person who held such sentiments as these could not with propriety practice infant baptism. Consequently, we find that he is charged by writers of those times with attempting to overthrow that rite. Deoduin, bishop of Liege (died A.D. 1075), says of Berengar, and of Bruno,

[1] Neander's *History of the Church*, iii. 525.

bishop of Angers, who had been one of his pupils—" as far as is in their power they overturn the baptism of little children." Guitmund, a Benedictine monk, and afterward archbishop of Aversa (died A.D. 1080), uses similar language, and expresses his horror at the "depth of all evil" into which such persons would be likely to fall, whom the devil should persuade, through Berengar, to renounce their baptism in infancy, since, as he supposed, they would hold themselves at liberty to plunge into every vice, in the assurance that whenever they might be baptized all would be cleansed away.[1] We cannot sympathize with Guitmund in that matter. We pity his ignorance. Berengar's teaching did not produce such effects.

Berengar died A.D. 1088. Later writers have stated that his followers were very numerous. It is even said that in the next century as many as 800,000 persons professed his sentiments. It is obvious, however, that any exact enumeration is impossible. As Berengarians the party was not of long continuance. But the principles remained, though the name was disused, and were spread over a large part of Europe.

In less than twenty years after Berengar's death, Peter of Bruys was preaching in the south of France with great power and blessing. I wish we had the materials for the history of this movement and Peter's own account of his doctrine. We know not by what means he was led to those thoughts and conclusions which issued in his assuming the bold position of a reformer. If the abbot of Clugny is to be believed, he had been a priest, an for some unmentioned reason had been dismissed

---

[1] *Biblioth. Maxima*, xviii. 441, 531.

from his parish; but the abbot refrains from any statement of facts.[1] Certainly Peter must have had a profound conviction of the utter worthlessness and injurious tendency of the religion of the age. He saw that people were "mad upon their idols," substituting the outward for the inward, the name for the reality. It seemed to him that nothing but a radical change would meet the necessity of the case. Seeing that the churches were held in so great reverence as consecrated buildings, the only places where worship should be celebrated, he taught that God's blessing was not limited to localities, and that prayer to him, if sincere, was as acceptable in a shop or in the market-place as in a church, in a stable as before an altar. Reproving the pomp and splendor, and the constant appeals to the senses by which the public services were characterized, especially the chants and the music, he instructed the people that "pious affections" were far more pleasing to God than loud vociferations. Instead of conniving at the adoration of the cross, or allowing any respect to be paid to it, he said that it should only be regarded as the representation of an instrument of cruelty, and therefore worthy of all detestation and fit to be destroyed. There was a practical demonstration of the effects of his instructions. The people assembled in great numbers on Good Friday, collected all the crosses they could lay their hands on, made a bonfire of them, roasted meat at the fire, and ate it publicly. Once more, Peter dissuaded his hearers from attempting to benefit the dead by prayers or by payment for priests' masses. No advantage, he told them, could accrue to the departed from anything of the kind.

[1] *Biblioth. Maxima*, xxii. 1058.

Baptism and the church were contemplated by Peter in the pure light of Scripture. The church should be composed, he constantly affirmed, of true believers, good and just persons; no others had any claim to membership. Baptism was a nullity unless connected with personal faith, but all who believed were under solemn obligation to be baptized, according to the Saviour's command

Peter was not merely what is now called a "Baptist in principle." When the truths he inculcated were received, and men and women were raised to "newness of life," they were directed to the path of duty. Baptism followed faith. Enemies said that this was *Anabaptism*, but Peter and his friends indignantly repelled the imputation. The rite performed in infancy, they maintained, was no baptism at all, since it wanted the essential ingredient, faith in Christ. Then, and then only, when that faith was professed, were the converts really baptized.[1]

Great success attended Peter's labors. At first he preached in thinly-populated places and villages. But, like his Divine Master, he "could not be hid." Multitudes flocked to hear him, and the towns and cities of Narbonne and Languedoc were enlightened by his ministry. This continued for twenty years. What an interesting chapter would it form in the history of the church if the record of the facts could be recovered! What striking conversions! What penetrating, powerful sermons! What revival meetings! What lovely manifestations of Christian fellowship! Doubtless such scenes were witnessed, and ministering angels rejoiced; and the news reached the saints in heaven, causing a fresh

---

[1] *Magdeburg. Centuriatores*, cent. xii. 331.

outburst of joyful acclaim. And again they sang, "Thou art worthy, for thou wast slain, and hast redeemed us to God by thy blood out of every kindred, and tongue, and people, and nation; and hast made us unto our God kings and priests; and we shall reign on the earth."

Instead of recitals which would have gladdened our hearts, we have but the meagre and melancholy jottings of a foe, written with the pen of prejudice. Peter the Venerable, abbot of Clugny, whose treatise against the Petrobrusians is our only authority on this subject, sums up all in these words: "The people are rebaptized, the churches profaned, the altars dug up, the crosses burned, flesh eaten in public on the very day of the Lord's passion, the priests scourged, the monks imprisoned, and compelled by threatenings and torments to marry wives."[1] When we bear in mind that in the first ebullitions of zeal during the Reformation in the sixteenth century the instruments and objects of superstition, as well as its abettors, sometimes received rather rough usage, the people thus evincing their indignation at the trickery which had been practiced upon them, we may wonder the less at any uproarious proceedings taking place four hundred years before. We are under no necessity, however, of believing that the "rebaptized" people committed the outrages spoken of. At such times there are always many to be found who are willing to attach themselves outwardly to an enterprise for the sake of some worldly advantage, and when they run into excesses the blame is laid on the cause with which they are connected. Yet, partial and unsatisfactory as Peter the Venerable's statement is, it indicates the extent and effect of the Reformer's

[1] *Biblioth. Maxima*, xxii. 1035.

efforts. Labbe, the Jesuit (also one of the editors of the
"Concilia"), evidently regarded Peter of Bruys as a man
by whose labors great injury was inflicted on Romanism.
These are his words: "Almost all the heretics who
came after Peter of Bruys trod in the steps of his heresy;
hence he may be deservedly called the parent of
heretics."[1]

Martyrdom awaited him. Having preached with his
accustomed fervor at St. Gilles, in Languedoc, the infuriated populace seized him and hurried him to the stake.
It was like the murder of Stephen—the act of a lawless
mob. Nor can we doubt that the Lord, whose presence
cheered the first martyr, comforted Peter of Bruys, and
enabled him to meet death, even in that terrible form,
with the composure of faith.

Such was the end of a Baptist minister in the twelfth
century. Peter's martyrdom is supposed to have occurred
about the year 1124. But the bereaved flocks were not
forsaken. Another shepherd was ready to take charge of
them.

I have again to complain of the paucity of materials
for our history. The little that is known of Henry of
Lausanne excites an earnest desire for fuller information.
But for even that little we are obliged to be dependent on
the reports of enemies whose trustworthiness cannot be
relied on. They were apt at defamation.

Henry was a monk, an inmate of the monastery of
Clugny, a town about forty-six miles from Lyons, in
France. The seclusion and inactivity of that mode of
life ill comported with his fervid spirit. He felt a consciousness of power, and longed to do something for the

[1] *Concil.* x. 1001.

cause of God. Being eminently gifted as a public speaker, he engaged in a preaching itinerancy. He commenced his labors at Lausanne in Switzerland, about the year 1116, and thence proceeded to the south of France. His first efforts were directed to the reformation of manners and morals. He declaimed against the vices of the clergy and the general dissoluteness that prevailed, and he preached so eloquently that all classes bowed beneath his rebukes, great numbers confessing their sins and entering upon a course of reform. At Mans, where, while the bishop was absent at Rome, he was permitted to occupy the cathedral, his influence over the people became so powerful that when the bishop returned they refused to receive him, and clamorously declared that they would adhere to Henry. Hildebert, however—that was the bishop's name—managed the affair with discretion, and Henry chose another field. He repaired to the district where Peter of Bruys had preached, and entered into his labors. By this time his own views were greatly enlarged. From opposing vice he proceeded to attack error. A treatise which he published, and which unfortunately is not now extant, contained a full exposition of his sentiments. It is said that on some points he went farther than Peter, but what they were is not stated. This is certain, that he fully agreed with him on the subject of baptism, and that those who received the truth were formed into " apostolical societies," or, as we should now say, Christian churches.

His success alarmed the church dignitaries of the country, who procured his arrest. He was condemned by the Council of Pisa in the year 1134, and sentenced to confinement in a monastery. Having obtained his liberty after a short imprisonment, he resumed the work of preaching, and for ten years the cities of Toulouse and Alby, and the district in which they are situated, enjoyed the benefit of his exertions. Astonishing results followed. Many nobles sanctioned and protected him. Multitudes were added to the churches, and, as in the times of the apostles, "a great company of the priests were obedient to the faith." The celebrated Bernard of Clairvaux says, in a letter to a nobleman, "The churches are without flocks, the flocks without priests, the priests are nowhere treated with due reverence, the churches are leveled down to synagogues, the sacraments are not esteemed holy, the festivals are no longer celebrated;" and he states in one of his sermons, that "Women forsake their husbands, and husbands their wives, and run over to this sect," and that "Clergymen and priests desert their communities and churches."[1] Stripping these expressions of their Romish meaning, the facts of the case clearly show themselves. Had Henry been the historian, he would have said, "God has blessed his work; priests and people have received the gospel; true churches are now formed; Christian ordinances have supplanted the old superstitions, and the commands of Christ, and his only, are obeyed."

Pope Eugenius heard of it, and sent Cardinal Alberic, accompanied by Bernard, to quash the movement. Bernard was reverenced as a great saint, and was accustomed to carry everything before him; but the Henricians knew Scripture as well and probably better than he, and quoted it against him with great effect. He met with poor suc-

[1] Epist. 240. In *Cantic. Sermones*, 65, 66. Opera, i. 438–440, iii. 415–432. Ed. Paris. 1667.

cess. But when preaching failed, force was employed. Henry was again seized. A council held at Rheims in the year 1148 condemned him, and he ended his days in prison. Samson, the archbishop of Rheims, disapproved of shedding blood for the faith, and so the perpetual dungeon was substituted for the stake. Henry languished in solitude and privation (for they put him on meagre diet) till the Master called him. The time of his death has not been recorded.[1]

Hildebert, bishop of Mans, styled Henry "a great snare of the devil and a celebrated champion of Antichrist."[2] These expressions are significant of extensive influence. And, indeed, it appears that his sentiments spread not only in Languedoc, where he chiefly labored, but in other parts of France. It is probable that his disciples traveled into Germany, and propagated the same doctrine there.

Wall says, in his "History of Infant Baptism," that Peter of Bruys and Henry were "the first Antipædobaptist preachers that ever set up a church or society of men holding that opinion against infant baptism, and rebaptizing such as had been baptized in infancy."[3] I do not admit the correctness of Mr. Wall's statements, because those churches can be traced a great way farther back. I was about to say, that we can trace their history as far back as the year 31, when the first church was formed at Jerusalem; but Mr. Wall's epithet, "Antipædobaptist," stands in the way. That church was not an

---

[1] Dr. Allix says that he was burnt at Toulouse, A.D. 1147, but he gives no authority for the statement. *Remark on the Albigenses,* chap. **xiv.**
[2] *Biblioth. Maxima.* xxi. 157.
[3] Vol. ii. p. 250. Third edition.

"Antipædobaptist" church, because Pædobaptists had not then appeared in the world. Infant baptism was then unknown. Mr. Wall, however, grants that there were Baptist, or, as he calls them, "Antipædobaptist," churches in the twelfth century. That is so far good. Some persons in these times wish to ignore all this, and make us start from the sixteenth century. Mr. Wall knew better.

It is much to be regretted that we are not furnished with any particulars respecting the order of worship or the mode of church government adopted by Peter and Henry. There can be no doubt that plainness and simplicity characterized the whole, and that there was a rigid adherence to the laws of the New Testament. They called Jesus "Master and Lord." They rendered obedience to his commandments, as interpreted and exemplified by the apostles, and were so scrupulously conscientious in these respects that the title "Apostolicals" distinguished them from others. How much pleasure it would afford us to read a full description of one of their meetings—and copies of the hymns they sang—and a sermon or two preached by Peter or Henry—and a few extracts from their church-books—that we might know in what manner they sought to "walk and to please God!"

Arnold of Brescia occupies a conspicuous place in history. By some writers he has been classed with "Baptist martyrs." There is not sufficient evidence to warrant such a statement. Arnold was a reformer, but not a separatist. Himself an ecclesiastic, he employed all his energies in attempting to restore his order to primitive plainness and purity, and thus to regain the moral influence which had been lost, and with it to promote a revival of scriptural piety. He declaimed loudly against the wealth and luxury of the clergy. He taught that they should not be possessors of worldly property, but be supported by tithes and the voluntary offerings of the people. So acceptable were his teachings that commotions were feared, and Arnold was banished from Italy. He pursued the same course in France, whither he had retired, and again he was banished. We then hear of him in Switzerland, where he was still indefatigable in his endeavors. The great Bernard, now called *Saint* Bernard, was unremitting in his efforts to stop Arnold's progress, and the language employed in his letters seems to imply that the reformer did not content himself with inveighing against the pomp and pride of the clergy, but exposed whatever evils he discerned, and labored to remove all the obstacles that stood in the way of religious restoration. His own life was a pattern of propriety. "Would that his doctrine," says Bernard, " were as sound as his life is austere. If you would know the man, he is one who neither eats nor drinks; like the devil, he hungers and thirsts only for the blood of souls."[1] Hard words, Bernard! very unlike a saint!

Arnold's sentiments became popular at Rome. He went there and thundered out well-deserved invectives against the union of secular and ecclesiastical power in the person of the pope. His Holiness, he said, ought to be a prelate only, not a prince. He exhorted the people to demand their ancient liberties, and restore the old form of government. They adopted his policy. The pope was required to resign his temporal power. Insurrection

[1] Epist. 195.

THE REVIVAL PERIOD.

followed. Rome was in a state of disturbance during the reigns of four successive popes, from 1143 to 1154. Arnold was there all the time. But Pope Adrian IV. quelled the storm. He laid Rome under an interdict. The terrified inhabitants promised to expel Arnold if the pontiff would remove it. Arnold fled. But he was taken prisoner in Tuscany, and conveyed back to Rome, where he was hanged, or, as some say, crucified. His body was burned, and the ashes thrown into the Tiber. This was in the year 1155.

The only authority for the ascription of Baptist sentiments to Arnold is Otto of Frisingen, who states in his Chronicle that Arnold was " said (*dicitur*) to be unsound in his views respecting the sacrament of the altar and the baptism of children."[1] The common histories give no support to this affirmation. Indeed, unless there has been an enormous suppression of facts, Arnold's attention was mostly confined to the points above mentioned. Bernard styles him "a flagrant schismatic." Baronius designates him " the patriarch of political heretics."

But Neander observes, "The inspiring idea of his movements was that of a holy and pure church, a renovation of the spiritual order, after the pattern of the apostolical church. . . . The corrupt bishops and priests were no longer bishops and priests—the secularized church was no longer the house of God. It does not appear that his opposition to the corrupt church had ever led him to advance any such remarks as could be interpreted into heresy; for, had he done so, men would, from the first, have proceeded against him more sharply, and his opponents who spared no pains in hunting up every-

---
[1] Labbe and Cossart, vi. 1012.

thing which could serve to place him in an unfavorable light, would certainly never have allowed such heretical statements of Arnold to pass unnoticed. But we must allow that the way in which Arnold stood forth against the corruptions of the church, and especially his inclination to make the objective in the instituted order, and in the transactions of the church, to depend on the subjective character of the men, might easily lead to still greater aberrations."[1] I cannot but acknowledge the correctness of these remarks, and am disposed to think that either Arnold's opposition originally extended to other particulars beside those specified, or that his followers separated from the church after his death. The "Arnoldists" were proscribed, with others, by Pope Lucius, A. D. 1183, and by the Emperor Frederic II., in a sanguinary edict against the various classes of heretics, issued in 1224.

We have not the means of determining how the societies established by Peter and Henry prospered after their death. None of the names of their successors have reached us. It can only be affirmed, generally, that the work continued to advance, as may be sufficiently gathered from the proceedings of sundry councils.

The heretics, as they were called, were very numerous at Cologne. Evervinus, provost of Steinfeld, wrote against them in 1146, and applied to Bernard for aid, who discoursed virulently on the points in debate, and made up in railing for the lack of sound argument.

Eckbert, abbot of St. Florin, published thirteen sermons in 1163, in which he labored hard to fix the charge

---

[1] *History of the Church*, iv. 149. See also the *Biographical Dictionary* of the Society for the Diffusion of Useful Knowledge, Art. "Arnold of Brescia."

of heresy on the Cathari, who, as usual, were accused of Manichæism. While both he and Evervinus affirm that the Cathari generally rejected baptism altogether, substituting for it the "*Consolamentum*," they agree in stating that a portion of them differed from the others in that respect. They rejected infant baptism only, on the ground that infants could not believe, and they taught that baptism should be administered to none but adults.[1]

The thirty "Waldenses," as they are called, who appeared in England about the year 1159, probably belonged to the same party. William, of Newbury, the chronicler, charges them with "detesting holy baptism," which may be fairly understood as implying the rejection of baptism as then practiced by Rome.[2]

In 1165 a council was held at Lombers, for the purpose of dealing with some persons who were known by the appellation of *boni homines* or "good men"—whether imposed on them by others, or assumed by themselves, does not appear—and who were manifestly Baptists. When asked what they thought about baptism, they answered that they would not say, but that they would reply "from the gospel and the epistles," meaning that they would adduce the Scripture testimony on the subject, and maintain the necessity of abiding by the word of God.[3] The bishops failed to convince them of their error.

In a bull issued by Pope Lucius III., he denounced all who held or taught any sentiments differing from those professed by the Church of Rome; and he particularly refers to baptism.[4] The Baptists gave a great deal of trouble to the Papists in those days.

[1] *Biblioth. Maxima*, xxiii. 601.   Gieseler, iii. 397.
[2] Labbe and Cossart, x. 1405.   [3] *Ibid.* 1470-1479.   [4] *Ib.* x. 1737.

The terrible storm which fell upon southern France in the crusade against the Albigenses doubtless swept away many of the Baptist churches, and scattered their surviving members. Notwithstanding the vigilance of the persecutors, great numbers escaped. Italy, Germany, and the eastern countries of Europe received them.

CHAPTER V.

Heretics of the Fourteenth and Fifteenth centuries—Wycliffe's Sentiments on Baptism—The Bohemians—Baptism among the Waldenses Church Government—Immersion.

THE references to heretics in the proceedings of councils during the fourteenth and fifteenth centuries are comparatively few in number and very general in their character. The particular opinions held are not specified, but directions are given to exercise constant vigilance lest heresies should creep in unawares, and magistrates are specially charged to apprehend all suspected persons, and to put in execution the laws against them if convicted. There was no lack of zeal in that respect. The civil powers were completely under the control of the clergy, who, while they indulged their own savage propensities, and sought by such means to perpetuate the reign of ignorance and delusion, continued to evade the responsibility. *They* did not torture and burn the heretics! How could it be supposed that ministers of mercy would have anything to do with deeds of blood? Oh no! They only delivered them up to the secular power! The base hypocrites would have hurled the thunders of excommunication against the secular power if the heretics had been spared. *They* did not burn them, but they delivered them up for the purpose of being burned! Were they not more than accessories to the murders?

Many of the reformers of this period inculcated truths, the legitimate consequences of which involved all, or nearly all, for which we now contend. When they argued that a Christian church should be a society of the pious, and that Christian ordinances belonged to believers only, they had but another step to take in order to appear as full Baptists. Take Dr. Vaughan's statement of John de Wycliffe's views:

"On baptism his expressions are at times obscure; but, according to his general language, the value of a sacrament must depend wholly on the mind of the recipient, not at all on the external act performed by the priest; and, contrary to the received doctrine, he would not allow that infant salvation was dependent on infant baptism."[1] Connect with this the charge brought against him by the Council of London, in 1391, as contained in one of the "articles" extracted from his "Trialogus," and which was to this effect—that those who held that infants dying without baptism could not be saved, were "presumptuous and foolish."[2] Now, if Wycliffe believed that the ordinances of Christianity require faith in those who observe them, he would necessarily see the futility of infant baptism, and the expression of even a doubt respecting the connection between infant baptism and salvation would be regarded in that age as equivalent to a denial of the divine authority of the rite. That great man, however, lived and died a priest of the Roman Catholic Church. But, as I before hinted, the light he had re-

---

[1] *John de Wycliffe, D.D., A Monograph*, p. 461.
[2] Labbe and Cossart, xi. 2080.

ceived would have guided him into Baptist paths had he followed it fully. Probably, if he had lived in France or Germany, he would have been at the head of one of the seceding parties. His writings perpetuated the beneficial influence exerted in his lifetime. It may be safely concluded that many of his immediate followers, and others who obtained possession of those writings, were induced thereby to extend their religious inquiries, and thus became more completely New Testament Christians than he was himself. That they labored incessantly in propagating the truth is manifest from the decrees of a council held at Oxford in the year 1408, by which the clergy were strictly enjoined not to allow any persons to preach in their churches without episcopal license, and to be prompt in denouncing to the proper authorities all who were chargeable with heresy. The parties so denounced were to clear themselves of the charge or be reconciled to the church, or in default of such clearance or reconciliation be committed to the civil power, in order to be " burned in a conspicuous place," for a terror to all others.[1] Notwithstanding such perils, the servants of God persevered in their efforts. They scattered abroad religious tracts, they taught the young in schools, and they preached in private houses when the churches were shut against them. Thus the English mind was prepared for the Reformation. A very full and interesting account of their proceedings is contained in " The Lollards," one of the volumes published by the London Religious Tract Society.

Some of them, perhaps the majority, opposed infant baptism. Indeed, it is expressly affirmed by several his-

---

[1] Labbe and Cossart, 2089–2102.

torians that they refused to baptize their new-born children, and that they were charged before the ecclesiastical authorities with maintaining that infants who died unbaptized would be saved. This was an unpardonable sin in the eyes of the Pædobaptists, and the Lollards suffered grievously for it.[1]

I stated in a former chapter that in the twelfth century Peter Waldo and many of his adherents retired to Bohemia to escape the fury of the persecution. Others followed them in succeeding centuries. There they served God according to their consciences. Diversities of opinion existed among them. All held that "in articles of faith the authority of Holy Scripture is the highest;" but, while some retained infant baptism, others rejected it, and among them the practice of believer's baptism prevailed.[2] "Authentic records in France," says Mr. Robinson, "assure us that a people of a certain description were driven from thence in the twelfth century. Bohemian records of equal authenticity inform us that some of the same description arrived in Bohemia at the same time, and settled near a hundred miles from Prague, at Salz and Laun on the river Eger, just on the borders of the kingdom. Almost two hundred years after, another undoubted record of the same country mentions a people of the same description, some as burnt at Prague, and others as inhabiting the borders of the kingdom; and a hundred and fifty years after that, we find a people of the same description settled, by connivance, in the metropolis, and in several other parts of the kingdom. About one hundred and twenty years later,

---

[1] *Martyr's Mirror*, p. 275.
[2] Jones' *History of the Waldenses*, ii. 44-46, 201.

we find a people in the same country living under the protection of law on the estate of Prince Lichtenstein, exactly like all the former, and about thirty or forty thousand in number. The religious character of this people is so very different from that of all others that the likeness is not easily mistaken. They had no priests, but taught one another. They had no private property, for they held all things jointly. They executed no offices, and neither exacted nor took oaths. They bore no arms, and rather chose to suffer than resist wrong. They held everything called religion in the Church of Rome in abhorrence, and worshiped God only by adoring his perfections and endeavoring to imitate his goodness. They thought Christianity wanted no comment, and they professed their belief of that by being baptized, and their love to Christ and one another by receiving the Lord's supper."[1]

There has been much dispute respecting the Waldenses. Some have represented them as being originally all Baptists. Others, on the contrary, persist in affirming that they were all Pædobaptists. Neither statement is correct. In the first place, we must inquire who are meant by the appellation "Waldenses." The old writers were extremely careless in the use and application of epithets After the rise of the Manichæans, as has been observed in a former chapter, it became the fashion to stigmatize all dissidents from the established order by that title, whether they harmonized with the Manichæans in profession and practice, or not. So in the twelfth and subsequent centuries, when Peter Waldo's success had issued in the formation of a new party bearing his name, that

---

[1] *Ecclesiastical Researches*, chap. xiii.

was the common appellation. Many treatises were writ ten "against the Waldenses," the authors of which evidently intended their remarks to apply to the Reformers of those times generally. It is obvious, then, that the statements which have been made respecting those Reformers are equally applicable to the Waldenses. There was no uniformity among them. A number of them, particularly in the early part of their history, judged that baptism should be administered to believers only, and practiced accordingly; others entirely rejected that ordinance, as well as the Lord's supper; a third class held Pædobaptism. If the question relates to the Waldenses in the strict and modern sense of the term, that is, to the inhabitants of the valleys of Piedmont, there is reason to believe that originally the majority of them were Baptists, although there were varieties of opinion among them, as well as among other seceders from the Romish Church.

But the language of some of their confessions cannot be fairly interpreted except on Baptist principles. One of them, ascribed to the twelfth century, contains the following articles: "We consider the sacraments as the signs of holy things, or as the visible emblems of invisible blessings. We regard it as proper and even necessary that believers use these symbols or visible forms when it can be done. Notwithstanding which, we maintain that believers may be saved without these signs, when they have neither place nor opportunity of observing them." Here, you see, the use of the sacraments is limited to believers; and, they add, in another article, "We acknowledge no sacraments, as of divine appointment, but baptism and the Lord's supper." How the Waldenses were led to change their practice, we need not now inquire : it is sufficiently manifest that their views harmonized with ours in the early stages of their history.

I have said nothing about church order and government. The reason is, that but little is known on those points. It is not safe to rely on the statements of adverse writers, who neither understood nor appreciated apostolic descriptions and precedents. Their own ecclesiastical affairs being managed without any reference to the New Testament, which was an unknown book to most of the Romish clergy, they were not in a position to form a correct judgment respecting Baptist societies, and were perpetually falling into mistakes. We may gather, however, from occasional hints and references, that Peter of Bruys and his successors formed the baptized into churches, after the apostolic pattern; that the churches were presided over by pastors, regularly chosen and ordained, as far as circumstances would allow, by whom the ordinances were administered; that all the brethren were encouraged to exercise their gifts by preaching or teaching; and that brotherly love was practically manifested by generous contributions in aid of the poor and afflicted, extensive hospitality, and spiritual sympathy in its manifold forms. The communion of saints among them was not a theory, but a habit.

I must now bring the account of this period to a close. It has been shown that there was a continuous protest against infant baptism from the eleventh to the sixteenth century; and that even those who did not substitute believer's baptism for it, or, rather, restore the ordinance to its primitive form, but who were driven into the other extreme, rejecting the sacraments, grounded their opposition to infant baptism on the necessary absence, in the case of infants, of Christian faith. All confessed the indissoluble connection between faith and baptism. All maintained the sole authority of Scripture in matters of religious belief and practice. All disavowed human traditions. All held that the churches of Christ should consist of truly pious men and women. All demanded and exercised the right of private judgment. Every one was at liberty to think, believe, profess, and worship as he pleased, without the interference of priests, kings, councils, popes, or any other earthly power. In a word, they taught that man is responsible in religion, not to his fellow-man, but to God. So have all Baptists taught in all ages.

Immersion was still the ordinary mode. The proof of this is abundant, both as contained in theological treatises and in decrees of councils.

Ebrard and Ermengard in their works "Contra Waldenses," written toward the close of the twelfth century, repeatedly refer to it.[1]

At the Synod of Exeter, A.D. 1277, explicit directions are given for the baptism of children, should there be danger of death immediately after birth; and immersion is strictly prescribed.[2]

The Ecclesiastical Constitutions contain frequent instructions respecting baptismal fonts, directing that they should be made large enough for the convenient immersion of a child. Records of the baptism of royal or noble personages illustrate these statements. "Prince Arthur, eldest son of Henry VII., was thus baptized." The Princess Elizabeth and Edward VI. were immersed. It was the universal practice.[3]

[1] *Biblioth. Maxima*, xxiv. 1542, 1610.
[2] Labbe and Cossart, xi. 1226.
[3] *Baptist Magazine*, Feb., 1850, p. 84.

THE REFORMATION PERIOD

CHRONOLOGICAL NOTES.

FROM A. D. 1517 TO A. D. 1567.

1519. Zuingli settled at Zurich.
1520. Papal Bull issued against Luther.
1521. Diet of Worms.
1522. German New Testament published.
1524. Danish New Testament published.—Insurrection of the Peasants in Germany.
1525. Helvetic New Testament published.—Tyndale's New Testament published.
1526. Swedish New Testament published.—Belgic Bible published.
1529. Diet of Spires.—Protest of the Reformers.
1530. Confession of Augsburg.—League of Smalcald.—Death of Cardinal Wolsey, November 29th.
1531. Death of Zuingli, Oct. 11th.—Death of Ecolampadius, Nov. 23d.
1534. Papal Supremacy abolished in England.—Insurrection at Munster.
1535. Coverdale's Bible published.
1536. Death of Erasmus, July 12th.—Martyrdom of Tyndale, Oct. 6th.
1539. The Reformation established in Denmark.
1540. Icelandic New Testament published.—Order of the Jesuits established.
1541. Swedish Bible published.
1545. Council of Trent opened, December 13th
1546. Death of Luther, February 18th.
1548. Finnish New Testament published.
1550. Danish Bible published.
1552. Polish New Testament published.
1553. Popery restored in England by Mary.
1555. Martyrdom of Bishops Hooper, Feb. 9th, Ridley and Latimer Oct. 16th.—Peace of Religion, Augsburg, Sept. 25th.
1556. Martyrdom of Cranmer, March 21st.—Death of Ignatius Loyola, July 31st.
1557. Geneva English New Testament published.
1558. Accession of Queen Elizabeth.
1559. The Reformation settled in England.—Establishment of the High Commission Court.—Rise of the Puritans.
1560. Death of Melanchthon, April 19th.—Geneva English Bible published.—Geneva French New Testament.
1561. Death of Menno Simon, Jan. 15th.
1563. Polish Bible published.—Close of the Council of Trent, Dec. 4th. —Croatian New Testament published.
1564. Pope Pius' Creed published.—Death of Calvin, May 27th.
1567. Publication of the Welsh New Testament.—The Reformation established in Scotland.

CHAPTER I.

Rise of the Reformation—Opinions held by the Baptists—Misrepresented by the Reformers—Their Wonderful Increase—Support under Sufferings.

THE period on which we are now entering is one of wondrous interest. The shackles with which the nations had been long bound were broken, and it was said "to the prisoners, Go forth—to them that were in darkness, Show yourselves." A great revival of religion took place all over Europe. Popery was renounced by a large portion of the German people, by the Swiss, the Dutch, the Danes, the Swedes, the Norwegians, the English, Welsh, and Scotch, and by great numbers in Austria, Hungary, Bohemia, Bavaria, Italy, and France.

When Luther blew the trumpet of religious freedom, the sound was heard far and wide, and the Baptists came out of their hiding-places, to share in the general gladness and to take part in the conflict. For years they had lived 'n concealment, worshiped God by stealth, and practiced the social duties of Christianity in the best manner they could, under the most unfavorable circumstances. Now, they hoped for peace and enlargement, and fondly expected to enjoy the co-operation of the Re formers in carrying into effect those changes which they knew were required in order to restore Christian churches to primitive purity. They were doomed to bitter disappointments. The Reformers had no sympathy with Baptist principles, but strove to suppress them. Papists and Protestants, Episcopalians and Presbyterians treated them in the same manner. The Baptists traveled too fast and went too far; if they could not be stopped by other means, the fire must be lighted or the headsman's axe employed Thus *the men* were silenced; the Emperor Charles V., whom historians have delighted to honor, ordered *the women* to be drowned, or buried alive. Hundreds were sent out of the world by these methods; thousands more lost their lives by the slower processes of penury and innumerable hardships. The demon of persecution reaped an immense harvest in those days.

Although there was not absolute uniformity of opinion among the Baptists, for they were shy of creeds, knowing how they had been used to serve the purposes of soul-bondage, certain important truths were viewed by all of them in the same light. Modes of expression varied, but they were substantially of one mind, those of Poland only excepted, who leaned to the system which was afterward termed " Socinianism." Baptist theology harmonized with that of the Reformation in regard to the leading doctrines of the gospel, such as justification by faith, the necessity of divine influence, etc. The sole authority of Scripture in matters of religion was carried out to its legitimate issues, and everything was rejected which would not abide the test, so that all rites and observances that were not expressly enjoined in the word of God were swept away at once. Steadfastly maintaining that be-

THE REFORMATION PERIOD.   153

lievers, and believers only, were the proper subjects of baptism, they pleaded for a pure church. The Reformers were astonished at this demand. They said that the thing was impossible; that there always had been tares among the wheat, and that so it would be till the end of time; that the good and the bad must be indiscriminately mixed in the Christian commonwealth. We need not wonder at this; Popery and Pædobaptism had blinded their eyes. They had never seen a New Testament church, and they practically kept out of sight the teachings of the New Testament on the subject, as it is quite necessary to do when the Pædobaptist theory is fully admitted; for if infants are baptized, and all who are baptized may claim church-fellowship, the church which is so formed must be a very different organization from that which was instituted at Jerusalem, when " believers were the more added to the Lord, multitudes both of men and women." Children, it will be perceived, are not mentioned. The historian seems to take special pains to exclude them, as if he desires his readers to note the difference between Judaism and Christianity, the former being the establishment of a national institute, which was kept up by the ordinary increase of the population—the latter the gathering together of individual servants of the Saviour, who " were born, not of blood, nor of the will of the flesh, nor of the will of man, but of God" (John i. 12, 13). One point more may be alluded to: the Baptists sternly asserted the rights of conscience. All men might believe and act in religion as they pleased, without the interference of the civil magistrate. *His* duties, they said, were confined to the preservation of good order and the protection of property and life; God had not given him the power to regulate religious affairs, nor authorized him to impose any mode of worship, or to punish such as might refuse to admit his usurpation. I have mentioned these principles before, but it seemed desirable to repeat the statement, because the Baptists of the sixteenth century have been singularly misrepresented.

In some other particulars there were also great differences between them and other dissidents from Rome. They would not take an oath. While they obeyed magistrates in all things civil, they regarded the magistrate's office as altogether needless among Christians, who, they said, would not commit crime, and therefore such officers would not be wanted among them; and besides, a magistrate could not discharge his duties but by force, which is not allowable to Christ's servants. Neither would they engage in war. They denounced it as utterly unlawful. The use of carnal weapons, whether for attack or defence, was abjured; hence they never resisted their persecutors. When the oppressions exercised by the rich and noble engendered hatred of the higher orders, some of the Baptists were disposed to plead for a general equality, or at any rate for such restraint on power and wealth as would take away the means of doing mischief. Among themselves, too, the spirit of true brotherhood so prevailed in acts of sympathy and kindness that they were regarded as advocates of the community of goods and opponents of separate personal property. On these accounts they were treated as enemies of civil society, fit only to be exterminated. But though they were more scrupulous than most religionists are now, their very peculiarities sprang from the love of peace. Such men could not be dangerous to the commonwealth. All they asked was to be let alone, that they might serve God according to their consciences. And yet they were hunted up and down like wild beasts.

Impartiality requires me to mention one opinion which some of them held. Unable to conceive how the Lord Jesus could be the Child of the Virgin without partaking of human depravity, they imagined that, though born of Mary, he did not "take flesh" of his mother. Joan Boucher was burned alive in the time of Edward VI. for maintaining this alleged heresy. It is not necessary to trouble the reader with any observations on it. It is often better to confess ignorance than to dogmatize. Suffice it to say, that among the Baptists of those days the matter in question was a harmless speculation. They believed that the Lord Jesus Christ was "God manifest in the flesh." That was enough. If they did not choose to adopt the current modes of expression, they were at any rate sound at heart. We ought to be very careful how we make a man "an offender for a word."

The Baptists of the sixteenth century, generally, were a goodly, upright, honorable race. They hated no man, but all men hated them. And why? Because they testified against the abominations of the times, and wished to accomplish changes which would indeed have revolutionized society, because it was constructed on antichristian principles, but which were in accordance with the word of God. An outcry was raised against them, as if they were "the offscouring of all things," and their blood was poured out like water. Even the Reformers wrote and acted against them. The writers of that age searched out the most degrading and insulting epithets that the language afforded, and applied them with malignant gratification. Latimer speaks of the "pernicious" and "devilish" opinions of the Baptists. Hooper calls those opinions "damnable." Becon inveighs against the "wicked," "apish Anabaptists," "foxish hypocrites," that "damnable sect," "liars," "bloody murderers both of soul and body," whose religious system he denounces as a "pestiferous plague," with many other foul-mouthed expressions which I will not copy. Bullinger designates them as "obstinate," "rebellious," "brain-sick," "frantic," "filthy knaves." Zuingli speaks of the "pestiferous seed of their doctrine," their "hypocritical humility," their speech, "more bitter than gall." But enough of this. Yet these men could appeal to those who witnessed their sufferings, and boldly declare, with the axe or the stake in view, none venturing to contradict, that they were not put to death for any evil deeds, but solely for the sake of the gospel.

It has been a common practice to ascribe to a whole community the follies or wrong-doings of a few. In the controversial works of the period now before us we meet with heaps upon heaps of representations respecting the opinions and conduct of the Baptists, which, if true at all, can only affect individuals, and ought not to be imputed to the body.

Notwithstanding the deadly onset that was made upon them from all quarters, they spread and increased most astonishingly. Leonard Bouwens, an eminent Baptist minister in Holland, who died in 1578, left in writing a list of upward of ten thousand persons whom he had baptized. Menno Simon and other laborers in the cause introduced "great multitudes" to the churches. The spirit of reform must have taken fast hold of the minds of the people, or they would not have embraced so readily a system, the profession of which was a sure passport to persecution in its most painful and revolting forms. Luther and his coadjutors opened the door of the temple of freedom to others, but remained themselves in the porch. They feared to penetrate into the interior. The Baptists passed by them, entered in, and explored the recesses of the hallowed place. For this they were reviled and oppressed. Thousands of them fell in the fight. But multitudes pressed after them, to be " baptized for the dead ;" and each could say,

> "I'll hail reproach and welcome shame,
> If thou remember me."

See how the Lord blessed his faithful servants. Algerius was burned at Rome in the year 1557. Thus he writes, a short time before his martyrdom:

"I will relate an incredible thing; that I have found infinite sweetness in the lion's bowels. Who will believe that which I shall relate? Who can believe it? In a dark hole I have found cheerfulness; in a place of bitterness and death, rest and hope of salvation; in the abyss or depth of hell, joy. Where others weep, I have found laughter; where others fear, I have found strength. Who will ever believe that in a state of misery I have had great pleasure; that in a lonely corner I have had glorious company; and in the hardest bonds, perfect repose? all these things (ye, my companions in Jesus Christ) the bountiful hand of God has granted me. Behold! he who at first stood far from me is now with me; and him whom I imperfectly knew, I now see clearly; him whom I formerly saw afar off, I now contemplate as present. He for whom I longed now stretches forth his hand; he comforts me; he fills me with joy; he drives bitterness from me, and renews my strength and consolation; he gives me health; he supports me; he helps me up; he makes me strong. Oh, how good the Lord is, who suffers not his servants to be tempted beyond their ability! Oh, how light, pleasant, and sweet is his yoke! Is any like unto God most high, who supports and refreshes the tempted, who heals the stricken and wounded, and restores them altogether? None is like unto him. Learn, my most beloved brethren, how gracious the Lord is; how faithful and compassionate is he who visits his servants in their trials; he who humbles himself, and condescends to stand by us in our huts and mean abodes. He grants us a cheerful mind and a peaceful heart." The letter is dated "from the most delightful pleasure-garden, the prison called Leonia, the 12th of July, 1557."[1]

You will read with much interest the following extracts from letters addressed by a pious mother—Soetgen Van den Houte, 1560—to her children, "written hastily" —in prison—"trembling with cold:"

"Love one another without strife or wrangling. Be affectionate the one to the other. The wisest must bear with the dull, and admonish them with kindness. The strong must have compassion on the weak, and assist him with all his power from love. . . . Love your enemies, and pray for them that speak evil of you and make you suffer. Rather suffer wrong than do wrong. Endure rather grief than put another to grief. Be your-

[1] *Baptist Martyrology*, published by the Hanserd Knollys Society, ii. 114, 122.

selves reproached rather than reproach another. Be rather belied than belie another. Let what is yours be taken from you rather than take what is another's. Be rather stricken than strike another. . . . Oh, my dear lambs, mind that you spend not your youthful days in vanity and pride; nor in tippling or feasting; but in sobriety and humility, in the fear of God, diligent in all good works, that you may be clothed with the adorning of the saints; that God may make you meet by his grace to enter into the marriage of the Lamb, and that we may see you there with joy. Your father and I have shown you the way, with many others besides. Take the example of the prophets and apostles. Even Christ himself went this way; and where the Head has gone before, there must the members follow."[1]

The husband of this good woman had won the crown of martyrdom before her. She followed soon after, and joined her companion before the throne. There "the noble army of martyrs" praise God. "They have washed their robes, and made them white in the blood of the Lamb." May we meet them there!

[1] *Baptist Martyrology*, 289-301.

CHAPTER II.

German Baptists—Thomas Munzer—The Peasant War—Michael Satler—Hans Schaffler — Salzburg — Wolfgang Brand-Hueber — The Burggraf of Alzey—Imperial Edicts.

ON the 10th of December, 1520, Luther burned the pope's bull against him, together with the decretals and other Papal documents, without the walls of Wittenburg, in the presence of an immense concourse of people. By that act he severed himself from the Church of Rome, and proclaimed the advent of a new order of things. The Baptists hailed it with joy, rightly judging that it indicated a great and favorable change of public opinion. They availed themselves of the advantages thus offered, and immediately engaged in active operations for the spread of truth. Luther had freed himself from the pope; they proclaimed freedom from Luther, and from all other human authority, as far as religion was concerned, and called on their fellow-countrymen everywhere to demand their rights.

This was more than Luther intended. Great and good man as he was, he had crotchets, like some other great men. He was willing that others should think for themselves, so that they thought as he thought. If they did not, he looked on them with suspicion, and they soon found it best to keep out of his way. His followers and flatterers regarded him with awe bordering on superstition. Sleidan, the historian, was struck with surprise at the boldness of Thomas Munzer, who, said he, "not only began to preach against the Roman pontiff, but against Luther himself!"[1] Doubtless that was "an iniquity to be punished by the judge." Reference to the earthly judge in religious affairs was too common in those days.

Believer's baptism and martyrdom were closely connected. The first witnesses for God in Germany, in the Reformation age, were Baptists. Hans Koch and Leonard Meyster were put to death at Augsburg in the year 1524.

You will find in most church histories doleful accounts of the German Anabaptists. Storck and Stubner, the writers tell you, pretended to prophesy, and demanded submission on the ground of their divine calling. They advocated a wild millenarianism, maintaining that the day of God's vengeance was at hand, and that the saints would put down all worldly rule and possess the earth. And Thomas Munzer, they say, not only held similar sentiments, but also headed the insurrection of the peasants, which brought so much misery on Germany, and ultimately on the poor peasants themselves.

Now, I have no desire to defend anything foolish or wrong. Granted that the men just spoken of were visionaries, and that their conduct was in some respects indefensible; but let it be further granted that *they* were not the Baptist body, and that for their follies that body was by no means responsible. As for the Peasant War,

[1] *De Statu Religionis*, lib. v. p. 265. Ed. 1785.

Giesler justly remarks that "no traces of Anabaptist fanaticism were seen" in it.[1] This is honorable and important.

But it is necessary to repeat the observation, that our accounts of these men are mainly derived from their enemies. Thomas Munzer is blackened in Pædobaptist histories. You would think him the very incarnation of all evil. Yet what are the facts? Just these: That he was a pious, learned man, and an eloquent preacher, whom the people followed amazingly, and that he was driven from place to place, because as fast as he learned the truth he preached it, sometimes to the great annoyance of Luther and his friends, whose misconceptions and errors, as he deemed them, he did not fail to expose. Let us listen to Robert Robinson:

"He had been a priest, but became a disciple of Luther, and a great favorite with the Reformed. His deportment was remarkably grave, his countenance was pale, his eyes rather sunk as if he was absorbed in thought, his visage long, and he wore his beard. His talent lay in a plain and easy method of preaching to the country-people, whom (it should seem as an itinerant) he taught almost all through the electorate of Saxony. His air of mortification won him the hearts of the rustics; it was singular then for a preacher so much as to appear humble. When he had finished his sermon in any village, he used to retire, either to avoid the crowd or to devote himself to meditation and prayer. This was a practice so very singular and uncommon that the people used to throng about the door, peep through the crevices, and oblige him, sometimes, to let them in, though he repeatedly assured

[1] *Ecclesiastical History*, v. 352.

them that he was nothing, that all he had came from above, and that admiration and praise were due only to God. The more he fled from applause, the more it followed him; the people called him Luther's curate, and Luther called him his 'Absalom,' probably because he 'stole the hearts of the men of Israel.'"[1]

The Peasant War was an ill-advised, badly-managed thing. But the peasants had right on their side. Their manifesto was a plain-spoken, noble document. It told a sad tale of oppression. The historian, Robertson, epitomizes it thus: "The chief articles were, that they might have liberty to choose their own pastors; that they might be freed from the payment of all tithes, except that of corn; that they might no longer be considered as the slaves or bondmen of their superiors; that the liberty of hunting and fishing might be common; that the great forests might not be regarded as private property, but be open for the use of all; that they might be delivered from the unusual burden of taxes under which they labored; that the administration of justice might be rendered less rigorous and more impartial; that the encroachments of the nobles upon meadows and commons might be restrained."[2] The conclusion is admirable. I copy it from Giesler, who has inserted the entire paper: "In the twelfth place, it is our conclusion and final resolution, that if one or more of the articles here set forth is not in agreement with the word of God, we will recede therefrom, if it be made plain to us on scriptural ground. Or if an article be now conceded to us, and hereafter it be discovered to be unjust, from that hour it shall be dead

[1] *Ecclesiastical Researches*, ch. xiv.
[2] *Charles V.*, book iv.

and null, and have no more force. Likewise, if more articles of complaint be truly discovered from Scripture, we will also reserve the right of resolving upon these."
It is said that Munzer assisted in preparing this document. If so, it does him honor. Whatever silly or extravagant opinions he fell into, he may be excused, for in those days very few public men escaped connection with some weakness or other. His conduct in joining the insurgents has brought heavy censure upon him. But he paid dearly for it. Taken prisoner after the battle in which the peasants were defeated, or rather slaughtered, for it was no fight, he was subjected to cruel tortures, after the fashion of the times, and put to death.

Though the Peasant War was not in itself a Baptist affair at all, occasion was taken from Munzer's connection with it to raise a storm of indignation against the Baptists, as if they were all rebels. The persecution raged fiercely, and it never wholly ceased during the period. Baptists worshiped God and preached the gospel at perpetual hazard of liberty and life. Still they held on their way. Sometimes they met in buildings far removed from general observation; sometimes in the woods, and not unfrequently long intervals passed between their meetings, so hot was the pursuit after them. One effect was produced which proved advantageous to their cause: they were "scattered abroad"—eastward, to Moravia, Hungary, and the adjoining countries—westward, to Holland. Everywhere numerous churches sprang up.

Sebastian Franck, a voluminous historian of those times, affirms that "within a few years not less than two thousand Baptists had testified their faith by imprison-

1 *Charles V.*, book v. 347-349.

ment or martyrdom."[1] Let us look at a few of the details.

Michael Satler had been a monk. He was converted to God, and became a preacher. He was put to death at Rottenburg, May 26, 1527. Thus ran his sentence: "That Michael Satler be delivered over to the executioner, who shall bring him to the place of execution and cut out his tongue; he shall then throw him upon a cart, and twice tear his flesh with red-hot pincers; he shall then be brought to the city gate, and shall have his flesh five times torn in like manner." This fiendish sentence was executed, and the body was afterward burned to ashes. Satler's wife and several other females who were arrested at the same time were drowned. A number of brethren who shared the imprisonment with them were beheaded.[2] Rottenburg was celebrated for such scenes. In 1528, Leonard Schoener was beheaded and burned there, and shortly afterward about seventy more. Schoener had been six years a barefooted monk, but had left the convent through disgust at the wickedness of the order. He learned the tailor's trade, and so gained his livelihood. After his conversion he joined the Baptists, and spent the remainder of his life in preaching the gospel and baptizing throughout Bavaria.[3]

At Schwatz, eleven miles from Rottenburg, Hans Schlaffer, who had been a Romish priest, was beheaded. "He was put to the test by cruel tortures, and examined by the priests concerning infant baptism; but he answered them from the Divine Scriptures, and showed, both by argument and by texts of Scripture, that it is commanded, and will be found throughout the New Tes-

[1] *Baptist Martyrology*, i. 49.   [2] *Ibid.* p. 27.   [3] *Ibid.* p. 47.

tament, that men should first teach the word of God, and they alone that hear, understand, believe, and receive it should be baptized. This is the Christian baptism, and no rebaptism. The Lord has nowhere commanded children to be baptized. They are already the Lord's. So long as they are innocent and inoffensive, they are in nowise to be condemned. They also asked him on what foundation the sect of the Anabaptists properly rests. To which he answered, Our faith, actions, and baptism rest on nothing else than the commandment of Christ" (Matt. xxviii. 18, 19; Mark xvi. 15).[1]

Leopold Snyder was beheaded at Augsburg in the same year. The sufferings in that city were very severe. "Not only were they beaten with rods, but their backs were branded, and one had his tongue cut out for his so-called blasphemy. The few who recanted were adjudged to a yearly fine, and were forbidden for five years the exercise of civil rights."[2]

Eighteen persons were burned in one day at Salzburg. Many more suffered in that city. Among them was a lovely young maiden of sixteen, who, refusing to recant, was taken in the arms of the executioner to the trough for watering horses, thrust under the water, and there held till life was extinct." "The Baptists there were called Garden-brethren, from their custom of meeting by night in the gardens and solitary places of the town, to escape the notice of their foes."[3]

Wolfgang Brand-Hueber and Hans Nidermair, both Baptist ministers, with about seventy others, were put to death at Lintz. "As to the said Wolfgang Brand-Hueber, there are still writings in the church which show

[1] *Baptist Martyrology*, p. 50. [2] *Ibid.* p. 54. [3] *Ibid.* p. 57.

how faithfully he taught the Christian community; likewise, that obedience and submission should be rendered to magistrates *in all things not contrary to God*. He held fast the true baptism of Christ, and the supper of the Lord; rejecting the baptism of infants, the sacraments [that is, the Romish sacraments], and other antichristian abominations, as his writings (still extant) sufficiently declare."[1]

Nearly three hundred and fifty persons suffered in various ways in the Palatinate, in the year 1529. The burggraf of Alzey was particularly active on the occasion. But his victims were steadfast. "While some were being drowned, or about to be led to execution, the rest who were to follow, and were awaiting death, sang until the executioner came for them. They remained altogether steadfast in the truth they had embraced; and secure in the faith they had received from God, they stood like valiant warriors. By them the nobles of this world and its princes were put to shame. On some, whom they would not altogether condemn to death, they inflicted bodily punishment; some they deprived of their fingers; others they branded with the cross on their forehead, and inflicted on them many cruelties; so that even the burggraf said, 'What shall I do? the more I condemn, the more they increase.'"[2]

These persecutions were the fruits of royal and imperial edicts. Ferdinand, king of Hungary and Bohemia, issued an edict in 1527, denouncing death to the Baptists. The priests were commanded to read it publicly in the churches four times a year for ten years. The Emperor Charles was equally embittered against them.

[1] *Baptist Martyrology*, i. 103.   [2] *Ibid.* 118.

The Edict of Worms, by which Luther was condemned, did not meet the case, but the deficiency was supplied at the Diet of Spires, in 1529. By the edict in which the decisions of the diet were embodied, it was "clearly ordained that all and every Anabaptist, or rebaptized person, whether male or female, being of ripe years and understanding, should be deprived of life, and according to the circumstances of the individual be put to death by fire, sword, or otherwise; and whenever found should be brought to justice, indicted, and convicted; and be no otherwise judged, tried, or dealt with, under pain of heavy and severe punishment."[1]

At the time of the publication of this edict, a number of Baptists—"nine brethren and three sisters"—were in prison at Alzey. "The mandate was then read to the prisoners, and as they would not yield, they were, without further trial, in fulfillment of the emperor's edict, led to execution; the brethren by the sword, but the sisters by being drowned in the horse-pond. While they were yet in confinement, a sister came to the prison to comfort the female prisoners. She said to them that they should valiantly and firmly cleave to the Lord, and not regard this suffering, for the sake of the everlasting joy that would follow. This visit becoming known, she also was speedily apprehended, and afterward burned, because she had comforted and strengthened the other prisoners."[2]

"But," says Sebastian Franck, "the more severely they were punished, the more they multiplied. Peradventure many were moved by the steadfastness with which they died, or perhaps God marked the endeavors of rulers and tyrants to root out heresy with the sword."[3]

[1] *Baptist Martyrology*, p. 116. [2] *Ibid.* p. 117. [3] *Ibid.* 125.

CHAPTER III.

Persecuting Tenets of the Reformers—German Diets—The Congregation at Steinborn—Leonard Bernkop—The Crown of Straw—Johannes Bair—Hans Pichner—Hans Breal—Baptists in Italy.

THE Baptists continued to spread in Germany, notwithstanding the odium that was attached to them in consequence of the Munster business. They were plundered, thrust into dungeons, banished, numbers of them beheaded or burned alive, yet still they made head against all opposition, and multiplied everywhere. It is stated that "between the Eifel mountains on the Rhine [in Westphalia] and Moravia, not less than fifty churches are said to have been existing at this period [about the year 1557], some of them having from five to six hundred members. Fifty elders and ministers gathered at one time at Strasburg, from a district of about a hundred miles in circumference, to consult together on the interests of Christ's kingdom."[1]

It is distressing to observe how completely the Reformers of those days were imbued with the persecuting spirit. At a diet held at Hombourg, in Hesse Cassel, in 1536, the opinions of many divines were adduced, sanctioning the punishment of the Baptists by the magistrates. Some

[1] *Baptist Martyrology*, ii. 125.

would have them scourged; some, branded; some, banished; but most of them held that death should be the infliction, and Luther, Melanchthon, and Bucer were of the number. See how sophistically the last-mentioned Reformer reasoned. A three days' discussion was held with the Baptists of Marburg. George Schnabet, one of their ministers, disputed with Bucer. "The Hessian Church is not the church of Christ," said Schnabet, "because it persecutes the poor, and banishes them from their possessions. The kingdom of God is joy and righteousness; but this church with great zeal commits injustice— it persecutes the innocent," etc. To this Bucer replied, "The church does not persecute; it is the magistrates, and they only certain mischievous Anabaptists. The church wishes to remain in peace; but these men despise the church." . . . "It is nowhere written," said Schnabet, "that unbelievers should be put to death." "Blasphemy must be punished," Bucer replied. "The disturbance of religion ought to be forbidden much more than any temporal mischief." "Unbelievers," Schnabet argued, "ought not to be punished; our enemies should be loved." "When the magistrate punishes an enemy," said Bucer, "he loves him. It is a father punishing his child."[1]

The Emperor Charles V. continued to evince his malignity by procuring cruel edicts at German diets. In 1544, at the Diet of Spires, when other Protestants were treated with leniency, severe measures were adopted against the Baptists. At Augsburg, in 1551, extermination was denounced against them. Nor was it a vain threat. Priests and people united to put into execution, and tremendous sufferings followed.

[1] *Baptist Martyrology*, i. 169, 170.

In several instances brethren who had been commissioned to visit other churches were discovered as they passed through the German territories, betrayed to the authorities, and died in prison or were publicly executed. It was a dangerous thing in these days to be a member of a deputation.

Torture was frequently employed, in order to wring from the sufferers the names and places of abode of their associates, or to force them, under the pressure of anguish, to renounce the faith.

In the year 1539, the Vienna police, aided by a detachment of cavalry, surprised a congregation at Steinborn, and captured nearly all of them. They were lodged in the castle of Falkenstein. After remaining in confinement about five weeks, during which time strenuous efforts were made by the priests to persuade them to abjure, it was notified to them that the women and children would be released, but that the able-bodied men would be sent to sea. The youths, and some that were weak or sickly, were reduced to bondage, and given to Austrian noblemen. Ninety men were sent away under a strong guard, bound two and two, to proceed on foot to Trieste, a journey of more than two hundred miles. "Man and wife were separated from each other, and children of tender years left behind; which flesh and blood could not have borne but by the power of God and for his sake. So deplorable was the separation that the king's marshal and others like him could not refrain from tears. . . . They were led about by his majesty's messengers through towns, villages, and the open country, from one jurisdiction to another. In their journeys they were constrained to suffer much, and various kinds of adversity and great affliction, but God always afforded them his gracious help, and in particular that every morning and evening, without hindrance, they could make and present their prayer to God, and durst, besides, without impediment, speak each one to the comfort of his brethren. This they received with great gratitude as a special favor and gift of God. By this means the people in many places were convinced of their innocence and piety; so that they who, at their first coming, regarded them as evil-doers, felt great compassion for them. To this, the king's servants who conducted them bare repeated testimony, and told them that they should not pass through the towns and country-places in silence, but might make known their faith by singing or in some other way. . . . God was thus pleased to reveal his word and truth in all places and lands, to make them known to the people who knew them not, and to cause their sound to be heard. As at all times, in a like manner, he graciously appoints means to draw men away from unrighteousness, so, by these witnesses of the faith and divine truth, who were led about into a great number and variety of places, amidst unknown and foreign tongues, where the truth was not heard, being unknown and hidden from the people, were some from Carniola and Italy led to inquire after the truth. Some were brought to the acknowledgment of the truth who, to this very day, serve God with an upright heart. But how these captive brethren, during their journeys and in many places, were treated, how they were driven and beaten, and with cords and chains were bound together, and what in consequence they suffered, were too long to be narrated. Yet, how great soever the oppression they endured, their hearts were always comforted by God."¹

When they had been in Trieste nearly a fortnight, they contrived to escape from the prison in which they were lodged. Fifteen of them were retaken, but the others eluded search, and arrived among their brethren in safety. They were "received with joy and thanksgiving, as a gift sent by God." The fifteen were never heard of any more.

Leonhard Bernkop was burned at Salzburg in 1542. "He was led to the place of execution, and a fire made on one side of him, so that he was, as it were, roasted; but he cleaved fast to the Lord. He said to the bloodhounds and the servants of the executioner, 'This side is roasted enough, turn me round; through the power of God, the suffering I feel is but little, and it is light compared with everlasting glory.'"²

Two young females who had been recently baptized at Bamberg, were apprehended, imprisoned, and severely tortured. But they did not swerve from the truth. When they were led out to die, wreaths of straw were placed on their heads, "by way of contempt and mockery." "Since Christ," said one of them to the other, "wore a crown of thorns for us, why should we not, in return, and for his honor, wear this crown of straw? Our faithful God will, instead of this, set a beautiful crown of gold and a glorious garland upon our heads." So they went cheerfully to the fire.³

Johannes Bair had been in prison nearly twenty years, when he wrote the following letter:

"Dear brethren, I have received the writing-desk, the

¹ *Martyrology* i. 189–193.   ² *Ibid.* 239.   ³ *Ibid.* 363.

account of our worship, faith, and teaching, and six lights, or candles, and pens; but the Bible, in particular, I have not received, though standing first in the list. Now, this is my prayer, that, if you have it, you will forward it me; for this above all things I wish to have, if it be according to the will of God. I suffer much for want of it, and have endured great hunger and thirst for the word of the Lord during many long years. Of this I make my complaint to God and his church, for it is full twenty years, save eight weeks, since the day of my miserable imprisonment.

"I, Johannes Bair, of Lichtenfels, of all men the most miserable and most forsaken, the prisoner of Jesus Christ our Lord, make again this my complaint before God and his angels, and also his servants, churches, and congregations. Now, my brethren and sisters, the best beloved of my heart in the Lord, beseech God for me, that he would deliver me out of this peril and great distress—a distress that is unspeakable. This God knows, and my poor self, and you likewise know it with me. Herewith be it commended to God. Written at Bamberg in a dark hole, in the year 1548."

Three years afterward he slept in the Lord in the prison, and obtained the martyr's crown.[1]

Here is a specimen of diabolical atrocity. Hans Pichner was "put to the rack, but all their tortures were unavailing. Very vexatious it was to them that they could extort nothing from him. Several times they stripped him, and let him hang in tortures for hours on the ropes. So strained did he become, that he could not set a step, nor stand upon his feet, nor bring his hand to his mouth

[1] *Martyrology*, i. 372.

to eat. Nevertheless he could not be turned aside, but remained steadfast in the Lord. Afterward they bound him hand and foot, and kept him confined in a dark prison or dungeon more than half a year. . . . After this they condemned him to death, and led him out to the place of execution, where he exhorted the people, who were numerously collected together, to repentance. He was then placed with his back against a stake, and so beheaded; for they had so dreadfully tortured and stretched him that he was unable to kneel."[1]

Take another case. Hans Breal was apprehended in the Tyrol in the year 1557. Having been repeatedly tortured, in the vain hope of compelling him to betray his brethren, he was at length placed in "a deep, dark, filthy tower, where he could neither see sun, moon, nor daylight. So that he could not tell whether it was night or day; sometimes he could tell that it was night by its being colder than before. The dungeon was moist and damp, so that his clothes became foul and rotted on his body, and for some time he was obliged to sit naked. He had nothing but a coarse blanket that had been given him; this he threw round his body, and sat in misery and darkness. His shirt was so much rotted as not to leave a single slip of it, except the collar of the neck, which he hung on the wall. When these children of Pilate had him brought out to see if he would recant, the brightness of the light was so painful that he was glad when they let him go down again into the dark tower. . . . Thus he lay in this foul dungeon, where worms and vermin were his companions, for a long time; he protected his head with an old hat, that from pity had been thrown

[1] *Martyrology*, ii. 59.

to him. No one had been confined in this tower for some years, so that the vermin had greatly increased, and caused him much terror until he had got used to it. The worms frequently ate his food. . . . Thus he lay in this foul tower the whole summer, until nearly Michaelmas day in the harvest. When they saw that the frost began to set in, they brought him out from thence, and led him into another prison, which could not possibly be worse. There he was obliged to stay for thirty-seven weeks, with one hand and one foot in the stocks, so that he was unable to lie down or sit, and could only stand. He also suffered much mocking and ridicule from the ungodly. . . . At length an order was issued by the council at Innspruck, which the magistrates brought to read to him. The contents were as follow: That since he was so obdurate, and would receive no instruction, he should be sent to sea, to which he must go the following morning; there he would find how the obstinate were stripped and flogged. But Hans answered that he would confide in the Lord his God, who was on the sea as well as on land, to help him and give him patience. He was then released from prison, and suffered to go about the castle for two days, that he might learn again to walk. This he could not easily do, so very infirm had he become through lying in prison and in the stocks, fastened by locks and chains; for in this state he had lain two years within five weeks, and had for a year and a half never seen the sun." [1]

Hans was committed to the charge of an officer, and they journeyed toward the sea. On the second day, while resting at a tavern, the officer became drunk, and Hans improved the opportunity to effect his escape. He re-

[1] *Martyrology*, ii. 99, 104.

THE REFORMATION PERIOD. 177

covered strength and health, rejoined his brethren, was called to preach the gospel, and died in peace in the year 1583

Thus God's servants suffered in Germany. There were Baptists in Italy in this period, some of whom attained the honor of martyrdom. Julius Klampherer, who had been a Romish priest, was drowned at Venice in 1561. Franciscus van der Sach, a minister, was drowned with another brother in the same city, in 1564. Hans George, Count of Grovtenstein, who had fled to Germany some years before, and had returned to Italy in 1566, in the hope of inducing his wife to share his exile, was betrayed by some who recognized him, and thrown overboard on the voyage to Venice. "By faith he forsook all things, disregarding rank, preferring rather to suffer affliction with the people of God than to enjoy the honors and rewards of this world among his own people."[1]

[1] *Martyrology*, 425.

CHAPTER IV.

Baptists in Switzerland—Zuingli—Concessions of Bullinger and Meshovius—Disputations—Drownings—Felix Mantz—Balthazar Hubmeyer—Louis Hetzer—Emigration to Moravia—Jacob Hutter.

THE sketch which has been already furnished describes the position of the Baptists in Germany. I will now trace their history in Switzerland.

Zuingli, the excellent Swiss Reformer, was at one time on the eve of becoming a Baptist. But he resisted the arguments in favor of our principles, and became a violent opposer. The government of Zurich adopted his policy. Zuingli was a good deal annoyed by the Baptists, for they not only pleaded for believer's baptism, but zealously maintained that none but real Christians were fit members of churches. The natural inference was, that as spiritual societies could not be governed by carnal men, the union of Church and State must be dissolved, and each party attend to its own affairs: the State, to things temporal; the Church, to things religious. This was going too far for Zuingli. He repudiated the idea of a spiritual church, regarding it as a sheer impossibility. He could not relinquish the notion that worldly power and law were requisite for the establishment of the faith. Hence he concluded that the Baptist theory must be treated as resistance to authority, and its supporters put down by the secular arm. Poor man! he fell a victim to his own principles. He was slain on the battle-field of Cappel, while in official attendance, as chaplain, on the Protestant army, fighting against the Papists, October 11th, 1531.

It was about the year 1523 that the Baptists first appeared in Switzerland. Their numbers rapidly increased. The appeal to Scripture on behalf of their sentiments was rendered more forcible by the innocence of their lives. Even Bullinger, who was strongly prejudiced against them, was compelled to confess it. "They had," said he, "an appearance of a spiritual life; they were excellent in character; they sighed much; they uttered no falsehoods; they were austere; they spake nobly and with excellence, so that they thereby acquired admiration and authority, or respect, with simple pious people. For the people said, 'Let others say what they will of the Dippers, we see in them nothing but what is excellent, and hear from them nothing else but that we should not swear or do wrong to any one, that every one ought to do what is right, that every one must live godly and holy lives; we see no wickedness in them.' Thus they have deceived many people in this land." Meshovius, adverting to the views of men at that time on this point, writes thus: "Some, they say, write what they wish of the Anabaptists, that they are given up to sedition, and plot the destruction of the Christian commonweal. But how false this is, is clearly manifest from their lives, actions, and doctrine, since they neither swear, nor blaspheme, nor seek their own things; but you will see them promote those only which are of Christ, which are con formable to the Scriptures; and will any one say that these are not true, nor especially worthy of a Christian man?"[1]

Public disputations were much in fashion at that time in Switzerland. They have rarely proved of any real service to the cause of truth, since it is obvious that the man who had the most fluent tongue, the readiest memory, the keenest wit, and the greatest amount of self-possession was most likely to prevail, whether he was attached to the right or the wrong side. Nor was it likely that either party would acknowledge defeat. Perhaps the only benefit that resulted from them was, that many persons had an opportunity of hearing the truth who would not otherwise have enjoyed it, and in some instances they were led to further inquiry, which issued in their joining the Reformers.

Three disputations were held at Zurich in the year 1525. In all of them, according to their adversaries, the Baptists were worsted, notwithstanding which they resolutely retained their sentiments, and declared themselves ready to seal them with their blood. But the magistracy did not rely on arguments. They issued an edict, prohibiting believer's baptism, enjoining the baptism of children, and threatening that the disobedient should be dealt with severely. And so they were. Some were imprisoned, some were banished. Still they persevered. Whereupon, in 1526, another edict was issued, ordering that if any baptized others, or submitted to baptism—re-baptism they called it—they should be " drowned without mercy."[2] Zuingli, I am sorry to say, approved this infamous enactment. It was no vain threat. Felix Mantz

[1] Quoted in Martyrology, i. 7, 8.   [2] Ibid. i. 121.

was drowned at Zurich in 1527. Jacob Falk and Heine Reyman were drowned in 1528. These three were ministers of the gospel. Anneken of Friburg, a Christian female, was drowned at that place in 1529, and her body was afterward burned. Many others suffered, whose names are not recorded. They did not inflict capital punishment at Basle, where the Baptists abounded, but they scourged them, threw them into dungeons, or banished them, hoping to wear them out by suffering. The great Erasmus resided there at that time. He bore honorable testimony on behalf of the sufferers. "The Anabaptists," said he, "although they everywhere abound in great numbers, have nowhere obtained the churches for their use. They are to be commended above all others for the innocence of their lives, but are oppressed by other sects, as well as by the orthodox," that is, Catholics.[1] Such were the men, according to an opponent, whom Protestants as well as Papists sought to exterminate. It is gratifying to know that, though they were treated so shamefully, their characters would endure the scrutiny of keen-eyed observers.

I mentioned Felix Mantz. He was a native of Zurich, and had received a liberal education. Having early adopted the principles of the Reformation, he became an intimate friend of Zuingli and other Swiss Reformers. But in the year 1522 he began to doubt the scriptural authority of infant baptism, and of the church constitution which then existed at Zurich, and suffered imprisonment in consequence. After this he preached in the fields and woods, whither the people flocked in crowds to hear him, and there he baptized those who professed faith.

[1] Letter to the Archbishop of Toulouse, *Ibid.* i. 165.

For this the Zurich magistrates denounced him as a rebel, and about the close of 1526 he was apprehended and lodged in the tower of Wellenberg. On the 5th of January, 1527, he was drowned. "As he came down from the Wellenberg to the fish-market," says Bullinger, "and was led through the shambles to the boat, he praised God that he was about to die for his truth. For Anabaptism was right, and founded on the word of God, and Christ had foretold that his followers would suffer for the truth's sake. And the like discourse he urged much, contradicting the preacher who attended him. On the way his mother and brother came to him, and exhorted him to be steadfast; and he persevered in his folly, even to the end. When he was bound upon the hurdle, and was about to be thrown into the stream by the executioner, he sang with a loud voice: 'In manus tuas, Domine, commendo spiritum meum.' ('Into thine hands, O Lord, I commend my spirit.') And herewith was he drawn into the water by the executioner, and drowned."

"It is reported here," says Capito, writing to Zuingli from Strasburg, on the 27th of January, 1527, "that your Felix Mantz hath suffered punishment, and died gloriously; by which the cause of truth and piety, which you sustain, is weighed down exceedingly."[1] No wonder. Persecution will "weigh down" any cause. And *Protestant* persecution is the most hateful of all.

Balthazar Hubmeyer requires a more lengthened notice. This eminent man was a Bavarian, born at Friedburg, about the year 1480. He studied in the high school of that city, intending to become a physician. But he

[1] *Martyrology*, i. 12-16.

THE REFORMATION PERIOD. 183

exchanged med'cine for theology, and in 1512, being already noted for learning and eloquence, he was appointed professor of divinity and principal preacher at Ingolstadt, where he labored between three and four years. In 1516 he removed to Ratisbon, and preached in the cathedral to immense throngs. His mistaken zeal was directed against the Jews, who were driven from the city, and their synagogue pulled down; on its site was built a chapel dedicated to the Virgin, and a wonder-working image placed over the door, to which vast numbers repaired in pilgrimage from the places adjacent. So blind was Hubmeyer at that time.

The blindness was not of long duration. The report of Luther's movements and of Zuingli's preaching at Einsidlen led him to inquiry, and the novelties of Rome were soon abandoned. Before he left Ratisbon he had made considerable progress in practical reformation. He had translated the Gospels and Epistles into German. He celebrated service in that language instead of Latin. He administered the Lord's supper in both kinds. He admonished the people to pray no more to the saints, and he destroyed images.

The next three years of his life were spent at Waldshut, a town in Baden, where he preached with great success. There also his religious views became matured, and he fully embraced Protestantism. In 1522 he returned to Ratisbon, and continued there a year, propagating the principles of the Reformation. When he resumed his residence at Waldshut he formed an acquaintance with the Swiss Reformers, particularly Zuingli and Ecolampadius, and enjoyed frequent opportunities of intercourse with them. He assisted in conducting the great disputation with the Papists at Zurich in the autumn of 1523. A visit to St. Gall was attended by a wondrous manifestation of blessing. He preached the word "in demonstration of the Spirit and of power." His labors at Waldshut were so successful that the other ministers yielded to the force of truth, and Romanism was abandoned. But Austrian influence was predominant in Baden, so that Hubmeyer soon found himself in a perilous position, and was compelled to seek concealment. After much suffering he repaired to Zurich, hoping to enjoy rest and refuge there.

But Zuingli was not now Hubmeyer's friend. Hubmeyer's researches had issued in the discovery that infant baptism is only a human tradition. He had communicated his thoughts to Zuingli and Ecolampadius, who were also in a doubting state of mind on that subject, and had sought their assistance. They remained Pædobaptists, while he, following his convictions, took the final step by which he was utterly estranged from his former brethren. He was baptized, with one hundred and ten others, in a village not far from Waldshut, by William Roubli, a Swiss Baptist. He himself baptized three hundred persons in the course of the next few months. A work on baptism, which he published about the same time, received a "virulent and violent" reply from Zuingli "I believe and know," Hubmeyer said, "that Christendom shall not receive its rising aright, unless baptism and the Lord's supper are brought to their original purity." Those were truthful words.

"About July, 1525, Hubmeyer entered Zurich, and sought a refuge at the Green Shield Hotel, with a few friends and faithful followers. His coming was soon known among his fellow-brethren, and soon also to the Council of Zurich. He was sought out, and immured in the cells of the court-house. For many days and weeks Zuingli and his old associates endeavored to shake his adhesion to the truth. At last the torture was applied. Protestant historians say a promise of recantation was willingly given and written with his own hand. Alas! how willingly! the pains of the rack were the sharp and effectual arguments. On the 22d of December he is led to the minster, and placed at a desk facing that from which Zuingli long and vehemently declaims against the heresies his friend is there come to confess. The sermon is past, and every eye turns to the rising form of the sick Balthazar. Though not old, his trials have told on his robust frame; and with a quivering voice he begins to read from the paper of recantation before him. As his articulation becomes distinct, he is heard to affirm that infant baptism is without the command of Christ. As the words continue to flow, and add certainty to the incredulous ears of the crowd in the thronged cathedral, murmurs float ominously in the resounding roof, increasing by degrees to audible expressions of approbation or of horror. Zuingli's voice rises above all. He quiets the coming storm, and Hubmeyer is rapidly conveyed to his cell in the Wellenberg.

"Redoubled efforts were afterward made to recall the mischief that had been done. Probably renewed tortures were applied or threatened; for in a few months the sufferer is said to have made a public recantation both at Zurich and St. Gall; but with so little satisfaction to his persecutors that, although released from prison, he was kept in the town under strict surveillance. About the middle of the year 1526, by the aid of distant friends, he succeeded in escaping from Zurich, and after preaching at Constance for a short time, he journeyed to Moravia, passing through Augsburg on his way. There he proclaimed the gospel freely, and in all the region round about, baptizing many, and forming churches of Christ after his word.

"In the year 1528 he was arrested, probably at Brünn, where he was teacher of the church, at the command of King Ferdinand, and sent to Vienna. After some days he was thrown into the dungeons of the castle of Gritsenstein. At his own request he was visited by Dr. Faber, of Gran, in Hungary, who had been in former days his friend. Their interviews, at which two other learned men assisted, lasted the greater part of three days. The substance of their discussions Faber afterward published, and hints that on several points Hubmeyer yielded to the cogency of his arguments. A written exposition of his views was afterward sent to King Ferdinand by Hubmeyer; but no material change in them could have taken place, since he was immediately sentenced to death. He steadfastly went to the scaffold, and on the 10th of March, 1528, from the midst of burning flames and embers, his spirit ascended to that region where those that have come out of great tribulation suffer and weep no more. The partner of his life was also partner of his sufferings; imprisoned with him, she, too, was led to Vienna, and in the river Danube found a watery grave."[1]

Hubmeyer was a learned man. He published several valuable works, and has the honor of being placed in the

---

[1] *Martyrology*, i. 61-75.

Romish Prohibitory Index, in the first class of proscribed authors.

Louis Hetzer, another Baptist minister, was beheaded at Constance, on the 4th of February, 1529. He also had been on intimate terms with Zuingli, Ecolampadius, and their associates, and was highly esteemed by them, till he became a Baptist. In conjunction with John Denk, he translated the Prophets from the Hebrew. Many other books were published by him. John Zwick, who was present at his death, said, "A more glorious and manful death was never seen at Constance. Very many of the opposite party who were present thought that he would have said something on account of our doctrine and against the preachers; but not a word. We were all with him to his end; and may the Almighty, the eternal God, grant to me and to the servants of his word the like mercy, in the day when he shall call us home!" Thomas Blaurer, another witness, observed: "No one has with so much charity, so courageously, or so gloriously laid down his life for Anabaptism, as Hetzer. He was like one who spake with God and died."[1] Slanderous reports respecting him, affecting both his morals and his religious opinions, were propagated after his death;[2] but they were the inventions of the enemy. "He was condemned," says the Chronicle of the Moravian brethren, "for the sake of divine truth."

I cannot give any statistics. The Baptists of Switzerland were very numerous, not only in Zurich, but also in

---

[1] *Martyrology*, i. 97–101.
[2] These calumnies are repeated in the *North British Review* for May, 1859, Art. "Socinianism." The writer ought to have known that they were not published till after Hetzer's death.

Berne, and in the Valtelline. They were compelled to meet in secret, in woods, and unfrequented places, or under cover of the night. No continuous records could be kept. Probably their church organizations were at that time very imperfect. It was not till a more advanced period of their history that they were enabled to secure the full benefits of orderly arrangements. But they did what they could. They obeyed the will of Christ as far as they had opportunity. Other Reformers opposed and even calumniated them. But they were a God-fearing, peaceable, upright, and holy people.

The persecution was so fierce in Germany and Switzerland that there seemed to be no safety but in emigration. In the year 1530 many thousands of Baptists, inhabitants of the Tyrol, Switzerland, Austria, Styria, and Bavaria, emigrated under the leadership of Jacob Hutter, and settled in Moravia. They bought farms, erected places of worship, and enjoyed for a time great prosperity, spiritually and temporally. Many other exiles joined them, so that their numbers were continually increased. But in 1535, Ferdinand, king of Bohemia, ordered their expulsion, and sent a military force to carry the order into effect. Their property was seized, and all the indulgence they could obtain was liberty to carry away their movables. They withdrew into the forests, and there lived as they could, worshiped God, and possessed their souls in patience. Hutter exhorted and comforted them. "Be ye thankful unto God," he said, "that ye are counted worthy to suffer persecutions and cruel exile for his name. These are the rewards of the elect in the prison-house of this world, the proofs of your heavenly Father's approbation. Thus did his people Israel suffer in Egypt, in the desert, and in Babylon. Thus have apostles and all the followers of the Lamb, some in prisons, in exile, and in persecutions, some in torments, in sufferings, and in martyrdoms, enjoyed the favor of their Lord, and have passed the more quickly to the paradise above. Sadness be far from you; put aside all grief and sorrow; reflect how great the rewards awaiting you for the afflictions ye now endure."

Jacob Hutter's letter to the marshal of Moravia, written in the name of the brethren, is worthy of an imperishable record. I will copy it entire, to show what manner of men the Baptists of the sixteenth century were:

"We brethren—who love God and his word, the true witnesses of our Lord Jesus Christ, banished from many countries for the name of God and for the cause of divine truth, and have hither come to the land of Moravia, having assembled together and abode under your jurisdiction, through the favor and protection of the Most High God, to whom alone be praise, honor, and laud for ever: we beg you to know, honored ruler of Moravia, that your officers have come unto us, and have delivered your message and command, as indeed is well known to you. Already have we given a verbal answer, and now we reply in writing: viz., that we have forsaken the world, an unholy life, and all iniquity. We believe in Almighty God, and in his Son, our Lord Jesus Christ, who will protect us henceforth and for ever in every peril, and to whom we have devoted our entire selves, our life, and all that we possess, to keep his commandments, and to forsake all unrighteousness and sin. Therefore we are persecuted and despised by the whole world, and robbed of all our property, as was done aforetime to the holy prophets, and even to Christ himself. By King Ferdinand, the prince of darkness, that cruel tyrant and enemy of divine truth and righteousness, many of our brethren have been slaughtered and put to death without mercy, our property seized, our fields and homes laid waste, ourselves driven into exile, and most fearfully persecuted.

"After these things we came into Moravia, and here, for some time, have dwelt in quietness and tranquillity, under thy protection. We have injured no one, we have occupied ourselves in heavy toil, which all men can testify. Notwithstanding, with thy permission, we are driven by force from our possessions and our homes. We are now in the desert, in woods, and under the open canopy of heaven; but this we patiently endure, and praise God that we are counted worthy to suffer for his name. Yet for your sakes we grieve that you should thus wickedly deal with the children of God. The righteous are called to suffer; but alas! woe, woe to all those who without reason persecute us for the cause of divine truth, and inflict upon us so many and so great injuries, and drive us from them as dogs and brute beasts. Their destruction, punishment, and condemnation draw near, and will come upon them in terror and dismay, both in this life and that which is to come. For God will require at their hands the innocent blood which they have shed, and will terribly vindicate his saints according to the words of the prophets.

"And now that you have with violence bidden us forthwith to depart into exile, let this be our answer. We know not any place where we may securely live; nor can we any longer dare here to remain for hunger and fear. If we turn to the territories of this or that sovereign, everywhere we find an enemy. If we go forward, we fall into the jaws of tyrants and robbers, like sheep before the ravening wolf and the raging lion. With us are many widows, and babes in their cradles, whose parents that most cruel tyrant and enemy of divine righteousness, Ferdinand, gave to the slaughter, and whose property he seized. These widows, and orphans, and sick children, committed to our charge by God, and whom the Almighty hath commanded us to feed, to clothe, to cherish, and to supply all their need, who cannot journey with us, nor, unless otherwise provided for, can long live—these we dare not abandon. We may not overthrow God's law to observe man's law, although it cost gold, and body, and life. On their account we cannot depart; but rather than they should suffer injury we will endure any extremity, even to the shedding of our blood. Besides, here we have houses and farms, the property that we have gained by the sweat of our brow, which in the sight of God and men are our just possession: to sell them we need time and delay. Of this property we have urgent need in order to support our wives, widows, orphans, and children, of whom we have a great number, lest they die of hunger. Now we lie in the broad forest, and, if God will, without hurt. Let but our own be restored to us, and we will live as we have hitherto done, in peace and tranquillity. We desire to molest no one, nor to prejudice our foes, not even Ferdinand the king. Our manner of life, our customs, and conversation are known everywhere to all. Rather than wrong any man of a single penny, we would suffer the loss of a hundred gulden (worth twenty pence sterling each), and sooner than strike our enemy with the hand, much less with sword, or spear, or halbert, as the world does, we would die and surrender life. **We carry no weapon**, neither spear nor gun, as is clear as the open day; and they who say that we have gone forth by thousands to fight, they lie, and impiously traduce us to our rulers. We complain of this injury before God and man, and grieve that the number of the virtuous is so small. We would that all the world were as we are, and that we could bring and convert all men to the same belief; then should all war and unrighteousness have an end.

"We answer further: that if driven from this land, there remains no refuge for us, unless God shall show us some special place whither to flee. We cannot go. This land, and all that therein is, belongeth to God of heaven: and if we were to give a promise to depart, perhaps we should not be able to keep it; for we are in the hand of God, who does with us what he will. By him we were brought hither, and peradventure he would have us here and not elsewhere to dwell, to try our faith and our constancy by persecutions and adversity. But if it should appear to be his will that we depart hence, since we are persecuted and driven away, then will we even without your command, not tardily but with alacrity, go whither God shall send us. Day and night we pray unto him that he will guide our steps to the place where he would have us dwell. We cannot and dare not withstand his holy will; nor is it possible for you, however much you may strive. Grant us but a brief space; peradventure our heavenly Father will make known to us his will, whether we are here to remain, or whether we must go. If this be done, you shall see that no difficulty, however great it may be, shall deter us from the faith.

"Woe, woe! unto you, O ye Moravian rulers, **who**

have sworn to that cruel tyrant and enemy of God's truth, Ferdinand, to drive away his pious and faithful servants. Woe! we say unto you, who fear more that frail and mortal man than the living, omnipotent, and eternal God, and chase from you, suddenly and inhumanly, the children of God, the afflicted widow, the desolate orphans, and scatter them abroad. Not with impunity will ye do this; your oaths will not excuse you, or afford you any subterfuge. The same punishment and torments that Pilate endured will overtake you, who, unwilling to crucify the Lord, yet from fear of Cæsar adjudged him to death. God, by the mouth of the prophet, proclaims that he will fearfully and terribly avenge the shedding of innocent blood, and will not pass by such as fear not to pollute and contaminate their hands therewith. Therefore great slaughter, much misery and anguish, sorrow and adversity, yea, everlasting groaning, pain and torment, are daily appointed you. The Most High will lift his hand against you, now and eternally. This we announce to you in the name of our Lord Jesus Christ; for verily it will not tarry, and shortly ye shall see that we have told you nothing but the truth of God, in the name of our Lord Jesus Christ, and are witnesses against you, and against all who set at naught his commandments. We beseech you to forsake iniquity, and to turn to the living God with weeping and lamentation, that you may escape all these woes.

"We earnestly entreat you, submissively, and with prayers, that you take in good part all these our words. For we testify and speak what we know, and have learnt to be true in the sight of God. We speak from a pure mind filled with the love of God, and from that true

Christian affection which we follow after before God and men. Farewell."[1]

The oppressor was melted for once. The order was recalled, and the Baptists enjoyed peace and freedom for some time longer. But in 1547 their expulsion was effected with indescribable misery and loss.

[1] *Martyrology*, i. 149-153.

CHAPTER V.

The Netherlands—Sicke Snyder—Furious Edict—The Inquisition-Severities of Philip II.—Torture—Lysken—Gerrit Hase-poot—Joris Wippe—Private Executions—Horrid Rackings.

IN the year 1525 many of the Baptists took refuge in the Netherlands, hoping to be able to serve God there in quietness. They might have done so, perhaps, if they could have refrained from preaching the gospel, and had forborne to propagate their distinctive tenets. But that was impossible. In the spirit of apostolic Christianity, they "went everywhere preaching the word." Numbers listened, were converted, baptized, and joined the persecuted sect at Amsterdam, Antwerp, Haarlem, and other places. Then the hand of oppression was heavy upon them. The Emperor Charles V., to whose dominions the Netherlands belonged, directed that the heretics should be treated with unsparing severity, and that the Baptists should be singled out for special manifestations of vengeance. The first martyr whose name is recorded was "Weynken Claes' daughter, of Monickendam, a widow," who was strangled at the stake and then burned, at the Hague, Nov. 20, 1527. She went to the place of execution "cheerfully, as if she were going to a festival."

Her last words were, "I cleave to God."[1] In the same year Jan Walen and two others were put to death at Haarlem. "Being bound to stakes with chains, and a fire being laid around them, they were slowly roasted, till the marrow was seen to ooze from the bones of their legs. They were thus burned and roasted upward, until death came to their release."[2]

Sicke Snyder—that is, Sicke, the tailor, his proper name being Freerks—was beheaded at Leeuwarden, in 1531. He had "received Christian baptism on confession of his faith, as a token of being a regenerate child of God, according to the instructions of Christ, seeking thus to live and to walk in obedience to his Maker. For this he became a prisoner in bonds at Leeuwarden, in Friesland, and experienced much suffering from the adversaries to the truth. And since he could by no torments be brought to apostatize, he was at the same place executed by the sword, displaying great firmness, bearing testimony to the true faith, and confirming it by his death and blood. . . . His sentence is thus recorded in the Criminal Sentence Book of the Court of Friesland: 'Sicke Freerks, on this 20th of March, 1531, is condemned by the court to be executed with the sword; his body shall be laid on the wheel, and his head set upon a stake, because he has been rebaptized, and perseveres in that baptism.'"[3]

In 1532 three were burned at the Hague. They were "fastened with chains to stakes, and a great fire having been made around them, they were roasted till they expired." At Amsterdam, "nine men were taken out of their beds by night, upon suspicion of Anabaptism, hurried away to the Hague, and after they had been impris-

[1] *Martyrology*, pp. 40–44.   [2] *Ibid.* p. 45.   [3] *Ibid.* 1. 136.

oned a fortnight, were there beheaded by order of the emperor. Their bodies were buried, but their heads put into a herring barrel and sent to Amsterdam, where they were set upon stakes."[1] By edicts published in the following year all persons were forbidden to harbor Baptist preachers in Holland; and obstinate Baptists, that is, those who refused to recant, were doomed to suffer the utmost penalty of the law. In obedience to these edicts the work of cruelty went on.

On the 10th of June, 1535, a furious edict was published at Brussels. Death by fire was the punishment of all Baptists who should be detected and should refuse to abjure. If they recanted they were still to die, but not by fire; the men were to be put to death by the sword, " the women in a sunken pit." Those who resisted the operation of the edict by failing to deliver up Baptists to the authorities, were to suffer the same punishment as accomplices. Informers were promised one-third of the confiscated estates. And all persons were forbidden " to claim or seek any grace, forgiveness, or reconciliation for the said Anabaptists, or rebaptizers, or to present, on their behalf, any petitions or requests; it being understood," says the emperor, " that it is not our will, nor will we permit, that any Anabaptists, or rebaptizers (because of their wicked opinions), shall be received into favor, but be punished as a warning to others, without any dissimulation, favor, or delay."[2]

A similar edict was published in September, 1540. And a novel expedient was adopted. The portraits of the principal Reformers, Baptists included, were placed at the gates of the cities, and in other public situations,

[1] *Martyrology*, pp. 133, 134.   [2] *Ibid.* 138–140.

that recognition and seizure might be more easily made. Large rewards were also offered for the apprehension of the ministers.[1]

The Inquisition was introduced into the Netherlands by Charles V. in 1550. Great consternation was excited, and some of the towns absolutely refused to publish the edict. So powerful were the remonstrances that the emperor consented to modify the provisions of the edict in certain respects; but there was no relaxation of severity toward the Baptists. "Protestants and Papists united to oppress and persecute them."[2]

When Philip II. succeeded his father, Charles V., on the abdication of the latter in the year 1556, he renewed the edict of 1550, with additional articles. "The publication of Baptist books was prohibited, and the right of disposing of their property, by sale or will, was taken away. Nor were magistrates or judges to moderate or lessen the penalties in the slightest degree."[3] In 1560, and again in 1563, these edicts were renewed and still farther extended, so that there might be no possibility of escape. An abstract of the proclamation issued in the last-mentioned year will serve to show the perilous state of society in the Netherlands at that time. No persons were to remove from Flanders to Holland without certificates from the priests and magistrates. Every settler was required to furnish proof that his children had been baptized according to the rites of Rome. Midwives were to be sworn to secure the christening of every infant at whose birth they might be present, and in case of any neglect to report it to the magistrates. Conventicles were to be diligently sought out and repressed. Parents

[1] *Martyrology*, i. 207.   [2] *Ibid.* p. 364.   [3] *Ibid.* i. 64-69.

were ordered to send their children to church and to school. Booksellers' houses and peddlers' packs were to be searched for heretical publications. All the people were enjoined to attend mass every Sunday and holiday. A month's continuous absence was to be punished at the discretion of the judges. No persons suspected of heresy were to be placed in offices of trust. In addition, as before stated, all the former enactments respecting burning, beheading, drowning, and burying alive remained in full force.[1]

The records of this period are truly heart-sickening. It is wonderful that any Baptists survived. And yet it is a fact that they were becoming stronger and stronger. Menno Simon, whose public labors commenced in 1537, preached, baptized, formed churches, published books, and traveled extensively, often exposed to great peril, as will be hereafter related; nevertheless, though a price was set on his head, the designs of the enemy were defeated, and Menno died in peace. Many other ministers were indefatigable in their zeal, among whom Dirk Philips and Leonard Bouwens deserve most honorable mention.

The Baptist Martyrology contains distinct notices of about four hundred brethren and sisters who were barbarously put to death in Holland and Flanders under the operation of the aforesaid edicts. The misery and ruin which befell their families cannot be described. Numbers more suffered, of whom no account has been preserved It was a season of " great tribulation."

Tjaert Reynerson, " a godly farmer," was beheaded at Leeuwarden in 1539, because he had " from compassion

[1] *Martyrology*, ii. 269, 342.

and brotherly love secretly harbored Menno Simon in his house in his great distress." He was frequently examined by torture before his execution, but would neither betray his minister nor deny the faith.[1]

Jan Claeson had forwarded the printing and publication of Menno Simon's works. For this he was condemned " to be executed by the sword; his body to be laid upon the wheel; the head set on a stake." Bestevaer, an aged brother, suffered with him. " The beloved brother, Jan Claeson, confirmed the word of God with his crimson blood, and was afterward given for food to the birds and wild beasts. . . . The aged Bestevaer, numbering eighty-seven years, likewise willingly resigned his gray head and beard to the stroke of these tyrants' sword for the truth of Jesus Christ. They now rest together under the altar."[2]

A number of Baptists met in secret at Rotterdam, in 1544, " to speak to each other for mutual edification and establishment in the truth of the holy gospel which they had received; likewise, with one mouth and lowly hearts to pray to the great God of heaven and earth for the forgiveness of their sins and the gift of the Holy Spirit, and also with one accord to praise and thank his most adorable name." They were betrayed, apprehended, tortured, and then put to death; the men, by the sword; and women were " thrown into a boat, and thrust under the ice till death followed." One of them " was a young female only fourteen years old. She composed the hymn which is found in the old hymn-book, beginning—

'To the wide world Immanuel came,
His Father's kingdom left, etc.' "[3]

[1] *Martyrology*, i. 207.   [2] *Ibid.* 262.   [3] *Ibid.* i. 263.

Richst Heynes was martyred in 1547. When the officers were sent to the house, her husband escaped. "But her they severely treated and cruelly bound, without any pity or compassion, although pregnant, and so near her confinement that the midwife was already with her. Notwithstanding all this they led her away, regardless of the tears and screams of her little children, to the prison at Leeuwarden, where, after three weeks' imprisonment, she was delivered of a son. . . . They afterward inflicted great torments on this sheep of Christ, and tortured her to such a degree that she could not raise her hands to her head. Thus was she treated in the inhuman rack, chiefly because she would not give evidence against her brethren. For these wolves were in nowise satisfied, but still thirsted for more innocent blood. But the faithful God, who is a refuge in time of need, and a shield for all those who trust in him, guarded her mouth, so that no one suffered through her. After all means had thus failed to separate her from Christ, she was condemned at the place above named, and like a brute beast was put into a sack, and plunged under water until life was extinct."[1]

The torture was constantly resorted to, either to force a recantation or to procure the discovery of the hiding-places of the brethren. The victims were stretched on the rack—or suspended by the hands, heavy weights being attached to the feet—or the thumb-screws were employed or a similar instrument applied to the ankles. The demons who inflicted these tortures paid no regard to sex, station, or age. The delicate maiden, the honored minister, the venerable confessor of threescore

[1] *Martyrology*, i. 292.

and ten and upward, were alike subjected to the brutal test.

In the year 1551, Jeronimus Segerson and another were burned at Antwerp. Segerson's letters written while in prison breathe a spirit of exalted piety and manly endurance. "I had rather," said he, "be tortured ten times every day, and then finally be roasted on a gridiron, than renounce the faith I have confessed."

Lysken, Segerson's wife, was drowned. The narrative of her examination and death is so interesting that I will transcribe the greater portion of it:

"Lysken, our sister, having long lain in bonds, has, at last, finished the period of her pilgrimage, remaining perfectly steadfast in the word of the Lord even to the end; the Lord be for ever praised! She very boldly and undisguisedly confessed her faith at the tribunal, before the magistrates and the multitude. They first asked her concerning baptism. She said, 'I acknowledge but one baptism, even that which was used by Christ and his disciples, and left to us.' 'What do you hold concerning infant baptism?' asked the sheriff. To which Lysken answered, 'Nothing but a mere infant's baptism, and a human institution.' On this the bench stood up, and consulted together, while Lysken, in the mean time, confessed, and explained clearly to the people the ground of her belief. They then pronounced sentence upon her. Lysken spoke in the following manner to the bench: 'Ye are now judges; but the time will come when ye will wish that ye had been keepers of sheep, for there is a Judge and Lord who is above all; he shall in his own time judge you. But we have not to wrestle against flesh and blood, but against the principalities, powers, and rulers of the darkness of this world.' The bench said, 'Take her away from the tribunal.'

"The people then ran earnestly to see her, and Lysken spoke piously to them. 'Know that I do not suffer for robbery, or murder, or any kind of wickedness, but solely for the incorruptible word of God.'"

She was then conducted back to prison, where two monks visited her, and endeavored, but in vain, to turn her from the faith. Next morning she suffered.

"On Saturday morning we rose early, some before day, some with the daylight, to see the nuptials which we thought would then be celebrated; but the crafty murderers outran us. We had slept too long, for they had finished their murderous work between three and four o'clock. They had taken that sheep to the Scheldt, and had put her into a sack, and drowned her before the people arrived, so that few persons saw it. Some, however, saw it. She went courageously to death, and spoke bravely: 'Father, into thy hands I commend my spirit.' Thus she was delivered up, and it came to pass, to the honor of the Lord, that by the grace of God many were moved thereby.

"When the people assembled, and heard that she was already dead, it occasioned a great commotion amongst them, for it grieved them as much as if she had been publicly executed. For the people said, 'Thieves and murderers they bring publicly before all men; but their treachery is thus more manifest.' Some simple-hearted people asked, 'Why must these persons die, for many bear a good testimony concerning them?' Some of the friends were present, and spoke openly to the people: 'The reason is, that they are more obedient to God's command than to the emperor's or men's; because they have heartily turned to the Lord their God, from lies to truth, from darkness to light, from unrighteousness to righteousness, from unbelief to the true faith, and have accordingly amended their lives, and been baptized, seeing they were true believers, according to the command of Christ and the practice of the apostles.' They further showed the people, from the word of God, that the Papists are they of whom the Apostle Paul prophesied—namely, the seducing spirits who teach the doctrines of devils; and moreover, that the righteous have had to suffer from the beginning, from the time of Abel to the present; that Christ also suffered and entered into the glory of his Father, and left us an example that we should follow in his footsteps; for 'all that will live godly in Christ Jesus must suffer persecution.'"[1]

Gerrit Hase-poot lived at Nymegen. During the heat of the persecution he fled to another place. After a time he returned to fetch his wife and children, but was seen by one of the sheriff's officers, who gave information to his master, on which he was taken into custody and condemned to die. "After his condemnation," says the historian, "his wife came to the town hall to speak to him once more, to take her leave of him and to say adieu to her beloved husband, carrying a little child on her arm, which, for sorrow, she was scarcely able to support When wine was presented to him, according to the custom of giving wine to those who were sentenced to death, he said to his wife, 'I desire not this wine, but hope to drink new wine, and to receive it above in my Father's house.' With great sorrow they were separated from

[1] *Martyrology* i. 427-431.

each other, bidding each other adieu in this world, for the wife could not longer stand, but became faint from grief. He was then led to death. On being taken from the wagon to the scaffold, he raised his voice, and sang the hymn—

> 'Father of heaven, on thee I call,
> Oh strengthen thou my faith.'

He then fell upon his knees and made his earnest prayer to God. When fastened to the stake, he threw the slippers from his feet, saying, 'It were a pity to burn these, for they may be of service to some poor person!' The strap with which he was to be strangled coming loose, not having been properly fastened by the executioner, he again lifted up his voice and sang the rest of the above hymn—

> 'Farewell, ye saints, farewell!
> What if I meet this end,
> Ere long the Lord shall come,
> Our only Leader, Friend:
> Joyous I wait the glorious day,
> With you to walk in white array.'

The executioner having adjusted the cord, this witness for Jesus fell asleep, and was then burnt."[1]

At the martyrdom of Joriaen Simons and Clement Dirks, at Haarlem, in 1557, there was a great burning of books. Joriaen was a colporteur, and had circulated a large number of Baptist works. "But when it was observed that the books began to blaze, such a tumult arose among the people that the magistrates hastily departed. The people then threw the books amongst the crowd,

[1] *Martyrology*, ii. 93.

who most eagerly caught them. Thus, through the providence of God, instead of the truth being extinguished, as was intended, it was the more spread by the reading of so great a number of these books."[1]

At length, even magistrates and executioners grew tired of the work, and disgusted at the cruelty of the bloodthirsty inquisitors. An instance of this occurred in 1558. Joris Wippe was a burgomaster at Menin, in Flanders. When he became a Baptist, he was obliged to leave that place. He settled at Dort, in Holland, engaged in business as a fuller, and was much esteemed by his fellow-citizens. When the magistrates were informed of his being a Baptist, and were compelled to take proceedings against him, they did all in their power to prevent his death; but the higher authorities overruled them. "When Joris was sentenced to die, the executioner lamented, with weeping eyes, that he must put a man to death who had often fed his wife and children, and would rather be discharged from his office than execute a man who had done him and others so much good, and never any harm. Joris was finally drowned in the prison by night, in a cask filled with water, by one of the thief-takers, who, at the magistrates' direction, performed the office of executioner, and threw him backward into the water. Thus he offered up his body to the Lord on the 1st of October, in the forty-first year of his age. The next day his body was suspended by the legs on a high gibbet, at the place of execution, for the sport of the people. Like his Master, Christ, he had to be numbered with the transgressors. The day following, some malefactors were whipped and banished. The executioner,

[1] *Martyrology*, ii. 108.

after executing justice on these, said, 'They crucified Christ, but Barabbas they released.'"[1]

Sometimes the execution took place privately, within the precincts of the prison. Andries Langedul and two others were beheaded at Antwerp in 1559, "not publicly, but in the prison. The other prisoners, of whom there were then many, could see it through the windows of their cells. When Andries knelt to receive the stroke of the sword, he put his hands together, saying, 'Father, into thy hands I commend'—but 'I commend my spirit' was not perfectly uttered; the rapid stroke of the sword prevented it." Several were drowned in the same city, the year following. "Peter Gomer the mason and Jacot the goldsmith, for the name of Christ, were drowned together in a tub." Lenaert Plovier and two young females "were thrust into sacks, put into wine-casks, and drowned by night in prison."[2]

Joos Verbeek, "a minister of God's word and his church," suffered at Antwerp in 1561. He was racked twice in four days. He was scourged till the blood flowed. His right hand having been "lamed by torture," his last letter to his wife was written with his left hand, "with great difficulty." He was burned in a straw hut, as was the common practice toward the end of the persecution. It was probably adopted to prevent bystanders from witnessing the manner in which the servants of God met death, and thus to repress all manifestations of sympathy. The martyrs were fastened to stakes inside the huts, and strangled, after which fire was applied, and the huts and the bodies were burnt together.[3]

Thirteen brethren and sisters who were apprehended

[1] *Martyrology*, i. 143. [2] *Ibid.* 250, 271, 272. [3] *Ibid.* ii. 304.

at Hallewin, on information given by a priest, and committed to prison at Lille, then called Ryssel, were shortly afterward all burnt alive, at three separate times. Jan de Swarte, a minister, his wife, and four sons, were of the number. "When Jan de Swarte was apprehended, the two youngest sons were not at home, but came in during the time. As they were approaching the house, the neighbors warned them, and told them who were in the house, and that their father and mother were arrested. The one said to the other, 'Let us not run away, but die with father and mother.' Meanwhile Jan de Swarte was led out of the house a prisoner, and seeing his sons said to them, 'Children, will you go with me to the New Jerusalem?' They said, 'Yes, father, we will;' and they were led captive with them. All these were conducted prisoners together to Ryssel, and there strictly guarded in the castle. Jan was placed by himself in a dungeon called Paradise. It was so small that he could not stand upright in it, nor lie down at full length.

"It happened one day that several brethren and sisters, moved by love and compassion, came from outside the town, and stood over against the castle, calling out over the fortification, and comforting the prisoners. Amongst them was a brother named Herman. Being observed by one of the city officers, who had gone out ecretly, he also was apprehended

"After ten days' imprisonment, Jan de Swarte, his son Klaes, and four others were executed. While going to death, the clock struck. Jan asked what it was o'clock. He was told four. On this he comforted himself, saying, 'By five o'clock we hope to be in our lodge, or rest.'"

A few days afterward, Klaesken, Jan de Swarte's wife,

THE REFORMATION PERIOD.

with her three sons, and Herman, were burned alive. The remaining two suffered a year's imprisonment, when they also were "cast alive into the fire, and burned to ashes."

The priest who had betrayed them "was very severely punished. For his flesh became so putrified, that pieces fell off from his body, or were sometimes cut off, and no cure could be found for it. . . . While he was lying ill, a man came to visit him. When the priest complained of his great misery, the man said to him, 'It is the coals of the fire at Ryssel.' This greatly displeased the priest; but he was obliged to endure such scoffing, as well as the punishments with which God had visited him. He at last died most miserably, as was of old the case with Antiochus and Herod."[1]

I will only add one more case. Christian Langedul, with three others, was burned at Antwerp in 1567. In his letters to his wife he gives an account of the manner in which they were tortured:

"We were all four, one after the other, sorely racked, so that we have at present little inclination to write. . . . Cornelius was the first taken: then Hans Symons. . . It was next my turn. You may conceive how I felt. As I approached the rack near the gentlemen, I was ordered to strip or to say where I lived. I looked sorrowful, as you may suppose. I said, 'Will you ask me any more questions besides that?' They were silent. I then thought, 'I know how it must be; they will not spare me.' I therefore undressed, and gave myself up to the gentlemen, fully prepared to die. They now cruelly racked me. I think two cords fastened on my thighs and

[1] *Martyrology*, 338–341.

legs broke. They also drenched me with water, pouring it into my mouth and nose. After releasing me, they inquired if I would now speak. They entreated me; then menaced me; but I did not open my mouth. God had shut it. They then said, 'Give him another taste of it.' This they did, calling out, 'Away, away; stretch him another foot.' I thought, 'You can but kill me.' While thus lying stretched out, drawn by cords on my head and chin, and on my thighs and legs, they said, 'Speak, speak.' They now chatted with one another about the account which J. T. had prepared of my linen, which amounted to six hundred and fifty pounds, the sum it would fetch by auction. . . . Again I was asked, 'Will you not speak?' I kept my mouth closed. They said, 'Say where you live, and where your wife and children are.' But I said not a word. 'What a dreadful thing!' said they in French; but I replied not, for the Lord kept the door of my lips. After they had long tried to make me speak, they at last released me.

"Matthew was tortured after me. He named his own house and the street where we live. He also said that we lived in a gateway, and I think there is no other gateway in the street but ours. You had better, therefore, immediately remove, if you have not left, for I think the magistrates will go there. Let no one go to the house who is in any danger of apprehension. He also mentioned the house of R. T., and the street in which F. V. lives. Do immediately the best you can in this matter. He is very sorry that he did so. Cornelius and Hans did not disclose anything."

"We were afraid that the margrave would come to torture Cornelius once more, and we also feared that we should again be tortured. We tremble much at the prospect, for the pain is frightful; we do not fear death near so much. Cornelius was so racked and scourged the second time that it required three men to carry him up stairs, who say that he could scarcely move a limb, only his tongue. He sent to us to say that if they come to him again he thinks that he must sink under it. As the margrave did not come yesterday, we expect him here to-day. The Lord help us! for the pain is excruciating!"[1]

While these horrible scenes were enacted, the Baptists of the Netherlands persevered in the faith. Neither fires nor floods appalled them. Menno Simon and other bold-spirited men risked their lives continually in the service of the gospel. They were always traveling from place to place, and by their itinerant labors an immense amount of good was accomplished. Converts were baptized and added to the churches in every part of the country. The servants of God were confirmed in the faith, useful publications were scattered abroad, and Anabaptism, as it was called, like the bush which Moses saw, though it was " burned with fire, was not consumed."

[1] *Martyrology*, ii. 426–438.

CHAPTER VI.

Biography of Menno Simon—Account of his Publications—Church Government among the Baptists—Missionary Excursions.

I PROPOSE now to give some account of Menno Simon, to whose labors the Baptists of Holland were so deeply indebted.

This great man was born at Witmarsum, in Friesland, in the year 1505. Very little is known of his early life. It is not known where he studied; but it is evident, both from his writings and from the admissions of his opponents, that he was a first-rate scholar. Mosheim says that he had acquired " learning enough to be regarded by many as an oracle." Though he was educated for the priesthood, he was entirely ignorant of the Scriptures, excepting such portions as are contained in the Missal and the Breviary. Nay more—he was not only ignorant but hostile, " speaking evil of things which he knew not," after the manner of the Romish priesthood of that age, who were irritated by the Reformers' constant appeal to the word of God, and refused to admit it, maintaining that the authority of the church was supreme. The fact that Luther and his coadjutors proposed to derive their religious views from the Bible led these sapient priests to identify the Holy Book with heresy, and therefore to refrain from perusing it. So Menno Simon afterward confessed.

But he was a thinking man. Having been ordained in 1528, he became vicar of Pingium, a village in Friesland. The celebration of the mass was of course a frequent duty. He had been taught to believe that when the priest uttered the words, "*Hoc est corpus meum*" ("This is my body"), the wafer was changed into the body of the Lord Jesus. His reason was shocked and disgusted. Could these things be true? Did Christianity teach them? Such questions could not be answered unless he examined the original record. He determined to do so, and in the year 1530 he read the New Testament. The perusal opened his eyes. He renounced transubstantiation. Continuing to read, more enlightenment followed. As he learned, he taught. He preached so differently that he began to be regarded as an evangelical minister. But as yet it was only light; spiritual life was wanting.

I mentioned in a former chapter the martyrdom of Sicke Snyder at Leeuwarden. Menno heard of it, and then for the first time was informed of the existence of the people called "Anabaptists." The effects produced on his mind, and the ultimate results, were thus stated by himself some years afterward:

"It sounded very strange in my ears to speak of a person being rebaptized. I examined the Scriptures with diligence, and meditated on them earnestly; but could find in them no authority for infant baptism. As I remarked this, I spoke of it to my pastor; and after several conversations he acknowledged that infant baptism had no ground in the Scriptures. Yet I dare not trust so much to my understanding. I consulted some ancient authors, who taught me that children must by baptism be washed from their original sin. This I compared with the Scriptures, and perceived that it set at naught the blood of Christ. Afterward I went to Luther, and would gladly have known from him the ground; and he taught me that we must baptize children on their own faith, because they are holy. This also I saw was not according to God's word. In the third place, I went to Bucer, who taught me that we should baptize children in order to be able the more diligently to take care of them and bring them up in the ways of the Lord. But this, too, I saw was a groundless representation. In the fourth place, I had recourse to Bullinger, who pointed me to the covenant of circumcision; but I found, as before, that according to Scripture the practice could not stand. As I now on every side observed that the writers stood on grounds so very different, and each followed his own reason, I saw clearly that we were deceived with infant baptism."

In 1530 Menno returned to Witmarsum, his native village, where he remained five years, discharging his duties as a Romish priest. "There," said he, "I preached and said much from the word of God, but without any influence from the Spirit, or any proper affection for the souls of men; and I made, by these my sermons, many young persons, like myself, vain boasters and empty talkers; but they had very little concern for spiritual things. . . . I entered with ardor into the indulgence of youthful lusts; and, like the generality of persons of similar pursuits, sought exclusively after gain, worldly appearance the favor of men, and the glory of a name." Nevertheless, he continued to inquire after truth, and the Lord graciously guided and blessed him. As his views became clearer, his heart was affected, and at length all the marks of genuine conversion appeared. Then came a time of trial. Should he retain his position as a priest, or forsake all and follow Christ? "If I continue in this state," he exclaimed, "and do not to the utmost of my ability expose the hypocrisy of false teachers, and the impenitent and careless lives of men, their depraved baptism and supper, with their other superstitions, what will become of me?" True to his convictions, he faithfully and fearlessly proclaimed the gospel.

"I began," he said, "in the name of the Lord, to teach publicly from the pulpit the doctrine of true repentance; to guide the people in the narrow path; to testify concerning sins and unchristian behavior, and all idolatry and false worship; as also concerning baptism and the supper, according to the sense and fundamental principles of Christ, as far as I at the time received grace from my God. Also, I warned every man against the Munster abominations in regard to a king, to polygamy, to a worldly kingdom, to the sword, etc., most faithfully, until the great and gracious Lord, perhaps after the course of nine months, extended to me his fatherly Spirit, help and mighty hand, so that I freely abandoned at once my character and fame among men, as also my antichristian abominations, mass, infant baptism, loose and careless life, and all; and put myself willingly in all trouble and poverty, under the pressing cross of Christ the Lord. In my weakness I feared God. I sought pious people, and of these I found some, though few, in good zeal and doctrine. I disputed with the perverted; and some I gained through God's help and power; but the stiff-necked and obdurate I commended to the Lord. Thus has the gracious Lord drawn me through the free favor of his great grace. He first stirred in my heart. He has given me a new mind. He has humbled me in his fear. He has led me from the way of death, and through mere mercy has called me upon the narrow path of life into the company of his saints. To him be praise for ever. Amen."

This reference to the "Munster abominations" serves to point out the peculiarity of his circumstances. He was fully a Baptist in principle; but the outrageous conduct of the men of Munster (about whom I shall have to speak at large in a subsequent chapter) had exposed all persons bearing the Baptist name to unmerited opprobrium; in fact, no man's life was safe who attached himself to that body. Menno distinguished, however, between the precious and the vile. Repudiating the monstrous dogmas and pretensions which characterized the Munster mania, against which he always earnestly protested, he embraced the sentiments held by the genuine Baptists, and joined one of their churches. This was in the year 1535.

During the first year after his baptism, Menno lived in retirement, meeting with the church from time to time, and diligently employing all the means in his power for the increase of knowledge and piety. But he could not be hid. The church recognized his talents for usefulness, and wisely determined to call him out to labor. I will again cite his own words:

"He who bought me with the blood of his love, and called me to his service, unworthy as I am, searches me, and knows that I seek neither gold, nor goods, nor luxury, nor ease on earth; but only my Lord's glory, my salvation, and the souls of many immortals. Wherefore I have had, now the eighteenth year, to endure such excessive anxiety, oppression, trouble, sorrow, and persecution, with my poor, feeble wife and little offspring, that I have stood in jeopardy of my life, and in many a fear. Yes, while the priests lie on soft beds and cushions, we must hide ourselves commonly in secret corners. While they are at all nuptials and christenings, and at other times make themselves merry in public with fifes, drums, and various kinds of music, we must look out for every dog, lest he be one employed to catch us. Instead of being greeted by all as doctors and masters, we must be called Anabaptists, clandestine holders-forth, deceivers, and heretics. In short, while for their services they are rewarded in princely style, with great emoluments and good days, our reward and portion must be fire, sword and death.

"What now I, and my true coadjutors in this very difncult and hazardous service, *have* sought, or *could* have sought all the well-disposed may easily estimate from the work itself and its fruit. . . . And through our feeble service, teaching, and simple writing, with the careful deportment, labor, and help of our faithful brethren, the great and mighty God has made so known and public in many cities and lands the word of true repentance, the word of his grace and power, together with the wholesome use of his holy sacraments; and has given such growth to his churches, and endowed them with such invincible strength, that not only have many proud hearts become humble, the impure chaste, the drunken temperate, the covetous liberal, the cruel kind, the godless godly; but also for the testimony which they bear, they fa thfully give up their property to confiscation and their bodies to torture and to death—as has occurred again and again to the present hour. These are no marks or fruits of false doctrine—with *that* God does not co-operate—nor under such oppression and misery could anything have stood so long, were it not the power and the word of the Almighty. Whether all the prophets, apostles, and true servants of God, did not through their service, produce the like fruits we would gladly let all the pious judge."

The issue was, that Menno became a Baptist minister. The last twenty-five years of his life were spent in toilsome and perilous efforts for the spread of the truth. Repeatedly compelled to change his abode, and living for the most part in a state of wandering and exile, his life was, no doubt, greatly embittered. Having married, too, at an early period of his ministry, his sufferings were increased by the exposure of his wife and children to the same distress as he himself endured. But he labored on without fainting, and God abundantly blessed him. Let us listen to him once more.

"Perhaps a year afterward, as I was silently employing myself upon the word of the Lord, in reading and writing, there came to me six or eight persons, who were of one heart and soul with me; in their faith and life, so far as man can judge, irreproachable; separated from the world, according to the direction of the Scriptures; subjected to the cross of Christ; and bearing a hearty abhorrence, not only of the Munster, *but also of all worldly sects, anathematizings, and corruptions.* With much kind entreaty they urged me in the name of the pious who were agreed with them and me in one spirit and sentiment, that I would yet lay a little to heart the severe distress and great necessities of the poor oppressed souls—for the hunger was great, and very few were the faithful stewards—and employ the talent, which, unworthy as I am, I had received from the Lord.

"As I heard this I was very much troubled; anguish and fearfulness surrounded me. For on the one hand, I saw my small gift; my want of erudition; my weak and bashful nature; the extremely great wickedness, willfulness, perverse conduct, and tyranny of the world; the powerful large sects; the craftiness of many spirits; and the heavy cross, which, should I begin, would not a little press me. On the other side, I saw the pitiable extreme hunger, want, and necessity of the devout, pious children; for I perceived clearly enough that they wandered, as the simple, forsaken sheep when they have no shepherd.

"At length, after much prayer, I resigned myself to the Lord and his people with this condition. They were to unite with me in praying to him fervently, that should it be his holy pleasure to employ me in his service to his praise, his fatherly kindness would then give me such a heart and mind as would testify to me with Paul: *Woe is me if I preach not the gospel!* But should his will be otherwise, that he would order such means as to permit the matter to rest where it was. '*For if two of you shall agree on earth as touching anything that they shall ask, it shall be done for them of my Father which is in heaven. For where two or three are gathered together in my name, there am I in the midst of them*' (Matt. xviii. 19, 20)."[1]

[1] The above account is extracted from Menno Simon's *Narrative of his Secession from Popery.*

Before his time the Baptists of Holland had been unable from various causes to realize, as completely as was to be desired, the advantages of church organization. Menno instructed them in these matters, and in establishing regular government and discipline. It might be said that he exercised a sort of apostolic supervision over them. At any rate, his labors and journeyings were apostolical. "He traveled in West Friesland," says Mosheim, "the territory of Groningen, and East Friesland, then in Guelderland, Holland, Brabant, and Westphalia, and the German provinces, along the shores of the Baltic, and penetrated as far as Livonia, and gathered an immense number of followers, so that he was almost the common father and bishop of all the Anabaptists." [1]

Such exertions could not fail to attract the special notice of the persecuting government of the Netherlands. A proclamation was issued, offering pardon (if the informer were a Baptist), the freedom of the country, and a large pecuniary reward, to any one who would deliver up Menno to the authorities.[2] Sometimes he was in imminent danger of being seized. On one occasion a Christian brother, in whose house he had taken shelter, was apprehended, cruelly tortured, and then put to death, because he would not betray the servant of God. Another narrow escape is thus narrated by his daughter:

"A traitor had agreed, for a specified sum of money, o deliver him into the hands of his enemies. He first sought to apprehend him at a meeting; in which, however, he failed of success, and Menno escaped in a wonderful manner. Soon after this, the traitor, in company

---

[1] *Ecclesiastical History*, cent. xvi. sect. 3, part 2, chap. vi. sect. 8.
[2] *Martyrology*, i. 242.

with an officer, passed him in a small boat on the canal. But the traitor kept quiet till Menno had passed them to some distance, and had leaped ashore in order to escape with less danger. Then the traitor cried out, 'Behold, the bird has escaped us!' The officer chastised him—called him a villain—and demanded why he did not tell of it in time; to which the traitor replied, 'I could not speak; for my tongue was bound.' The lords were so displeased at this that they punished the traitor severely—a warning and lesson to all bloodthirsty traitors."[1]

At last Providence appeared for him. The lord of Fresenburg, a territory between Holland and Lubeck, had frequently visited the Netherlands, had witnessed the persecution of the Baptists, and admired their piety and steadfastness. When they were driven from their homes, he allowed them to settle on his estates. Great numbers availed themselves of the privilege. Flourishing settlements were founded, and many Baptist churches established. There Menno also found a peaceful retreat, and pursued his labors without molestation. A printing establishment was founded there, whence his numerous works were issued. And there he died, on the 15th of January, 1561, in the village of Odesloe. His remains were deposited in his own garden.

No account of the manner of his death has been preserved. But his "doctrine, purpose, and manner of life" were "fully known." The "end" of such a man was undoubtedly "peace."

Menno Simon was a voluminous writer. His works have been collected and published in a handsome folio volume. I will mention the principal treatises contained in it.

[1] *Martyrology*, i. 244.

I. "An evident demonstration of the saving doctrine of Jesus Christ." In this work he discusses the following subjects: 1. The time of grace. 2. Repentance. 3. Faith, which he defines, "An embracing of the gospel through the agency of the Holy Spirit." He shows that the believer relies upon Christ and his grace; that he embraces his promises; and that he is justified, not by works, but by faith, which is not of men, but the gift of God; and that this faith is not without fruits, but worketh by love. 4. Baptism. He defends the confining of baptism to believers from Matt. xxviii. 19, Mark xvi. 16, and by the arguments usually adduced by Baptists, and replies to the arguments in favor of Pædobaptism. In this chapter he employs a very severe style of writing. It was common to the authors of that and the next age. The Reformers, and after them, the Puritans, treated their adversaries with very little courtesy; and certainly they received none from their opponents. 5. The Lord's supper. 6. Secession from the Church of Rome. 7. The calling of ministers in the church. 8. The doctrines to be preached by ministers, showing that the Scripture is the only rule of faith. 9. The life of ministers, and their support. He denies the lawfulness of ministerial stipends. This was one of his mistakes. In this chapter also, he cautions magistrates, learned men, and the common people, against false ministers, meaning those who had identified themselves with insurrections against the civil power. He shows that the only sword which the Christians ought to use is the sword of the Spirit, and that with this sword Christ so protects his church that the gates of hell shall not prevail against it. He also admonishes the church under persecution to walk in the practice of all Christian virtues.

II. "Fundamental doctrines from the word of God." This treatise closely resembles the first. He writes very clearly and fully on the spirituality of the kingdom of Christ, and contends that none but the regenerate are true members of the church.

III. "A consolatory admonition to the people of God under persecution." Having adverted to the ordinary topics of consolation, he warns his brethren very earnestly against taking up arms in defence of religion.

IV. "The doctrine of excommunication." It is shown that excommunication is designed to bring sinners to repentance, and preserve the church in its purity. This is well. But when Menno goes on to maintain that the pious must withdraw altogether from the excommunicated, and have no dealings with them—and that excommunication dissolves all society between father and children, brothers and sisters, husbands and wives—union with Christ by faith being infinitely more important than any earthly union—we cannot but confess that his scheme was far harsher than the New Testament would warrant. There was much disputing on this subject between the men of severe measures and their moderate brethren: but the latter were in the minority during the period now under consideration.

V. "Reply to Gellius Faber, minister at Embden." All the peculiarities of the Baptists were stated and defended in this work. Faber had not only written against them, but had also stirred up persecution and inflamed the minds of the people. Hence Menno hits him hard. Faber, too, gives sturdy blows. They were both rough men.

VI. "A piteous supplication of poor Christians, addressed to magistrates," etc.

VII. "A brief vindication of miserable Christians and dispersed strangers, etc., addressed to all divines and preachers in the Netherlands." In these two works Menno defends himself and his brethren against the accusations brought against them. He exposes the calumnies of their foes, and indignantly remonstrates with magistrates and ministers for allowing themselves to be led away by misrepresentations and lies, invented for no other purpose than the accomplishment of the ruin of innocent people.

VIII. The most interesting of all Menno Simon's works is the "Narration of his Secession from Popery," in which he traces and describes the various experiences through which he passed, and the struggles he endured ere he attained full deliverance.[1]

In common with the Baptists of that period, generally, Menno Simon held that no Christian should undertake the office of magistrate, or bear arms, or bind himself by oath. Whatever may be thought of these sentiments, now, it is evident that they originated in the views entertained by Baptists respecting the purity of the church. Maintaining that a church of Christ should consist exclusively of pious persons, they concluded, necessarily, that such persons would not be law-breakers, that they would abhor all violence, and that their word might be relied on. Among *them*, therefore, no magistrate would be required. Their principles would be incompatible with the

---

[1] See *London Baptist Magazine*, vol. x. pp. 361–368, 401–406, containing a Memoir of Menno Simon, by the late Rev. William Rowe, of Weymouth.

employment of force, even in self-defence. It would be outrageous to call upon *them* to confirm any statement by an oath, since the word of true men ought always to be taken. All this may be admitted. Menno Simon and his friends seem to have forgotten, however, that they were living "in the world," and that there were certain duties incumbent on them as members of society. Yet these were harmless notions, and might have been borne with. They would have been, had forbearance been the temper of the age.

It is manifest that the doctrinal opinions of the Baptists of this period harmonized, with a few exceptions not of great moment, with those entertained by the Reformers of all persuasions. With regard to the constitution and government of Christian churches, they and the Reformers materially differed. According to the latter, infant baptism formed the basis of church-membership, and the church and the nation were identical. The Baptists, on the contrary, would admit no members to their churches but on personal profession of repentance and faith, on which profession the parties were baptized. All their subsequent arrangements were founded on these prerequisites. Every church was a family of believers. When they sat down at the table of the Lord, they felt that they were one in Christ and "members one of another." The church, in their estimation, was a holy society. All the rule and discipline tended to the preservation of that holiness. So Baptists have thought and practiced from the beginning.

I do not find any material difference between them and ourselves in regard to the organization and management of churches. The opposition was so violent that they were compelled to meet in secret, and at such times as they were able. Doubtless, whenever it was practicable, they spent the Lord's Day together in spiritual exercises, "according to the commandment." On those occasions, if ministers were present, they preached and taught, and administered the ordinance of the Lord's supper: if not, there was mutual exhortation, with prayer and praise. Care was taken to ascertain who among them were possessed of suitable gifts; and these, after a season of probation, were solemnly set apart to the ministerial office, by prayer and imposition of hands. Sometimes they sent out brethren on missionary tours, to gather together scattered disciples or comfort afflicted churches. This proved not unfrequently a perilous task. Several instances of martyrdom are recorded, resulting from the discharge of the duty. The itinerant missionary was apprehended as a suspected man; for the fact of his being a stranger, and often a foreigner, was sufficient to arouse suspicion. Examination disclosed the secret, and death followed.

I will give you a few extracts from the "Martyrology," which will illustrate this part of the subject.

Joriaen Simons and Clement Dorks, together with Mary Jones, "fell into the hands of the tyrants at Haarlem," in 1557. "From the very gates of their prison they made known the word of the Lord, for the reformation of all.' When called on to declare their faith, they said, "that they had been baptized on a confession of their faith, according to the command of Christ," and that "infant baptism was not from God, but in opposition to his word." They observed the supper of the Lord "agreeably to the institution of Christ, after his own usage and blessing when with his apostles." They "could not acknowledge the Pope and the Romish Church to be the church of God." They acknowledge "no other punishment of offenders in the church than evangelic excommunication, thereby to separate the bad from the good, that a pure church might be presented to the Lord, in which there might be nothing impure or defiled."[1]

It was observed of two godly women who were beheaded at Ghent, in 1564, that "they had separated themselves, agreeably to the direction of the holy Scriptures, from the Popish Church of Antichrist, as corrupted with many impurities, and filled with the unfruitful works of darkness, and doctrines, and commandments of men, in opposition to the holy word of the Lord. They had also united themselves with the true members of Christ, and with them, according to their weak ability, endeavored to observe the Lord's commandments and ordinances. They were therefore deprived of life by the persecutors and haters of the truth."[2]

In 1559, "Jan Bosch, commonly called Jan Durps, was a pious, worthy man, a linen-weaver by trade, living at Maestricht. Though the truth was very much obscured by the Papacy, yet the light of divine grace shone into his mind, and genuine gospel truth was brought home to him. He repaired to the church of God, and yielded the obedience which Christ the Son of God prescribed and commanded. After he had for a season adorned his Christian calling, the church ordained him, and the charge of it was entrusted to him, that by reading and exhortation he should serve them. After many refusals he consented,

[1] *Martyrology*, ii. 166.   [2] *Ibid.* 357.

and discharged his duty with fidelity, and employed his talents to the best of his ability."[1]

"Jan de Swarte, a man of excellent character, from Nipkerke, and his wife and children, came to the knowledge of the truth, and were united to the church of God. He was afterward chosen and ordained to be a minister of the church. In this office he, according to his ability, and in meekness, so conducted himself—not only as deacon by caring for the poor, but also, according to the gift he had received from God, in the dispensation of the word of exhortation—that he became greatly endeared to all that knew him."[2] I have noticed his martyrdom in a previous chapter.

"In the year 1560, the brother Claes Felbinger, a locksmith, a willing servant of the word of God—he was then on trial—was apprehended," and put to death. This brother "was called to the ministry of the gospel in the year 1556, but had not received the imposition of hands."[3] "In the year 1562, the brother Franciscus van der Sach, a native of Rovigo, in Italy, a minister of the word of God, being still on probation, with another, his fellow-messenger, named Antonius Walsch, was apprehended at Capo d'Istria." He was subsequently drowned at Venice, as I have before stated.[4]

The following cases illustrate the statement respecting the dangers attending missionary excursions in those days. "In the beginning of the year 1536, Jeronimus Kels, of Kufstein, with Michiel Zeepsieder, of Walt, in Bemen, and Hans Overacker, of Etschland, were commissioned to go into the earldom of the Tyrol; but being come to

---

[1] *Martyrology*, ii. 240.   [3] *Ibid.* 338.
[2] *Ibid.* 279.   [4] *Ibid.* 335.

Vienna, in Austria, they were seized, having been betrayed by the innkeeper with whom they lodged. While at supper, the people there sought to discern who they were by drinking their healths; and when they found out their views, by their declining to respond to the toasts, the landlord sent for paper, and wrote a letter in Latin, which, among other words, contained the following: 'Here are three persons, who, I think, are all Anabaptists.' They were arrested, and died in the fire at Vienna."[1] In 1537, "Juriaen Vaser, by desire of some zealous brethren, was sent to Pogstall, in Austria, where he joyfully began to teach the word of the Lord, notwithstanding that he was just come out of prison at Metlyng. He gathered the faithful together, and formed a church agreeably to God's command. But he could not escape the foils of a crafty knave, who, feigning a desire to learn from him, as a minister, the nature and ground of the truth, brought with him many servants, whom he ordered to lay hold and capture this Juriaen Vaser, when a suitable opportunity should occur. This was faithfully performed."[2] Vaser was beheaded. In the year 1545, "Brother Hans Blietel, having been sent by the church to Riet, in Bavaria, was there apprehended; for money had been offered by them of Riet to any one that should take him. There was in consequence a traitor who gave him good words, affected much zeal, wished ardently to be with him, and drew him to his house. The brother thought it was for the welfare of his soul, and went with him." The wretch endeavored to extort money from him, and, failing in that, betrayed him to the magistrates, who condemned him to the flames. "When the dear

---

[1] *Martyrology*, i. 157.   [2] *Ibid.* 161.

brother Hans reached the place of execution outside the city, he thought upon the church, and called out with a loud voice, in the midst of the assembled people, asking if there was any one present who would have courage to inform the church of God in Moravia, that 'I, Hans Blietel, have been burned for the sake of the gospel, at Riet, in Bavaria.' A zealous man, full of piety, then discovered himself. His zeal was inflamed by this question, and as he could not get near Hans, he called out to him and said that he would tell and make known to the church in Moravia that he had been burned at Riet for the faith." [1]

[1] *Martyrology*, 268. The *Martyrology* is an abridgement of a large folio volume, in Dutch, by T. J. Van Braght, a Mennonite minister. The first edition was published at Dordrecht, in 1660; the second, illustrated by more than a hundred engravings, at Amsterdam, in 1685. A full translation of the work, by J. Daniel Rupp, was published at Lancaster, Pennsylvania, in an octavo volume of 1048 pages, in 1837. The late Rev. Benjamin Millard, of Wigan, was the author of the translation issued by the Hanserd Knollys Society.

CHAPTER VII.

Baptists in England—Proclamation of Henry VIII.—Latimer's Sermon before Edward VI.—Baptists excepted from "Acts of Pardon"—Royal Commissions against them—Ridley—Cranmer—Joan Boucher—Rogers—Philpot—Bishop Hooper's Scruples—George Van Pare—Protestant Persecutions Inexcusable—Congregations in Essex and Kent—Bonner—Gardiner—Disputations in Jail—Queen Elizabeth's Proclamation against Baptists—Bishop Jewel—Archbishop Parker—Dutch Baptists.

WHEREVER the Reformation prevailed, Baptist sentiments sprang up with it. So it was in England. In 1534, when Henry VIII. assumed the headship of the English Church, he issued two proclamations against heretics. The first referred to certain persons who had presumed to dispute about baptism and the Lord's supper, some of whom were foreigners: these were ordered to depart the realm within eight or ten days. The second stated more explicitly that foreigners who had been baptized in infancy, but had renounced that baptism and had been rebaptized, had entered England, and were spreading their opinions over the kingdom. They were commanded to withdraw within twelve days, on pain of suffering death if they remained. Either some of them did remain, or others visited England the following years, for ten were burned, by pairs, in different places, in 1535, and fourteen more in 1536. In 1538, six Dutch Baptists were detected and imprisoned; two of them were burned. Bishop Latimer refers to these circumstances in a sermon preached before Edward VI., in the year 1549. "The Anabaptists," said he, "that were burnt here in divers towns in England—as I heard of credible men, I saw them not myself—went to their death even *intrepide*, as ye will say, without any fear in the world, cheerfully. Well, let them go."[1] That good man was blind on the subject of religious freedom, as the Reformers generally were. He and his fellow-laborers might think for themselves; but if others ventured to do so, and thought themselves into Baptist principles, the fire was ready for them, and even Latimer could say, "Well, let them go." Let us be thankful that the "times of that ignorance" have passed away.

There is some reason to believe that a Baptist church existed in Cheshire at a much earlier period. If we may credit the traditions of the place, the church at Hill Cliffe is five hundred years old. A tombstone has been lately dug up in the burial-ground belonging to that church, bearing date 1357. The origin of the church is assigned, in the "Baptist Manual," to the year 1523. This, however, is certain, that a Mr. Warburton, pastor of the church, died there in 1594. How long the church had been then in existence, there are no written records to testify.[2]

Henry VIII. had a keen scent for heresy. He claimed to be an infallible judge in that matter, as free from error

---

[1] *Sermons*, p. 160. Parker Society's Edition.
[2] These statements are made on the authority of the Rev. A. Kenworthy, the present pastor of the church.

as the Pope himself. And so he was, no doubt; the one was as good as the other. Baptists were particularly distasteful to him. In the year 1538, Peter Tasch, a Baptist, was apprehended in the territories of the landgrave of Hesse. It was discovered, on searching him, that he was in correspondence with Baptists in England, and expected soon to go thither in order to aid them in propagating their opinions. The landgrave gave information to the king, who immediately appointed a commission, of which Cranmer was chairman, charging the commissioners to adopt severe measures against the alleged heretics if they should be detected, to burn all Baptist books, and, if they did not recant, to burn the Baptists themselves. They were not slow to obey the king's commandments. On the 24th of November, three men and one woman escaped the fire by bearing fagots at St. Paul's Cross; that is, they were brought before the people, assembled opposite the great cross outside St. Paul's Cathedral, London, and walked in procession, each with a bundle of fagots on the shoulder, to signify that they had deserved to be burned; after which they confessed and renounced their supposed errors. Three days after a man and a woman were committed to the flames in Smithfield. All these were natives of Holland. Fuller, the church historian, writes of them in his peculiarly quaint style. He says, "Dutchmen flocked faster than formerly into England. Many of these had active souls; so that whilst their hands were busied about their manufactures, their heads were also beating about points of divinity. Hereof they had many rude notions, too ignorant to manage them themselves, and too proud to crave the direction of others. Their minds had a by-stream of activity more than what sufficed to drive on their vocation; and this waste of their souls they employed in needless speculations, and soon after began to broach their strange opinions, being branded with the general name of Anabaptists."[1] This is amusing enough And yet it is a melancholy specimen of the ignorance in which some men, otherwise well-informed and even learned, have been contented to remain. Instead of examining Baptist sentiments for themselves, they have taken them at second hand, and pronounced them "needless speculations" and "strange opinions."

The hatred of Baptists was farther shown by excepting them from general acts of pardon. Such acts were published in 1538, 1540, and 1550; but those who held that "infants ought not to be baptized" were excluded from the benefit. Thieves and vagabonds shared the king's favor, but Baptists were not to be tolerated.

Protestantism nominally flourished in the reign of Edward VI. But there were many un-Protestant doings. The use of the Reformed liturgy was enforced by the pains and penalties of law. Ridley, himself, a martyr in the next reign, was joined in a commission with Gardiner, afterward notorious as a persecutor of Protestants, to root out Baptists. Among the "Articles of Visitation," issued by Ridley in his own diocese, in 1550, was the following: "Whether any of the Anabaptists' sect or other, use notoriously any unlawful or private conventicles, wherein they do use doctrines or administration of sacraments, separating themselves from the rest of the parish?"[2] It may be fairly gathered from this article

[1] *Church History*, book v. sect. 1, 11.
[2] Cardwell's *Documentary Annals of the Church of England*, i. 91.

that there were Baptist churches in the kingdom at that time.

A royal commission was issued by Edward VI., empowering thirty-one persons therein named, Cranmer at the head and Latimer as one of its members, to proceed against all heretics and contemners of the Book of Common Prayer. The "wicked opinions" of the Baptists are specifically mentioned, and the commissioners—or rather, *inquisitors*, for such they were—were directed, in case the persons accused should not renounce their errors, to deliver them up to the secular power, that is, to death. Joan Boucher, or "Joan of Kent," as she was sometimes called, was the first victim. She was a Christian lady, well known at court, and very zealous in her endeavors to introduce Christian truth among its inmates. Strype says, " She was at first a great disperser of Tindal's new Testaments, translated by him into English, and printed at Colen [Cologne], and was a great reader of Scripture herself; which books she also dispersed in the court, and so became known to certain women of quality, and was more particularly acquainted with Mrs. Anne Ascue [Anne Askew, cruelly tortured, and afterward burned alive, in the year 1546]. She used, for the more secresy, to tie the books in strings under her apparel, and so passed with them into court."[1] But she maintained the opinion held by many of the foreign Baptists, that the Redeemer, though born of the Virgin Mary, and truly man, did not take flesh of the substance of her body. For this she was condemned to die. A year elapsed between the trial and the execution, during which many efforts were employed, but in vain, to con-

[1] *Memorials of the Reformation*, ii. 368. Edit. 1816.

vince her of her error. Archbishop Cranmer, Bishop Ridley, and others, visited her frequently for that purpose. It was at length determined to burn her. It is said that the young king hesitated long, and would not have consented that the warrant should be issued had it not been for the persuasion of Cranmer. He wept as he gave his consent, and told the primate that *he* must answer for it at the bar of God, if it should prove to be a wrongful deed. The archbishop did not relent. The final sentence bears his name and that of Latimer. On the 2d of May, 1550, Joan Boucher was burned in Smithfield. Bishop Story preached on the occasion, and, as Strype says, "tried to convert her;" but his misrepresentations and calumnies were so gross that she told him he "lied like a rogue," and bade him "go and read the Scriptures." It was doubtless needful advice.

John Rogers, who was the first martyr in Mary's reign, approved this execution. When some one remonstrated with him on the subject, and particularly urged the cruelty of the mode of death, he replied that "burning alive was no cruel death, but easy enough." Archdeacon Philpot, in his sixth examination before the queen's commissioners, Nov. 6, 1555, six weeks before his own martyrdom, said, "As for Joan of Kent, she was a vain woman (I knew her well), and a heretic indeed, *well worthy to be burnt.*"[1] It is distressing to record such utterances.

In Edward the Sixth's time Hooper was appointed bishop of Gloucester. His consecration was delayed for some months on account of his scruples against the epis-

---

[1] *Examinations and Writings*, p. 55. Parker Society's Edition.

copal habits, which he justly regarded as popish. He had learned the truth, which is known now as an elementary principle, but was then little understood, except by Baptists, that in the service of the church nothing should be admitted for which we cannot adduce apostolic precept or precedent, or which is contrary to any apostolic teaching. He was unwilling to defer to church authority or long-continued custom. Ridley was astonished at his brother's difficulties. In writing on the subject he affected to be very logical, and he was not sparing in rhetorical flourishes, but there was more sophistical declamation than either logic or rhetoric. Thus the bishop writes: "If this reason should take place, 'The apostles used it not, *ergo* it is not lawful for us to use it'—or this either, 'They did it, *ergo* we must needs do it'—then all Christians must have no place abiding, all must, under pain of damnation, depart with [part from] their possessions, as Peter said they did ['Behold, we have left all things,' etc.]; we may have no ministration of Christ's sacraments in churches, for they had no churches, but were fain to do all in their own houses; we must baptize abroad in the fields, as the apostles did; we may not receive the holy communion but at supper, and with the table furnished with other meats, as the Anabaptists do now stiffly and obstinately affirm that it should be; our naming of the child in baptism, our prayer upon him, our crossing, and our threefold ab-renunciation, and our white chrisom [or vesture], all must be left, for these we cannot prove by God's word, that the apostles did use them. And, if to do anything which we cannot prove they did be sin, then a greatest part is sin that we do daily in baptism. What followeth then other things, than to receive the Anabaptists' opinion, and to be baptized anew? Oh, wicked folly and blind ignorancy!"[1]

Ridley's argument was, "If you take such ground, you had better become an Anabaptist at once. But that would be a shocking thing. Therefore you must admit, in these things, the authority of the church, and yield submission to it." So, in utter contradiction to true Protestantism, did the bishop reason. The other alternative, viz., that the Baptists were right, which ought to have been granted, he either had not eyes to see or honesty to admit.

One point adverted to by Ridley may require explanation. The Baptists, according to him, taught that the Lord's supper should be celebrated at the close of a meal. Their practice, it is to be supposed, agreed with the theory. They observed that the ordinance was instituted while our Lord and his apostles were still at the Passover supper-table; and they inferred that the Lord's supper should be preceded by a meal, taken in common by the assembled disciples. We may think them mistaken, but this is clear, that the Baptists evinced therein their scrupulous regard to the directions, express or implied, of the word of God. Positive institutions should be observed, in their judgment—and were they not right?—as nearly as possible in the exact manner in which they were enjoined. The original precept should be literally obeyed, the original precedents followed. This is the characteristic distinction of the Baptist body. Can it be controverted?

George Van Pare, a Dutch Baptist, was burned in

[1] Reply to Bishop Hooper in *Bradford's Letters, Treatises, etc.*, p. 362. Parker Society.

Smithfield on the 13th of January, 1551. He was charged with Arianism, but it is testified that he was a man of fervent piety and active benevolence. His behavior at the stake was eminently Christian. The condemnatory sentence was signed by Cranmer, Ridley, and Coverdale!

Whatever opinion we may entertain respecting the doctrinal views held by Joan Boucher and Van Pare, there can be no difficulty in deciding on the conduct of Cranmer and his associates. Nor need we seek excuses for them. It is customary to plead in their behalf the general prevalence, in that age, of Church-and-State principles of the most *ultra* kind, and to maintain that at a time when everybody believed that the magistrate was bound to do the church's bidding, and, therefore, to rid the country of those whom the church might condemn, it could not be expected that any ecclesiastics would differ from their brethren, or be disinclined to carry out the common policy. I am not disposed to admit the force of this reasoning. The Apostle Paul " verily thought within himself that he ought to do many things contrary to the name of Jesus of Nazareth" (Acts xxvi. 9): but neither did he, after he became a Christian, nor do we, who walk in the light of the nineteenth century, justify the desolation he caused at Jerusalem, on the ground of his ignorance and prejudice. He *might* and he *ought* to have known better, and it was his sin that he did not inquire impartially respecting Christianity before he persecuted it. So it was with Cranmer, Calvin, and other Protestant persecutors. Rome had trained them in savageness. But she had also brought them up in the fooleries of her superstition, and instructed them to cleave to will-worship and merit When they forsook those sandy foundations, that they might build on Christ, it was because they had learned from the New Testament the doctrine of justification by faith. Why did they not also derive from the same New Testament the great truth that the kingdom of the Saviour is " not of this world," and that, therefore, the use of carnal weapons in its propagation or defence is absolutely forbidden? These truths were as fully taught by the apostles as were the doctrines of faith and grace. The Baptists were clear on these subjects. They understood the nature and limitations of magisterial rule. They anticipated Dr. Watts:

> "Let Cæsar's dues be ever paid
> To Cæsar and his throne;
> But consciences and souls were made
> To be the Lord's alone."

They acted on their convictions, and withdrew from a corrupt church to worship God according to his word. In doing so they committed no crime against the state. For that act they were responsible to God only. The state had no control over them. As long as they were peaceable subjects and obeyed the laws, they rightfully claimed protection. In regard to religion, they rightfully demanded freedom and independence. The Reformers had put forth the same demand in seceding from Rome. It is true that they coupled with it the false step of asking leave of the civil magistrate to secede, and having fallen into that error, required that no one should secede from *them*, because the magistrate, as tutored by them, forbade it. But, I ask again, where was the New Testament all the while? and how was it that they did not see in it the spiritual church—and the spiritual King—and the absolute unlawfulness of calling for "fire from heaven," or devising other mischief against those who differed from them? The Baptists saw all this. Cranmer and his party might have seen it. In refusing to see it they were guilty of treachery to Protestant principles.

But they could not put down the Baptists, who grew and flourished in spite of them. Congregations were discovered at Bocking in Essex, at Feversham in Kent, and other places. Their number must have been considerable, as four ministers were arrested when the discovery was made. The names of the ministers were Humphrey Middleton, Henry Hart, George Brodebridge, and —— Cole. At the time of their apprehension they were assembled at Bocking. Besides the ministers, about sixty members of the congregation were apprehended. Their Christian organization appears to have been correct and complete. They met regularly for worship and instruction; the ordinances of the gospel were attended to; contributions were made for the support of the cause; and so great was their zeal that those who lived in Kent were known to go occasionally into Essex to meet the brethren there—a journey of fourscore miles, which, in the sixteenth century, was no small undertaking. When they were brought into the ecclesiastical court, they were examined on forty-six articles, and charged with Pelagianism and other errors. Their religious sentiments, or those imputed to them, would be now called Arminian. This, however, is clear, that they were "Anabaptists." They held also "that we are not to communicate with sinners." In other words, they advocated believer's baptism, and contended for the purity of Christian churches. What became of the others I do not know, but Mr. Middleton was committed to prison, where he remained till the death of Edward VI. The Kentish members of these congregations suffered continual annoyance and persecution in various ways. Cranmer did all he could to suppress the Baptist movement.

We cannot but regret that so little is known of this interesting band of disciples. Strype asserts that they "were the first that made separation from the Reformed Church of England, having gathered congregations of their own." As they confessed that they had not communed in the parish churches for two years, their separation must have taken place about the year 1548, which was before the Presbyterians or Independents were known in England. The Baptists were the vanguard of the Protestant Dissenters in that country.[1]

There were many Baptists among the sufferers in Queen Mary's reign. Some endured painful imprisonments; some passed to heaven through the fire. Humphrey Middleton, one of the ministers mentioned above, was burned at Canterbury, July 12, 1555. We should have known more about these good men had the historians of the times been more faithful. Even the venerable John Fox allowed his prejudices so far to influence him that he kept back information respecting Baptist martyrs. But "their record is on high."

Bishop Bonner bestirred himself diligently. In his "Articles of Visitation," issued in the year 1554, he directed inquiry to be made—"whether there be any that is a Sacramentary or Anabaptist, or libertine, either in reiterating baptism again, or in holding any of the opin-

[1] Strype's *Memorials*, ii. 381. *Baptist Magazine*, February, 1866, pp. 113-115.

ions of the Anabaptists, especially that a Christian man or woman ought not to swear before a judge, nor one to sue another in the law for his right, and that all things should be common."¹ The last item, we need here only say, was a calumny—or rather, perhaps, a misapprehension of the brotherly hospitality that prevailed among the Baptists. In a "declaration to be published to the lay people of his diocese concerning their reconciliation," he affirmed that England had been "grievously vexed" and "sore infested" with "sundry sorts of sects of heresies," among which he expressly mentions "Anabaptists."² Next year he published a book of homilies, in one of which he warned the people against the Baptists. "Certain heresies," said he, "have risen up and sprung in our days, against the christening of infants"—a practice which "the most wholesome authority of the church doth command."³

Bishop Gardiner was chancellor of the university of Cambridge. In 1555 he published fifteen articles, which were to be signed by all persons desirous of enjoying the privileges of the university. The fourth was to this effect, that "baptism is necessary to salvation, even for infants; that all sin, actual as well as original, is taken away and entirely destroyed, in baptism; and that the said baptism is never to be repeated."⁴ This language betrays the existence of Baptists in Cambridge, and the bishop's fear lest persons holding their opinions should repair thither for education from other parts of the kingdom.

¹ *Documentary Annals*, ii. 156.   ² *Ibid.* ii. 170.
³ Underhill's "Historical Introduction" to *Tracts on Liberty of Conscience*, p. cxxv.
⁴ *Documentary Annals*, i. 195.

Henry Hart, one of Humphrey Middleton's colleagues, was committed to the King's Bench prison, London, with other Baptists. The prisons of the metropolis were crowded with Protestants at that time, many of whom, such as Bradford, Philpot, and others, glorified God in the flames. But the spirit of disputation was so powerful in them that there was hot controversy in the very jails. Mr. Hart and his friends, as I have before observed, differed from other Reformers on what is called the Arminian question. Those differences led to fierce disputes, and occasioned considerable loss of temper. Ridley, Bradford, and Philpot were men eminent for piety; we venerate them to this day; their names will be fragrant in all time coming. But in their zeal for truth they sometimes forgot the claims of charity, and in reference to baptism they held and inculcated tenets of a truly un-Protestant character. Philpot must surely have felt the weakness of his cause when he pleaded thus: "Since all truth was taught and revealed to the primitive church, which is our mother, let us all that be obedient children of God, submit ourselves to the judgment of the church for the better understanding of the articles of our faith and of the doubtful sentences of the Scripture. Let us not go about to show in us, by following any private man's interpretation upon the word, another spirit than they of the primitive church had, lest we deceive ourselves; for there is but one faith and one Spirit, which is not contrary to himself, neither otherwise now teacheth us than he did them. Therefore let us believe as they have taught us of the Scriptures, and be at peace with them. according as the true catholic church is at this day."[1]

[1] *Examinations and Writings*, p. 273.

Notwithstanding the vigilant ferocity of Bonner and his associates, the Baptists held their ground in Kent and Essex, and it was found impossible to root them out. Commissioners were sent to Colchester in 1558, with full power to proceed against heretics, and they had entered on their duties with activity and ardor, hoping to make a thorough clearance, when, for some unexplained reason, a letter of recall was despatched. Dr. Chedsey, one of the commissioners, expressed his feelings on the occasion in the language of an inquisitor's regret. He was vexed at the loss of his prey. "We be now," he said, writing to the Privy Council, "in the midst of our examination and articulation. And if we should give it off in the midst, we should set the country in such a roar that my estimation, and the residue of the commissioners, shall be for ever lost. . . . Would to God the honorable council saw the face of Essex as we do see. We have such obstinate heretics, Anabaptists, and other unruly persons here, as never was heard of."[1]

Bradford, as I have said, was one of those who disputed, while in prison, with his fellow-sufferers. He was ingenuous enough to acknowledge that though he regarded them as heterodox in their opinions, they were men of unquestionable and even signal piety: "he was persuaded of them that they feared the Lord, and therefore he loved them."

No sooner had Elizabeth ascended the throne than she began to display the despotic tendencies by which her reign was distinguished. In that respect she closely resembled her father. She would reform, to a certain extent, but not so far as to allow her subjects to think and act for

[1] Strype's *Memorials*, v 265.

themselves. She would prescribe to them what they should believe, and how they should worship, under penalty of her high displeasure if they dared to go beyond the allotted bounds. The nation generally submitted in meekness. Some few chafed under the yoke, yet continued to wear it. Others remonstrated against ecclesiastical impositions, and asked for freedom in things indifferent. It seemed to them a monstrous thing, especially at a time when there were so few able and faithful ministers, to demand rigorous uniformity, not only in theological opinions, but also in the cut and wear of caps and gowns, and in liturgical services. But Elizabeth was not to be diverted from her purpose. She had made up her mind to go so far and no farther. And she was determined, as far as lay in her power, to check the progress of her subjects. The "Act of Uniformity," passed in the year 1559, declared her will and defined their duty. The Puritan clergy grumbled, but the queen said "Silence!" And so it was. They must be silent or withdraw; and if, having withdrawn, they reduced their reforming principles to practice, they incurred all the terrors of the High Commission Court.

It was not to be expected that Baptists would find any favor with Elizabeth. Many had fled from foreign countries to England, hoping to enjoy there the peace and freedom elsewhere denied them. They had settled chiefly in London and "other maritime towns." But the queen would not suffer them to remain. A proclamation was issued, September 2d, 1560, declaring that her majesty "willeth and chargeth all manner of persons, born either in foreign parts or in her majesty's dominions, that have conceived any manner of such heretical opinion as the

Anabaptists do hold, and mean not by charitable teaching to be reconciled, to depart out of this realm within twenty days after this proclamation, upon pain of forfeiture of all their goods and chattels, and to be imprisoned and further punished as by the laws, either ecclesiastical or temporal, in such case is provided."[1] This was a severe and cruel measure. In those days of slow traveling, the proclamation would not reach some of the outposts till the twenty days had nearly expired; and the poor people would have little time to dispose of their immovable property, and of such goods as they could not conveniently take away with them. In all cases there was doubtless a great sacrifice.

Bishop Jewel supposed that the hated sectarians were effectually got rid of. Writing to Peter Martyr, under date of November 6, 1560, he said: "We found at the beginning of the reign of Elizabeth a large and inauspicious corps of Arians, Anabaptists, and other pests, which I know not how, but as mushrooms spring up in the night and in darkness, so these sprang up in that darkness and unhappy night of the Marian times. These, I am informed, and I hope it is the fact, have retreated before the light of purer doctrine, like owls at the sight of the sun, and are now nowhere to be found; or, at least, if anywhere, they are no longer troublesome to our churches."[2] But he was mistaken. Many Baptists contrived to elude the proclamation. Next year, Parkhurst, bishop of Norwich, was complained of by Secretary Cecil for "winking at schismatics and Anabaptists."[3]

---

[1] *Documentary Annals*, i. 293.
[2] *Zurichs Letters*, i. 92. Parker Society.
[3] *Documentary Annals*, i. 338.

Six years after, 1567, "Articles of Visitation" were issued by Archbishop Parker, in which it was directed that inquiry should be made whether any persons did "say, teach, or maintain, that children, being infants, should not be baptized."[1] It is evident, therefore, that persons holding those views were still in the realm. And they continued to seek shelter in England from persecution, while the queen and her minions were indefatigable in attempts to ferret them out and drive them away. Another proclamation appeared in 1568, in which it is stated that "great numbers of strangers from the parts beyond the seas," some of whom were supposed to be "Anabaptists," did "daily repair to her Majesty's dominions, but that she did 'in nowise mean to permit any refuge' to them."[2] Permitted or not, however, they were there, and they were neither idle nor unsuccessful. Collier, the ecclesiastical historian, says, "The Dutch Anabaptists held private conventicles in London, and perverted a great many."[3]

[1] *Documentary Annals*, 340. [2] *Ibid.* 343.
[3] *Ecclesiastical History of England*, vi. 162.

CHAPTER VIII

The Enormities Perpetrated at Munster and other Places—Injustice of Ascribing them to Baptist Sentiments.

MUCH has been said of the black deeds of Munster in the year 1534, and of some transactions of a similar kind in Holland about the same time. Perhaps some readers have been taught to consider those events as deeply disgraceful to the Baptist cause.

I have no wish to throw a veil over that part of the history. Let the facts be set forth in all their horrid enormity, as Pædobaptist historians have portrayed them. Then let them be fairly contemplated in the light of impartial truth.

The facts must first be stated. There had been fierce contests in Westphalia between the Roman Catholic authorities and the Protestants. The former would have exterminated the latter, but their numbers and their power prevented it. Their superiority over their opponents was shown in the terms of the agreement which had been recently entered into between them and the bishop of Munster, who was also its prince. The Protestants secured for their worship the six parish churches, leaving to the bishop and his co-religionists only the cathedral and a monastery. The bishop, however, had left the city, not choosing to remain there under such circumstances. It could not be surprising that Munster became the resort of many religious fugitives, whom persecution had driven from their homes, and who hoped to find a peaceful and safe refuge in that city. Nor could it be wondered at, in that age of excitement, that among the fugitives were found men of discordant and even outrageous opinions. Some of them were Baptists. Rothman, one of the Reformed preachers, and a man of high repute and great influence, embraced their views, and their numbers were daily increased, both by immigration and conversion. Just at that time, in January, 1534, Jan Matthys and Jan Bockelson arrived at Munster. They were fiery fanatics, strong in the belief that the restoration of all things was at hand, that the Lord's kingdom was to be established by the sword, that the saints were to take possession of the earth, and that they and their associates were the saints. Bernhard Knipperdolling, a wealthy burgher, invited them to his house, and entered into all their schemes. The fruits of their activity were soon manifest. Proselytes multiplied on every hand. At length they had secured the adhesion of the majority of the inhabitants. Tumults and conflicts followed, and the result was the expulsion of all who would not favor the designs of Matthys and Bockelson. The remainder of the narrative shall be given substantially in the words of Ranke, the well-known modern historian:

"The Anabaptists were thus not only the masters of the city, but its sole occupants. What their adversaries had scrupled to do to them, they inflicted with fanatical eagerness. They divided the city among themselves;

and communities from different parts of the country took possession of the religious houses. The movable property of the exiles was collected together, and seven deacons were appointed by Matthys to distribute it gradually to the faithful, according to their several necessities."

All the pictures and statues in the cathedral, works of art generally, and even musical instruments, were destroyed. "The rule which had been laid down as to the property of the exiles was very soon applied to the possessions of the faithful. They were ordered, under pain of death, to deliver up their gold and silver, their jewels and effects, to the chancery, for the common consumption. . . . While the idea of property was abolished, each man was to continue to exercise his craft. Regulations are extant, in which journeymen shoemakers and tailors are specially mentioned; the latter being enjoined to take heed that no new garment or fashion be introduced. . . . Meat and drink were provided at the common cost; the two sexes, 'brethren and sisters," sat apart from each other at meals; they ate in silence, while one read aloud a chapter from the Bible."

Matthys being killed in a tumult, Bockelson took upon himself the management of affairs. He soon showed symptoms of the wildest fanaticism. At first he assumed the name and office of the prophet. He was a second Moses—the people were the " new Israel"—twelve elders were appointed to judge them. " Six were to sit to administer justice every morning and afternoon; the prophet Jan Bockelson was to proclaim their sentences to the whole people of Israel, and Knipperdolling to execute them with the sword." A table of laws was prepared, drawn chiefly from the books of Moses. Unconditional submission was required. If any refused it, they were denounced as the "wicked," who were to be "rooted out of the earth," and Knipperdolling was authorized to put them to death at once without trial. "Preceded by four heralds, with a drawn sword in his hand, he traversed the streets, carrying terror wherever he went."

Bockelson's next step was to introduce polygamy. He married Matthys' widow, and many more women. The contagion spread. Rothman, the preacher, took four wives. All the females in the city were soon appropriated.

The climax was reached when Bockelson procured himself to be appointed king. The millennium, it was said, was just at hand. Christ would then reign with his saints over the whole earth for a thousand years. "The kingdom of Munster would endure until the commencement of that millennium, and ought therefore to foreshadow it, and be an image of it." Bockelson declared "that in him the kingdom announced by Christ was incontestably come—that he sat upon the throne of David. He wore round his neck a chain of gold, to which hung the symbol of his dominion—a golden globe transfixed with two swords, the one of gold, the other of silver, above the handles of which was a cross." Thrice a week he appeared in the market-place, thus attired, and administered justice. As he rode through the city, all persons were required to fall on their knees at his approach

On one occasion, when the Lord's supper was celebrated by the whole population, Bockelson fancied that one of the persons present "had not on a wedding garment." He ordered him out, followed him, cut off his head, and then "returned cheerful and delightful to the feast." At another time, one of his wives having determined to leave him, he led her into the market-place, beheaded her with his own hands, and induced his other wives to dance round the corpse, exclaiming, "To God alone in the highest be honor."

It did not last long. The bishop of Munster, aided by some of the German princes, besieged the city. Tremendous sufferings were endured by the inhabitants, and great numbers died of starvation. At length the city was taken by assault. A fearful carnage took place. Rothman and other leaders were killed. Bockelson, Knipperdolling, and another were taken prisoners, and torn to death by red-hot pincers. The Baptists who remained alive were banished; not one was allowed, not even a woman, to live in Munster.[1]

While these things were taking place at Munster, similar outrages were attempted in Holland, particularly at Leyden and Amsterdam, in which cities certain Anabaptists, so called, endeavored to effect revolutions and to set up the new kingdom. Extravagance and immoralities marked their proceedings, as at Munster, but they were fortunately unsuccessful.

The question now arises, How far were the Baptists, as a religious body, responsible for these transactions? To this I reply:

1. That not only among the Baptists, but also among other Reformers of that age, there were persons who were led away by wild notions and unaccountable delusions. It was a time of universal excitement—of new thoughts and new feelings. In the sudden transition from gross

[1] Ranke's *History of the Reformation in Germany*, book vi. chap. ix.

darkness to the blaze of noonday, it is not surprising that men's vision should prove feeble, imperfect, or even deceptive. Popery had chained down the mind: when the fetters were broken, it ought not to have been wondered at if a period of erratic and wayward movement followed. For my own part, I think that, under all the circumstances, the conduct of the Reform leaders was marvelously sober.

2. That although certain Baptists embraced erroneous notions about the millennium and other absurd theories, the whole body cannot be held responsible for such things, since they were discountenanced by the majority. The fair representation would be, that some persons professing Baptist sentiments fell into these evils, but that the denomination as a whole was entirely free from them. They are properly enough ascribed by Brandt to "a new sect of enthusiastical Anabaptists" which arose at that time, widely differing from the "well-meaning" people who bore the same name.[1]

3. That the men of Munster should have been treated as maniacs. Motley says of some who suffered at Amsterdam, that they were "furious lunatics, who certainly deserved the madhouse rather than the scaffold."[2] The remark is as applicable to the Germans as to the Dutch. It was insanity produced by intense feeling, a phenomenon not unusual in times of excitement, from whatever cause that excitement might spring. Taught to abandon the old formalism, and to regard Christianity as essentially identified with life and power, and as requiring personal choice and action, the Baptists were conscious of an engagedness of heart in religion which was peculiar

[1] *History of the Reformation*, abridged, i. 38.
[2] *History of the Dutch Republic*, i. 80.

to such sentiments. The opposition they met with caused them to cling more closely to the truth, and to study it with greater earnestness. Firmly believing the promises of Scripture, they looked forward to the triumph of New Testament principles, and that triumph, they foresaw, would occasion a complete revolution in society, and particularly a dissolution of the union between church and state, since, in proportion as their views prevailed, the right of the civil magistrate to interfere in religious matters would be denied, and such interference abolished. Then persecution would cease, and the peaceful dominion of the Saviour would prevail. The majority of the Baptists were content to labor and suffer in the propagation of these truths, confidently expecting their ultimate prevalence. They employed spiritual means for the accomplishment of a spiritual end. So far from allowing the use of carnal weapons in the cause of religion, they held all war to be unlawful. But some few, men of warm imagination and weak judgment, were overpowered by their visionary hopes, and thought themselves authorized to establish a new government on the ruin of the existing order of things. It was at first the fire of enthusiasm —then, frenzy—at last, stark madness. But it was a temporary mania, and soon subsided. The disorders and outrages which attended it, and the disturbances which ensued in various parts of Europe, must be ascribed solely to the individuals who were implicated in them. The Baptists in general were wholly free from participation in riot or rebellion.

4. That not only at Munster, but in many other places, there was a deadly struggle going on between despotism, civil and religious, on the one hand, and freedom on the

other. Numbers of the Germans were prepared to follow any leader who would show them the path of deliverance from their hateful bondage; nor were they very scrupulous as to the means that might be employed. Their efforts failed. As it happened in some instances that Baptists had taken the lead or acquired pre-eminence, they were made to bear all the discredit, and patriotic risings were stigmatized as Baptist insurrections, whereas in fact the majority of those who were termed rebels had no connection with the Baptists, in a religious point of view.

It is observable, also, that the Baptist martyrs of this period frequently and indignantly rebutted the calumny cast upon them, and maintained that they were not answerable for the disgraceful doings at Munster and other places.

"They also asked him (Brother Dryzinger, A. D. 1538), if it were true, that if we should become numerous, we would rise up against them and strangle them, if they would not join us? He told them, 'If we did so, *we should be no Christians, but only such in name.*'"[1]

Speaking of the word of God, Hans, of Overdam (martyred A. D. 1550), said, "That is our sword; it is sharp and two-edged. But we are daily belied by those who say that we would defend our faith with the sword, as they of Munster did. The Almighty God defend us from such abominations!"[2]

"Were they not your people," said the lady of the governor of Friesland, to Jaques Dosie, "that disgracefully and shamefully took up the sword against the magistrates at Amsterdam and Munster?" "Oh no, madam,"

[1] *Martyrology*, i. 180. [2] *Ibid.* i. 335.

Jaques replied; "those persons greatly erred. But we consider it a devilish doctrine to resist the magistrates by the outward sword and violence. We would much rather suffer persecution and death at their hands, and whatever is appointed us to suffer."[1]

5. I will only remark, in conclusion, that the history of these transactions has been written by enemies. We live in an age of impartial historical criticism. It is not improbable, therefore, that discoveries will yet be made which will enable future historians to tell the tale of the so-called Anabaptists of Munster much more clearly and fully than their predecessors.

At any rate, this is certain, that the atrocities and impurities perpetrated at Munster were not more justly traceable to Baptist sentiments than the massacres of the Waldenses and the enormities of the Inquisition would be to Pædobaptism.

[1] *Martyrology*, 357.

THE TROUBLOUS PERIOD.

CHRONOLOGICAL NOTES.

FROM A. D. 1567 TO A. D. 1688.

1568. The Bishop's Bible published.
1571. The Basque New Testament published.
1572. Massacre of Protestants at Paris, Aug. 24th.—Death of John Knox, Nov. 24th.
1574. The Hungarian New Testament published.
1580. Rise of the Brownists.
1581. The Slavonish Bible published.
1582. The Rhemish New Testament published.
1584. The Icelandic Bible published.
1587. Death of John Fox, the Martyrologist, April 18th.
1588. The Spanish Armada.—The Welsh Bible published.
1598. Edict of Nantes.
1600. Rise of the Arminian Controversy.
1605. Death of Theodore Beza, Oct 13th.—Gunpowder plot, Nov. 5th.
1609. Douay Bible published.
1611. English Authorized Version published.
1618. Synod of Dort.
1620. Settlement of the Puritans in New England.
1637. Harvard University Founded.
1638. Episcopacy abolished in Scotland.
1641. Massacre of Protestants in Ireland.—Episcopacy overthrown in England.
1643. Assembly of Divines convened.—Baptist Confession of Faith published.
1645. Archbishop Laud beheaded, Jan. 10th.
1648. Peace of Westphalia.
1649. Rise of the Quakers.
1653. Persecution of the Waldenses.
1658. Death of Oliver Cromwell, Sept. 3d.
1660. Episcopacy restored in England.
1661. Episcopacy restored in Scotland.
1662. Act of Uniformity, England, Aug. 24th.
1664. Conventicle Act.
1665. Five Mile Act.—Great Plague in London.
1666. Great Fire of London.
1672. Corporation Act.
1673. Test Act.
1674. Death of John Milton, Nov. 8th.
1683. Death of Dr. Owen, Aug. 24th.
1684. Death of Archbishop Leighton, Feb. 1st.
1685. Revocation of the Edict of Nantes.
1686. Persecution of the Waldenses.
1688. Death of John Bunyan, Aug. 30th.—Glorious Revolution in England.

CHAPTER I.

Baptists Persecuted by all other Sects—Liberal Policy of William, Prince of Orange—The "Union of Utrecht"—Differences of Opinion—Persecution in Moravia and in Switzerland.

I CALL this "The Troublous Period," because, while the Baptists were fast increasing in those parts of Europe in which they had already appeared, their history presents one continued scene of disturbance and suffering, inflicted not only by the Papists, from whom nothing else could have been expected, but by their fellow-Protestants. The Episcopalians and Presbyterians of England, the Lutherans of Germany, and the Reformed in Switzerland, differing from one another and refusing intercommunion, agreed in persecuting the Baptists. They were the "sect everywhere spoken against." -It would have been well if the opposition had vented itself in hard words only: our forefathers would have borne it with Christian meekness, "not rendering evil for evil, or railing for railing " But their co-religionists persecuted them with relentless malice, even to the spoiling of their goods, imprisonment, and death. These things must not be concealed. I hold it to be the special duty of the historian to record with impartial and scrupulous accuracy the atrocities prepetrated by those who professed the principles of the Reformation. When a Papist persecutes, he acts in accordance with the well-known assumptions of the great apostasy; and however we may deplore it, we do not wonder, for it is not in the nature of popery to practice the charity of the gospel. But Protestant persecution deserves to be branded with double infamy. It is an outrage on Protestant principles, and should be held up to universal indignation.

The fires of martyrdom were frequently lighted in Holland during the early part of this period. But the establishment of the Dutch Republic quenched them. The prince of Orange understood religious freedom, and availed himself of the opportunity which his position gave him to assert the natural rights of his countrymen and the claims of conscience. The Baptists had aided him in the struggle with Spanish tyranny. Their integrity and peaceableness could be trusted. He steadfastly and successfully resisted the endeavors of those who sought to exclude them from the general toleration.

In 1572 a considerable sum of money had been carried to the prince, who was then at Dillenberg, by J. Cortenbosch and Peter Bogaert, Baptists (the latter was a minister), as the offering of the brethren. They performed this service at the risk of their lives. When he asked them what he could do in return, they replied that all they wanted was a due share of his favor should he be established in the government. He assured them that all men should be regarded by him as equals, and that they had no cause for fear.[1]

William, Prince of Orange, was a man of right noble spirit. "He resolutely stood out against all meddling

[1] *Ottii Annales*, ad ann. 1572.

with men's consciences or inquiring into their thoughts. While smiting the Spanish Inquisition into the dust, he would have no Calvinist Inquisition set up in its place. Earnestly a convert to the Reformed religion, but hating and denouncing only what was corrupt in the ancient church, he would not force men, with fire and sword, to travel to heaven upon his own road. Thought should be toll-free. Neither monk nor minister should burn, drown, or hang his fellow-creatures when argument or expostulation failed to redeem them from error. It was no small virtue, in that age, to rise to such a height. We know what Calvinists, Zwinglians, Lutherans have done in the Netherlands, in Germany, in Switzerland, and almost a century later in New England. It is, therefore, with increased veneration that we regard this large and *truly catholic* mind." But it was " impossible for the prince thoroughly to infuse his own ideas on the subject of toleration into the hearts of his nearest associates. He could not hope to inspire his deadly enemies with a deeper sympathy. Was he not himself the mark of obloquy among the Reformers, because of his leniency to Catholics? Nay, more, was not his intimate counselor, the accomplished Saint Aldegonde, in despair because the prince refused to exclude the Anabaptists of Holland from the rights of citizenship? At the very moment when William was straining every nerve to unite warring sects, and to persuade men's hearts into a system by which their consciences were to be laid open to God alone—at the moment when it was most necessary for the very existence of the Fatherland that Catholic and Protestant should mingle their social and political relations, it was indeed a bitter disappointment for him to see wise statesmen of his own creed unable to rise to the idea of toleration. 'The affair of the Anabaptists,' wrote Saint Aldegonde, 'has been renewed. The prince objects to exclude them from citizenship. He answered me sharply, that their yea was equal to our oath, and that we should not press this matter, *unless we were willing to confess that it was just for the Baptists to compel us* to a divine service which was against our conscience.' It seems hardly credible that this sentence, containing so sublime a tribute to the character of the prince, should have been indited as a bitter censure, and that, too, by an enlightened and accomplished Protestant." [1]

Notwithstanding the ignorance and bigotry of those with whom he was associated, William held on his way. When the "Union of Utrecht," the foundation of the Dutch Commonwealth, was formed, it was expressly provided that "every individual should remain free in his religion, and that no man should be molested or questioned on the subject of divine worship." [2]

That auspicious event took place in the year 1579. Then "the churches had rest." From that time the Dutch Baptists, or Mennonites, as they have been commonly called, enjoyed a good measure of prosperity. Their numbers greatly increased. In those very cities where their predecessors were so cruelly butchered they were held in high respect, and often discharged with credit the duties connected with the civic affairs to which they were appointed. Their scruples against oath-taking were met by substituting in their case a solemn affirmation, as is the practice now in England with regard to the Quakers and some other religious bodies. In

Motley's *Rise of the Dutch Republic*, ii. 362, 206.   [2] *Ibid.* p. 412.

lieu of personal service in the army, they paid an annual tax.

During their troubles, it was impossible to carry into effect any educational plans. When peace was restored, the desirableness of securing an educated ministry became a matter of earnest consideration. Sound views were entertained, and a college was established at Amsterdam, which has proved a great blessing to the denomination.

Certain divergences of opinion among them occasioned bitterness of feeling and estranged brethren from one another. These manifestations of human weakness were to be lamented. Their injurious effects were felt by all parties, and at length they agreed to bear with one another, and to cease to regard their differences as hindrances to mutual fellowship. Those differences related chiefly to the manner in which the human nature of the Saviour was produced, and to the effects of exclusion from the church. As to the former, a resolution was passed at a synod held in 1615, declaring that harmony on that subject was not essential. The harshness which characterized the discipline of the churches in the early period of their history gradually gave way to a more Christian policy, and exclusion was not held, by the Mennonites in general, as involving the severance of domestic and social relations. There was another point in which they differed—the washing of one another's feet—which some of them regarded as an apostolical ordinance of perpetual obligation. This, too, was placed among things indifferent. But some of the Mennonites hold it to this day.

The progress of the Baptists in the central countries of

Europe is indicated by the number of publications on the baptismal controversy which issued from the press in the seventeenth century. There would have been no need of those works if Pædobaptism had not been in danger. The concurrent testimony of the authors of that age proves that in the German states, in Prussia, and in Poland, Baptist principles were spreading among the people, in spite of continual efforts to suppress them.

In a former chapter I gave an account of the persecution of the Baptists in Moravia. They had re-entered that country, and lived without molestation for a number of years. Their industrious habits, their honesty, and integrity commanded great respect. But the Jesuits, who had obtained complete control over the Emperor Ferdinand II., persuaded him that it would be for the glory of God and for his own welfare to expel them. They had done no wrong; they owed no arrears of taxes; they were loyal and peaceable, and the district in which they lived was improving fast under their good management. But they were heretics. They would not wear the yoke of Rome, for they were the Lord's freemen. That was enough. The crime of thinking for oneself in matters of religion is unpardonable; it must be visited with the "great curse," and its perpetrators must be put out of the way. In this case extermination, which would have been preferred, was impossible; it was not politic, and might not be safe, to attempt the destruction of from twenty to forty thousand of the best subjects of the kingdom. The milder measure of expulsion was resolved on, and the craft and cruelty of the Jesuits were strikingly displayed in carrying it into effect. It was summer, harvest-time was near, and the vintage would follow shortly afterward. Humanity would have dictated that if justice required the banishment of those men, they should have the opportunity of gathering in the produce of their labors, and so be provided with the means of sustenance for themselves and their families during the coming winter. But Jesuitism knows nothing of humanity. Goaded on by his spiritual advisers, Ferdinand issued an edict in the year 1621, declaring that his conscience would not permit him to allow the continuance of the heretics any longer in his dominions, and ordering them all to depart within three weeks and three days, on pain of death if they were found even on the borders of the country after the expiration of the allotted time.

"Heaven had smiled on their harvest labors," says Robinson; "their fields stood thick with corn, and the sun and the dew were improving every moment to give them their last polish. The yellow ears waved a homage to their owners, and the wind whistled through the stems, and the russet herbage softly said, 'Put in the sickle, the harvest is come.' Their luxuriant vine leaves, too, hung aloft by tendrils mantling over the clustering grapes like watchful parents over their tender offspring; but all were fenced by an imperial edict, and it was instant death to approach. Without leaving one murmur upon record, in solemn, silent submission to the Power that governs the universe and causes 'all things to work together for good' to his creatures, they packed up and departed. In several hundred carriages they conveyed their sick, their innocent infants sucking at the breasts of their mothers who had newly laid in, and their decrepid parents whose work was done, and whose silvery locks told every beholder that they wanted only the favor of a grave. At the borders they filed off, some to Hungary, others to Transylvania, some to Wallachia, others to Poland; greater, far greater for their virtue than Ferdinand for all his titles and for all his glory."[1]

Robinson adds, that "the Jesuit who executed this business says ten thousand stayed in Moravia, and became Catholics." That may be set down as a glaring falsehood, for Baptists and the Church of Rome are the spiritual antipodes to each other. The truth was, that though the greater part obeyed the edict, some ventured to remain. They had to endure tremendous persecution for the first seven years, after which the activity of the bloodhounds slackened, and the Baptists were enabled to live in comparative peace. But freedom of worship was denied them. They met as they could, in small companies, in woods, and caves, and unfrequented places. God was with them.

Protestant Switzerland was disgraced by unremitting opposition to the truth. The history of the Baptists in that country is a sad tale of woe. Swiss Presbyterians had won freedom for themselves, but they were determined not to grant it to others. It seemed as if the ghost of Zuingli haunted them, urging them on in their antichristian career. Notwithstanding all the efforts that had been made, the Baptists had multiplied among them, and it was impossible to drive them out. Many emigrated to Moravia, but the majority preferred to remain in their own homesteads; and they could not be silent and quiet. They felt that they had as much right as others to worship God according to their consciences, and they acted accordingly. When edicts were issued against them they

[1] *Ecclesiastical Researches,* p. 526.

said, ' We ought to obey God rather than men," and refused to acknowledge the authority of the magistrate in things spiritual. If they were sent to prison, they broke out whenever they could get opportunity; if they were put in irons in order to prevent escape, they made good use of the files with which their friends supplied them, and so extricated themselves, to the astonishment of their jailers; and on one occasion they contrived to throw a quantity of opium into their keepers' wine, and took leave of them while they slept. It was a most perplexing case. Both magistrates and clergy were at fault. The magistrates said to the clergy," Answer these men's arguments—preach better—live better—make it impossible for our Swiss to become Baptists." The clergy replied, " All we can do and say is in vain. Our people *will* listen to the heretics. You must inflict sharper punishments."

They tried it. Some were sent to the galleys. John Landis, a Baptist minister, was put to death. All Baptists were required to leave the country. On their refusal, their property was confiscated, and held by the government for the benefit of such of their children or heirs as should conform to the established religion. All persons were forbidden to show them hospitality. It can easily be imagined that such barbarous proceedings must have occasioned a vast amount of suffering.

The preceding statements relate chiefly to Zurich. But the Baptists were similarly treated in Berne and in the other cantons. " All men hated them."[1]

[1] *Ottii Annales*, passim.

CHAPTER II

Dutch Baptists Persecuted in England—Account of Hendrick Terwoort and Jan Pieters—Their Martyrdom—Their Religious Sentiments—Whitgift's Invectives against the Baptists.

DURING the persecution which ranged in the Netherlands under the Duke of Alva, butcher-general of the Inquisition in that country, numbers fled to other parts of the Continent, or to England, for refuge and safety. In England, at any rate, they ought to have been safe. But the demon of persecution ruled there. At London, on the 3d of April, 1575, a small congregation of Dutch Baptists convened in a private house, outside the city gates ("without Aldgate"), was interrupted while at worship by a constable, and twenty-five persons were taken before a magistrate, who committed them to prison, but released them after two days' confinement, on their giving bail for their appearance whenever summoned.

Information being given to the queen, a royal commission was issued to Sandys, bishop of London, and some others, to examine the parties and proceed accordingly. They appeared before the commissioners in pursuance of the summons. Their confession of faith was rejected, and they were required to subscribe to four articles, condemnatory of their own principles.

"They proposed to us four questions," says one of the prisoners, "telling us to say yea or nay—

"1. Whether Christ had not taken his flesh and blood of the Virgin Mary?

"We answered; He is the Son of the living God.

"2. Ought not little children to be baptized?

"We answered; Not so; we find it not written in Holy Scripture.

"3. May a Christian serve the office of a magistrate?

"We answered; That it did not oblige our consciences; but, as we read, we esteemed it an ordinance of God.

"4. Whether a Christian, if needs be, may not swear?

"We answered; That it also obliged not our consciences; for Christ has said, in Matthew, *Let your words be yea, yea; nay, nay.* Then we were silent.

"But the bishop said, that our misdeeds therein were so great that we could not enjoy the favor of God. O Lord! avenge it not. He then said to us all, that we should be imprisoned in the Marshalsea."

In the Marshalsea prison—now called the "Queen's Bench"—to which they were then conveyed, many efforts were made by the ministers of the Dutch Church and others, to persuade them to submit and recant. "Master Joris came to us and said, If we would join the church, that is, the Dutch Church, our chains should be struck off, and our bonds loosed. The bishop, he said, had given him command so to do. But we remained steadfast to the truth of Jesus Christ He is indeed our Captain, and no other; yea, in him is all our trust. My dear brethren, and sweet sisters, let us persevere until we conquer. The Lord will then give us to drink of the new wine. O Lord, strengthen our faith. As we have received the Lord Jesus Christ, let us go forward courageously, trusting in him." Five of them were overpowered, and consented to join the Dutch Church. They made a public recantation in St. Paul's churchyard on the 25th of May, standing there before thousands of people, with faggots bound to their shoulders, as in popish times. A few days after, the remainder appeared again before the commissioners. "We remembered the word of the Lord," says Gerrit van Byler: "*When they shall lead you before lords and princes, fear not what you shall say, for in that hour it shall be given you.* So we trusted in the Lord. The questions were again proposed, and subscription demanded; but we said, That we would cleave to the word of the Lord." Upon this they were declared to be incorrigible heretics, sentenced to death, and given over to the secular arm to be punished.

Bishop Sandys was the spokesman on the occasion. The sentence accorded with his theology. In a sermon preached by him before the Parliament, this passage occurs: "Such as teach, but teach not the good and right way; such as are open and public maintainers of errors and heresy; such, in the judgment of God, are thought unworthy to live. *Let the false prophet die* [Deut. xiii. 5]. Elias and Jehu did not think themselves imbrued, but rather sanctified with such blood. I have no cruel heart; blood be far from me. I mind [desire] nothing less. Yet needs must it be granted that the maintainers and teachers of errors and heresy are to be repressed in every Christian commonwealth."[1]

[1] *Sermons*, p. 40. Parker Society.

Fourteen women and a youth were put on board a vessel and sent out of the country. The youth was whipped from the prison to the wharf. The remaining five were consigned to Newgate, where they were put in heavy irons, thrust into a damp and filthy dungeon, swarming with vermin, and not allowed to associate with other prisoners, lest the thieves and murderers in the jail should be corrupted by Anabaptist contamination! One of their number, Christian Kemels, sank under the inhuman treatment. He died in the dungeon, after eight days' confinement. He was " released by death, trusting in God his dying testimony filled us with joy."

The queen was entreated to spare them. But she resented such interference with her prerogative, and would only consent to a month's reprieve, and that in compliance with the intercession of John Fox, the martyrologist, whose truly pathetic and eloquent letter to her majesty on the subject has been often printed and generally admired. Admirable it was, in some respects. It was a gushing forth of Christianized humanity, quite peculiar in that age of steel-clad religion. But good old John was still in the dark. He did not understand soul-freedom. According to him, Baptists had no right to hold and profess their opinions. They were ranked with those "fanatical sects" which " are by no means to be countenanced in a commonwealth," but ought to be " suppressed by proper correction." He did not ask therefore for their release. All he complained of was, " the *sharpness* of their punishment." He would have it changed. "There are excommunications and close imprisonment; there are bonds; there is perpetual banishment, burning of the hand, and whipping, or even slavery itself." But " to *roast alive* the bodies of poor wretches, that offend rather through blindness of judgment than perverseness of will, in *fire* and *flames*, raging with *pitch* and *brimstone*," he denounced as "a hard-hearted thing," and more agreeable to the practice of the Romanists than the custom of the gospelers. If, however, the queen would not consent to recall the sentence, he implored her to grant "a month or two, in which we may try whether the Lord will give them grace to turn from their dangerous errors; lest with the destruction of their bodies their souls be in danger of eternal ruin."[1]

Fox wrote also to the prisoners, urging them to acknowledge their errors, to give up their "frantic conceptions," and telling them that they had "disturbed the church by their great scandal and offence." He sent them a copy of his letter to the queen. In their reply to him they say: "We are sorry that you do not understand our matter, and that you have another opinion of us than we wish, since you think that by our curiosity and obstinacy we have not only given offence to the church of God, but also provoked God himself, and frustrated our salvation. What reason you have thus to think of us we know not; nevertheless, we can assure you that we seek with our whole hearts to serve the one God, and Christ, in a good conscience, and to edify our neighbor as far as in us lies. Therefore we gladly receive what the Holy Scripture testifies, and wish to be permitted to adhere to the plainness and simplicity of the word of God, and not to be urged farther with subtle questions, which our feeble understandings are not able to comprehend, nor by Scripture to justify."

[1] Crosby's *History of the Baptists*, i. 70–73.

The prisoners transmitted to the queen a confession of their faitl , accompanied by a "supplicatton," from which I copy the following extract:

"We testify before God and your majesty, that were we in our consciences able by any means to think or understand the cortrary, we would with all our hearts receive and confess it; since it were a great folly in us, not to live rather in the exercise of a right faith, than to die, perhaps in a false one. May it also please your majesty in your wisdom and innate goodness to consider, that it were not right, but hypocrisy in us to speak otherwise than with our hearts we believe, in order to escape the peril of temporal death; that it is impossible to believe otherwise than we in our consciences think; and also that it is not in our power to believe this or that, as evil-doers who do right or wrong as they please. But the true faith must be implanted in the heart of man by God; and to him we daily pray, that he would give us his Spirit, to understand his word and gospel.

"Above all, it is evident to your majesty that we have not sought to stir up any rebellions or seditions against your majesty; but much more, have daily besought the Lord for your happy reign, and the welfare both of your soul and body. Lastly, we have not endeavored to spread our faith in the land. This we could not do, for we are only unlearned tradespeople, unskilled in divinity."

All was in vain. The Baptists remained firm. The queen would not relent. On the 15th of July she signed the warrant for the execution of two of them, commanding the sheriffs of London to burn them alive in Smithfield.

A copy of the warrant is now before me. There is

also before me a copy of the warrant for the burning of Archbishop Cranmer in Queen Mary's days. These warrants are substantially alike. In fact, they are almost couched in the same language, word for word. Mary, the Papist, dooming to death the Protestant, and Elizabeth, the Protestant, ordering the execution of the Baptist, advance the same pretensions and adopt the same forms of speech. Both of these call their victims "heretics." Both assume to be "zealous for justice." Both are "defenders of the Catholic faith." Both declare their determination to "maintain and defend the holy church, her rights and liberties." Both avow their resolve to "root out and extirpate heresies and errors." Both assert that the heretics named in the warrants had been convicted and condemned "according to the laws and customs of the realm." Both charge the sheriffs to take their prisoners to a "public and open place," and there to "commit them to the fire," in the presence of the people, and to cause them to be "really consumed" in the said fire. Both warn the sheriffs that they fail therein at their peril. Herod and Pontius Pilate forgot their differences when they united in crucifying the Saviour. Papists and Protestants agree in murdering his followers.[1]

Hendrick Terwoort and Jan Pieters were the two whom the queen appointed to death. Terwoort was a young man, about twenty-five years of age. He was a goldsmith and in good circumstances. He was married some eight or ten weeks before his imprisonment. Pieters was aged, poor, and nine children depended on his daily toil. His first wife had been martyred at Ghent in Flanders;

[1] *Documentary Annals*, i. 201, 394.

his second wife was the widow of a martyr. A statement of his circumstances was laid before Sandys, in order to induce him to get permission for Pieters to leave the country with his wife and children ; but the bishop was inaccessible to pity.

On Lord's Day, the 17th of July, they were informed that the warrant for their execution had arrived. "Upon Tuesday," says Gerrit van Byler, "a stake was set up in Smithfield, but the execution was not that day. On Wednesday many people were gathered together to witness the death of our two friends, but it was again deferred. This was done to terrify, and draw our friends and us from the faith. But on Friday our two friends, Hendrick Terwoort and Jan Pieters, being brought out from their prison, were led to the sacrifice. As they went forth, Jan Pieters said, 'The holy prophets, and also Christ, our Saviour, have gone this way before us, even from the beginning, from Abel until now.'" A vast multitude had collected together on the occasion, but few of whom, probably, sympathized with the sufferers. Some preachers were sent to the place of execution to prevent the expression of sympathy by maligning them. One of them exclaimed, "These men believe not on God." "We believe," replied Pieters, "in one God, our heavenly Father Almighty, and in Jesus Christ, his Son." When they were bound to the stake, the articles were again offered to them, and life and pardon promised if they would subscribe. Pieters answered for them both, "You have labored hard to drive us to you, but now, when placed at the stake, it is labor in vain." One of the preachers said, in excuse, "That all such matters were determined by the council, and that it was the queen's intention they should die." "But," rejoined Pieters, "you are the teachers of the queen, whom it behooves you to instruct better; therefore shall our blood be required at your hands." No answer could be given to this. Fire was applied, and the souls of the martyrs ascended to God. "How utterly absurd," says the Dutch martyrologist, "do all such cruel proceedings and sentences as are here seen, appear, when contrasted with the Christian faith! The Christian host is described as sheep and lambs, sent forth among cruel and devouring wolves. Who will be able, with a good conscience, to believe that these English preachers were the true sheep of Christ, since in this matter they brought forth so notably the fruit of wolves?"[1]

This was a black affair. It was essentially unjust and cruel, and admitted of no palliation. These Baptists owed no allegiance to Elizabeth. They were not her subjects. They were refugees, and claimed her protection as exiles for religion's sake from their native land. They were living peaceably, doing harm to none. No rioting or disturbance was laid to their charge. All that could be alleged against them was, that they did not go to the parish churches, but exercised Christian freedom, and worshiped God as they understood the Scriptures to teach them. For this they were burned to death by a Protestant queen.

I am willing to believe that Elizabeth was influenced by her bishops. Sandys and Whitgift were furious against the Baptists. They misrepresented and calumniated them continually. They held them up to public

---

[1] Von Braght's *Bloody Theatre, or Martyr's Mirror*, translated by J Rupp, pp. 915-929.

scorn and indignation, as professing sentiments incompatible with the well-being of society. The queen was instructed by these men to regard the Baptists as hostile to her royal authority. That was touching her in a tender part. The womanly heart was strangely hardened, and she refused to show mercy.

Elizabeth could not plead ignorance respecting the sentiments of the Baptists. In the confession of faith which Terwoort and Pieters sent to her, a revised copy of which was signed by them the day before their martyrdom, they thus plainly stated their views:

"We believe and confess that magistrates are set and ordained of God, to punish the evil and protect the good; which magistracy we desire from our hearts to obey, as it is written in 1 Peter ii. 13, 'Submit yourselves to every ordinance of man for the Lord's sake.' 'For he beareth not the sword in vain' (Romans xiii. 4). And Paul teaches us that we should offer up for all 'prayers, and intercessions, and giving of thanks; that we may lead a quiet and peaceable life in all godliness and honesty. For this is good and acceptable in the sight of God our Saviour, who desires that all men should be saved' (1 Tim. ii. 1–4). He further teaches us 'to be subject to principalities and powers, to obey magistrates, and to be ready to every good work' (Titus iii. 1). Therefore we pray your majesty kindly to understand aright our meaning; which is, that we do not despise the eminent, noble, and gracious queen, and her wise councils, but esteem them as worthy of all honor, to whom we desire to be obedient in all things that we may. For we confess with Paul, as above, that she is God's servant, and that if we resist this power, we resist the ordinance of God; for 'rulers are not a terror to good works, but to the evil.' Therefore we confess to be due unto her, and are ready to give, tribute, custom, honor, and fear, as Christ himself has taught us, saying, 'Render unto Cæsar the things that are Cæsar's, and unto God the things that are God's' (Matt. xxii. 21). Since, therefore, she is a servant of God, we will kindly pray her majesty that it would please her to show pity to us poor prisoners, even as our Father in heaven is pitiful (Luke vi. 36). We likewise do not approve of those who resist the magistrates; but confess and declare with our whole heart that we must be obedient and subject unto them as we have here set down."[1]

But it availed them nothing. They were Baptists The queen was told that the Baptists were incorrigible heretics, and that she would be doing God service if she put them to death. So she lighted again the flames of Smithfield.

I have referred to Sandys and Whitgift. Their writings teem with invectives against the Baptists. In his controversy with Thomas Cartwright, the Puritan, Whitgift endeavored to show that the arguments employed by Cartwright in defence of separation from the Church of England were similar to those used by the "Anabaptists," a sect which was "hated" by "all estates and orders of the realm." He collected a number of extracts from the writings of Zuingli, Calvin, Bullinger, and others, and adopted them as containing true descriptions of the opinions and practices of the "hated" party, adding observations of his own to the same effect. He says that they make contentions wheresoever they come;

[1] *Bloody Theatre*, as above.

that the churches are disquieted by them, and magistrates contemned and despised; that "they do with as spiteful words and bitter speeches condemn the Church of England as they do the Papistical Church;" that they count all them as wicked and reprobate which are not of their sect; that they are "great hypocrites;" that they constantly "invent new opinions, and run from error to error"—that they are "stubborn and willful, wayward and forward, without all humanity"—that they seek to "overthrow commonweals and states of government"—that they "reject all authority of superiors"—that they seek "to be free from all laws, and to do what they list," and finally, that all this is "most true, and therefore no slander."[1] No comment on these monstrosities is required. They are fair specimens of the controversial style of the age.

Doubtless, it was an unpardonable sin in the Baptists that they condemned the interference of the civil power with religion. They were remarkably clear on that subject. Whitgift unwittingly does them justice. He observes that they taught that "the civil magistrate hath no authority in ecclesiastical matters, and that he ought not to meddle in cases of religion and faith"—that "no man ought to be compelled to faith and religion"—and that "Christians ought to punish faults, not with imprisonment, not with the sword, or corporal punishment, but only with excommunication." These are scriptural truths, which the bishops aforesaid labored to suppress, because their own nefarious proceedings were inconsistent with them.

When Terwoort and Pieters were led out to die, Gerrit

[1] *Works*, i. 78-110.

van Byler and Hans van Straten were left in Newgate, uncertain as to their fate. How long they remained there is not known. It is said that they were heavily ironed because they had endeavored to escape by filing asunder the bars of their dungeon. At length they were discharged, probably because the government was unwilling to incur the odium of another burning.

CHAPTER III.

Severity of Elizabeth's Government—Bigotry of James I.—The Hampton Court Conference—Emigration—John Smyth's Church—Their Confessions—Bartholomew Legate—Extracts from Baptist Publications on Liberty of Conscience—The King's Distress at their Increase.

SO great was the severity of Elizabeth's government that the separatists of all classes were scattered about, and forced to hold their meetings in utmost privacy. The Baptists, having been especially marked out for expulsion, could scarcely meet at all. Consequently, but little is known of them during the remainder of this reign. There is no doubt, however, of their continued existence. One writer refers to "Anabaptist conventicles" in London and other places. Another intimates his suspicion that there were some even in the Church of England who held their sentiments. A congregation was discovered in London in 1588, whose views and practices point them out as "Anabaptistical." Strype says that they were accustomed to meet together on Lord's Days, and listen to exhortations from the word of God; that they dined together, collected money to pay for the food, and sent the surplus to such of their brethren as were in prison; that they used no form of prayer; that they refused to regard the Church of England as a true church;

that they denied the authority of the queen, and of all magistrates, in religious affairs, and that they held it unlawful to baptize children. At a still later period a Baptist is mentioned as being in prison at Norwich, and in peril of death, solely on account of his religious opinions.[1]

James I. was as bigoted and despotic as Elizabeth While in Scotland he had affected great zeal for Presbyterianism. When he subscribed the Solemn League and Covenant in 1590, "he praised God that he was born in the time of the light of the gospel, and in such a place, as to be king of such a church, the sincerest [purest] kirk in the world. 'The Church of Geneva, said he, 'keep Pasch and Yule [Easter and Christmas]; what have they for them? They have no institution. As for our neighbor Kirk of England, their service is an evil-said mass in English; they want nothing of the mass but the liftings. I charge you, my good ministers, doctors, elders, nobles, gentlemen, and barons, to stand to your purity, and to exhort the people to do the same; and I, forsooth, as long as I brook my life, shall maintain the same.'"[2] But on his rising to the higher dignity of king of Great Britain, he suddenly became enamored of Episcopacy. Kingcraft, in which he thought himself an adept, harmonized better with bishops than with presbyters Bishops seemed to be the natural allies of sovereigns. "No bishop, no king," was James' motto. Like all new converts, he evinced remarkable fervor of attachment, and was ready to do anything on behalf of the cause. The Puritan clergy, that is, those who wished for more liberty, and desired to assimilate the government of the church to

---

[1] *Broadmead Records*, Introduction, pp. lxxii., lxxiii.
[2] Neal's *History of the Puritans*, ii. 2.

the Genevan model, asked for a hearing. The result was, the event known in history as the Hampton Court Conference. It was no conference, however, for the king had made up his mind beforehand. His behavior was rude and overbearing. Nine bishops, with other dignitaries, appeared in support of the Church of England, and of things as they were; Dr. Raynolds, with three other ministers, represented the Puritans. Their demands were comprised in four particulars: "1. That the doctrines of the church might be preserved pure, according to God's word. 2. That good pastors might be planted in all churches, to preach in the same. 3. That the book of Common Prayer might be fitted to more increase of piety. 4. That church government might be sincerely ministered, according to God's word." In support of these requests, Dr. Raynolds adduced many weighty considerations, and argued with great modesty and forbearance, though often interrupted and insulted by the king. "Well, doctor," said James, "have you anything else to offer?" "No more," Dr. R. replied. "If this," rejoined the king, "be all your party have to say, I will make them conform, or I will hurry them out of the land, or else worse."[1]

The Puritans saw that there was nothing to hope for from the government, and took measures accordingly. Many crossed over to Holland. Among them were some of the Brownist persuasion, afterward called Independents, and now Congregationalists. Churches of that order were established at Leyden, Amsterdam, and other places. Such as could not leave their own country worshiped God in private, and kept themselves quiet,

[1] Neal, *ut sup.* p. 10.

hoping, though as it were against hope, for better times. Of that class were many Baptists. Enoch Clapham, a writer of that age, speaks of them as "leaving the public assemblies, and running into woods and meadows, and meeting in bye stables, barns, and haylofts for service."[1]

John Smyth had been a clergyman of the Church of England, and held the living of Gainsborough, Lincolnshire. On leaving that church he became a minister among the Brownists, who esteemed him so highly that Bishop Hall calls him their "oracle in general." After a toilsome and perilous service of about fifteen years, during which he and his friends had suffered much from Elizabethan tyranny, it was deemed necessary to abandon the field, in order to preserve life and liberty. In the year 1606 he joined a party of emigrants who settled in Amsterdam. There they united with an English church which had been formed some time before. But Mr. Smyth's connection with that church was not of long duration. He had left the Church of England for the Brownists, and now more mature reflection led him to take another step. The Brownists denied that the Church of England was a true church, and therefore they reordained all ministers who went over to them from that church, accounting its ordinances null and void. But they did not rebaptize. This appeared to Mr. Smyth an inconsistency. He thought that if the ordination was invalid, the baptism was no less so. Investigation followed, which was extended to the whole question of baptism, and issued in the conviction that believers are the only subjects of the ordinance, and that immersion is essential to it. Some of Mr. Smyth's friends

[1] Crosby, i. 88.

shared in the conviction. There has been much dispute respecting the manner in which they proceeded, some maintaining that Smyth baptized himself and then baptized the others. It is a thing of small consequence. Baptists do not believe in apostolic succession, as it is commonly held. But the probability is, that one of the brethren baptized Mr. Smyth, and that he then baptized the others. The number of these brethren soon increased greatly. A church was formed, of which Mr. Smyth was chosen pastor. At his death, which took place in 1611, Mr. Thomas Helwys was appointed in his place. In the above-mentioned year, before Mr. Smyth's death, the church published a Confession of Faith, in twenty-six articles. I will transcribe those which relate to the constitution of the church and the ordinances:

"10. That the church of Christ is a company of faithful people, separated from the world by the word and Spirit of God, being knit unto the Lord, and one unto another, by baptism, upon their own confession of the faith and sins (1 Cor. i. 2; Ephes. i. 1; 2 Cor. vi. 17; 1 Cor. xii. 13; Acts viii. 37; Matt. iii. 6).

"11. That though in respect of Christ the church be one, yet it consisteth of divers particular congregations, even so many as there shall be in the world; every of which congregation, though they be but two or three, have Christ given them, with all the means of their salvation, are the body of Christ, and a whole church; and therefore may and ought, when they are come together, to pray, prophesy, break bread, and administer in all the holy ordinances, although as yet they have no officers, or that their officers should be in prison, or sick, or by any other means hindered from the church (Ephes. iv. 4; Matt.

xviii. 20; Romans viii. 32; 1 Cor. iii. 22; xii. 27; **xiv** 23; 1 Peter iv. 10; ii. 5).

"12. That as one congregation hath Christ, so have all. And that the word of God cometh not out from any one, neither to any one congregation in particular, but unto every particular church, as it doth unto all the world. And therefore no church ought to challenge any prerogative over any other (2 Cor. x. 7; 1 Cor. xiv. 36; Col. i. 5, 6).

"13. That every church is to receive in all their members by baptism, upon the confession of their faith and sins wrought by the preaching of the gospel, according to the primitive institution and practice. And, therefore, churches constituted after any other manner, or of any persons, are not according to Christ's Testament (Matt. xxviii. 19; Acts ii. 41).

"14. That baptism, or washing with water, is the outward manifestation of dying unto sin, and walking in newness of life; and therefore in nowise appertaineth to infants (Rom. vi. 2, 3, 4).

"15. That the Lord's supper is the outward manifestation of the spiritual communion between Christ and the faithful, mutually to declare his death until he come (1 Cor. x. 16, 17; xi. 26).

"19. That every church ought, according to the example of Christ's disciples and primitive churches, upon every first day of the week, being Lord's Day, to assemble together, to pray, prophesy, praise God, and break bread, and perform all other parts of spiritual communion, for the worship of God, their own mutual edification, and the preservation of true religion and piety in the church (John xx. 19; Acts ii. 42; xx. 7; 1 Cor. xvi. 2). And they ought not to labor in their callings, according to the equity of the moral law, which Christ came not to abolish, but to fulfill (Exod. xx. 8, etc.).

"20. That the officers of every church or congregation are either elders, who by their office do especially feed the flock concerning their souls; or deacons, men and women, who by their office relieve the necessities of the poor and impotent brethren, concerning their bodies (Acts xx. 28; 1 Peter v. 2, 3; Acts vi. i. 4).

"21. That these officers are to be chosen when there are persons qualified according to the rules in Christ's Testament, by election and approbation of that church or congregation whereof they are members, with fasting, prayer, and laying on of hands; and there being but one rule for elders, therefore but one sort of elders" (1 Tim. iii. 2, 7; Titus i. 6, 9; Acts vi. 3, 4; xiii. 3; xiv. 23).[1]

Shortly after the publication of the Confession, Mr. Helwys, accompanied by most of the members of the church, returned to England. They feared that if they remained longer abroad in a foreign country, it would be regarded as cowardice. They considered, too, the circumstances of the brethren who had continued in their own land, and who were "as sheep without a shepherd." So they went back to their native shores, and established themselves in London, meeting for worship in strict privacy. They had encountered a great risk in returning at such a time. The fires of persecution had been lighted again, and men burned to ashes for heresy. On the 18th of March, 1612, Bartholomew Legate, an Arian, suffered at the stake in Smithfield; on the 11th of April, in the

[1] *Confessions of Faith* (Hanserd Knollys Society), pp. 1-10.

same year, Edward Wightman was put to death at Lichfield in the same manner. This man, if the warrant for his execution may be believed, was a wholesale heretic, for he was charged with "the wicked heresies of Ebion, Cerinthus, Valentinus, Arius, Macedonius, Simon Magus, of Manes, Photinus, and of the Anabaptists and other arch-heretics; and moreover, of other cursed opinions, belched, by the instinct of Satan excogitated, and heretofore unheard of." He maintained "that the baptism of infants is an abominable custom," and "that Christianity is not wholly professed and preached in the Church of England, but in part." *There* was his real delinquency. But the public, even in those days, would have protested against burning a man merely for his Baptist and anti-Church of England principles. It was found necessary, therefore, to blacken the victim to such an extent that he might appear perfectly hideous and fit only for the fire. But Bishop Neile, of Lichfield, and his coadjutors, who acted as royal commissioners on the occasion, were manifestly "forgers of lies." No sane man could possibly hold the multifarious opinions imputed to Wightman. Crosby appropriately remarks that "many of the heresies they charge upon him are so foolish and inconsistent that it very much discredits what they say;" and that "if he really held such opinions he must either be an idiot or a madman, and ought rather to have had their prayers and assistance than be put to such a cruel death."[1]

Another person, said to be a "Spanish Arian," was also condemned to die; but so much sympathy had been expressed by the people at the other executions that "he

[1] *History*, i. 108, Appendix, pp. 1-7.

was suffered to linger out his life in Newgate, where he ended the same;" for "King James politicly preferred," says Thomas Fuller, "that heretics hereafter, though condemned, should silently and privately waste themselves away in the prison, rather than to grace them, and amuse others, with the solemnity of a public execution, which in popular judgment usurped the honor of a persecution." Fuller had before observed that "such burning of heretics much startled common people," and that "the purblind eyes of common judgments looked only on what was next to them—the suffering itself—which they beheld with compassion, not minding the demerits of the guilt, *which deserved the same.*"[1] Thus wrote a Protestant clergymen of the seventeenth century; but murder is murder, however perpetrated, whether by the sword, the fire, or the slower process of the dungeon.

Though the Baptists were debarred the use of the pulpit, the press did them good service. Two tracts published by them soon after the events just recorded were honorable alike to their good sense and pious feeling. The first appeared in 1614. It was entitled, "Religion's Peace, *or*, a Plea for Liberty of Conscience," and is the earliest published work on the subject in the English language. Of the author, Leonard Busher, no account has been preserved. It may be gathered from the tract itself that he had formerly belonged to the Brownists. He was acquainted with the Greek original of the New Testament, and was a diligent student of the sacred volume. Two other tracts were written by him, which poverty prevented him from printing. One was entitled, "A Scourge of Small Cords, wherewith Antichrist and

[1] *Church History*, book x. cent. 17, sect. 14.

his Ministers might be driven out of the Temple of God;" the other, "A Declaration of certain False Translations in the New Testament." Our authorized version had been published but three years, and here was revision already threatened!

"Religion's Peace" contains an address to the king and parliament, earnestly pleading for pardon, and "certain reasons against prosecution."

I will copy a few passages, that it may be seen how a Baptist thought and wrote, and was bold enough to publish, in the early part of the seventeenth century, on this important question.

"Christ's kingdom is not of this world, therefore it may not be purchased nor defended with the weapons of this world, but by his word and Spirit. No other weapons hath he given to his church, which is his spiritual kingdom. Therefore Christ saith, 'He that will not hear the church, let him be to thee as a heathen and a publican.' He saith not, 'Burn, banish, or imprison him;' that is Antichrist's ordinance.

"It is not only unmerciful, but unnatural and abominable, yea monstrous, for one Christian to vex and destroy another for difference and questions of religion. And though tares have overgrown the wheat, yet Christ will have them let alone till harvest, 'lest while you go about to pluck up the tares, you pluck up also the wheat with them;' as your predecessors have done, who thought they had gathered up the tares and burned them, but you see now that they have burned the wheat instead of tares. Wherefore, in all humility and Christian modesty, I do affirm that through the unlawful weed-work of persecution, which your predecessors have used, and by your majesty and parliament is still continued, there is such a quantity of wheat plucked up, and such a multitude of tares left behind, that the wheat which remains cannot yet appear in any right visible congregation.

"It is not the gallows, nor the prisons, nor burning, nor banishing that can defend the apostolic faith. Indeed, the king and state may defend religious peace [that is, protect all parties in the exercise of religion] by their sword and civil power, but not the faith, otherwise than by the word and Spirit of God.

"They cannot be Christ's bishops and preachers that persuade princes and people to such antichristian tyranny and cruelty; and it is very evident that those bishops and ministers which give over men and women to the magistrate to be persuaded by persecution, do show clearly that their doctrine is not good, and that they want the word and Spirit of God, and therefore flee to the magistrate's sword for the forcing of them to their faith and discipline.

"I do verily believe that if free liberty of conscience be granted that the spiritual kingdom of these idol-bishops will in time fall to the ground of itself, as the idol Dagon fell before the ark. For through the knowledge of God's word all godly people will withdraw themselves, in all peaceable and godly wise, from the spiritual obedience of these spiritual lords and idol-bishops, and quietly betake themselves unto the obedience of the only spiritual Lord, Jesus Messiah."[1]

It is much to be regretted that we have no knowledge

---

[1] *Tracts on Liberty of Conscience*, Hanserd Knolly's Society, pp. 18, 24, 54, 60, 66.

of the life and labors of the good man who penned these plain and pithy sentences.

The other treatise was somewhat larger. It was issued in 1615. The original title was, "Objections answered by way of Dialogue; wherein is proved by the law of God, by the law of our land, and by his majesty's many testimonies, that no man ought to be persecuted for his religion, so he testify his allegiance by the oath appointed by law." In an edition published in 1662 it was entitled "Persecution for Religion, Judged and Condemned." The author was a member of Mr. Helwys' church. The work is constructed in the form of a dialogue, in which "Antichristian" defends the interference of the magistrate in the affairs of religion, and his power to proscribe and punish; "Christian" replies to his argument—and "Indifferent Person" listens to the discussion. That question being settled, "Indifferent Person" is represented as inquiring into the grounds of Baptist tenets and practices, which are so clearly explained that he declares himself convinced, and intimates his intention to join the persecuted sect.

The argument against persecution is handled in a masterly manner. And it is observable that the author takes the most liberal position. He avows his abhorrence of *all* persecution, and would grant religious freedom even to the Papists, in which respect he is far in advance of all the religionists of his time. "For the Papists," he observes, "may it not be justly suspected that one chief cause of all their treasons hath been because of all the compulsions that have been used against their consciences, in compelling them to the worship practiced in public, according to the law of this land; which being taken away, there is no doubt but that they would be much more peaceable, as we see it verified in divers other nations, where no such compulsion is used; for if they might have freedom in their religion unto their faithful allegiance to the king, the fear of the king's laws, and their own prosperity and peace would make them live more inoffensively in that respect."[1] In the discussion on Baptist sentiments, an interesting inquiry is started. Thus the dialogue proceeds.:

"*Indifferent Person.* May none be admitted to the church to partake in the ordinances, except they be baptized?

"*Christian.* If any teach otherwise, he presumeth 'above that which is written,' and therefore ought to be held 'accursed.' For there never was a true church since Christ's manifesting in the flesh, joined together of unbaptized persons, though some have vainly published the contrary.

"*I.* True, I think that cannot be denied, where the persons were never baptized; but now the members of the Church of Rome, from whence the baptism of the Church of England cometh, are baptized; therefore why need they again be baptized?

"*C.* If they be baptized with Christ's baptism, I will acknowledge they need not again be baptized; but that the baptism of the Church of Rome is Christ's baptism can never be proved; for Christ requireth that only his disciple should baptize his disciple, and into his body; none of which is Rome's baptism. For Christ's adversaries washed with water those that are not Christ's disciples, into the body, not of Christ, but of Antichrist."

[1] *Tracts*, as above. p. 114.

Having proved that the Romish and English Churches are altogether corrupt, neither of them administering true baptism, and both being founded on anti-biblical principles, "Christian" is asked, "Who then shall baptize after Antichrist's exaltation?" That is, how shall baptism be recovered, where it has been lost through the long prevalence of antichristian rule? The answer is thus given: "We and others affirm, that any disciple of Christ, in what part of the world soever, coming to the Lord's way, he by the word and Spirit of God preaching that way unto others and converting—he may and ought also to baptize them." Again; having referred to the command given to every Israelite to go and build the Temple after the captivity (Ezra i. 3, 5), he adds—" So now, every spiritual Israelite with whom the Lord is, and whose spirit the Lord stirreth up, are commanded to go and build, and the Lord will prosper them in rising up and building, though some be more excellent in the business than others; the beginning of which spiritual building is first to beget men anew by the immortal seed of God's word, so making them living stones, and thereupon to couple them together a spiritual house unto God, upon the confession of their faith by baptism, as the Scriptures of the New Testament everywhere teach."[1]

These extracts will serve to show that our Baptist forefathers were distinguished for mental vigor and independence. They had shot ahead of their religious contemporaries, too many of whom, instead of sympathizing with them, caricatured their principles and excited popular fury against their persons.

How severely the Baptists suffered in the reign of

[1] *Tracts*, pp. 158-166.

James I. may be gathered from a statement made by one of them in 1620: "Our miseries are long and lingering imprisonments for many years in divers counties of England, in which many have died and left behind them widows and many small children; taking away our goods, and others the like, of which we can make good probation; not for any disloyalty to your majesty, nor hurt to any mortal man, our adversaries themselves being judges; but only because we dare not assent unto, and practice in the worship of God, such things as we have not faith in, because it is sin against the Most High." This passage is taken from a tract entitled "A Most Humble Supplication of many of the king's majesty's loyal subjects, ready to testify all civil obedience, by the oath of allegiance or otherwise, and that of conscience; who are persecuted (only for differing in religion), contrary to divine and human testimonies."[1] After an interval of several years, a parliament was about to assemble. The "Humble Supplication" was written on that occasion, and it was hoped that the patriotic men, who had signified their intention to seek redress of all grievances and the restoration of freedom, would hear the complaints of persecuted Christians. The treatise was probably written by the author of "Persecution Judged and Condemned;" but the arguments are more systematically arranged than in that work. The following are the titles of the chapters: "1. The rule of faith is the doctrine of the Holy Ghost contained in the sacred Scriptures, and not any church, council, prince or potentate, nor any mortal man whatsoever. 2. The interpreter of this rule is the Scriptures, and the Spirit of God in whomsoever. 3. The Spirit of

[1] *Tracts*, p. 190.

God, to understand and interpret the Scriptures, is given to all and every particular person that fear and obey God, of what degree soever they be; and not to the wicked. 4. Those that fear and obey God, and so have the Spirit of God to search out the mind of God in the Scriptures, are commonly, and for the most part, the simple, poor, and despised, etc. 5. The learned in human learning do commonly and for the most part err, and know not the truth, but persecute it, and the professors of it; and therefore are no farther to be followed than we see them agree with truth. 6. Persecution for cause of conscience is against the doctrine of Jesus Christ, King of kings. 7. Persecution for cause of conscience is against the profession and practice of famous princes. 8. Persecution for cause of conscience is condemned by the ancient and later writers, yea, by Puritans and Papists. 9. It is no prejudice to the commonwealth if freedom of religion were suffered, but would make it flourish. 10. Kings are not deprived of any power given them of God when they maintain freedom for cause of conscience."

"The author of these arguments against persecutions," says Roger Williams, "as I have been informed, being committed by some then in power close prisoners to Newgate, for the witness of some truths of Jesus, and having not the use of pen and ink, wrote these arguments in milk, on sheets of paper brought him by the woman, his keeper, from a friend in London, as the stopples of his milk bottle.

"In such paper, written with milk, nothing will appear; but the way of reading it by fire being known to this friend who received the papers, he transcribed and kept together the papers, although the author himself could not correct nor view what himself had written."[1]

This appeal was presented in vain. The persecution continued. Messrs. Dodd and Cleaver, two authors of the time, who published in partnership a pamphlet, in 1621, entitled "The Patrimony of Christian Children," assign as reasons for engaging in this controversy, "that those of the contrary opinion were very industrious, and took great pains to propagate their doctrine; that divers persons of good note for piety had been prevailed upon by them; that several had entreated their help and assistance; and that they had been engaged already in private debates about this matter."[2] Another person, writing in 1662, states "that they [the Baptists] separated from the church, and writ many books in defence of their principles, and had multitudes of disciples; that it was their custom to produce a great number of Scriptures to prove their doctrines; that they were in appearance more holy than those of the Established Church."[3]

It would appear, therefore, that the Baptists were an active and growing body. This is further evident from a letter addressed to the clergy by Archbishop Abbot in 1622, in which he tells them that his majesty was "much troubled and grieved at the heart, to hear every day of so much defection from our religion, both to Popery and Anabaptism, or other points of separation, in some parts of this kingdom;" and that he attributed these defections, in great measure, to the "lightness, affectedness, and unprofitableness of that kind of preaching which hath been of late years too much taken up in court, university,

[1] *Bloody Tenet of Persecution*, p. 36. Hanserd Knollys Society.
[2] *Crosby*, i. 141. [3] *Ibid.* p. 139.

city and country. The usual scope of very many preachers," it is added, "is noted to be a soaring up in points of divinity, too deep for the capacity of the people, or a mustering up of much reading, or the displaying of their own wit, or an ignorant meddling with civil matters, as well in the private of several parishes and corporations, as in the public of the kingdom, or a venting of their own distastes, or a smoothing up of those idle fancies which in this blessed time of a long peace do boil in the brains of unadvised people; or lastly, a rude or undecent railing, not against the doctrines (which when the text shall occasion the same is not only approved, but much commended by his royal majesty), but against the persons of Papists and Puritans. Now the people bred up with this kind of teaching, and never instructed in the catechism and fundamental grounds of religion, are for all this airy nourishment no better than 'abrasæ tabulæ,' new table books, ready to be filled up with the manuals and catechisms of the Popish priests, or the papers and pamphlets of Anabaptists, Brownists, and Puritans."[1]

I think the king was right. The preachers of the day had not been educated, for the most part, in the best school, and knew not how to engage the sympathies of the people. Puritans and Baptists were much more likely to gain the popular ear. It was said of our Lord, that "the common people heard him gladly."

[1] *Documentary Annals*, ii. 204.

CHAPTER IV.

Character of Charles I.—Sufferings during his Reign—First Particular Baptist Church—Samuel Howe—Dr. Featley's Book—Baptist Confessions of Faith—Toleration hated by the Presbyterians—Their Attempts to put down the Baptists—Milton's Lines—The Assembly of Divines—Outcry against Immersions—Parliamentary Declaration in favor of the Baptists—Fearful "Ordinance" against them—Their Activity during the Commonwealth and the Protectorate—Cromwell's Baptist Officers—The "Triers"—Baptists in Ireland.

CHARLES I. succeeded his father, James I., in 1625. In religion he was a Romish Protestant. Politically, he believed in the one-man system of government, regarding the people as ciphers, and lost his life by pertinaciously laboring to put it in practice. Morally, he was made up of negations; he wanted principle, sincerity, and steadfastness. The Church of England used to call him a "martyr," but the annual service in commemoration of his death is now discontinued. *We* may call him a "martyr-maker." His reign up to the time of the assembling of the Long Parliament, was distinguished by unremitting persecution of all dissenters from the Established Church, and of all who still remained in the church, but scrupled conformity to some of its ceremonies and laws. The High Commission Court, first established by

Queen Elizabeth, to which court was entrusted the exercise of the royal authority in things ecclesiastical, was in reality a Protestant Inquisition. It possessed absolute power to fine, imprison, and otherwise punish all alleged delinquents, and from its decisions there was no appeal. So severe were the proceedings of that tribunal that great numbers fled the country to avoid them—some to Holland, some to New England.

The Baptists had their share in those sufferings, but the particulars have been imperfectly recorded. One case, casually mentioned in Neal's "History of the Puritans," may be regarded as an index of their condition. Among the ministers whose imprisonment for religion is noticed, the name of Mr. Thomas Brewer occurs, "a Baptist preacher," whose confinement extended to fourteen years. What times were those, when a man was suffered to lie in jail fourteen years for being a "Baptist preacher!"[1]

In the year 1633 an event occurred which requires specific notice. This was the formation of the first Particular or Calvinistic Baptist Church in England. Hitherto the Baptists favored the Arminian views. William Kiffin gives the following account: "There was a congregation of Protestant Dissenters of the Independent persuasion in London, gathered in the year 1616, whereof Mr. Henry Jacob was the first pastor, and after him succeeded Mr. John Lathorp, who was their minister at this time. In this society several persons, finding that the congregation kept not to their first principles of separation, and being also convinced that baptism was not to be administered to infants, but to such only as

[1] *Neal*, ii. 329.

professed faith in Christ, desired that they might be dismissed from that communion, and allowed to form a distinct congregation, in such order as was most agreeable to their own sentiments. The church, considering that they were now grown very numerous, and so more than could in these times of persecution conveniently meet together, and believing also that those persons acted from a principle of conscience, and not obstinacy, agreed to allow them the liberty they desired, and that they should be constituted a distinct church; which was performed the 12th of September, 1633. And as they believed that baptism was not rightly administered to infants, so they looked upon the baptism they had received in that age as invalid; whereupon most or all of them received a new baptism. Their minister was Mr. John Spilsbury. What number they were is uncertain, because in the mentioning of the names of about twenty men and women, it is added, 'with divers others.'"[1]

As the time of enlarged freedom drew near, the tyrant's increased in rage. Seventeen canons were passed by the convocation of the clergy in the early part of 1640, the fifth of which was directed "against sectaries." Having ordered that Popish recusants who refused to conform should be excommunicated, and that the civil power should be requested to aid in carrying the sentence into effect, these words were added: "The synod decrees, that the canon above-mentioned against Papists shall be in full force against all Anabaptists, Brownists, Separatists, and other sectaries, as far as they are applicable."[2]

An excommunicated person is forbidden what is called

[1] *Crosby*, i. 148.   [2] *Ibid.* p. 151.

Christian burial. Samuel Howe, a Baptist minister, who died in prison about this time, while under excommunication, was buried in the highway; interment in consecrated ground, so called, being refused. Mr. Howe was a popular preacher, but uneducated, and on that account, it seems, vilified by some, who were unable to distinguish between university learning and absolute ignorance; and who chose to regard those who had not received college education as disqualified for the ministerial office, notwithstanding their religious attainments, or even their profound acquaintance with Scripture. In this latter respect Mr. Howe excelled most men. But in defending himself from their attacks he certainly exceeded the bounds of moderation. In a treatise which he published, entitled, "The sufficiency of the Spirit's teaching, without human learning," he attempted to show, not only that human learning is an insufficient guide in religion, but that it is "dangerous and hurtful." The following lines appear on the title-page:

> "What *How?* how now? Hath *How* such learning found,
> To throw Art's curious image to the ground?
> Cambridge and Oxford may their glory now
> Veil to a Cobbler, if they know but *How*."

Nevertheless, Mr. Howe was a good and useful man. Roger Williams has this reference to him: "Amongst so many instances, dead and living, to the everlasting praise of Christ Jesus, and of his Holy Spirit, breathing and blessing where he listeth, I cannot but with honorable testimony remember that eminent Christian witness and prophet of Christ, even that despised and yet beloved Samuel Howe, who being by calling a cobbler, and without learning (which yet in its sphere and place he honored), who yet, I say, by searching the Holy Scriptures, grew so excellent a textuary, or Scripture-learned man, that few of those high rabbies that scorn to mend or make a shoe, could aptly or readily, from the Holy Scriptures, outgo him. And however, through the oppressions upon some men's consciences even in life and death, and after death, in respect of burying, as yet unthought of and unremedied—I say, however he was forced to seek a grave or bed in the highway, yet was his life, and death, and burial—being attended with many hundreds of God's people—honorable and (how much more on his rising again) glorious."[1] The barbarity attending his burial was characteristic of the age.

Immediately after the commencement of the contest between Charles I. and the Long Parliament, freedom in religion advanced with rapid strides. The chief restraints of law being removed by the abolition of the High Commission Court and the downfall of the hierarchy, all parties claimed and exercised liberty of worship. The Baptists increased very fast, greatly to the chagrin of the Presbyterian party, which was then in the ascendant. A book published in 1644, by Dr. Featley, may be taken as the exponent of the feelings entertained toward them. Dr. Featley had been engaged in a public disputation with the Baptists, and he printed an account of it, in which he claimed the victory. The book was entitled, "The Dippers Dipt, or the Anabaptists ducked and plunged over head and ears at a Disputation in Southwark." He calls the Baptists an illiterate and sottish sect—a lying

---

[1] *The Hireling Ministry none of Christ's*, p. ii., quoted in Ivimey's *History of the Baptists*, i. 155.

and blasphemous sect—an impure and carnal sect—a bloody and cruel sect—a profane and sacrilegious sect. His malice is thus expressed in the "Epistle Dedicatory": "Of all heretics and schismatics, the Anabaptists ought to be most carefully looked unto and severely punished, if not utterly exterminated and banished out of the church and kingdom. . . . They preach, and print, and practice their heretical impieties openly; they hold their conventicles weekly in our chief cities and suburbs thereof, and there prophesy by turns. . . . They flock in great multitudes to their Jordans, and both sexes enter into the river, and are dipt after their manner with a kind of spell, containing the heads of their erroneous tenets. . . . And as they defile our rivers with their impure washings, and our pulpits with their false prophecies and fanatical enthusiasms, so the presses sweat and groan under the load of their blasphemies." I cannot help thinking that these are the words of a defeated champion, venting his spite against his opponents.

Dr. Featley was a man of influence, and it was therefore judged expedient to furnish an antidote to his book. This was done by the publication of a Confession of Faith, on the part of seven London churches. It appeared in the year 1644, under the following title: "The Confession of Faith of those churches which are commonly (though falsely) called Anabaptists; presented to the view of all that fear God, to examine by the touchstone of the word of truth: as likewise for the taking off those aspersions which are frequently both in pulpit and print (although unjustly) cast upon them." It was a fair digest of Baptist principles, showing that in all important points of theology, Christian ordinances and church government excepted, the Baptists agreed with other evangelical Protestants. The compilers were particularly careful to state in full the views on magistracy held by the churches, in order to disabuse men of the absurd notions still cherished by many, who were fain to charge the Baptists with revolutionary tendencies, similar to those of Munster. The concluding paragraph is admirably written. It is as follows: "Thus we desire to give unto Christ that which is his, and unto all lawful authority that which is their due; and to owe nothing to any man but love; to live quietly and peaceably, as it becometh saints, endeavoring in all things to keep a good conscience, and to do unto every man (of what judgment soever) as we would they should do unto us; that as our practice is, so it may prove us to be a conscionable, quiet, and harmless people (no ways dangerous or troublesome to human society), and to labor and work with our hands that we may not be chargeable to any, but to give to him that needeth, both friends and enemies, accounting it more excellent to give than to receive. Also we confess that we know but in part, and that we are ignorant of many things which we desire and seek to know; and if any shall do us that friendly part to show us from the word of God that we see not, we shall have cause to be thankful to God and them. But if any man shall impose upon us anything that we see not to be commanded by our Lord Jesus Christ, we should in his strength rather embrace all reproaches and tortures of men, to be stripped of all outward comforts, and, if it were possible, to die a thousand deaths, rather than to do anything against the least tittle of the truth of God, or against the light of our own consciences. And if any shall call what we have said heresy, then do we with the apostle acknowledge, that 'after the way they call heresy, worship we the God of our fathers,' disclaiming all heresies (rightly so called), because they are against Christ, and to be steadfast and immovable, always abounding in obedience to Christ, as knowing our labor shall not be in vain in the Lord."[1]

The seven churches by which this Confession was published met in the following places, viz.: Devonshire Square; Broad Street, Wapping; Great St. Helens; Crutched Friars; Bishopsgate Street; Coleman Street; and Glaziers' Hall. The first-mentioned church has existed from that time to the present. The others have been long extinct.

I have said that Presbyterianism was in the ascendant. But the Presbyterians of the seventeenth century held toleration in abhorrence. It was in their eyes the quintessence of all heresy.

The great Richard Baxter says: "My judgment in that much-disputed point of liberty of religion, I have always freely made known. I abhor unlimited liberty and toleration of all, and think myself easily able to prove the wickedness of it."[2]

The President of the Scotch Parliament writes thus to the Parliament of England (Feb. 3, 1645): "It was expected the honorable houses would add their civil sanction to what the pious and learned Assembly have advised; and I am commanded by the Parliament of this kingdom to demand it, and I do in their names demand it. And the Parliament of this kingdom is persuaded that the piety and wisdom of the honorable houses will

[1] *Confessions of Faith*, pp. 13-48.   [2] Ivimey, i. 169.

never admit toleration of any sects or schisms contrary to our Solemn League and Covenant."[1]

The London Presbyterian clergy bear their testimony against "the error of toleration, patronizing and promoting all other errors, heresies, and blasphemies whatsoever, under the grossly-abused notion of liberty of conscience;" and that they consider it a great grievance, "that men should have liberty to worship God in that way and manner as shall appear to them most agreeable to the word of God, and no man be punished or discountenanced by authority for the same. We, the ministers of Jesus Christ," say they, "do hereby testify to our flocks, to all the kingdom, and to the Reformed world, our great dislike of Prelacy, Erastianism, Brownism, and Independency; and our utter abhorrency of Anti-Scripturism, Popery, Arianism, Socinianism, Arminianism, Antinomianism, Anabaptism, Libertinism, and Familism; and that we detest the forementioned toleration, so much pursued and endeavored in this kingdom, accounting it unlawful and pernicious."[2]

The Lancashire ministers declare their "harmonious consent" with their brethren in London as follows: "A toleration would be putting a sword into a madman's hands; a cup of poison into the hand of a child; a letting loose madmen with firebrands in their hands, and appointing a city of refuge in men's consciences for the devil to fly to; a laying a stumbling-block before the blind, a proclaiming liberty to the wolves to come into Christ's fold to prey upon the lambs: neither would it be to provide for tender consciences, but to take away all conscience."[3]

[1] Neal, iii. 310.   [2] *Ibid.* 300.   [3] Crosby, i. 190.

These sentiments were reduced to practice as far as possible. In 1645 an ordinance of Parliament was published, enacting "that no person be permitted to preach, who is not ordained a minister, either in this or in some other Reformed church, except such as, intending the ministry, shall be allowed for the trial of their gifts, by those who shall be appointed thereunto by both houses of Parliament." The ordinance was to be sent to Sir Thomas Fairfax, with the "earnest desire and recommendation" of the houses, that it should be "duly observed in the army."[1] The Baptists were particularly aimed at, because there were great numbers of preachers among them, and they were of course destitute of ordination, in the Presbyterian sense of the word. Next year the Corporation of the city of London interfered in the matter, by presenting a memorial to Parliament, called "The City Remonstrance," in which they prayed "that some strict and speedy course might be taken for the suppressing all separate and private congregations; that all Anabaptists, Brownists, heretics, schismatics, blasphemers, and all other sectaries, who conform not to the public discipline established, or to be established by Parliament, may be fully declared against, and some effectual course settled for proceeding against such persons; and that no person disaffected to the Presbyterial government, set forth or to be set forth by Parliament, may be employed in any place of public trust."[2] But the Baptists and others in the army procured a counter-petition, which was very numerously signed, "applauding the labors and successes of the Parliament in the cause of liberty, and praying them to go on with managing the affairs of the

[1] Crosby, i. 192.   [2] *Ibid.* p. 184.

kingdom according to their wisdom, and not to suffer the free-born people of England to be enslaved on any pretence whatever, nor to suffer any set of people to prescribe to them in matters of government or conscience."¹ Nevertheless, the intolerant principle prevailed, and in December, 1646, a second parliamentary ordinance appeared, forbidding all unordained persons to " preach or expound the Scriptures in any church or chapel, or any other public place," and directing that all ministers, or others, who should " publish or maintain, by preaching, writing, printing, or any other way, anything against or in derogation of the church government which is now established by authority of both houses of Parliament," should be apprehended, and " due punishment " inflicted on them.² Many Baptists suffered under this ordinance, by imprisonment and otherwise. Had it been rigidly executed, there would have been extensive disturbances of the public peace, for the intolerance of the Presbyterian party excited general disgust and loathing. Milton's thoughts and feelings on the subject were expressed with more force than elegance. There is stinging truth in his lines entitled, " On the new Forcers of Conscience under the Long Parliament:"

> " Because you have thrown off your Prelate lord,
> And with stiff vows renounced his Liturgy,
> To seize the widowed whore Plurality
> From them whose sin you envied, not abhorred ;
> Dare ye for this adjure the civil sword
> To force our consciences that Christ set free,
> And ride us with a classic hierarchy
> Taught ye by mere A. S and Rotherford ?

Neal, iii. 328. ² Crosby, i. 194.

> Men whose life, learning, faith, and pure intent
> Would have been held in high esteem with Paul,
> Must now be named and printed Heretics
> By shallow Edwards and Scotch what d'ye call:
> But we do hope to find out all your tricks,
> Your plots and packing worse than those of Trent,
> That so the Parliament
> May with their wholesome and preventive shears
> Clip your phylacteries, though bauk your ears,
> And succor our just fears,
> When they shall read this clearly in your charge,
> *New Presbyter is but old Priest writ large.*" [1]

These Presbyterian outrages were also exposed by Samue. Richardson, one of the pastors of the Calvinistic or Particular Baptist Church, the formation of which has been mentioned. Mr. Richardson's pamphlet was entitled, "The necessity of Toleration in matters of religion; or, certain questions propounded to the synod, tending to prove that corporal punishments ought not to be inflicted upon such as hold errors in religion, and that in matters of religion men ought not to be compelled, but have liberty and freedom." The "questions" are such as no persecutor, Roman Catholic or Protestant, Episcopalian or Presbyterian, could satisfactorily answer; and the observations interspersed are so pithy and pungent, that the good cause must have derived great benefit from the publication. "Sit still quietly," the author says, "and be humbled, for your folly in calling persecution discipline and just-deserved censure; and in calling your priesthood and presbytery a holy order, and yet are but

---

[1] Todd's *Milton*, vi. 92-97. "Bauk," for "balk," means to "spare," to "leave untouched." "The mild and gentle Parliament will content itself with only clipping away your Jewish and persecuting principles." — *Warburton.*

the pope's priesthood. And we had as good be under the pope as under your Presbyterian check. . . . You would all be tolerated, and would have none tolerated but yourselves; you would suffer none to live quietly and comfortably but those of your way. Is this to do as you would be done by?"[1]

The Assembly of Divines sat from 1643 till 1649. Their Confession of Faith and Catechisms will live as long as theological literature lasts. With the exception of those portions in which religious liberty, church government, and Christian baptism are treated, they are invaluable. The assembly not only sustained infant baptism, but also enjoined sprinkling as the mode of administering the ceremony. It was a close division— twenty-five were for the injunction of sprinkling, twenty four against it. That majority of one was obtained by Dr. Lightfoot's influence, to whose authority as an Oriental scholar and biblical critic great deference was paid. The minority were not willing to legislate on the subject, and would have left it to the option of ministers. But it seems that there was a dread of possible consequences; for if any infants should be immersed, a suspicion might get abroad that sprinkling was insufficient. This might lead to the conclusion that those who had been only sprinkled ought to be baptized. The inquiry might then be extended to adults, and so the interests of the Baptists might be furthered. It was judged prudent to prevent all this by positive enactment.

There was a wonderful outcry against immersion. Even Baxter allowed himself to use expressions which might be laughed at, were it not for the melancholy fact

[1] *Tracts,* p. 284.

that in his case—for he could not be ignorant on the subject—prejudice and passion prevailed over Christian charity, and impelled him to adopt a course which in his sober moments he must have condemned. Take a specimen or two: "That which is a plain breach of the sixth commandment, *Thou shalt not kill*, is no ordinance of God, but a most heinous sin. But the ordinary practice of baptizing over head, and in cold water, as necessary, is a plain breach of the sixth commandment; therefore it is no ordinance of God, but a heinous sin, and, as Mr. Craddock shows in his book of gospel liberty, the magistrate ought to restrain it, to save the lives of his subjects." . . . "In a word, it is good for nothing but to despatch men out of the world that are burdensome, and to ranken churchyards. I conclude, if murder be a sin, then dipping ordinarily over head in England is a sin; and if those who make it men's religion to murder themselves, and urge it upon their consciences as their duty, are not to be suffered in a commonwealth, any more than highway murderers; then judge how these Anabaptists, that teach the necessity of such dipping, are to be suffered." Poor Baxter! Had he never read the *ninth* commandment?[1]

Samuel Oates' case is another illustration of the intense hatred against everything Baptist which was at that time indulged in. This excellent minister, who was for some time pastor of one of the London churches, was much blessed in his labors. While engaged in a home missionary tour in the county of Essex, in the year 1646, his preaching was attended with such success that hundreds were converted and baptized. One of the converts hav

---

[1] Ivimey, i. 193.

ing died a few weeks after, Mr. Oates was actually committed to prison, put in irons, and indicted for murder! It would seem hardly credible that this charge could be seriously entertained; but malice and bigotry stick at nothing. Mr. Oates' persecutors were disappointed, as it clearly appeared on the trial that the young woman baptized was in good health for some time after her baptism. The jury returned a verdict of "not guilty," but the attempt to destroy a Christian minister by such means was an ugly symptom.[1]

Verily the times were odd and strange! The same Parliament which denounced preachers who had not been regularly ordained, and ordered the magistrates to seize them, issued, in the following year, a declaration in favor of the Baptists! How it came to pass I know not. Perhaps some thought that they had gone too far, and honestly desired to retrace their steps; or possibly the growing numbers and influence of the denomination inspired a salutary fear, especially as it was known that there were many Baptists in the army. These words were found in the "Declaration," issued March 4, 1647: "The name of Anabaptism hath indeed contracted much odium, by reason of the extravagant opinions and practices we abhor and detest. But for their opinion against the baptism of infants, it is only a difference about a circumstance of time in the administration of an ordinance, wherein in former ages, as well as this, learned men have differed both in opinion and practice. And though we could wish that all men would satisfy themselves, and join with us in our judgment and practice on this point, yet herein we hold it fit that men should be convinced by

---
[1] Crosby, i. 236.

the word of God, with great gentleness and reason, and not beaten out of it with force and violence."[1]

It was but a momentary gleam of light. As if terrified at what they had said—

> "They back recoiled,
> E'en at the sound themselves had made,"

and in May, 1648, passed a law more fearfully barbarous than any which had for a long time found a place in the statute-book. I refer to the "Ordinance of the Lords and Commons assembled in Parliament, for punishing blasphemies and heresies." By this law it was enacted that all persons found guilty of Atheism, Deism, or Socinianism, and refusing to abjure, should *suffer death*, as in case of felony. If they abjured, they were to remain in prison till they found sureties that they would not maintain their errors any more; then, if they afterward recanted, and were convicted a second time, they were to be executed. It was also enacted that all persons convicted before two justices of the peace of maintaining and defending certain specified opinions held by Papists, Arminians, Antinomians, Quakers, or Baptists, should be ordered to renounce their errors in the parish church, and in case of refusal, to be committed to jail till they should find sureties that they would not maintain or defend such opinions any more. This was equivalent to a sentence of imprisonment for life. The Baptist sentiment condemned was thus expressed: "That the baptizing of infants is unlawful, or such baptism is void, and that such persons ought to be baptized again;" it is added, "and in pursuance thereof shall baptize any per-

[1] Crosby, i. 196.

sol formerly baptized." Even the Episcopalians were included in the condemnation, for the same penalties were provided for those who should maintain "that the church government by presbytery is antichristian or unlawful."[1]

It is no apology for this vile law that it was practically a dead letter, and was intended to terrify or prevent rather than to punish. The good sense and Christianity of the people would not suffer it to be executed; but the Presbyterians, whose handiwork it was, were fully prepared for the experiment, if power had been entrusted to them. Here again we see "*old priest writ large.*"

During the Commonwealth the Baptists evinced much zealous activity in the cause of the Saviour. The ministers were indefatigable, the people fervent and steadfast. If now and then the fervor evaporated into fanaticism, or something like it, and if diversity of opinion on comparatively minor points caused a multiplication of small parties, an excuse may be found in the peculiar state of the times. And surely it was better that the waters should be in motion, or even troubled, than stagnant and corrupted. We are not required to defend all the measures adopted by our forefathers, any more than to employ their quaint modes of speech. But it would be well for us to imitate their diligence, their prayerfulness, their strict regard to the authority of the Saviour, their endeavors for mutual edification. They labored "in season, out of season." Those of them who were in Cromwell's army took care not to blink their principles there. Prayer and preaching were duly attended to, by officers as well as by privates. A serious, orderly deportment prevailed.

[1] Crosby, i. 199–205.

In camp and in garrison they observed good discipline; in the field their prowess was unquestioned. They were the Havelocks of the seventeenth century.

Under the Protectorate the Baptists were not only unmolested, but prosperous. Some of them disapproved of the new government, preferring the commonwealth; and some joined the Fifth Monarchy men, who held visionary notions respecting the kingdom of Christ. Hence the Protector was thought to look coolly on them, and to wish to lessen their influence, particularly in the army. But the main body were satisfied with the existing order of things, and diligently improved their opportunities.

Crosby has republished a letter from some Baptists in the army to the Protector, in which they accuse him of designing to get rid of them, or, as they expressed it, "to purge the army of the Anabaptists." They were not very careful in the choice of words. These are some of the "queries" they put to "his highness:" "Whether your highness had come to the height of honor and greatness you are now come to, if the Anabaptists, so called, had been so much your enemies as they were your friends?" "Whether the Anabaptists were ever unfaithful, either to the Commonwealth in general, or to your highness in particular? And if not, then what is the reason of your intended dismission?" "Whether the Anabaptists may not as justly endeavor to eat out the bowels of your government, as your highness may endeavor to eat them out of their employments?" "Whether the Anabaptists did not come more justly into their employments in the army than your highness into the seat of government?" "Whether the Anabaptist will not be in a better condition in the day of Christ, that keeps his covenant with God and man, than your highness will be if you break with both?" "Whether *an hundred of the old Anabaptists*, such as marched under your command in '48, '49, '50, etc., be not as good as *two hundred* of your new courtiers, if you were in such a condition as you were at Dunbar in Scotland?" "Whether your highness' conscience was not more at peace, and your mind more *set upon things* above, when you loved the Anabaptists, than it is now, when you hate their principles, or their service, or both?" "Whether your highness' court is not a greater charge to this nation than the Anabaptists in the army? And if so, whether this be the ease which you promised the people?"[1]

This is plain dealing. But Cromwell accomplished his purpose, as regarded his own regiment, the principal officers in which were dismissed, avowedly because they were Baptists. The probability is that they were strong republicans, and were afraid of the old tyranny.

The discontents of the Irish Baptists, some of whom objected to the Protectorate, regarding the title of "Lord Protector" as "applicable to God alone," were allayed by a judicious letter addressed to them by Messrs. Kiffin and Spilsbury. It is inserted in the volume of "Confessions of Faith," published by the Hanserd Knollys Society.[2]

Three Baptist ministers—John Tombes, Henry Jessey, and Daniel Dyke—were appointed "Triers," that is, they were members of a committee so called, constituted by the government for the examination of candidates for church livings, and the removal of "ignorant and scandalous" clergymen. The ministers above mentioned, and

[1] Crosby, iii. 231–242.   [2] Pp. 322–326.

several more, accepted the charge of parishes. I do not vindicate their consistency in consenting to receive tithes and other payments, by which parish ministers are supported in the Church of England; but the impartial reader will give due weight to the considerations which have been alleged in their defence, viz.: that the scarcity of qualified ministers warranted them in taking this step, as they were thereby put in a position to preach the gospel to thousands who would have been otherwise destitute of the means of grace; that they were bound to no forms and ceremonies, and allowed to conduct worship in whatever manner they pleased; and that some of them retained their own churches, and continued to minister to them, occupying the parish pulpits on only one part of the Lord's Day.

Statistics were not much thought of in those days. I am unable to furnish an exact account of the number of Baptist churches in England at the time of the Restoration. It may suffice to remark that there were churches of our denomination in about thirty English counties, and that they were numerous in Wales. The principal churches in Ireland were at Dublin, Waterford, Kilkenny, Clonmel, Cork, and Limerick.

I will here introduce some passages of a letter written by Mr. Thomas Patient, who was then preaching at Kilkenny, and addressed to "the Lord General Cromwell." It is strikingly characteristic of the spirit of the times:

"It is a great honor to be made use of in the hand of God, to do him special service for church and commonwealth, to have a spirit like unto Christ, which is a public spirit. He came not to be served, but to serve, and to lay down his life a ransom for many. Oh, therefore, my beloved in the Lord, still let this be the joy of your heart, in all your difficulties and great undertakings, that you are in such a work and service, which I know God hath made you sensible of, hath tended much to the preservation and peace of his church, and free passage of the gospel, and I hope at last will appear to be for the public good of the commonwealth.

"My constant prayers are at the throne of grace for you, that you may be kept upright with God, and in nothing left to sin and dishonor God, his name being so much concerned in it. Therefore, as God hath formerly given you the experience of the benefit of a humble walking with God, I beseech you, in the bowels of Christ, still keep a close watch over your own heart, and labor to walk under the sense of that body of death and your daily infirmities, and to see a need of godly repentance daily, and humiliation, and fresh strength from Christ by faith, by which you may be kept and preserved in a fresh, sweet, and comfortable communion with God; for his presence will be all your happiness.

"Be sure to prize God's holy word, and all the rest of God's holy ordinances, and in so much as may be, neglect not to practice them, that you by your constant godly example may provoke others to holiness and the fear of the Lord."[1]

[1] *Confessions of Faith*, etc., pp. 311-315.

CHAPTER V.

Character of Charles II. and James II.—Commencement of Persecution—Venner's Rebellion—Disclaimer by Baptists—Severe Sufferings—John James—Act of Uniformity—The Aylesbury Baptists—Benjamin Keach Pilloried—Conventicle Act—Five-Mile Act—Their Effects.

WE are now entering upon a dark time. The reigns of Charles II. and James II. were inglorious in all respects. Those kings were despicable as men, despotic as rulers. In religion, the first was a hypocrite, the second a bigot. The former was traitorous to British interests for the sake of his pleasures and his pride; the latter was willing to offer up British freedom on the altar of the Papacy. Martyrdom, in various forms, gained fresh laurels while they occupied the throne of which they were utterly unworthy.

Charles II. had pledged his royal word at Breda, before his restoration, "that no man should be disquieted or called in question for differences of opinion in matters of religion, which did not disturb the peace of the kingdom." Like a true son of his father, he broke his promise. It was doubtless given with a mental reservation which a Jesuit would applaud.

The Savoy Conference, like the Hampton Court Conference in the reign of James I., was a mere sham. The design was, first to cheat and then to insult. The Episcopalians and Presbyterians who attended the conference held several meetings, and partially discussed the points at issue, but without any good result. No Baptists were there. The conference was opened April 15, 1661, and closed July 25.

The religious condition of the kingdom was very peculiar. "Ignorant and scandalous" ministers had been ejected by wholesale during the Commonwealth and under the Protectorate. Their successors were a motley group. The majority were Episcopalians, but there were many Presbyterians, some Independents, and a few Baptists. A large number of the Presbyterians would have submitted to the restored establishment, if they had been allowed to retain discretionary power with reference to portions of the ritual. They particularly objected to wearing the surplice; to the sign of the cross in baptism; to kneeling at the Lord's supper; to the indiscriminate administration of the Lord's supper to sick persons; to the form of absolution; to the language of the burial service; and to the declaration required of all clergymen that there was nothing in the Common Prayer Book, the Book of Ordination, or the Thirty-nine Articles contrary to the word of God. But the temper of the times was rigid and fierce. The hierarchical party, flushed with victory and confident of complete success, refused all consideration. They would not abate a jot, except in matters of the most trivial importance. A few verbal alterations were made in the Liturgy; a new edition of the Prayer Book was published, containing forms of prayer for the 30th of January and the 29th of May, with other additions, and the Parliament, subservient to the wishes of the king and the priesthood, passed the "Act of Uniformity," which went into operation August 24, 1662.

We are now prepared for a tale of woe. The history of our denomination from 1660 to 1688 is not so much a history of progress as of endurance. Persecution commenced immediately after the king's return. The clergymen ejected during the Commonwealth and the Protectorate, with the exception of such as had "justified the late king's murder or declared against infant baptism," were restored to their livings by act of Parliament. Though the High Commission Court was not re-established, it was presumed that the old laws of Elizabeth were in force again, and magistrates in every part of the kingdom were eager to execute them.

The Baptists saw the storm coming, and took measures accordingly. They asked for no indulgence, no emoluments. They sought no office. All they wanted was freedom of worship. They recognized but one course of action in things civil: they were prepared to be obedient subjects. With these views they approached the throne. First, a petition was presented to the king, July 26, 1660, setting forth the sufferings inflicted on the churches in Lincolnshire. "We have been much abused," they say, "as we pass in the streets and as we sit in our houses; being threatened to be hanged if but heard praying to our Lord in our own families, and disturbed in our so waiting upon him by uncivil beating at our doors and sounding of horns; yea, we have been stoned when going to our meetings; the windows of the place where we have met have been struck down with stones: yea, [we have been] taken as evil-doers, and imprisoned, when peaceably met together to worship the Most High in the use of his most precious ordinances. . . . And as if all this were too little, they have to fill up their measure very lately indicted many of us at the sessions, and intend, as we are informed, to impose on us the penalty of twenty pounds [each], for not coming to hear such men as they provide us."[1] Accompanying this was a Confession of Faith, drawn up by Thomas Grantham, said to be "owned and approved by more than twenty thousand." Another petition, entitled, "The humble petition and representation of the sufferings of several peaceable and innocent subjects, called by the name of Anabaptists, inhabitants in the county of Kent, and now prisoners in the jail of Maidstone, for the testimony of a good conscience," dated Jan. 25, 1661, not only represented the case of the prisoners, but of their brethren in the county of Kent, who were already suffering severely.[2] These petitions produced no favorable results. The king, indeed, replied to the first, "That it was not his mind that any of his good subjects who lived peaceably should suffer any trouble on account of their opinions in point of religion," and he made fair promises. But the work of violence still went on. Some of the principal Baptist ministers were lodged in prison during the year 1660. In November of that year, John Bunyan entered Bedford jail, which was destined to be his abode for twelve years. In every part of England power was leagued with cruelty and lawlessness for the extermination of freedom.

The ridiculous affair called "Venner's Rebellion" oc-

[1] Ivimey, i. 276.
[2] *Tracts on Liberty of Conscience*, pp. 297-308.

curred on the 7th of January, 1661. Thomas Venner preached in a small meeting-house in Coleman Street, London. He "warmed his admirers with passionate expectations of a fifth universal monarchy under the personal reign of King Jesus upon earth, and that the saints were to take the kingdom themselves." On the day above mentioned about fifty of them marched out of their meeting-house, well armed, "with a resolution to subvert the present government or die in the attempt." In the tumult that followed, they lost about half their number. The remainder surrendered; "Venner and one of his officers were hanged before their meeting-house door, Jan. 19, and a few days after nine more were executed in divers parts of the city." A proclamation was issued the day after the insurrection prohibiting all meetings of Baptists, Quakers, and Fifth Monarchy men for religious worship, unless in the parish churches or in private houses, and then limited to "the persons there inhabiting." The reason assigned was, that the parties abovementioned had met under religious pretexts, but in reality for treacherous purposes; and the insurrection gave a plausible color to the proceeding. But the proclamation, though not issued till after the rebellion, had been ordered five days before; and the rebellion was eagerly laid hold of in justification of the act, which was manifestly an unauthorized stretch of power. That, however, gave little concern to Charles II. or his unscrupulous advisers. The document was a characteristic specimen of Stuart knavery and audacity.[1]

The Baptists hastened to disclaim all sympathy with

[1] *Documentary Annals.* ii. 302. *Tracts*, pp. 313-316. Neal's *Puritans* iv. 310.

Venner. A "Humble Apology of some commonly called Anabaptists, in behalf of themselves, and others of the same judgment with them, with their protestation against the late wicked and most horrid treasonable insurrection and rebellion," signed by thirty ministers and others, at the head of whom were William Kiffin and Henry Denne, was presented to the king the day after the outbreak. But none of their number were compromised, and Venner himself had declared that if he succeeded "the Baptists should know that infant baptism was an ordinance of Jesus Christ."[1]

Two publications were issued in 1661. The objects of both were the same, namely, to establish the iniquity of persecution—to claim for the Baptists the rights of religious freedom—and to declare their willingness, as loyal subjects, to obey the king and his officers in all things lawful.

The first was entitled "A Plea for Toleration of opinions and persuasions in matters of religion, differing from the Church of England." It was written by "John Sturgion, a member of the baptized people." The reasons against persecution are concisely given, and are expressed in a bold, nervous style.

The second pamphlet was entitled "Sion's groans for her distressed; or, sober endeavors to prevent innocent blood," etc. The names of seven Baptist ministers are appended to the "Epistle to the Reader." They were all sufferers as well as laborers. One of them, Joseph Wright, spent no less than twenty years in prison for the truth's sake. The others were—Thomas Monck, who labored in Buckinghamshire; George Hammon and William

[1] Crosby, ii. 65. *Confessions of Faith, etc.*, pp. 343-348.

Jeffrey, in Kent; Francis Stanley, in Northamptonshire; William Reynolds, in Lincolnshire; and Francis Smith.

It is not likely that the king saw these or any other publications in which the principles of the Baptists were explained and advocated. Nor is it probable, had he seen them, that they would have induced him to change his policy. Immediately after Venner's insurrection, Hanserd Knollys and many more were apprehended and lodged in Newgate and other London prisons. "Above four hundred," says Crosby, "were crowded into Newgate, besides many more in the other prisons belonging to the city and parts adjacent." Vavasor Powell, then preaching in Wales, was treated in the same manner, and many of his brethren in the principality shared his fate. Throughout the kingdom the Baptists were exposed to outrage. "They have been haled from their peaceable habitations," says John Sturgion, "and thrust into prisons, almost in all counties in England, and many are still detained, to the utter undoing of themselves and families, and most of them are poor men, whose livelihood, under God, depends upon the labor of their hands. So that they lie under a more than ordinary calamity, there being so many thrust into little rooms together that they are an annoyance each to other, especially in the city of London, where the lord mayor crowds them very close together, that it hath been observed the keepers have complained they have had too many guests. And whilst they suffer there, some of their wives and tender babies want bread at home."[1]

The execution of John James was a horrible illustration of royal malice. John James was a Sabbatarian Baptist

[1] *Tracts*, p. 328.

His meeting-house was in Bullstrake Alley, Whitechapel, London. On the 19th of October, 1661, he was dragged from his pulpit and committed to Newgate, on the charge of uttering treasonable words against the king. The principal witness against him was one Tipler, a journeyman pipe-maker, a man whose character was so well known that the magistrate before whom Mr. James was taken refused to receive his deposition, unless some other witness would corroborate it. Others were found who confirmed Tipler's testimony; but one of them afterward confessed that "he had sworn against Mr James he knew not what." In fact, there can be little doubt that the witnesses were suborned, probably bribed, to commit perjury. There is the more reason to believe this, because when the lieutenant of the Tower read the information laid against Mr. James in the presence of his congregation, and asked them how they could hear such doctrine, they all replied, "that they never heard such words, as they shall answer it before the Lord, and they durst not lie." But the death of the victim was predetermined. It was no difficult matter to procure a verdict against him. He was tried and convicted on the 19th of November, and sentenced the next day to be hanged, drawn, and quartered.

So flagrant was the injustice that his wife was advised by her friends to present a petition to the king for his life, setting forth the facts which I have mentioned, and entreating his majesty's interposition. But they had miscalculated. Charles treated the heart-broken woman with gross brutality. "With some difficulty she met the king, and presented him with the paper, acquainting him who she was. To whom he held up his finger, and said, 'Oh! Mr. James—he is a sweet gentleman;' but following him for some further answer, the door was shut against her. The next morning she attended again, and an opportunity soon presenting, she implored his majesty's answer to her request. Who then replied, 'That he was a rogue, and should be hanged.' One of the lords attending him asked her of whom she spake. The king answered, "Of John James, that rogue; he shall be hanged; yea, he shall be hanged.'"[1]

On the 26th of November Mr. James was dragged on a hurdle, after the manner of traitors, from Newgate to Tyburn, the place of execution. His behavior under those awful circumstances was dignified and Christian. In his address to the multitude, referring to his denominational sentiments, he said, "I do own the title of a baptized believer. I own the ordinances and appointments of Jesus Christ. I own all the principles in Hebrews vi. 1, 2." He charged his friends to continue their religious assemblies, at all risk. His closing exhortations were remarkably solemn and impressive, reminding the people of the days of the old martyrs. "This is a happy day," said one of his friends: "I bless the Lord," he replied, "it is so." When all was ready, he lifted up his hands, and exclaimed, with a loud voice, "Father, into thy hands I commit my spirit." So he died. His quarters were placed over the city gates, and his head was set upon a pole, opposite the meeting-house in which he had preached the gospel.[2]

I have mentioned the Act of Uniformity. It received the royal assent on the 19th of May, 1662, and went into operation on the 24th of August following. By this act,

[1] Crosby, ii. 17.   [2] Ivimey, i. 325-327.

five things were required of all ministers then in possession of livings, as essential to their continuance in the Establishment: 1. Reordination, if they had not been episcopally ordained before. 2. A declaration of "an feigned assent and consent to all and everything contained in the Book of Common Prayer, and administration of the sacraments, and other rites and ceremonies of the church"—a new and corrected edition of which was then published, but which great numbers of the clergy could not possibly *see* before the time specified—affirming that there was nothing in it contrary to the word of God; with a promise to use the prescribed form and no other. 3. An oath of canonical obedience and subjection to the bishop. 4. Abjuration of the Solemn League and Covenant. 5. A declaration of the unlawfulness of taking up arms against the king and government *upon any pretence whatsoever.*

The interval that elapsed between the time when the act was passed and the day on which it was to take effect was a period of anxious suspense, both to the people and their ministers. It was a trial of character. Some came to an immediate decision, and left their livings before the appointed day; others waited till the time had expired; and when at length the 24th of August came, there were found more than *two thousand* worthy, learned, pious ministers ready to say, "We ought to obey God rather than men." And they acted on the principle. Regardless of consequences, they sacrificed all to truth and to God, and cast themselves on Providence for supply and defence, exhibiting to the world and to future ages a noble example of disinterested virtue and conscientious integrity. The loss which they sustained was by no means trivial; they were not only forbidden to exercise their ministry under severe penalties, but they were left without any visible means of subsistence. No provision was made for them, no mercy was shown to them; on the contrary, one persecuting decree was followed by another, and the governing powers seemed only to be engaged in racking their brains to devise some new method of vexing and tormenting their more worthy fellow-countrymen.

On the list of the ejected ministers stand the names of Richard Baxter, John Howe, Joseph Alleine, John Owen, Stephen Charnock, John Flavel, and many more, whose writings are still rendering service to the cause of God. About thirty of the ejected belonged to the Baptist denomination. The Church of England sustained a blow from that ejectment from which she has scarcely yet recovered. Her best men were driven away. Uniformity was the idol set up, and all who would not bow down to it were sacrificed without mercy.

The hand of power was heavy on the Nonconformists in every part of England. In Buckinghamshire the persecution raged with intolerable fierceness. So numerous were the prisoners that the magistrates were obliged to hire two large houses for their accommodation, the county jail being too small. On one occasion, in 1664, the Baptist minister of Aylesbury and eleven of his congregation were seized, among whom were two women. They were placed before the justices at the quarter sessions, and advantage was taken of the 35th of Queen Elizabeth to require them either to conform to the Church of England and take the oaths of allegiance and supremacy, or to abjure the realm; and they were told that if they would not do either, they would be declared guilty of felony and sentence of death would be passed on them. Unawed by this prospect, they replied, that as they could not comply with the requisitions, they threw themselves on the mercy of the court; on which they were sentenced to be hanged, and sent back to jail till the day of execution. The sentence would have been executed, had not measures been promptly taken to lay the case before the king and obtain his interference. The son of one of the condemned persons hastened to London, and by the assistance of William Kiffin procured an interview with the lord chancellor, who immediately proceeded to the king. Implacable as Charles had proved himself to be in John James' case, he saw that the wholesale murder contemplated at Aylesbury would bring his government into disrepute, and might stir up resentment not easily to be appeased. He was willing enough to worry his subjects into submission, or at least to attempt to do so, by confiscation and the dungeon; but the thought of sacrificing twelve lives at once to the demon of intolerance was too shocking even for Charles II. A reprieve was placed in the hands of the applicant, and at the next assizes his majesty's pardon was produced by the presiding judge, and the prisoners were released.

Let me now give an instance of interference with the freedom of the press. Benjamin Keach, a Baptist minister, wrote a small book for children, entitled, "The Child's Instructor; or, a New and Easy Primer." In the catechetical portion of the book Baptist sentiments were inculcated. It was affirmed that "believers, or godly men and women only, who can make confession of their faith and repentance," should be baptized. The personal reign of the

Saviour on earth for a thousand years, held at the time by some Baptists, was taught. And, which was peculiarly offensive, Mr. Keach said, that "Christ's true ministers have not their learning and wisdom from men, or from universities, or human schools; for human learning, arts and sciences are not essential to the making of a true minister; but only the gift of God, which cannot be bought with silver or gold. And also, as they have freely received the gift of God, so they do freely administer; they do not preach for hire, for gain or filthy lucre; they are not like false teachers, who look for gain from their quarters, who eat the fat, and clothe themselves with the wool, and kill them that are fed; those that put not into their mouths they prepare war against. Also, they are not lords over God's heritage; they rule them not by force and cruelty, neither have they power to force and compel men to believe and obey their doctrine, but are only to persuade and entreat; thus is the way of the gospel, as Christ taught them."

For this he was indicted at the assizes. The language of the indictment may amuse the reader. "Thou art here indicted by the name of Benjamin Keach, of Winslow, in the county of Bucks, for that thou, being a seditious, heretical, and schismatical person, evilly and maliciously disposed, and disaffected to his majesty's government of the Church of England, didst maliciously and wickedly, on the first day of May, in the sixteenth year of the reign of our sovereign lord the king, write, print, and publish, or cause to be written, printed, and published, one seditious and venomous book, entitled, 'The Child's Instructor; or, a New and Easy Primer;' wherein are contained, by way of question and answer, these damnable positions, contrary to the Book of Common Prayer and the Liturgy of the Church of England."

The trial took place October 9, 1664. Chief Justice Hyde, afterward Lord Clarendon, presided, and conducted himself with a malignity wholly unbefitting his office. Under his direction a verdict of "guilty" was recorded, and the judge then proceeded to pass sentence, in the following terms: "Benjamin Keach, you are here convicted for writing, printing, and publishing a seditious and schismatical book, for which the court's judgment is this, and the court doth award: That you shall go to jail for a fortnight, without bail or mainprise; and the next Saturday to stand upon the pillory at Aylesbury, in the open market for the space of two hours, from eleven of the clock to one, with a paper upon your head with this inscription—'For writing, printing, and publishing a schismatical book, entitled, "The Child's Instructor; or, a New and Easy Primer."' And the next Thursday to stand in the same manner, and for the same time, in the market of Winslow; and there your book shall be openly burnt before your face, by the common hangman, in disgrace of you and your doctrine. And you shall forfeit to the king's majesty the sum of twenty pounds, and shall remain in jail until you find sureties for your good behavior, and appearance at the next assizes, there to renounce your doctrines, and make such public submission as shall be enjoined you."

The punishment of the pillory was abolished by act of Parliament in the year 1837. The instrument so called was an upright frame placed on a scaffold, upon which the offender stood, his head appearing through one hole of the frame, and his hands fixed in two others. As this punishment was generally reserved for persons guilty of perjury and other infamous crimes, the mob were accustomed to pelt them with rotten eggs or various kinds of filth, and even with stones and brickbats, so that death sometimes ensued. To such an exposure the lord chief justice of England delivered up a worthy minister of the gospel. The sentence was duly carried into execution, and the sheriff, who was himself a fierce opposer of the truth, took care that the judge's directions should be obeyed to the very letter.

It was market-day at Aylesbury. The town was thronged. People flocked thither from all parts of the country to see the new and strange spectacle. But though many of them were prepared to deride and sneer, the usual expressions of popular indignation were wanting. Hitherto the pillory had been reserved for the vilest criminals. But Mr. Keach was a good man, and a preacher of the gospel. They could not find it in their hearts to pelt *him*.

Precisely at eleven o'clock he was placed in the pillory. Many friends attended him, and stood around the instrument of torture for the purpose of sympathy and encouragement. And there, too, stood his wife, and "frequently spoke in vindication of her husband, and of the principles for which he suffered." A true "helpmeet."

"Good people," said he, "I am not ashamed to stand here this day, with this paper on my head; my Lord Jesus was not ashamed to suffer on the cross for me; and it is for his cause that I am made a gazing-stock. It is not for any wickedness that I stand here, but for writing and publishing his truth." "No!" exclaimed an Episcopal clergyman who was standing by; "it is for writing and publishing *errors*." "Sir," replied Mr. Keach, "can you prove them errors?" He would have answered, but he was too well known by the multitude. "One told him of his being pulled drunk out of a ditch. Another upbraided him with being lately found drunk under a haycock. At this time all the people fell to laughing, and turned their diversion from the sufferer in the pillory to the drunken priest; insomuch that he hastened away with the utmost disgrace and shame."

When the uproar had subsided, the voice from the pillory was heard again. Having somehow slipped one of his hands out of the hole, he took his Bible from his pocket and said, "Take notice, that the things which I have written and published, and for which I stand here this day a spectacle to men and angels, are all contained in this book." The jailer snatched the book from him, and replaced his hand in the hole.

Still the voice came from the pillory: "A great concernment for souls was that which moved me to write and publish those things for which I now suffer, and for which I could suffer far greater things than these. It concerns you therefore to be very careful, otherwise it will be very sad with you at the revelation of the Lord Jesus from heaven; for we must all appear before his tribunal."

The officers interposed, and he was compelled to be silent for a time. But again he ventured: "Oh! did you but experience the great love of God, and the excellencies that are in him, it would make you willing to go through any sufferings for his sake. And I do account this the greatest honor that ever the Lord was pleased to confer upon me."

The sheriff was furious, and declared that he should be gagged if he did not hold his tongue. So he refrained from speaking. Yet he could not forbear uttering these words: "This one 'yoke' of Christ, which I can experience, is 'easy' to me, and a burthen which he doth make 'light.'"

When the two hours had expired, he was released, and "blessed God with a loud voice for his great goodness unto him."

That day week he was exposed to the same indignity at Winslow, where he lived, and bore it with equal patience and manliness. There also his book was publicly burned, according to the sentence.[1]

In 1664 the *Conventicle Act* was passed. The principal clause was to this effect: "That if any person above the age of sixteen shall be present at any meeting, under color or pretence of any exercise of religion, in any other manner than is allowed by the liturgy or practice of the Church of England, where shall be five or more persons than the household, he shall for the first offence suffer three months' imprisonment, upon record made upon oath, under the hand and seal of a justice of peace, or pay a sum not exceeding five pounds: for the second offence six months' imprisonment, or ten pounds: and for the third offence, the offender to be banished to some of the American plantations for seven years, or pay one hundred pounds, excepting New England or Virginia; and in case they return, or make their escape, such persons are to be adjudged felons, and suffer death without benefit of clergy."[2]

[1] *Crosby*, ii. 186–208. [2] *Neal*, iv. 394.

The procedings under this act were summary. There was no trial by jury. A single justice of the peace was empowered to levy the fines, or commit the offenders to jail, or even banish them for seven years, and there was no appeal from his decision. Under the operation of this law vast numbers suffered in every part of the kingdom. Those who were banished were sent to the West Indies, where they endured very hard treatment.

Next year the *Five-Mile Act* was passed. It was entitled, " An Act to restrain Nonconformists from inhabiting corporations." All Nonconformist ministers were required to take the following oath : " I, *A. B.*, do swear, that it is not lawful upon any pretence whatsoever to take arms against the king ; and that I do abhor that traitorous position of taking arms by his authority against his person or against those that are commissioned by him, in pursuance of such commissions ; and that I will not at any time endeavor any alteration of government, either in church or state." The Earl of Southampton justly observed that this was an oath which " no honest man could take." But those ministers who refused to take it were forbidden to go within five miles of any city or town that sent members to Parliament, or within five miles of any place where they had formerly exercised their ministry before their ejectment. The fine for every offence was forty pounds. They were also declared "incapable of teaching any public or private schools :" fine forty pounds. And in addition to the fines, any two justices of the peace might " commit the offender to prison for six months."

The object of this inhuman act was to silence the ministers, or compel them to conform for fear of starvation

"But the body of Nonconformist ministers refused the oath, choosing rather to leave their habitations, their relations and friends, and all visible support, than destroy the peace of their consciences. Those ministers who had some little estate or substance of their own retired to remote and obscure villages, or such little market towns as were not corporations, and more than five miles from the places where they had preached; but in many counties it was difficult to find such places of retirement, for either there were no houses untenanted, or they were annexed to farms which the ministers were not capable of using, or the people were afraid to admit the ministers into their houses, lest they should be suspected as favorers of nonconformity. Some took advantage of the ministers' necessities, and raised their rents beyond what they were able to give. Great numbers were thus buried in obscurity; but others, who had neither money nor friends, went on preaching as they could, till they were sent to prison, thinking it more eligible to perish in a jail than to starve out of one, especially when by this means they had some occasional relief from their hearers, and hopes that their wives and children might be supported after their death. Many who lay concealed in distant places from their flocks in the day-time, rode thirty or forty miles to preach to them in the night, and retired again before daylight. These hardships tempted some few to conform" (says Mr. Baxter), "contrary to their former judgments; but the body of Dissenters remained steadfast to their principles, and the church gained neither reputation nor members."[1]

The Conventicle Act having failed to accomplish its

[1] *Neal*, iv. 402.

purpose, and the time specified for its operation having expired, a severer law was passed in the spring of 1670. All persons attending conventicles were to be fined five shillings for the first offence, ten shillings for the second; the preachers were to be fined twenty pounds for the first offence, forty pounds for the second; the owners of the houses, barns, buildings, or yards in which the meetings were held, were to be fined twenty pounds each time; the fines were to be "levied by distress and sale of the offender's goods and chattels;" the money was to be divided into three parts—one-third for the king, one-third for the poor, and "the other third to the informer or his assistants, regard being had to their diligence and industry in discovering, dispersing, and punishing the said conventicles;" and in case of the poverty of the ministers, the fines imposed on them were to be levied "on the goods and chattels of any other present." Any justice of the peace refusing to carry the act into execution was to be fined five pounds; and it was expressly declared, "That all clauses in the act should be construed most largely and beneficially for the suppressing of conventicles, and for the justification and encouragement of all persons to be employed in the execution thereof."[1]

If the first act scourged the Dissenters with whips, the second was a scorpion plague. They were plundered and imprisoned without remorse. To their disgrace be it spoken, Archbishop Sheldon and many of the bishops exerted themselves in every possible way to enforce the act. They sent circulars to the clergy, directing them to stimulate and aid the civil authorities; and some of the bishops went in person to the places where meetings were

[1] Neal, 426.

supposed to be held, in order to encourage the constables, or ensure the rigorous discharge of their duty.

The activity of the informers was excited by the promised share of the penalties. Their infamous trade became lucrative, and many of them amassed large sums, mercilessly filched from the servants of God. A more degrading and detestable occupation cannot well be imagined. They spent their time in prowling about the retired streets and by-lanes of towns, or in exploring the recesses of woods, and wild, desolate places, if happily they might hear the voice of singing or prayer, or watch the movements of some straggler, hastening to join his brethren. With savage glee they darted upon the secret assembly, gloating over their confusion and distress, and specially rejoicing when they seized the preacher, because of the heavier fine. They accompanied the constables when they executed warrants of distress on property; and they attended the sales of the goods seized, taking care to get bargains for themselves. They scrupled not to take the bed from under the sick; they robbed of their bread children whose fathers were languishing in prison. The law created their calling, and encouraged them in diligently pursuing it. Magistrates urged them on. Clergymen and country squires applauded their cleverness, and judges on the bench commended them for their zeal There was an unholy alliance against truth and righteousness, in which the titled and the learned were willing to associate themselves with the meanest, the wickedest, and the most brutal of men.

The prisons were crowded. Families were ruined. Houses were desolated. Estates were impoverished or abandoned. Numbers fled their native shores, and sought in Holland or in the American wilderness for "freedom to worship God."

I will give the details of one case. On Lord's Day, the 29th of May, 1670, the Baptists of Lewes, in Sussex, met for worship in a house about a mile from the town. Two persons watched them and became informers. The minister was fined twenty pounds, and forty of the hearers five shillings each; but as the minister was poor, his fine was imposed on five members of the congregation. All the fines were recovered by levying distresses on property, which was done forthwith.

Walter Brett was a grocer; his fine, six pounds five shillings. The constables took from him two barrels of sugar which cost him more than fifteen pounds.

Thomas Barnard was fined six pounds five shillings, and his brother five pounds five shillings. Six cows were taken from them, worth twenty-seven pounds.

Richard White, brazier, was fined three pounds fifteen shillings; for which, brass kettles and other articles were seized, the value of which was upward of ten pounds.

John Tabret's fine was two pounds fifteen shillings; a cow was taken for it.

John Price and wife were fined ten shillings, to pay which sum four cheeses were taken. Price told the constables that "he never sold anything to so great an advantage, for this would bring him an hundred fold." (See Matt. xix. 29.)

The same system of excessive and heartless distraint was pursued in levying the fines of five shillings each upon the other hearers. Five pairs of shoes from one shoemaker; three pairs from another; three hats from a haberdasher; a horse from a butcher; the sheets from a poor mason's bed, and his wife's under-apparel—and so on.

Shortly after this a meeting was held in a house about three miles from Lewes. The owner was fined twenty pounds, and to meet it they took from him the whole of his stock, being six cows, two young bullocks, and a horse.[1]

[1] Ivimey, i. 366–377.

CHAPTER VI.

History of the Broadmead Church, Bristol.

PERHAPS we shall obtain a clearer view of the actual condition of the Baptists in the reign of Charles II. from the history of one church than from any other source. We are fortunately furnished with such a history. The records of the church at Broadmead, Bristol, have been published by the Hanserd Knollys Society. I will give an extract of the narrative:

This church was founded in 1640. The members met regularly for worship, whether they could obtain the services of a minister or not, the gifted brethren helping by prayer and exhortation. In 1651, Mr. Ewins, who had been a minister in the Episcopal Church, became their pastor. Under his ministry the church prospered. In addition to the Lord's Day exercise, they met on Thursday evenings in private houses for free conference on the Scriptures and mutual exhortation. Those meetings were found very profitable.

But in 1661 their troubles began. On the 27th of July in that year, Mr. Ewins was apprehended while preaching. He was released on the 25th of September following, and immediately recommenced his work. Next year he endured another short imprisonment. A heavier trial came upon them in 1663. Mr. Ewins and several others were arrested on the 4th of October, and indicted at the quarter sessions for a riot. Various fines were imposed—Mr. Ewins was fined £50—and the parties adjudged to lie in prison till the fines were paid. So the prison became the parsonage till the following September, when a compromise was effected, and on payment of part of the money the prisoners were released. Mr. Ewins had not been idle, however. The people were accustomed to gather around the prison, and their pastor preached to them from the window of the room which he occupied, on the fourth story. "The word of the Lord was precious in those days."

Hitherto they had met in a "chapel called the Friars," but now they were compelled for a time to worship in private houses. The constables frequently disturbed them, and many were imprisoned and fined. Sometimes, when they learned that the officers were coming, they evaded them by taking refuge in a cellar, and sometimes by climbing into a garret. Still they resolutely kept up their assemblies. "In the year 1665," they say, "we had many disturbances, and divers imprisoned, but the Lord helped us through it." Their firmness was remarkably shown by a resolution passed to the effect that *those who absented themselves from worship through fear should be dealt with as disorderly members.* The names of all the members were engrossed on parchment, and the roll was called once a month, when they met for the Lord's supper, "to see who doth omit their duty." Not many were willing to expose themselves to church censure, but now and then a case occurred, and the delinquents were excluded " for neglecting their duty of assembling, through fear."

When the plague broke out in Bristol, in 1666, a stop was put to the persecution. There was peace for four years. In 1667 the church obtained another " public meeting-place." It was " a large warehouse, up one pair of stairs." Mr. Ewins died April 26th, 1670. In the following month the police made their appearance again, and took some members of the congregation to the magistrates, who fined them. This was repeated several Lord's Days; but they secured the preacher by breaking a hole in the wall, so that he could stand in a room of the adjoining house, and preach without being seen. Thus their enemies were baffled. The opposition becoming more violent, they adopted another course. They nailed up the doors of the meeting-house, and " we were fain," the record states, " to meet in the lanes and highways for several months."

Another interval of tranquillity was enjoyed. They invited Mr. Thomas Hardcastle, who had been preaching some time in London, to become their pastor. He was in prison when the invitation reached him. After his release he visited the church, and subsequently accepted the charge, in 1671. In that year they procured " the meeting-house at the lower end of Broadmead, where the heretics called Quakers had formerly used to meet; it being four great rooms made into one square room, about sixteen yards long and fifteen yards broad." There Mr. Hardcastle preached upward of three years without any disturbance.

But in 1674 there came a new bishop to Bristol, " one Guy Carleton "—" though aged and gray, a violent man against good people that separated from that which he called the church." . . . "He resolved to destroy all our meetings, and said he would not leave a track of a meeting in Bristol; but would make us all come to church, as he called it." With him was leagued George Hellier, a lawyer, who took up the trade of an informer, and found it more lucrative than his profession. He spent the Lord's Days in going from one meeting-house to another, in search of prey. His chief object was to seize the minister, partly in the hope of suppressing the meetings thereby, and partly for the sake of the heavy fine. Mr. Hardcastle was apprehended Feb. 4, 1675, and committed to jail for six months. But the meetings were not discontinued, although arrests took place nearly every Lord's Day. In order to protect the preacher, a curtain was prepared, by which, when drawn, a portion of the room was separated. About fifty persons could sit behind the curtain, the preacher being placed among them, undistinguished. Care was taken that a number of "women and maids" should sit on the staircase, "so that the informers could not quickly run up." By this contrivance, whenever Hellier and his minions were approaching, notice was given, the curtain was drawn, the service ceased, and the whole congregation, according to a preconcerted arrangement, commenced singing a psalm. When the informers entered at such a time, they were utterly confused. It was impossible to tell who had been preaching; and singing psalms was no crime. But "justice had fallen in the streets," and they rarely failed to drag away some of the congregation to prison, and to procure the infliction of fines upon them.

Mr. Hardcastle was released from prison at the end of

six months; but on the second Lord's Day after his release, he was apprehended while preaching, and sent to jail again. During this second term of imprisonment he wrote a weekly letter to the church, which was read at the Lord's Day meetings. These letters have been preserved. They are admirably adapted to the instruction and comfort of a people under such trying circumstances. And they were much needed. Toward the end of the year the meetings were "grown very poor and lean, through fines, imprisonments, and constant worrying of us every day." On one occasion the bishop himself was among the constables!

I will transcribe a few passages from Mr. Hardcastle's letters:

"It has been our great error that we have not trusted in the power of God. We have reasoned about the worst that men can do, but have not believed the best that God can do. Sense and carnal reason must be left behind in the things of God."

"The preaching of the gospel is the ordinance of Christ, and so is the imprisonment of the preachers of the gospel; but I never knew that forbearing to preach, for fear of a prison, did ever convince or establish any one."

"Keep your consciences, keep your confidences, keep your communions, and all is well enough."

"Wicked men, and ungodly men, are prevented of doing that mischief they design against the people of God, when they trust in his power. And godly men are disappointed of that good which they expect from other men, when, by such expectings, their faith in the omnipotence of God is weakened and divided."

"Precious faith makes sin rare to a believer; and to

see sin most vile, makes faith most precious, because it keeps a due distance between the precious and the vile. Now, common and counterfeit faith makes no such distinctions, no such separation; knows no such awe and tenderness; admits of the prevalency of corruptness with the eminency of privileges, the power of ungodliness with the form of godliness; sees no such unhandsomeness, nor uncomeliness, to have the money-changers in the temple; does not think that there is such need of that strictness, niceness, and circumspection amongst believers. This creed-faith, baptism-faith, supper-faith—in a word, this tradition, profession, conviction-faith, that is a stranger to this preciousness and power—will in case make no great matter of handling and taking up a sin, or letting fall a duty, if men see not or say nothing. Outward profession and performances are its paint; natural conscience, credit, interest, custom, or company are its pulleys."

"The Lord will save his people with a 'notwithstanding.' How is this?

"1. Notwithstanding their own unworthiness, imperfections, backslidings, and unfitness for mercies.

"2. Notwithstanding their fears, faintings, despondencies, unbelief, and positive conclusion against themselves, their hopes, and the returns of mercy.

"3. Notwithstanding all the improbabilities, and growing oppositions and obstructions that seem to lie in the way of their peace and deliverance.

"4. Notwithstanding the power, prevalency, expectations, interests, and insultings of their enemies.

"5. Notwithstanding many tokens and testimonies of his own displeasure and indignation against them, and a kind of resolution not to show mercy to them any more. See Hosea ii. 4-7, 14, 15, 23; Judges x. 11-17. I must conclude with this: Peter was afraid, and he began to sink; our fears are the great cause of our sinkings. But when he began to sink, Christ came to his relief, and saved him; he will make you to cry out, but he will not suffer you to perish. The Lord increase your faith."

"The kingdom of God is that which is primarily promised, and principally to be sought after. Other things are consequential and cautionary; secondary helps, made use of as lesser means; baits, not business. A little of them helps a traveler on his journey more comfortably; but a great deal proves his burden and his hindrance. Heaven is the great deed of settlement; the earth is but the loose money to bear the charges—the staff to walk to the kingdom."

From the beginning of 1676 to the middle of 1680 there was a lull in the storm. Mr. Hardcastle died in 1678, and was succeeded by Mr. George Fownes in September, 1679.

Interruption of their worship was resumed in July, 1680, and continued at times through that year and the next. In December, 1681, Mr. Fownes and a large number of the brethren were seized and sent to prison. He preached to them there. Twenty-four of them were brought up at the quarter sessions, and obliged to give bail for their appeaance when called on to answer an indictment for a breach of the peace, with which they were most unrighteously threatened. Mr. Fownes was detained, but the brethren were determined to test the legality of his imprisonment, and procured a writ of *habeas corpus*, by which means his cause was taken to the Court of King's Bench at London, and he was ultimately discharged, although he was still prevented from preaching in public, by the operation of the Five-Mile Act.

The years 1682 and 1683 were the darkest times to them. They held their meetings in private houses, in the fields, or in the woods, wherever they could best escape the vigilance of the authorities. Mayor, aldermen, and constables could hardly have gone to church at all in those years, for all their time was spent in hunting after Dissenters' meetings. A few brief extracts from the records will show how our ancestors fared:

1682. *Jan.* 29.—The church met at four different places. Many of them "went in the afternoon on Durdham Down, and got into a cave of a rock toward Clifton, where Brother Thomas Whinnell preached to them."

March 12.—"Met in the fields by Barton Hundred, and Mr. Samuel Buttall of Plymouth preached in the forepart of the day, and Brother Whinnell in the evening. It was thought there were near a thousand persons in the morning."

March 19.—"Met in the lanes beyond Baptist Mills."

April 13.—"Met in the rain in a lane."

April 20.—"A day of prayer, from nine to five in the evening, at Mr. Jackon's over the Down, in peace."

May 4.—"Information was brought to a petty session for Gloucestershire, against Brother Jennings, for preaching in the lanes, and a warrant granted for levying five pounds, or else goods, or person."

June 11.—"Brother Fownes being come from London, but not daring to come into the city because of the Corporation Act, met with us, and preached in Kingswood, near Scruze Hole, under a tree, and endured the rain."

July 2.—" Our pastor preached in another place in the wood. Our friends took much pains in the rain, because many informers were ordered out to search; and we were in peace, though there were near twenty men and boys in search."

July 16.—" Brother Fownes first, and Brother Whinnell after, preached under a tree, it being very rainy."

August 20.—" Met above Scruze Hole, in our old place, and heard Brother Fownes preach twice in peace. Brother Terrill had caused a workman to make banks on the side of the hill to sit down on, several of them like a gallery; and there we met also on the 27th, in peace. On both days we sang a psalm in the open woods."

"On the 7th of December we met for our lecture at Mr. Shuter's on Redcliffe Hill in peace, taking a great deal of care in going and coming, the women wearing neither white aprons nor pattens."

1683. *Jan.* 21.—" We met at eight in the morning, and though there were seven on horseback and twenty on foot to seek after us, we escaped, having broken up at ten."

March.—" This week about one hundred and fifty Dissenters were convicted by our recorder, on the statute of 23d Eliz., for £20 a month, for not coming to church."

March 25.—Mr. Fownes, though "very ill, went to the meetings in the wood; but after three quarters of an hour we were surrounded by horse and foot, the former in ambush." Mr. Fownes was arrested and **sent** to Gloucester jail for six months.

April 22.—" We went out at four in the morning, and were in peace."

November 14.—" A day of prayer, having some hours together in the wood, between London and Sodbury Road: the enemy came upon us unawares, and seized about eight persons; but the brethren escaped to admiration. The bushes were of great service to us." A number of the sisters were taken: "they got Justice Fitz Herbert to come, and upon examination he could get little out of them, and could not learn who was the preacher; so they were let go."

December 20.—" Watkins the marshal, and others, went with warrants from Justice Herbert to Brother John Morgan, in Temple street, and took his yarn and what goods they could find, for seven pounds ten shillings. And the day before took away Margaret Seymour's trunk and clothes, with about thirty pounds, for seven pounds odd money, for being at our meeting in the fields."

December 30.—" Being a hard frost, and snow on the ground, we met in the wood, and though we stood in the snow, the sun shone upon us, and we were in peace."

1684. *March* 4.—" We took our sad state into consideration; and Brother Terrill signified that our duty lay in three things: 1st. To watch over one another, that none draw back to the world's worship. 2d. That every one sanctify the Lord's Day. 3d. That we endeavor to edify one another as members, and also do what we can for others' souls. And, considering what is above, and that writs are daily expected to levy £20 a month, £240 per annum a man, upon us, for not coming to church, or imprison us if it be not paid, there being thirteen brethren present, we agreed to have circular meetings at five places, where the brethren were to exercise their gifts, and twice in a day, at nine in the morning and at one in the afternoon. These five places were, 1st, Brother Dickson or Davis; 2d, Brother Clark or Robert Lewis; 3d, Brother Whinnell; 4th, Brother Ellis or J. Cornish; 5th Brother Terrill. And also three places for prayer and repetition; viz., Brother Gwilliam's, Brother Bodenham's, Brother Reeve's. And because some might be sick or otherwise detained, we appointed six or seven to a place, and the first four were to be taken in, and that those that were shut out were to go to the places of repetition. And none were to go to a place but once a day, and not to the same place every Lord's Day; but round, so they came to the same once in five weeks. And by this means near one hundred might hear every Lord's Day, and in a few weeks have the benefit of all the church's gifts. And besides, Brother Whinnell would repeat again at some house in the evening, and on week-days at other places. Thus we kept within the law, which allowed four besides the family. And on the ninth of March we began this circular meeting."

April 10.—" Brother Warren was fined £10 for a riot, being at a meeting near Roe Gate, and fees 47*s*., which he paid in the hall at Gloucester. But Lugg was forsworn in it, for he swore it was on the 27th, and it was on the 29th day that the meeting was. Old Brother Cornish was bound to appear again next sessions, and several others. Some were fined 40*s*. and their fees, and released. Sister Fowles was put in prison at Gloucester Some were fined five marks, as Mr Jos. Wey; some £5, as the justices pleased, and to lie in prison till paid. About this time Pug Read died miserably, being an in former about twenty years old : had his skull broke, as said, by one of his companions ; he was one that broke into Mr. Terrill's house."

September 16.—" Several of our brethren, Brother Hunt, William Dickason, etc., and many more, were summoned by the apparitor to the bishop's court, for not receiving the Lord's supper."

October 7.—" Nearly twenty more friends were indicted for eleven months' not coming to church." . . . " And Brother Fownes being brought into court, was by Powell, the chairman, called a ringleader, turbulent, seditious, and told he must find six hundred pounds' bail to appear next sessions at Bristol, and be of good behavior, or lie in prison."

October 10.—" New mayor and sheriff being chosen, James Twyford, sheriff, threatens to find out our little meetings, and he would be like death—spare none."

1685. *January* 13.—" At the quarter sessions, Brother Fownes was treated as before, and Justice Powell, the chairman, told him Sir Richard Hart, of Bristol, should say he was a dangerous man. So they still kept him there at Gloucester, prisoner."

" On the 29th of November, 1685, *our pastor, Brother Fownes, died in Gloucester jail*, having been kept there for two years and about nine months a prisoner, unjustly and maliciously, for the testimony of Jesus and preaching the gospel." He was originally committed for six months, but they would not release him unless he would give bond for his good behavior, which meant that he would not preach again. This, of course, he would not do.

Thus the enemy prevailed, and the servants of God were brought low. Truly, they were " perilous times."

CHAPTER VII.

Declaration of Indulgence—Confession of Faith—Fierce Persecution—Thomas Delaune—The Duke of Monmouth's Rebellion—Account of the Hewlings—Mrs. Gaunt—The Dark Time—Another Declaration of Indulgence—William Kiffin—The Glorious Revolution.

THERE were some intervals of rest during this period. King Charles was bent on removing the restrictions imposed on Roman Catholics, and on several occasions the severity of the persecution was relaxed, in the hope that some general measure would be introduced in Parliament embracing all parties. In 1672 he issued a "Declaration of Indulgence," by which, in the exercise of the prerogative, the operation of the penal enactment was suspended during the royal pleasure. Many Nonconformist ministers availed themselves of it, and took out licenses to preach.

But the Dissenters generally refused to receive the "Declaration," declaring it an unlawful exercise of the prerogative, and fearing the consequences that might follow the admission of Roman Catholics to power. They did more. They submitted without a murmur to the Test Act, which was passed in 1673, and by which all persons who accepted office of any kind under the government were required to take the Lord's supper according to the rites of the Church of England, and to subscribe a declaration against transubstantiation. The primary object of that act was the exclusion of Roman Catholics from power, and that being accomplished, it was expected that the door would be opened to Protestant Dissenters by a repeal of the test, as far as they were concerned. But bigotry kept the door shut till the year 1828, and the Lord's supper was all that time "an office key, a picklock to a place."

In the midst of the uncertainties and perils of the times, a meeting of ministers and delegates was summoned in 1675, to consider the propriety of taking steps for the education of candidates for the ministry. Whether the meeting was held or not, I am not able to say; but the proposal itself, under those circumstances, indicates moral courage as well as enlightened views.

Two years after, a Confession of Faith was published, under the following title: "A Confession of Faith, put forth by the elders and brethren of many congregations of Christians (baptized upon profession of their faith) in London and the country. With an Appendix concerning baptism."

In doctrinal points the language of the Assembly's Confession is for the most part adopted, while on baptism and church government the views of our denomination are very clearly and fully expressed. The alleged grounds of infant baptism are critically examined in the appendix, and their insufficiency proved. "Let it not therefore be judged of us (because much hath been written on this subject, and yet we continue this our practice different from others) that it is out of obstinacy; but rather, as the truth is, that we do herein, according to the best of our understandings, worship God, out of a pure mind, yielding obedience to his precept, in that method which we take to be most agreeable to the Scriptures of truth and primitive practice. . . . It would not become us to give any such intimation as should carry a semblance that what we do in the service of God is with a doubting conscience, or with any such temper of mind, that we do thus for the present with a reservation that we will do otherwise hereafter upon more mature deliberation; nor have we any cause so to do, being fully persuaded that what we do is agreeable to the will of God. Yet we do heartily propose this, that if any of the servants of our Lord Jesus Christ shall, in the spirit of meekness, attempt to convince us of any mistake, either in judgment or practice, we shall diligently ponder his arguments, and account him our chiefest friend that shall be an instrument to convert us from any error that is in our ways; for we cannot wittingly do anything against the truth, but all things for the truth."[1]

This is thoroughly Baptist language. So we have always held and professed. We are "ready to give an answer to any man that asketh us a reason of the hope that is in us," and we trust that we shall ever be thankful to any man who will convince us of error or show us "a more excellent way."

The persecution raged furiously in the latter years of the reign of Charles II. It seemed to be the settled policy of the Court to crush the Nonconformists. Informers fattened on them. Judges and magistrates encouraged the informers, and were in their turn urged to greater diligence and zeal in their infamous career by the

[1] *Confessions of Faith, etc.*, p. 232.

clergy, even by bishops. Some of the Nonconformists were cited to the spiritual courts and excommunicated, which was tantamount to ruin, as an excommunicated person was out of the protection of the law. Others were prosecuted for attending conventicles or for not going to church, and their property was seized for the payment of fines. So numerous were these cases that in the small town of Uxbridge and its neighborhood (fifteen miles from London) " two hundred warrants of distress were issued." The ministers, particularly, were hunted down like wild beasts. Many of them were under the necessity of selling their household furniture and books, in order to provide food for their starving families. It has been estimated that property to the amount of two millions sterling in value was taken from the Nonconformists during the reigns of Charles II. and James II.

The prisons were crowded, and great numbers died in confinement—as really put to death—murdered—as if they had been hanged or shot. I will select one instance:

Thomas Delaune was a native of Ireland. His parents were Roman Catholics. The gentleman on whose estate they lived noticing in young Delaune an aptness for study, sent him to a friary at Kilcrash, about seven miles from Cork, for education. Having remained there nine years, he obtained a situation at Kingsale, as clerk to a Mr. Bampfield, who was largely engaged in the pilchard fishery. Mr. Bampfield's efforts were blessed to his conversion from Popery and sin. After some years he found it necessary to leave Ireland, his religious zeal having excited persecution. He settled ultimately in London, as a schoolmaster, and was well known as a pious, learned, and exemplary man. He enjoyed the friendship of Benjamin Keach, William Kiffin, and other Baptist ministers, by whom he was much esteemed.

Dr. Benjamin Calamy, one of the royal chaplains, published a sermon, entitled "A Scrupulous Conscience." He challenged the Nonconformists to a discussion of the points at issue between the Church of England and themselves, and invited them to propose their doubts and difficulties, that the truth might be ascertained. Mr. Delaune accepted the challenge, and wrote his "Plea for the Nonconformists," in which the subject is handled with consummate ability. "The book," says Defoe, "is perfect in itself. Never author left behind him a more finished piece; and I believe the dispute is entirely ended. If any man ask what we can say, why the Dissenters differ from the Church of England, and what they can plead for it, I can recommend no better reply than this. Let them answer, in short, Thomas Delaune, and desire the querist to read the book." Before the work was finished at press, it was seized by a king's messenger, and its author lodged in jail. He was first "committed to Wood Street Compter, and lodged among the common-side prisoners, where he had a hard bench for his bed, and two bricks for his pillows." Thence he was removed to Newgate, and placed among the felons, whose "horrid company," as he wrote to Dr. Calamy, gave him "a perfect representation of that horrid place which you describe when you mention hell." He was afterward allowed to associate with prisoners of a better sort. Before his trial he appealed to Dr. Calamy for friendly interference on his behalf. The doctor, as he reminded him, had invited discussion, and in writing the book he had but responded to his challenge. But instead of the treatment which one scholar ought to expect from another, he was cast into prison. He "would fain be convinced by something more like divinity than Newgate." "I had some thoughts," he said in another communication, "that you would have performed the office of a divine, in visiting me in my place of confinement; either to argue me out of my doubts, which your promised *Scripture* and *reason*, not a *mittimus* or *Newgate*, could easily do. To the former I can yield. To the latter it seems I must. This is a severe kind of logic, and will probably dispute me out of this world." But Dr. Calamy was deaf to his appeal, and ungenerous enough to abstain from exercising any influence on behalf of his opponent.

Mr. Delaune was tried at the Old Bailey in January, 1684, for " a certain false, seditious, and scandalous libel against the king and the Book of Common Prayer." He entreated that the question might be thoroughly and fairly examined. "I desire," he said, "that the entire paragraphs may be read, from which the crimes charged against me are inferred. If fragments only be produced, from which no perfect sense can be deduced, I shall be unfairly dealt with. The coherence of sense in a continued discourse, not scraps and broken pieces of sentences, can demonstrate the scope of an argument. If what I have written be true, it is no crime, unless truth be made a crime. If false, let Dr. Calamy or any of the guides of your church confute me, as he promised in his sermon aforesaid, by good Scripture and good reason; then will I submit. If the latter method be not taken, I must repeat it, 'tis very hard, my lord, 'tis very hard."

No doubt it was " hard, very hard." But Jeffreys was on the bench! A verdict of " guilty" was recorded, and the sentence ran thus: "Thomas Delaune fined a hundred marks, and to be kept prisoner, etc., and to find good security for his good behavior for one whole year afterward; and that the said books and seditious libels by him published shall be burnt with fire before the Royal Exchange, London."

The sentence consigned him to a slow and painful martyrdom. I quote Defoe again, who wrote a recommendatory preface to the seventeenth edition of the "Plea:"

"The expensive prosecution, depriving him of his livelihood, which was a grammar school, and long imprisonment, had made him not only unable to pay his fine, but unable to subsist himself and his family.

"He continued in close confinement in the prison of Newgate about fifteen months, and suffered there great hardships by extreme poverty, being so entirely reduced by this disaster that he had no subsistence but what was contributed by such friends as came to visit him.

"His behavior in this distress was like the greatness of mind he discovered at his trial. And the same spirit which appears in his writings appeared in his conversation, and supported him with invincible patience under the greatest extremities. But long confinement and distresses of various kinds at last conquered him. He had a wife and two small children, all with him in the prison, for they had no subsistence elsewhere. The closeness and inconvenience of the place first affected them, and all three, by lingering sorrow and sickness, died in the prison. At last, worn out with trouble, and hopeless of relief, and too much abandoned by those who should have taken some other care of him, this excellent person sank under the burden, and died there also I cannot refrain saying such a champion, of such a cause, deserved better usage. And it was very hard, such a man, such a Christian, such a scholar, and on such an occasion, should starve in a dungeon; and that the whole body of Dissenters in England, whose cause he died for defending, should not raise him £66 13s. 4d. to save his life."

"Had I been a minister," said John Sharp, pastor of the Baptist church at Frome, Somersetshire, soon after the Revolution of 1668, "I would have taken a horse, and rode till my skin was off, but I would have got the money to pay his fine."[1]

"I am sorry to say," Defoe observes, "he is one of near *eight thousand Protestant Dissenters* that perished in prison in the days of that merciful prince, King Charles II., and that merely for dissenting from the church in points which they could give such reasons for as this 'Plea' assigns; and for no other cause were stifled, I had almost said, murdered, in jails for their religion."

Soon after the accession of James II., the Duke of Monmouth's rebellion broke out, and involved great numbers in ruin. Some Baptists were compromised in it. That was not to be wondered at. James II. was a Papist and a tyrant. He was known to be a cold-hearted, bloodthirsty man It was not believed that the liberties of England would be safe in his keeping. Besides this, some of the insurgents regarded Monmouth as the legitimate son of Charles II., and therefore the right heir to the throne; while others deemed it better to overlook the stain of his birth, and thus secure a Protestant succession, than to expose the kingdom to the misrule of a popish

[1] Ivimey, ii. 556.

despot. Had the enterprise succeeded, they would have been applauded as patriots; by its defeat, their names were handed down to posterity as traitors. Numbers of them suffered the vengeance of the law. The brutal Judge Jeffreys presided at the trials, and hurried off his victims to the gibbet by the shortest process, and with all the glee of a practiced butcher.

The fate of two young men excited unusual commiseration. Benjamin and Thomas Hewling were grandsons of William Kiffin, whose daughter their father had married. The father having died, Mr. Kiffin took charge of the family, and assisted the surviving parent in giving them an excellent education and training. William was at a seminary in Holland when the Duke of Monmouth planned his ill-fated expedition. He accompanied the duke to England. Benjamin, "conversing with those that were under great dissatisfaction, seeing popery encouraged, and religion and liberty like to be invaded, did furnish himself with arms, and went to the said duke." After the disastrous battle of Sedgemoor, the two brothers attempted to escape by sea, but were driven back by contrary winds, and compelled to land and surrender themselves prisoners. After a short confinement in Exeter jail, they were conveyed to London, where they were lodged in Newgate, and remained there three weeks, when they were sent back into the West for trial.

Their grandfather labored hard to save them. Every thing was venal in those days. "It being given out," says Mr. Kiffin, "that the king would make only a few who had been taken examples, and would leave the rest to his officers, to compound for their lives, I attempted, with my daughter, their mother, to treat with a great man, agreeing to give him three thousand pounds if he would obtain their deliverance. But the face of things was soon altered, so that nothing but severity could be expected. Indeed, we missed the right door, for the Lord Chief Justice [Jeffreys] finding that agreements were made with others, and so little attention paid to himself, was the more provoked to use all manner of cruelty to the poor prisoners; so that few escaped, and amongst the rest those two young men were executed."[1]

Their sister was indefatigable in her endeavors on their behalf. When all other means had failed, she determined to present a petition to the king. "For this purpose she was introduced by Lord Churchill, afterward the celebrated Duke of Marlborough. While they waited in the antechamber for admittance, standing near the chimney-piece, Lord Churchill assured her of his most hearty wishes of success to her petition. 'But, madam,' said he, 'I dare not flatter you with any such hopes, for that marble is as capable of feeling compassion as the king's heart.'"[2]

So it proved. The king's heart was hard as adamant. The Hewlings were executed—William, at Lyme, September 12th, 1685; Benjamin, at Taunton, on the 30th of the same month. How they spent the last few days of their lives, and how they died, has been admirably told by their sister, of whose narrative I will give here a brief abstract:

"At Salisbury, the 30th of August, I had the first opportunity of conversing with them. I found them in a very excellent composure of mind, declaring their ex-

[1] *Life of Kiffin*, p. 63. [2] *Ibid.* p. 64.

perience of the grace and goodness of God to them in all their sufferings, in supporting and strengthening and providing for them, turning the hearts of all in whose hands they had been both at Exeter and on shipboard, to show pity and to favor them; although since they came to Newgate they were hardly used, and now in their journey loaded with heavy irons and more inhumanly dealt with. They with great cheerfulness professed that they were better and in a more happy condition than ever in their lives, from the sense they had of the pardoning love of God in Jesus Christ to their souls, wholly referring themselves to their wise and gracious God to choose for them life or death, expressing themselves thus: 'Any thing what pleaseth God; what he sees best, so be it. We know he is able to deliver; but if not, blessed be his name, death is not terrible now, but desirable.'"

"The sixth of September, Mr. Benjamin Hewling was ordered to Taunton, to be tried there. Taking my leave of him, he said, 'Oh, blessed be God for afflictions! I would not have been without them for all this world.'

"I remained still at Dorchester, to wait the issue of Mr. William Hewling, to whom, after trial, I had free access, and whose discourse was much filled with admirings of the grace of God which had been manifested toward him in calling him out of his natural state. He said, God by his Holy Spirit did suddenly seize upon his heart when he thought not of it, in his retired abode in Holland, as it were secretly whispering in his heart, 'Seek ye my face,' enabling him to answer his gracious call and to reflect upon his own soul, showing him the evil of sin and the necessity of Christ, from that time carrying him on to a sensible adherence to Christ for justification and eternal life. Hence he found a spring of joy and sweetness beyond the comforts of the whole earth."

"When I came to him the next morning, when he had received news that he must die the next day, and in order to it was to be carried to Lyme that day, I found him in a more excellent, raised, and spiritual frame than before. He was satisfied, he said, that God had chosen best for him. 'He knows what the temptations of life might have been. I might have lived and forgotten God; but now I am going where I shall sin no more. Oh, it is a blessed thing to be freed from sin and to be with Christ! Oh how great were the sufferings of Christ for me, beyond all I can undergo! How great is the glory to which I am going! It will soon swallow up all our sufferings here!'

"As they passed through the town of Dorchester to Lyme, multitudes of people beheld them with great lamentations, admiring his deportment at his parting with his sister. Passing on the road, his discourse was excedingly spiritual, taking occasion from everything to speak of the glory they were going to. Looking at the country as he passed, he said, 'This is a glorious creation; but what then is the paradise of God to which we are going! It is but a few hours, and we shall be there, and be for ever with the Lord.'

"At Lyme, just before they went to die, reading John xiv. 8, he said to one of his fellow-sufferers, 'Here is a sweet promise for us: *I will not leave you comfortless; I will come unto you.* Christ will be with us to the last!' One taking leave of him, he said, 'Farewell till we meet in heaven. Presently we shall be with Christ. Oh, I would not change condition with any one in the world. I would not stay behind for ten thousand worlds.'

"Afterward he prayed for three quarters of an hour with the greatest fervency, exceedingly blessing God for Jesus Christ, adoring the riches of his grace in him, in all the glorious fruits of it toward him, praying for the peace of the church of God, and of these nations in particular; all with such eminent assistance of the Spirit of God as convinced, astonished, and melted into pity the hearts of all present, even the most malicious adversaries, forcing tears and expressions from them; some saying, they knew not what would become of *them* after death, but it was evident *he* was going to great happiness.

"When just departing out of the world, with a joyful countenance, he said, 'Oh, now my joy and comfort is that I have a Christ to go to;' and so sweetly resigned his spirit to Christ.

"An officer who had shown so malicious a spirit as to call the prisoners 'devils' when he was guarding them down, was now so convinced that he afterward told a person of quality that he was never so affected as by his cheerful carriage and fervent prayer, such as he believed was never heard, especially from one so young; and said, 'I believe, had the Lord Chief Justice been here, he would not have let him die.'

"The sheriff having given his body to be buried, although it was brought from the place of execution without any notice given, yet very many of the town, to the number of two hundred, came to accompany him; and several young women of the best of the town laid him in his grave in Lyme churchyard, September 13th, 1685.

"When I came to Taunton to Mr. Bejamin Hewling, he expressed himself to this effect: 'We have no cause to fear death if the presence of God be with us; there is no evil in it, the sting being taken away. It is nothing but our ignorance of the glory the saints pass into by death which makes it appear dark to ourselves or our relations: if in Christ, what is the world that we should desire an abode in it? It is all vain and unsatisfying, full of sin and misery.' He also intimated his own cheerful expectations soon to follow (he had just heard of his brother's death), discovering then and all along great seriousness and sense of spiritual and eternal things, complaining of nothing in his present circumstances but want of a place of retirement to converse more uninterruptedly with God and his own soul; saying that his lonely time in Newgate was the sweetest in his whole life.'

"When there was a general report that no more should die, he said, 'I do not know what God hath done contrary to our expectations; if he doth prolong my life, I am sure it is all his own, and by his grace I will wholly devote it to him.' But on the 29th of September, between ten and eleven at night, we found the deceitfulness of this report, they being then told that they must die the next morning, which was very unexpected as to the suddenness of it. But herein God glorified his power, grace, and faithfulness, in giving suitable support and comfort by his blessed presence, which appeared upon my coming to him at that time and finding him greatly composed. He said, 'Though men design to surprise, God doth and will perform his word, to be a very present help in trouble.'

"The next morning, when I saw him again, his cheerfulness and comfort were much increased, waiting for the sheriff with the greatest sweetness and serenity of mind. . . . With a smiling countenance, he discoursed of the glory of heaven. . . . His hope and comfort still increasing, with the assurance of an interest in that glorious inheritance to the possession of which he was now going, he said, ' death was more desirable than life, and he would rather die than live any longer here.' . . . Then, reading the Scriptures and musing with himself, he intimated the great comfort which God conveyed to his soul in it; saying, 'Oh, what an invaluable treasure is this blessed word of God. In all conditions, here is a store of strong consolation.' One desiring his Bible, he said, ' No; this shall be my companion to the last moment of my life.'

"Thus praying together, reading, meditating, and conversing of heavenly things, they waited for the sheriff, who, when he came, void of all pity and civility, hurried them away, scarcely suffering them to take leave of their friends. Notwithstanding this, and the doleful mourning of all about them, the joyfulness of his countenance was increased. Thus he left the prison, and thus he appeared in the sledge, where they sat about half an hour before the officers could force the horses to draw; at which they were greatly enraged, there being no visible obstruction from weight or way. At last the mayor and sheriff haled them forward themselves, Balaam-like, driving the horses.

"When they came to the place of execution, which was surrounded with spectators, many that waited their coming said, that when they saw him and them come with such cheerfulness and joy, and evidence of the presence of God with them, it made death appear with another aspect. They first embraced each other with the greatest affection; then two of the elder persons praying audibly, they joined with great seriousness. Then he [Benjamin] required leave of the sheriff to pray particularly; but he would not grant it, and only asked him whether he would pray for the king. He answered, 'I pray for all men.' He then requested that they might sing a hymn. The sheriff told him it must be with the rope round their necks; which they cheerfully accepted, and sung with such heavenly joy and sweetness that many who were present said it both broke and rejoiced their hearts. Thus in the experience of the delightfulness of praising God on earth, he willingly closed his eyes on a vain world, to pass to that eternal enjoyment.

"All present of all sorts were exceedingly affected and amazed. Some officers who had before insultingly said, 'Surely these persons have no thoughts of death, but will find themselves surprised by it,' now acknowledged that they saw he and they had something extraordinary within, which carried them through with so much joy. Others said that they were so convinced of their happiness that they would be glad to change conditions with them. The soldiers in general, and all others, lamented exceedingly, saying, 'It was so sad a thing to see them so cut off that they scarcely knew how to bear it.' Some of the most malicious in the place, from whom nothing but railing was expected, said, as they were carried to their grave in Taunton church, 'These persons have left sufficient evidence that they are now glorified spirits in heaven.' A great officer also in the king's army has often been heard to say, 'If you would learn to die, go to the young men of Taunton.'"[1]

The execution of Mrs. Gaunt was another horrible affair. It is one of the blackest in the catalogue of crimes with which James II. stands charged in history.

Elizabeth Gaunt was a Baptist lady, resident in London. Her life was a series of charitable acts. She was constantly engaged in visiting the jails, and administering succor, according to her means, to the distressed and unfortunate. On the discovery of the Rye House plot, one Burton, who was deeply implicated in it, and for whose apprehension a reward of 100*l*. was offered, found shelter in her house. She assisted him to escape to Holland, where he lived some months. He returned to England with the Duke of Monmouth, and was at the battle of Sedgemoor. After wandering about some time he obtained concealment in the house of John Fernley, a barber, in Whitechapel, London. Fernley was a poor man, but though he knew of the reward that had been offered for Burton's apprehension, he would not betray him. Much as he wanted money, his honor was not to be sold. That noble feeling cost him his life. The wretch Burton learned that the king was peculiarly exasperated against those who harbored traitors. He informed against both his protectors. They were brought to trial and convicted. Fernley was hanged, Mrs. Gaunt was burned alive, that being then the punishment of females for this offence. The only witnesses against her were the villain Burton and her own maid-servant; but the girl was ignorant of Burton's character and position, and could only testify to the concealment, so that

[1] *Life of Kiffin*, pp. 66–78.

the law's demand; requiring two witnesses, was not satisfied. But the judge who presided at the trial over ruled the exception taken on this account, and a verdict of "guilty" was brought in, in opposition to right. The good woman suffered the terrible punishment in such a manner as to excite strong sympathy in her favor. Bishop Burnet says, "She died with a constancy, even to cheerfulness, that struck all who saw it. She said charity was a part of her religion as well as faith; this at worst was feeding an enemy. So she hoped she had reward with Him for whose sake she did this service, how unworthy soever the person was who made so ill a return for it. She rejoiced that God had honored her to be the first that suffered by fire in this reign, and that her suffering was a martyrdom for that religion which was all love. Penn the Quaker told me that he saw her die. She laid the straw about her for burning her speedily, and behaved in such a manner that all the spectators melted in tears."[1]

This execution took place October 23d, 1685. When she left the prison for the place of burning, Mrs. Gaunt gave a paper to the keeper of Newgate, from which I extract the following paragraphs:

"Let none think hard or be discouraged at what hath happened unto me; for He doth nothing without cause in all that he hath done unto me; he being holy in all his ways and righteous in all his works; and it is but my lot in common with poor desolate Zion at this day. Neither do I find in my heart the least regret for anything I have done in the service of my Lord and Master, Jesus Christ, in securing and succoring any of his poor sufferers that

[1] *History of his Own Times,* iii. 62.

have showed favor, as I thought, to his righteous cause; which cause, though it be now fallen and trampled on, yet it may revive, and God may plead it at another time more than ever he hath yet done, with all its opposers and malicious haters. And I desire to bless his holy name that he hath made me useful in my generation, to the comfort and relief of many desolate ones; that the blessing of many who were ready to perish hath come unto me, and I have helped to make the widow's heart leap for joy. And I bless his holy name that in all this, together with what I was charged with, I can approve my heart to him, that I have done his will, though it doth cross man's."

Having mentioned several persons engaged in the prosecution, whose malice and cruelty had aggravated her sufferings, she proceeds: "All which, together with the great one of all [James II.], by whose power all these and multitudes more of cruelties are done, I do heartily and freely forgive, as against me; but as it is done in an implacable mind against the Lord Jesus Christ, and his righteous cause and followers, I leave it to him who is the avenger of all such wrong, and *who will tread upon princes as upon mortar, and be terrible to the kings of the earth.*"[1]

The darkest time in the history of the Dissenters during this period was the interval between the autumn of 1685 and the summer of 1686. Macaulay says: "Never, not even under the tyranny of Laud, had the condition of the Puritans been so deplorable as at that time. Never had spies been so actively employed in detecting congregations. Never had magistrates, grand juries, rectors,

[1] Ivimey, i. 456–458.

and churchwardens been so much on the alert. Many Dissenters were cited before the ecclesiastical courts. Others found it necessary to purchase the connivance of the agents of the government by presents of hogsheads of wine and of gloves stuffed with guineas. It was impossible for the sectaries to pray together without precautions such as are employed by coiners and receivers of stolen goods. The places of meeting were frequently changed. Worship was performed sometimes just before break of day and sometimes at dead of night. Round the building where the little flock was gathering together, sentinels were posted to give the alarm if a stranger drew near. The minister in disguise was introduced through the garden and back-yard. In some houses there were trap-doors, through which, in case of danger, he might descend. Where Nonconformists lived next door to each other, the walls were often broken open, and secret passages were made from dwelling to dwelling. No psalm was sung; and many contrivances were used to prevent the voice of the preacher, in his moments of fervor, from being heard beyond the walls. Yet, with all this care, it was often found impossible to elude the vigilance of informers. In the suburbs of London, especially, the law was enforced with the utmost rigor. Several opulent gentlemen were accused of holding conventicles. Their houses were strictly searched, and distresses were levied to the amount of many thousands of pounds. . . . Dissenting ministers, however blameless in life, however eminent for learning and abilities, could not venture to walk the streets for fear of outrages, which were not only not repressed, but encouraged, by those whose duty it was to preserve the peace. Some divines of great fame were in prison. Among these was Richard Baxter. Others, who had, during a quarter of a century, borne up against oppression, now lost heart, and quitted the kingdom. Among these was John Howe."[1]

Then the king suddenly changed his policy. Assuming power to suspend the laws by the exercise of the royal prerogative, he first caused licenses to be issued, which protected the parties holding them from all persecuting annoyances, and permitted them to reoccupy their places of worship; and this was followed in April, 1687, by the celebrated "Declaration of Indulgence," removing, during his majesty's pleasure, all restraints on Nonconformity, whether Protestant or Popish. The design of these acts was the establishment of popery, but it was cloaked by a pretended regard for liberty of conscience.

Some few of the Baptists were induced to join in an address to the king, thanking him for this unlooked-for freedom. The majority, however, viewed his proceedings as altogether unconstitutional, and would not compromise themselves by taking any step which might be construed as an admission of their legality. While they availed themselves of the newly-acquired liberty, they regarded it as the restoration of a right of which they had been unjustly deprived, and not as the bestowment of a boon.

Hoping thereby to gain assistance in carrying into effect his ulterior purposes, James II. courted the Dissenters. Among them was William Kiffin. The king had taken away the charter of the city of London, and undertaken to remodel the government of the city by arbitrary appointments of his own. "Kiffin, says Noble, in his *Memoirs of the House of Cromwell*, "was per-

[1] *History of England*, vol. i. chap. v.

sonally known both to Charles and James; and when the latter of these princes, after having arbitrarily deprived the city of the old charters, determined to put many of the Dissenters into the magistracy, under the rose he sent for Kiffin to attend him at Court. When he went thither in obedience to the king's commandment, he found many lords and gentlemen. The king immediately came up to him, and addressed him with all the little grace he was master of. He talked of his favor to the Dissenters in the court style of this season, and concluded by telling Kiffin that he had put him down as an alderman in his new charter. 'Sire,' replied Kiffin, 'I am a very old man, and have withdrawn myself from all kind of business for some years past, and am incapable of doing any service in such an affair to your majesty in the city. Besides, Sire,' the old man went on, fixing his eyes steadfastly on the king, while the tears ran down his cheeks, ' the death of my grandsons gave a wound to my heart which is still bleeding, and will never close but in the grave.' The king was deeply struck by the manner, the freedom, and the spirit of this unexpected rebuke. A total silence ensued, while the galled countenance of James seemed to shrink from the horrid remembrance. In a minute or two, however, he recovered himself enough to say, 'Mr. Kiffin, I shall find a balsam for that sore,' and he immediately turned about to a lord in waiting."[1]

Every one knows what followed. The English were not to be cajoled. They had no taste for Popery and arbitrary power. The deliverer came. The tyrant fled. The persecution ceased. Thanks be to God for the Revolution of 1688!

[1] Vol.ii. p. 463.

CHAPTER VIII.

Principles and Practices of the Denomination—Human Tradition Renounced—Freedom of Conscience Demanded—Personal Piety requisite to Church Fellowship—Purity of Discipline—Cases Cited—Mode of Public Worship—Plurality of Elders—Communion—Singing—Laying on of Hands—The Lord's Day.

HAVING thus brought down the history of the English Baptists to the end of the "troublous" period, I will close this portion of the narrative by a few observations on the character and state of the denomination, and some biographical notices of the principal ministers.

The distinguishing principle of the Baptists was clearly discerned by our British forefathers, and consistently maintained. They owned no master but Christ, no rule but his word. Hence they were ranked among Protestants. When Protestants required submission to human forms, whether the Common Prayer Book or the Directory, they separated themselves and became Dissenters. Differing from other Dissenters on some important points, they separated themselves again, following the light of the word, and endeavoring to render strict obedience to all the Lord's injunctions. They acknowledged no authority in any "traditions of the elders." They abhorred all "will-worship."

They claimed the right to profess what they believed, and to reduce their faith to practice, and they demanded that all others should be allowed to exercise the same right; for religious freedom, in its broadest sense, was regarded by them as the inalienable patrimony of all mankind. No exceptions were made. The magistrate was bound, in their judgment, to protect all, and to interfere with none, however foolish, superstitious, or perilous to souls their opinions might be deemed, as long as they obeyed the laws in things civil, and refrained from disturbing the peace of society. As I have before remarked, they were in this respect far in advance of other religious communities, the Friends excepted; and they had published their sentiments before the Friends were known.

Closely allied to these views was their requirement of true piety as an indispensable prerequisite to church membership. Whenever infant baptism is an introduction, directly or indirectly, to the fellowship of the church, the process of corruption is at work. In national establishments it is unavoidable. No such communities can be pure. But Baptists have always maintained that religious character is essential to union with a Christian church. The measures they adopt, in accordance with New Testament precepts and precedents, afford the best guarantee for purity. They open the doors to the godly—all besides are excluded. If they are sometimes mistaken in their judgments—if, now and then, a fanatic or a hypocrite creeps in undetected—they are reminded that even in apostolic times such cases occurred, and they take the earliest opportunity to expel the intruder.

The discipline of the English Baptist churches was in harmony with their doctrines. It was a commentary on 2 Cor. vi. 17. As they would not admit any to fellowship, knowingly, who did not appear to be the subjects of regenerating grace, so they placed members under censure, or excluded them, for immorality or any unscriptural or disorderly conduct, without respect of persons. I will adduce a few examples illustrative of their care in this matter.

The Broadmead Church would not admit Mrs. Bevis to fellowship, "by reason of her selling of drink, and some defects in her conversation about her husband's debts that he had contracted." The same church has this record of "Sister Watkins:" "Tidings came to the ears of the church that she walked disorderly and scandalously in the borrowing of money, up and down, of many persons—of some ten shillings, of some twenty shillings, of some more, some less, as she could get them to lend—and took no care to pay it again, promising people and not performing, spending much if not most of her time going up and down; and so did not work, or but little, to endeavor honestly to live and eat her own bread. And thus, she walking disorderly and scandalously in borrowing, contrary to the rule (2 Thess. iii. 6, 10–12), the church, after her crime was declared, and proved to her face by divers in the church, and that they had heard she had so served some not of the congregation, they consented all universally to withdraw from her. Then the ruling elder, Brother Terrill, declared to her, before the church, how that for her so sinning against the Lord, she rendered herself among the wicked ones, as Psalm xxxvii. 21; and, therefore, the church, in faithfulness to the

Lord and to her soul, must withdraw from her, seeing she had by several of the members been admonished once and again, and by several together witnessing against her evil in so doing; yet she had lately done the like, so that there was a necessity upon them to do their duty. And also acquainted her that if the Lord should hereafter give her repentance of the evil that she should reform to the satisfaction of the congregation, they should be willing to receive her into full communion again. And then the sentence, by the said ruling elder, was passed upon her, viz.: That in the name of our Lord Jesus Christ, and by the authority he had given to the church, we did declare, that Sister Watkins, for her sin of disorderly walking, borrowing and not paying, making promises and not performing, and not diligently working, was withdrawn from, and no longer to have full communion with this church, nor to be partaker with them in the holy mysteries of the Lord's supper, nor privileges of the Lord's house [that is, 'if she doth come to the meeting, not to be suffered to stay when any business of the church is transacted']; and the Lord have mercy upon her soul."[1]

The Fenstanton Church made an order, "that if any members of the congregation shall absent themselves from the assembly of the same congregation upon the first day of the week, without manifesting a sufficient cause, they shall be looked upon as offenders and be proceeded against accordingly;" and "it was desired that if any member should at any time have any extraordinary occasion to hinder them from the assembly, that they would certify the congregation of the same beforehand,

[1] *Broadmead Records* pp. 211, 413.

for the prevention of jealousies, etc." Several members were excluded by the same church, at different times for marrying irreligious persons, or such as were not "members of the congregation." Joan Parker was excommunicated for "absenting from the assembly of the congregation," for "running from her service, without the consent either of her master or dame, and letting herself to another man," and for "contempting all reproof." John Blows, a preacher, was not only absent on a day appointed for fasting and prayer, but was that day "at a great foot-ball play, he being one of the principal appointers thereof." Being called to account for it, he was at first disposed to justify himself, but at length confessed that he had been wrong, and " promised to abstain from the like for time to come." Nevertheless, as he had "dishonored the Lord," "grieved the people of God," and "given occasion to the adversary to speak reproachfully," it was resolved that "he should not be suffered to preach until further fruits meet for repentance did appear."[1]

The church at Warboys withdrew from Mary Poulter, "for forsaking the assembling with the church and neglecting holy duties, and walking disorderly in pride and vanity;" and from John Christmas, "for not loving Ann his wife as he ought, and for speaking hateful and despising words against her, giving her occasion to depart from him by his unkindness." But "John Christmas, afterward sending for Ann his wife again and promising amendment, after her coming again to him, desired to be a partaker with the church, in holy duties, was joined in fellowship again." "Mary Drage, for

[1] *Fenstanton Records*, pp. 126, 169, 244.

sundry times dissembling with the church, and out of covetousness speaking things very untrue, at length it being plainly proved against her in her hearing, and she having little to say for herself, was withdrawn from." "Thomas Bass, for telling of lies and swearing, was withdrawn from." "Ellen Burgess, for lying and slandering of her relations, and counting them and her mother witches, which we have no ground to believe, was withdrawn from."[1]

The church at St. Alban's withdrew from "Brother Osman," because one day in harvest-time "he did very shamefully with others betray his trust, and left his work, his master not being there, and went to an alehouse, where he spent most part of the day sinning against God, and spending his money, which should relieve his family, unto excessive drinking." A few months afterward he "did, in the presence of the congregation, publicly declare his fall, acknowledge his sin, and manifest great trouble for the same. The church gladly embraced him again, believing that God had given him repentance to the acknowledgment of the truth; he was admitted to his membership." "Sister Searly was by the church accused as to matter of fact. In the first place, she, selling strong water, let a person drink to excess; and, secondly, did give herself in marriage to a wicked drunkard, contrary to the rule of our Lord, who saith, 'Let her marry to whom she will, only in the Lord.' Thirdly, and was married in the national way with common prayer, with all the Romish ceremonies to it. All these things being considered, the church did

[1] *Fenstanton Records*, pp. 274, 278.

think it their duty to withdraw their communion, and yet she lieth under admonition."[1]

Their religious services were simple. When the pastor was present, he preached; but in the times now under review he was often in jail, or was compelled to hide himself from the pursuers. Then, prayer and exhortation occupied the time; any brother who felt disposed was at liberty to exhort. Generally, however, there was a sermon by a ruling elder or some gifted brother. Singing was not commonly practiced: many of the Baptists refused to join in that part of worship. In some of the churches the Lord's supper was observed weekly, or whenever they could meet unmolested on the Lord's Day; in most the monthly observance prevailed.

There was a plurality of elders in many of the churches. As numbers increased, they judged it conducive to profit to increase the number of teachers, and thus avoid the inconvenience and loss which must accrue from placing a large church under the care of a single pastor. Probably there were not more than a hundred and fifty churches in England during this period, and many of them were small. But there were two or more pastors at Bedford, at Luton, at Farringdon, at St. Alban's, at Portsmouth, at Bessel's Green, at Ashford [four]; at Glazier's Hall, Devonshire Square, and Mile End Green, London; at Norwich, at Hooknorton, at Bridgewater, at Bristol, and doubtless at other places. This shows a very commendable care for the spiritual interests of the churches.

In some of the churches there were "ruling elders," sometimes called "teachers," who preached when their

[1] Ivimey, ii. 177.

services were required, and presided at the church meetings in the absence of the pastor. In the Broadmead Church, Thomas Jennings, who appears to have been an ordained minister, was the "usual administrator" of baptism; but any preacher, ordained or not, might baptize.

Strict communion was practiced in the majority of the churches, none but baptized believers being admitted to the Lord's table. In some, however, the want of baptism was not regarded as a bar to fellowship, so that there was satisfactory evidence of piety. The Broadmead Church, the churches at Bedford, Luton, Gamlingay, Hitchen, Tottlebank, and many in Wales—especially those founded by Vavasor Powell—were so constituted.

Under the Commonwealth and the Protectorate, the freedom which was enjoyed was improved by the churches. Itinerating excursions were frequently made by acceptable preachers, whose aim was not so much to proselytize men to their sect as to convert them to God. Great numbers were converted by their instrumentality. And the stated labors of many of the pastors were extensively blessed. The good work prospered in those days.

Freedom implies the right to differ. We must not be surprised at the lack of uniformity among our ancestors. There were controversies among them, which were not always carried on with courtesy and forbearance; those qualities were but little valued in the seventeenth century. The greatest virulence was displayed in the disputes about doctrines. The advocates of Arminianism contended with the Calvinists. The former charged the latter with uncharitableness, and were in their turn accused of latitudinarianism. Each looked on the other with a jaundiced eye. This controversy has ceased to rage. There have been tacit concessions on both sides, or, at least, an abandonment of certain extreme views—perhaps it would be better to say, incautious expressions.

The question of communion was another cause of agitation. Bunyan's gentle temper was sadly ruffled by it. His zeal for open communion led him to speak in such disparaging terms of "water baptism" as no other writer of our denomination in that age would have ventured to employ. He was ably answered by D'Anvers and Kiffin.

Singing in worship was another subject of dispute. Strange as it may appear to us, many good men refused to join in it or allow it. Benjamin Keach had great difficulty in introducing the practice in the church under his care. He wrote a book in defence of his views, entitled, *The Breach repaired in 'God's Worship; or, Singing of Psalms, Hymns, and Spiritual Songs proved to be a Holy Ordinance of Jesus Christ.* Ivimey observes, that, "in the present day, when this practice is universal, it will appear unaccountable that our forefathers should require arguments to prove the following particulars, viz.: What it is to sing; that there can be no proper singing without the voice; 'tis not simple heart-joy, or inward rejoicing without the voice; no metaphorical singing mentioned in Scripture; no mental singing, as there is no mental praying; the essence of singing no more in the heart or spirit than the essence of preaching, etc.; singing is a musical modulation or tuning of the voice, etc., etc.—with a number of other particulars equally curious, and, to us, self-evident. Crosby says: 'Though he had very great success in this controversy, yet it brought upon him much trouble and ill-will. When he was convinced that singing the praises of God was a holy ordinance of Jesus Christ, he labored earnestly and with a great deal of prudence and caution to convince his people thereof; and first obtained their consent to the practice of it at the conclusion of the sacrament of the Lord's supper, and had but two of the brethren in the church who opposed him therein. After his church had continued in this practice about six years, they further consented to practice the same on public thanksgiving days, and continued therein about fourteen years; and then, by a regular act of the church, in a solemn manner, agreed to sing the praises of God on every Lord's Day, excepting about five or six persons that dissented therefrom: and, if I am not mistaken, this was the first church that thus practiced this holy ordinance. But, so far was Mr. Keach, or the church, from imposing on the consciences of those few that dissented (though the church then consisted of some hundreds) that they agreed to sing when prayer was concluded after the sermon; and if those few who were not satisfied could not stay the time of singing, they might freely go out, and the church would not be offended at them; for they did not look upon singing the praises of God as an essential of communion, nor for the *being*, but for the comfort and *well*-being of a church.' Notwithstanding this care and consideration, however, the malcontents would not yield. They withdrew, and founded another church, upon the same principles, *singing only excepted;* so difficult was it to remove long-standing prejudices." [1]

Laying on of hands after baptism was practiced by

[1] *History*, ii. 298–301.

some, but strongly objected to by others; and sometimes churches differing from each other on this subject refused intercommunion. In a Confession of Faith prepared by the General Baptists, and presented to Charles II. in 1660, the following is the twelfth article: "That it is the duty of all such who are believers baptized to draw nigh unto God in submission to that principle of Christ's doctrine, to wit, prayer and laying on of hands, that they may receive the promise of the Holy Spirit (Heb. vi. 1, 2; Acts viii. 12, 15, 17; 2 Tim. i. 6), whereby they may mortify the deeds of the body (Rom. viii. 13), and live in all things answerable to their professed intentions and desires, even to the honor of him who hath called them out of darkness into his marvelous light."[1] Thomas Grantham, a celebrated minister in that connection, thus explains it: "That as God has promised to give the Holy Spirit to all that are called of the Lord, so he hath appointed a solemn way wherein his servants and handmaids are to wait upon him for the reception thereof, which way is the prayers of the church performed by her ministers or pastors with laying on of hands, and this, as a principle of Christ's doctrine, belonging to them in the minority of their Christian state."[2] The practice was first introduced about the year 1645.

Some few believed in the perpetuity of the Jewish sabbath; but the majority observed the first day of the week, in common with Christendom in general.

Here and there, a church observed the washing of feet, and had a love-feast before the Lord's supper.

But, though in these and some other points the English Baptists were not altogether agreed among themselves, in

---

[1] *Confessions of Faith, etc.*, p. 113.   [2] *Fenstanton Records*, p. 157.

one thing there was entire union. They were of one mind in resisting Antichristianism, even "unto blood." They were united in pleading for the rights of conscience, and they shrank not from suffering. They could not all subscribe the same confession, nor take part in the same ceremonies; but they were "of one heart and one soul" in readiness to "endure all things" for the truth's sake. The plunderings and imprisonments they suffered were frightful, and will never be fully known on earth. Some of their ministers were very cruelly dealt with. Francis Bampfield was eight years in Dorchester jail, and spent the last year of his life in Newgate, where he died. John Miller was confined ten years in the same jail. Henry Forty was twelve years in prison at Exeter. John Bunyan was in Bedford jail twelve years. Joseph Wright lay in Maidstone jail twenty years. George Fownes died in Gloucester jail. Thomas Delaune, and many other servants of God, died in Newgate.[1]

[1] For fuller particulars the reader is referred to Dr. B. Evans' *Early English Faptists*.

CHAPTER IX.

Biographical Notices—John Smyth, Thomas Helwys, and John Spilsbury—Henry Denne—Francis Cornwell, A. M.—Christopher Blackwood—Major-General Harrison—Colonel Hutchinson.

I WILL now proceed to give some account of the principal English Baptist worthies of the seventeenth century.

It is much to be regretted that we know so little of the personal history of John Smyth, Thomas Helwys, and John Spilsbury. All the information I have been able to gather respecting Mr. Smyth has been already communicated. I am not able to add much to the notice of Mr. Helwys, whose settlement in London has been recorded in a former chapter. He wrote several small treatises, which were much prized. His sentiments on persecution, and on the unlawfulness of the magistrate's interference in religious affairs, were so unacceptable to John Robinson, the celebrated Independent minister, to whose church the New England Pilgrims had belonged, that he published a reply, showing that, though he and his friends suffered so much from that interference, they were not willing to give it up. Mr. Robinson held that the magistrate might " use his lawful power lawfully for the furtherance of Christ's kingdom and laws." He observed: "It is true, they [the magistrates] have no power against the laws, doctrine, and religion of Christ; but for the same, if their power be of God, they may use it lawfully, and against the contrary."[1] This is a surrender of the whole case. Mr. Helwys' views, which were fully expressed in *Persecution Judged and Condemned*, were far sounder and more scriptural. Crosby says, "How long Mr. Helwys lived, and continued the elder of this church of Baptists in London, I cannot find. The books wrote against them at this time show that they went on with great courage and resolution; and, notwithstanding the severities used against them by the civil power, increased very much in their numbers."[2]

Neither can I satisfy curiosity respecting Mr. John Spilsbury, the pastor of the first Particular or Calvinistic Baptist Church, which met in Broad Street, Wapping, London. I can only say that his signature is fixed to the Confession of Faith published in 1646, and to sundry other public documents, the last being the "Humble Apology of some commonly called Anabaptists," presented to Charles II. in 1660, as a disclaimer of sympathy with Venner's insurrection. I observe that, though he joined William Kiffin in a letter to the Baptists in Dublin, persuading them to submit quietly to the Protectorate, he afterward united with a number of others in an address to Cromwell, earnestly protesting against his assumption of the kingly title. It may be concluded that Mr. Spilsbury was a man of influence in the denomination. How long he lived after the Restoration does not appear. Hercules Collins became pastor of the church in Broad Street in 1677. Whether he was Mr. Spils-

[1] *Tracts*, p. 92.   [2] *History*, i. 275.

bury's immediate successor, I have not the means of deciding.

HENRY DENNE was a man of note. He was educated in the University of Cambridge, where he acquired a respectable standing. Having received ordination from the bishop of St. David's about the year 1630, he was presented to the living of Pyrton, in Hertfordshire, which he held for ten years, greatly to the profit of the inhabitants, by whom he was justly esteemed as an instructive and faithful preacher. In 1641 he was appointed to preach at a visitation held at Baldock, and he determined to embrace the opportunity of exposing the evils which had long grieved and vexed him, particularly " the sin of persecution, the vices of the clergy, and the corruptions in doctrine and worship which he apprehended to be in the Established Church." His text was John v. 35. After an ingenious introduction, he proceeded to execute his purpose, and laid on the lash quite freely. The pride and covetousness of the clergy, their pluralities, their neglect of duty by non-residence, and other evils, were held up to view, and reformation boldly demanded. " I must call upon those in authority," he said, " to make diligent search after these foxes. If the courts had been so vigilant to find out these as nonconformable ministers, surely by this time the church would have been as free f om *them* as the land from *wolves*. But they have preferred the traditions of men before the commandments of Almighty God. I tell you, that conformity had ever sped the worse for their sakes, who, breaking the commandments of God, think to make amends with conformity to the traditions of men."[1]

[1] Crosby, i. 298–301.

We cannot be surprised at hearing that soon after this he announced his change of sentiments. In the early part of 1643 he was baptized by Mr. Thomas Lamb, pastor of the church in Bell Alley, Coleman Street, London. His gifts were thankfully recognized by the church, and by their direction he engaged in a mission to the counties of Staffordshire and Cambridgeshire, where he preached the gospel with great success and formed many churches. This roused the ire of the Presbyterian authorities. He was arrested and imprisoned at Cambridge. By the interference of a friend this case was brought before Parliament, in order to which he was removed to the Peterhouse, Aldersgate Street, London. The notorious Dr. Featley was in the same prison, as a royalist. Mr. Denne challenged him to a disputation. They met and fought, in the usual way, with propositions and syllogisms, till the doctor was tired, and withdrew from the conflict. Mr. Denne carried on the war with his pen, and published a reply to Dr. F.'s famous book, *The Dippers Dipt*, etc.

He was soon released, and was appointed minister of Eltisley parish, Cambridgeshire, from which place, as a centre, he itinerated in various directions, preaching and baptizing. In 1645 he visited the county of Kent, and his labors were blessed to many.

The opposition Mr. Denne met with issued in his leaving Eltisley. He then entered the army, and served several years. But he did not desist from preaching, nor was it necessary, for praying and preaching were no strange things among the Parliamentary soldiers. "Cornet Denne" was his military title, but "Parson Denne" was the appellation by which he was known among his associates. I cannot tell whether he saw any fighting or not, nor in what parts of England the regiment to which he was attached was from time to time quartered. The only recorded event is his narrow escape from death as a mutineer In May, 1649, he took part in a mutiny of the troops, partly occasioned by the men's unwillingness to join the expedition to Ireland, and partly by discontent with the existing state of affairs. Prompt measures were taken, and the revolt was quelled; but Mr. Denne and three others were sentenced to be shot. "Cornet Denne, being a man of parts, and one who had been esteemed for piety and honesty, received his sentence with great manliness and fortitude of spirit, yet with so much relenting and acknowledgment of the just hand of God, the justice of the sentence, and his submission thereunto, that he seemed to rejoice with willingness to suffer under so righteous a sentence, and he professed openly, that although his heart could not accuse him of an evil meaning, yet he was convinced of the evil of the action, and dangerous consequences of it; that if they had but continued three or four days longer, the land had been plunged in misery and ruin." Cornet Tompson and Corporals Church and Perkins were shot; and "Cornet Denne being called out, came with much composure of spirit, expecting to die, but the general having commanded the Lieutenant-general Cromwell to let him know at the place of execution that his excellency had extended mercy to him, he soberly and suddenly replied, 'I am not worthy of such a mercy; I am more ashamed to live than afraid to die'—weeping bitterly."[1] He afterward endeavored to repair the mischief by publishing a pamphlet in which the origin and objects of the

[1] *Fenstanton Records*, Introductory Notice, pp. xii., xiii.

mutiny were stated, and the deplorable consequences which would have followed if it had not been suppressed were faithfully set forth.

It is not likely that he continued long in the army after this. We next find him in his place as a member of the church at Fenstanton in 1653, taking part in certain disciplinary proceedings. At one of their meetings Henry Denne began to speak, saying, "Brethren, I desire you to consider the word of Christ, saying, *Go ye therefore, and teach all nations, baptizing them in the name of the Father, Son, and Holy Spirit; teaching them to observe whatsoever things I have commanded you, and lo! I am with you alway, even unto the end of the world* (Matt. xxviii. 19); which last words are often used by us, yet I think not too often. But I desire that we may seriously consider the former, viz., *Go, teach all nations, baptizing them*, etc., [or] as Mark saith, *Go, preach the gospel to every creature;* and so, whether we are not as much bound to observe them as any. And if it appeareth that we are, then I pray consider whether we are not in a great fault, in being so negligent in sending forth persons to divulge the gospel, in those many places that are ignorant thereof. Truly, I conceive that we are much to blame, and especially seeing there are many towns hereabouts that have no teacher; and who can tell but that the Lord may work in this opportunity?"[1] The result was that Mr. Denne and another member were sent out on a missionary excursion, an account of which was given to the church on their return. Next year he went again into Kent, and spent some time at Canterbury. His labours there were

[1] *Fenstanton Records*, p. 71.

so acceptable that the church invited him to settle among them. The Fenstanton Church consented, appointed another brother to attend him on the journey, and "money and horses were provided for them." He arrived in safety and was received with gladness. "He is provided of an house," the Canterbury Church said, in a letter to that of Fenstanton, dated Feb. 19, 1655, "and we doubt not of a comfortable being and subsistence amongst us."[1] He was regarded as one of the chief men of the denomination. In 1658 he was engaged in a disputation on baptism with Dr. Gunning, a celebrated divine of the day, afterward bishop, successively, of Chichester and Ely. It was held in the church of St. Clement Danes, Strand, London, and was attended by some thousands of persons. Mr. Denne published an account of it, and soon after baptized the lady at whose instance the disputation took place. Her doubts were removed by Mr. Denne's arguments.

Nothing more is known of Mr. Denne except the publication of two small pamphlets. His signature appears among those to the *Humble Apology*, etc., issued after Venner's insurrection. Crosby supposes that he died in the year 1661, and states that an Episcopal clergyman composed the following epitaph for his tomb:

"To tell his wisdom, learning, goodness unto men,
 I need to say no more—But here lies Henry Denne."[2]

FRANCIS CORNWELL, A.M., was educated at Emmanuel College, Cambridge. Neal says that "he was one of the most learned divines that espoused the cause of the Baptists." This took place under singular circumstances.

[1] *Fenstanton Records*, p. 135.   [2] *History*, i. 306.

Mr. Cornwell was vicar of Marden, Kent, where he had refused to conform to certain ceremonies imposed by Archbishop Laud, and for his refusal he was committed to Maidstone jail. While there, a woman who visited h.m intimated that she had some doubts respecting the lawfulness of infant baptism. He endeavored to remove them by the best arguments he could think of, but failed to satisfy her. This led him to further inquiry, the result of which was that he abandoned infant baptism, and was baptized by Mr. William Jeffery, an eminent Baptist minister. After his release from prison he was called on to preach a sermon at a meeting of ministers at Cranbrook. This was in 1644. He chose for his text Mark vii. 7, and "took the liberty of declaring his sentiments freely in this point; and told them pædobaptism was an antichristian innovation, a human tradition, and a practice for which there was neither precept, nor true deduction from the word of God."[1] Much discussion followed, and great indignation was manifested; but Mr. C. Blackwood, one of the ministers present, who had taken down the sermon in short-hand, having promised to furnish a reply to it, the further consideration of the subject was postponed till their next meeting. Instead of replying, however, Mr. Blackwood followed Mr. Cornwell's example, finding it impossible to refute him, and was also baptized by Mr. Jeffery. Mr. Cornwell was very zealous for Baptist principles. His work on baptism, entitled *A Vindication of the Royal Commission of King Jesus*, was distributed among the members of the House of Commons, and produced great excitement. He soon left the Establishment, and formed a Baptist church in the

[1] *History*, i. 346.

neighborhood of Cranbrook, over which he presided till his death.

CHRISTOPHER BLACKWOOD was an able preacher. He was born in 1606, graduated at Cambridge in 1624 and became curate of Rye, in Sussex. When he embraced Baptist principles, he became pastor of a church which met at Spillshill House, near Staplehurst, Kent. After laboring there some years, he went into the army, accompanied the forces sent to Ireland, and was for some time pastor of a church at Dublin, exercising, as it would seem, a general superintendence over the other Baptist churches in that country. In a letter sent to Secretary Thurloe, in the year 1655, he is styled "The Oracle of the Anabaptists in Ireland." He appears to have returned to England about the time of the Restoration, as his name is affixed to the Baptist declaration against Venner's rebellion. In 1661 he went to Holland, where he remained a year. Shortly after his return he resumed his residence in Dublin, where he died in 1670. He was a learned man, well read in the Fathers. Both he and Mr. Cornwell were warm advocates of soul-freedom, and protested in their writings against the intolerance of the Presbyterian party. His first publication was entitled *The Storming of Antichrist in his two Last and Strongest Garrisons—Compulsion of Conscience and Infants' Baptism.*[1]

MAJOR-GENERAL HARRISON was one of Cromwell's best soldiers, and for a time enjoyed his entire confidence. He commanded the troop of horse appointed to convey Charles I. from the Isle of Wight to Hurst Castle. He

[1] See *Baptist Magazine* for June, July, August, and September, 1867, for a valuable collection of letters written by Mr. Blackwood.

was one of the king's judges. He assisted Cromwell in dissolving the Long Parliament. He was a member of the Council of State under the Commonwealth. But he was a stern republican, and therefore entirely opposed to the Protectorate. He had also embraced the Fifth Monarchy principles. On these accounts Cromwell degraded him and placed him in confinement. At the Restoration he was excepted from clemency. Ten of the regicides (as the king's judges were called) were hanged, drawn, and quartered. Major-General Harrison was one of them. He suffered with great calmness and intrepidity, declaring at the place of execution "that he was fully persuaded that what he had done was the cause and work of God, which he was confident God would own and raise up again, how much soever it suffered at that time."

Mr. Ivimey says that "though Major-General Harrison was a Baptist at the time of his trial and execution, yet he was not at the period of the king's death;" and that "there is no evidence of any Baptist being among the king's judges."[1] This is not quite clear. Thurloe, in his *State Papers*, referring to Harrison's refusal to submit to the Protectorate, in December, 1654, calls him "the most eminent man of the Anabaptist party." He could scarcely have been worthy of that appellation if he had not been for some time connected with the Baptist denomination.

Harrison is generally described by historians as a fanatic. It is certain that he was an impulsive being, and somewhat tinctured with vanity. But there can be no doubt that he was sincerely and soberly in earnest,

[1] Vol. i. 293.

although it may be admitted that he was a singular man even in those singular times. We must not measure the seventeenth century by the nineteenth. A modern writer says of Harrison: "For the integrity of his life, and the Christian heroism with which he endured a cruel and ignominious death, he may deservedly be classed, if he may not challenge priority, with a More, a Russell, a Sydney."[1]

Here is an extract from a letter written by him to Cromwell on occasion of his taking the command of the army sent to invade Scotland in 1650: "Oh that a spirit of faith and supplication may be poured forth on you and your army! There is more to be had in this poor simple way than even most saints expect. My lord, let waiting upon Jehovah be the greatest and most considerable business you have every day; reckon it so, more than to eat, sleep, or council together. Run aside sometimes from your company, and get a word with the Lord. Why should you not have three or four precious souls always standing at your elbow, with whom you might now and then turn into a corner? I have found refreshment and mercy in such a way. Ah! the Lord of compassion own, pity your burdens, care for you, stand by and refresh your heart each moment! I would I could in any kind do you good. My heart is with you, and my poor prayers to my God for you." In a former part of the letter he had said, "I doubt not your success, but I think faith and prayer must be the chief engines."[2]

Cromwell loved such talk. "In such spirit," says Carlyle, "goes Oliver Cromwell to the wars. 'A God-

---

[1] *Burton's Diary*, by Rutt, iv. 432, note.
[2] *Fenstanton Records*, pp. 315-317.

intoxicated man,' as Novalis elsewhere phrases it. I have asked myself, if anywhere in modern European history, or even in ancient Asiatic, there was found a man practicing this mean world's affairs with a heart more filled by the idea of the Highest! Bathed in the eternal splendors—it is so he walks our dim earth; this man is one of few. He is projected with a terrible force out of the eternities, and in the times and their arenas there is nothing that can withstand him."[1]

COLONEL HUTCHINSON was a man of a noble mind and a warm heart. He is immortalized in the *Memoirs* written by his widow, and well known to all students of English history. It is valuable on historical accounts, as elucidating sundry misty paragraphs in other writers. But its great charm consists in the exquisite delineations of character with which it abounds. Mrs. Hutchinson gives us a full-length portraiture of her excellent husband, drawn, it is true, by the hand of affection, and therefore some may be disposed to deem it flattering; but there is such an air of truthfulness in the narrative that it is impossible to doubt the general correctness of the picture. There are also many discriminating sketches of other persons who figured prominently in the scenes of that struggle for freedom which Clarendon calls "The Great Rebellion."

The colonel was for some time governor of Nottingham, under the Parliament. He afterward sat in the House of Commons, where he was always listened to with great respect. Having been one of the king's judges, he was in great peril at the Restoration. But he had powerful connections, and he had conciliated the regard

[1] Cromwell's *Letters and Speeches,* ii. 173.

of his enemies by acts of moderation and kindness when he was in office. His life was spared; yet he was treated as a suspected person, whom any one might vex and annoy with impunity, and whom, on any pretext, the government might put in durance. So it proved. He was suddenly apprehended on a charge of complicity in some treasonable plot, and committed to the Tower, whence he was conveyed to Sandown Castle, near Deal. There was no legal investigation—no trial. The accusation was utterly false; but it was determined to put him out of the way. The keen air of the sea-coast was ill-suited to the delicate state of his health; added to which, the accommodations of the prison were of the most miserable kind. The physician declared that "the place killed him." He died in confinement, September 11, 1664.

Mrs. Hutchinson has given an account of the manner in which she and her husband were converted to Baptist principles. It occurred at Nottingham in the year 1647.

"When formerly the Presbyterian ministers had forced him, for quietness' sake, to go and break up a private meeting in the cannonier's chamber, there were found some notes concerning pædobaptism, which were brought into the governor's lodgings; and his wife having then more leisure to read than he, having perused them and compared them with the Scriptures, found not what to say against the truths they asserted, concerning the misapplication of that ordinance to infants; but being then young and modest, she thought it a kind of virtue to submit to the judgment and practice of most churches, rather than to defend a singular opinion of her own, she not being then enlightened in that great mistake of the national churches. But in this year she, happening to be with child, communicated her doubts to her husband, and desired him to endeavor her satisfaction; which while he did, he himself became as unsatisfied, or rather satisfied against it. First, therefore, he diligently searched the Scriptures alone, and could find in them no ground at all for that practice; then he bought and read all the eminent treatises on both sides, which at that time came thick from the presses, and was still more satisfied of the error of the Pædobaptists. After this, his wife being brought to bed, that he might, if possible, give the religious party no offence, he invited all the ministers to dinner, and propounded his doubt and the ground thereof to them. None of them could defend their practice with any satisfactory reason, but the tradition of the church from the primitive times, and their main buckler of federal holiness, which Tombes and Denne had so excellently overthrown. He and his wife then, professing themselves unsatisfied in the practice, desired their opinions, what they ought to do. Most answered, to conform to the general practice of other Christians, how dark soever it were to themselves; but Mr. Foxcraft, one of the assembly, said that except they were convinced of the warrant of that practice from the word, they sinned in doing it: whereupon that infant was not baptized. And now the governor and his wife, notwithstanding that they forsook not their assemblies, nor retracted their benevolences and civilities from them, yet were they reviled by them, called fanatics and Anabaptists, and often glanced at in their public sermons. And not only the ministers, but all their zealous sectaries, conceived implacable malice against them upon this account; which was carried on with a spirit of envy and persecution to the last, though he, on his side, might well have said to them, as his Master said to the old Pharisees: 'Many good works have I done among you: for which of these do you hate me?'"[1]

[1] *Memoirs of Col. Hutchinson*, pp. 299-301.

CHAPTER X.

Biographical Notices continued—Henry Jessey, A. M.—John Canne—Vavasor Powell—Abraham Cheare.

HENRY JESSEY, A. M., was a native of Yorkshire, and son of an Episcopal clergyman. Having been carefully prepared for university studies, he entered St. John's College, Cambridge, in the seventeenth year of his age, and continued there six years. He was a hard student. In addition to a competent knowledge of classics and mathematics, he acquired great proficiency in Hebrew and Rabbinical lore, and was well skilled in Syriac and Arabic.

He was converted to God while at the university—a rare occurrence at that time. After his ordination he officiated for a short time in a country parish, but was removed on account of his nonconformity to some of the rites and services enjoined. In 1637 he became pastor of an Independent church in London. He had not been long there when the Baptist controversy broke out among them. Many of his congregation withdrew and joined Baptist churches. Being led thereby to study anew the points in debate, he was convinced of the unlawfulness of sprinkling, announced the fact to his people in 1642, and for two years *dipped* the children that were brought to him. Further thought and inquiry issued in a conviction that believers only are the proper subjects of baptism. Before he took the final step he conferred with Dr. Goodwin, Philip Nye, and other eminent Independent ministers, but their arguments for infant baptism failed to give him satisfaction. He followed the dictates of conscience, was baptized by Hanserd Knollys in June, 1645, and became pastor of a church which is supposed to have met in Woodmonger's Hall, London. He labored there till his death.

Mr. Jessey was a hard student. He continued to be so all his days. Biblical criticism was his principal study. A large amount of his time was devoted to a revision of our authorized version of the Scriptures. Crosby gives the following account of his labors in this department:

"Besides his constant labors in the work of the ministry, there was another profitable work wherein his soul was engaged, and in which he took great pains for divers years; and this was no less than the making a new and more correct translation of the Holy Bible.

"He was very industrious, in the first place, to understand fully those languages in which it was written: the Hebrew and Greek Testaments he constantly carried about him, frequently calling one his 'sword and dagger,' and the other his 'shield and buckler.' And besides the Hebrew and Greek, he studied the Syriac and Chaldee dialects, which the unlearned Jews spoke in their captivity. But notwithstanding his qualifications in this and many other respects, he had not the vanity to think this a work fit for any single man to encounter with, and therefore sent letters to many learned men of this and other nations, desiring their assistance and joint labors with him in this great design. And by his persuasions many persons of great note for their learning, faithfulness, and piety, did engage in it; particularly Mr. Rowe, the Hebrew professor of Aberdeen, took great pains with him herein. The writer of Mr. Jessey's life says, that he made it the master study of his life, and would often cry out, 'Oh that I might see this done before I die!'

"In that book there is a specimen given of the errors he took notice of in the present translation, the rules he observed in correcting them, and the progress that was made in this work.

"It appears that it was almost completed, and wanted little more than the appointing commissioners to examine it, and authorize its publication, which was what he always intended, and of which he had from the first some assurances given him. But the great turn that was given to public affairs, both in Church and State, by the Restoration, caused this great and noble design to prove abortive."[1]

Under the Protectorate, Mr. Jessey was appointed one of the "Triers." He officiated also at St. George's Church, Southwark, every Lord's Day morning, preaching to his own people in the afternoon, and at other places during the week.

Being an unmarried man, he was able to gratify his benevolent disposition to a large extent. His charities were very liberally bestowed. About thirty families were chiefly sustained by him. Applications for aid pressed upon him daily, and if they were deserving he seldom refused them. On one occasion he interested himself in behalf of the poor Jews resident in Jerusalem, who had

[1] *History* i. 313.

fallen into great destitution through the failure of customary remittances from Europe. He succeeded in enlisting the sympathies of London merchants and others, and remitted upward of 300*l*. (fifteen hundred dollars) for their relief.

On account of the high esteem in which he was held, and his well-known learning and admirable judgment, his opinion was frequently sought on a great variety of subjects. Such demands on his time were thereby occasioned that he affixed the following notice to his study door

"Amice, quisquis huc ades;
Aut agito paucis, aut abi:
Aut me laborantem adjuva."

"Whatever friend comes hither,
Despatch in brief, or go,
Or help me busied too."
By Henry Jessey.

At the Restoration, Mr. Jessey was quickly ejected from St. George's Church. Twice he suffered imprisonment. But he did not live to see the "great and sore troubles" of the times of Charles II. and his brother. He died September 4, 1663, and was followed to his grave by thousands of mourners.

"He spent his last days and nights in searching his heart, humbling his soul, extolling free grace, and exhorting all about him to keep close to God, to persevere in faith, and prepare for trials; adding for their encouragement the long experience he had had of the goodness of the Lord in all times and conditions. The last evening but one before his departure, having a mind to walk, he was led about the room, and often repeated this expression, 'God is good; he doth not lead me whither I would not, as he did Peter: good is the Lord to me.' Being soon tired, he sat down on his bed, and one who sat by him said, 'They among whom you have labored can witness that you have been a faithful servant of Christ; making his glory your utmost end, for the good of their souls.' But he replied, 'Say no more of that; exalt God—exalt God.' He spent the first part of his last night in blessing God and singing praises to his name, and fell asleep about eleven o'clock. Waking again between two and three, he fell into a wonderful strain of abasing himself, and admiring the love of God, 'that he should choose the vilest, the unworthiest, and the basest,' which last word he repeated many times, and then cried out, "Oh, the unspeakable love of God, that he should reach me, when I could not reach him!" And when the cordial ordered for that night was brought, he said, 'Trouble me not—upon your peril, trouble me not!' He was then as if he had seen some glorious vision, or had been in a rapture. . . . The last words he was heard to speak were these: 'He counted me worthy.' And when the sound of his words ceased, his lips were observed still to move, and he seemed to be inwardly adoring that God whom in his health he served, feared, and praised, and made his boast of continually—whose law he preached, and whose goodness he proclaimed Such was his habitual sense of the goodness of God that, when he met an acquaintance, it was a common thing for him (after the usual salutations) to say, 'Verily God is good—blessed be his name—stick to him.' . . . He was so great a scripturist, that if one began to rehearse any passage, he could go on with it, and name the book, chapter, and verse where it migh: be found. The original languages of the Old and New Testaments were as familiar to him as his mother tongue."[1]

JOHN CANNE was another worthy champion of the truth. He was born about the year 1590, and for a short time ministered in the English Church. In 1621 he was chosen pastor of a church which afterward met in Deadman's Place, Southwark, and which had been formed but a little time before. The church met at first stealthily in private houses, to avoid persecution, which at length became so fierce that Mr. Canne found it necessary to withdraw from England for a time. He fixed his residence at Amsterdam, where he was chosen pastor of "the ancient English Church." In that city he published in 1634 his work entitled *The Necessity of Separation*, justifying dissent from the Church of England, and enforcing that duty. During a visit to England in 1641 he formed the church at Broadmead, Bristol. He returned to his pastoral duties at Amsterdam, but visited his native land again after the death of Charles I., and probably spent several years, wholly or partially, in England. It appears that he was dissatisfied with the Protectorate, and as he was a man whose influence might be dreaded, he was not suffered to propagate his opinions undisturbed. He was banished from Hull, where he had been preaching for some time, and after some wanderings fixed his residence at London. Having embraced Fifth Monarchy principles, although he had no sympathy with the political schemes of their advocates, he was apprehended, in April, 1658, at a meeting held in Coleman Street, and committed to prison, but acquitted on his trial. Once

[1] Palmer's *Nonconformists' Memorial*, i. 133.

more he sought refuge at Amsterdam, and exercised his ministry there till his death, in the year 1667.

Though Mr. Canne was a "baptized man," as he is styled in the records of the Broadmead Church, he maintained and practiced open communion. The Rev. Charles Stovel, of London, who edited *The Necessity of Separation* for the Hanserd Knollys Society, says, in a letter to the author, recently received: "I see nothing in his works to indicate a very decided baptistical zeal. I should judge that he was, separating from all hierarchies, a free communionist, in the widest meaning of that designation that could comport with fellowship in vital religion."

Believing that "Scripture is its own best interpreter," he prepared an edition of the Bible, with marginal references, judiciously selected, and excellently adapted to assist thoughtful inquirers in the search for truth. It was first published at Amsterdam in 1644, and afterward, repeatedly, both in that city and in England. The Rev. Christopher Anderson says: "The first English Bible, with scriptural references on the margin throughout, was prepared and printed in that city [Amsterdam] by John Canne. He proceeded on the principle that 'Scripture was the best interpreter of Scripture,' and his parallels, therefore, are parallels of *sense*, and not of sound, as too many have been since his day. . . . A good reprint would prove a very valuable and salable book."[1]

VAVASOR POWELL has been not inappropriately termed "the Whitefield of Wales." That excellent man was born at Knocklas, in Radnorshire, in the year 1617. He received a good education, and was well skilled in the

[1] *Annals of the English Bible*, ii. 559.

learned languages; but he was such a wild youth that even his young associates called him *dux omnium malorum*—leader in all mischief. Nevertheless, he was considered in those times good enough for a clergyman, and was accordingly ordained, and admitted to a curacy, although, as he afterward confessed, he "slighted the Scriptures, and was a stranger to secret and spiritual prayer, and a great profaner of the Sabbath." But he did not long continue in that state. God "called him by his grace." The books and sermons of Puritan ministers were blessed to his conversion. Having left the Established Church, and joined the Nonconformists, he engaged in ministerial labor with great zeal. He was an eloquent and popular preacher, and had the honor to be persecuted with no small malice. On one occasion, when he had been preaching at a house in Brecknockshire, he was seized, together with sixty or seventy of his hearers, by a rude mob, who placed their prisoners in the church, as it was too late at night to take them to a magistrate. Mr. Powell improved the opportunity, and preached in the church at midnight from Matt. x. 28. Next morning they went to the magistrate, who was not at home when they arrived. Mr. Powell thought that time ought not to be wasted, and therefore preached again, greatly to the chagrin of his worship, who found his house so unceremoniously turned into a conventicle. His daughter had been impressed by the sermon, and interceded for the release of the prisoner, which was reluctantly granted.

The opposition was so violent that, in 1642, Mr. Powell went to London, where he preached to many congregations with much acceptance. Next year he settled at Dartford, in Kent, and was "blessed with great success in his labors, being instrumental in bringing many souls to Christ, and gathering a congregation in that town." After remaining there nearly three years, he was strongly urged to return to Wales, the number of faithful ministers in that country being then very small. He went accordingly, in 1646, and spent fourteen years in his native land, traveling from place to place, preaching incessantly, and planting churches. "He frequently preached in two or three places in a day, and was seldom two days in a week throughout the year out of the pulpit —nay, he would sometimes ride a hundred miles in a week, and preach in every place where he might have admittance, either night or day; so that there was hardly a church, chapel, or town-hall in all Wales where he had not preached, besides his frequent preaching in fairs and markets, upon mountains and in small villages; for, if he passed at any time through any place where there was a concourse of people, he would take the opportunity of preaching Christ and recommending to them the care of their souls, and another world." [1]

In 1649 he was appointed one of the commissioners, under authority of an act passed "for the better propagation and preaching of the gospel in Wales, for the ejecting of scandalous ministers and schoolmasters, and redress of some grievances." He discharged his duty in that office honestly and conscientiously, though it occasioned him much ill-will. The good effects were apparent in every part of the principality.

At the Restoration, Vavasor Powell became a marked man. Such representations were made against him that in August, 1660, orders were issued by government to

[1] Crosby, i. 376.

suppress his congregations. In the following January, immediately after Venner's insurrection, he was thrown into prison, with many more, and continued there nine weeks, when, at the coronation, a general pardon was granted and he was released.

But the term of freedom was short. Preach he would, notwithstanding all prohibition. It was impossible to stop him unless he was shut up in jail, and there was no difficulty about that in the days of Charles II. Upon a vague charge of "sedition, rebellion, and treason," preferred by the high sheriff of Montgomeryshire, he was arrested. The sheriff had no evidence to produce, and the prisoner ought to have been released at the sessions, but a pretext was found for retaining him, because he refused to take the oaths of allegiance and supremacy. Soon after he was taken to London, and appeared before the king and council, by whom he was committed to the Fleet prison, where he remained nearly two years. For twelve months he was not allowed to leave his chamber, under the window of which was a dunghill. His health was so impaired by the noisome effluvia that he never thoroughly recovered. Thence he was conveyed to Southsea Castle, near Portsmouth, and was confined there five years more. At the end of that time he obtained his liberty by a writ of *habeas corpus*. Crosby remarks that this took place "upon the removal of Chancellor Hyde" [Lord Clarendon], implying that the imprisonment w s altogether illegal, and that the chancellor had illegally prevented the victim, as well as many others, from regaining liberty.

Mr. Powell repaired immediately to Wales, and recommenced preaching. He was not permitted to labor long.

One George Jones, an Episcopal clergyman, and a man of infamous character, lodged a false information against him, to the effect that several of his congregation went armed to their meetings, as if for the purpose of resisting the authorities. This was levying war! Again the minister of Christ was shut up in jail. The charge could not be substantiated. They then tendered the oaths. He refused to take them, and offered to give bail for his appearance at the next sessions. His request was denied, and he was remanded to prison. A writ of *habeas corpus* was obtained, and he was taken before the Court of Common Pleas, at London: yet, although the court unanimously decided that "the return was false and illegal," they committed Mr. Powell, in defiance of all law and justice, to the Fleet prison, where he lay till his death, October 17th, 1670.

The Lord was with him there, and gave him " songs in the night." Nor was he wholly useless. He had opportunities for intercourse with his brethren, and he could use his pen for the advancement of the cause. One of the last acts of his life vas a correspondence with the Broadmead Church, respecting Mr. Hardcastle, who afterward became their pastor. It was singularly illustrative of the hardness of the times. Vavasor Powell, a prisoner, recommends to the church a ministering brother, himself a prisoner!

"We are appointed and commanded," he observed, "to be partakers of the afflictions of the gospel (1 Thess. iii. 3). To be some of the forwardest therein is an honor, which I perceive God is calling you to; therefore rejoice, and so much the more as tribulations abound (2 Cor. vii. 4). Our trials are like to be sharp, but it is to be hoped so much the shorter. However, what are the worst and greatest we can endure here, in comparison of the weight of glory, and crown of righteousness, prepared and reserved for those who continue faithful to the end? An interest in God through Christ, his presence with, power under, Spirit in, and promises to us, are sufficient to carry us comfortably through fire and water; herein let us remember one another, and all the Israel of God, who are in several countries now intended by men to be sheep for the slaughter, though the thought of the Lord may be otherwise."[1]

"During the time of his last illness," says Crosby, "though his physician ordered he should be kept from speaking much, yet so zealously was he affected for the glory of God, and with the love of Christ, that neither his pains, bodily weakness, nor the tender advice of friends, could possibly restrain him; but he would, notwithstanding all, break forth into high and heavenly praises, sometimes by prayer, and sometimes by singing.

"His patience under all his pains was very great. He would under the greatest pain bless God, and say he would not entertain one bad thought of God for all the world. The sight of the pardon of sin and reconciliation with God was so clear, and without interruption, even to the last, that it was as a fire in his bosom till he spake of it; and very hardly would he be restrained at any time; and when he had spent his strength in speaking, then would he compose himself to get a little more strength, that he might go on to speak further of the grace of God toward him, and to give seasonable

[1] *Broadmead Records*, p. 108.

advice to all about him; and so continued till God took away his strength and speech from him."[1]

Among the publications issued by him were two, which were probably written in jail. One was entitled, "The Bird in the Cage, Chirping;" the other, "The Sufferer's Catechism."

ABRAHAM CHEARE was not a scholar, but he was one of the working, suffering men of the seventeenth century, whom the Lord honored and blessed. He was a native of Plymouth, and was a fuller by trade. Whether he had been a minister in one of the Pædobaptist denominations, or whether his preaching abilities showed themselves immediately after his conversion, I am not able to decide. This only is recorded, that he was invited to the pastorate of the church at Plymouth in the same year in which he was baptized, viz., 1648. Though the Baptists in that town were "a poor, despised people," they were respectably numerous, the invitation to Mr. Cheare being signed by one hundred and fifty members. It is probable that many of them resided in the neighboring villages, and that Mr. Cheare had a somewhat extensive diocese. He was a diligent and faithful overseer. After thirteen years of peaceful labors, during which many souls were converted, and a good degree of religious prosperity was enjoyed by the church, Mr. Cheare entered on his course of sufferings. In 1661 he was confined for three months in Exeter jail, for "encouraging religious assemblies." Referring to this imprisonment, in a letter written some time afterward, he says, "Some from our neighboring parts are sent to the place of ancient experience [the prison], where they have a stock of prayers and presence

[1] *History*, i. 380.

to begin upon; they begin on straw, learning to endure hardness as good soldiers. The Lord make that word good to them which *often* hath been, in *that place*, sweet to me (Exod. xxiii. 25; Eccles. iv. 14)."

The Act of Uniformity was the death-knell of Christian freedom. Not only the ejected ministers, but all others who refused obedience, were subjected to persecution. Mr. Cheare became again an occupant of Exeter jail, and lay there three years, " enduring great inhumanities from merciless jailers," yet enjoying the consolations of the gospel in an eminent degree. Writing to a friend, who had known something of persecution, he says: " I received yours of the 11th of the seventh month, and in it a testimony of teaching and supporting grace and presence continued to you abroad, which he is pleased not to deny his poor worms here, in these holes of the earth, where violence hath thrust us in as so many slaughter-houses of men; but overruling grace makes them as the presence-chambers of the great King, where he brings and feasts his favorites with the best things, and proclaims among them, ' Thus shall it be done to them whom the King delights to honor.' This honor have not all, that yet are saints; much less have any this mercy, who either through the fear or formality of their unconverted souls are enforced shamefully to put off that profession which hypocritically they did put on in a day of seeming prosperity; not but these walls, as a draw-net, do enclose bad and good; but at length a discovery is made more manifest; he chooseth in this furnace of affliction, a week in a *prison* giving plainer discovery of a man's spirit than a month in a *church*."

He was released in 1665, and returned to his work

but had scarcely entered on it when his enemies obtained an order for his perpetual banishment. He was placed on the small island of St. Nicholas, whence he had a full view of his former abode, and doubtless often gazed on it with sadness. But he was not alone. Other Christian friends shared his exile. Their discomforts were many; the military guard which was constantly in attendance prevented them from engaging in religious exercises; and Mr. Cheare had the additional trial of a severe fit of sickness, which lasted nine months, and brought him to the brink of the grave. Yet, though "cast down," he was not "destroyed." Divine comforts sustained him, and the sympathy of his brethren on the mainland was practically shown in contributions for his support. They were not long needed. Another fit of sickness came on, under which he rapidly sank. At even-tide it was light. His dying experience afforded a beautiful illustration of the power of the gospel. It cheered those who watched around his bed, and the published record edified many. He exchanged exile for a heavenly home March 5, 1668.[1]

[1] Ivimey, ii. 103-116.

CHAPTER XI.

Biographical Notices continued—John Tombes, B.D.—Francis Bampfield, A.M.—Henry D'Anvers—Edward Terrill—Dr. Du Veil—John Bunyan.

JOHN TOMBES, B.D., was an eminently learned man. His writings in defence of believers' baptism were numerous and weighty. Educated at Magdalen Hall, Oxford, he was appointed to the "Catechetical Lecture" in that hall, on the death of his tutor, when he was but twenty-one years of age, and discharged the duty to the satisfaction of all concerned. About the year 1631 he obtained the living of Leominster in Herefordshire, where he preached and labored ten years. His zeal for "a reformation in the church, and the purging out of all human inventions in the worship of God," exposed him to the fury of anti-reformers. When the king's forces occupied Leominster, Mr. Tombes was driven out of the place and most of his property plundered. After a short stay in Bristol he repaired to London, where he preached, first in Fenchurch Street, and afterward in the Temple Church. But he had been studying the subject of baptism several years. Doubts respecting the authority of infant baptism troubled him while he held the lectureship at Oxford. He sought satisfaction with great earnestness and diligence. The Scriptures were carefully examined; the best writings on both sides were read, and frequent conferences were held with learned ministers, for which there was ample opportunity at that time, as the Assembly of Divines was then sitting. But his scruples took faster hold of him, and at length he yielded to the conviction of the nullity of infant baptism. Dismission from his situation in the Temple followed the publication of one of his works on the subject. He then retired into the country, and became minister of Bewdley, Worcestershire. There in 1646 he was baptized, and formed a Baptist church, to which he ministered separately, still retaining the charge of the parish; but the want of sympathy between him and the people occasioned his removal, and he returned to Leominster, at which place he closed his public ministry soon after the Restoration. I have before stated that he was appointed one of the triers in Cromwell's time. The terms of uniformity were too hard for him. He withdrew into private life. "Having not long before married a rich widow at Salisbury, by whom he enjoyed a good estate, he resolved to live in rest and peace in his old age."[1] The latter end of his life was spent in communion with the Church of England, although he refused to accept any benefice or dignity, or to occupy any public position. With singular inconsistency, as it seems to me, he still wrote against baptism.

Mr. Tombes wrote fourteen treatises on baptism. The principal one was entitled, *Antipædobaptism, or a full review of the dispute about Infant Baptism.*

FRANCIS BAMPFIELD, A.M., was one of the "excellent

[1] Crosby, i. 290.

of the earth" in those days. He received his education at Wadham College, Oxford, where he spent upwards of seven years in the pursuit of knowledge. About the year 1639 he entered into the ministry of the Church of England. The celebrated Bishop Hall ordained him. Shortly afterward he obtained a living in Dorsetshire, and a prebendal stall in Exeter Cathedral. In 1655 he removed to Sherborne, where he labored, as in his former location, with exemplary diligence, and was greatly endeared to the people of his charge.

But he had long been dissatisfied with the National Establishment. The corruptions and abuses inherited from Rome were not to be borne with. They could not, in his opinion, be classed among " things indifferent," for they struck at the authority of the Redeemer, as sole Head of the church, and were totally inconsistent with the spirituality of his kingdom. The enactment of the Act of Uniformity, in 1662, brought Mr. Bampfield to a decision. He took leave of his flock, and commenced preaching as a Nonconformist.

In less than a month he was committed to prison, and there, too, he preached the gospel. His imprisonments were numerous. One of them lasted eight years. He was then an inmate of Dorchester jail, where he continued his ministerial efforts, and had the happiness of forming a church. He preached in jail almost every day. As soon as he was liberated he resumed his public work by itinerating in several counties. In March, 1676, he became pastor of a Sabbatarian Baptist church, meeting in Pinner's Hall, London, which had been gathered by his instrumentality. In the record of the formation of the church, it is stated that " the persons who then agreed to join together in church-communion, according to the order of the gospel, under the conduct of the said Mr. Francis Bampfield as their pastor, laid their church state upon the only sure foundation, and agreed to form and regulate it by the only certain rule and measure, expressing the nature and constitution of this church in the following terms: 'We own the Lord Christ to be the one and only Lord and Lawgiver to our souls and consciences; and we own the holy Scriptures of truth, as the one and only rule of faith, worship, and life, according to which we are to judge in all cases.' Accordingly, these principles were subscribed by the pastor and divers brethren on behalf of the rest."[1]

This was his last station. Here he met with the usual disturbances, the congregations being often broken up by the officers of miscalled justices. On February 17, 1683, while he was preaching, a constable entered and interrupted him. "I have a warrant from the lord mayor to disturb your meeting," said the constable. "I have a warrant from Jesus Christ to go on," replied the preacher, and was proceeding with his discourse, when he was seized and taken, with six of his brethren, to the lord mayor, who fined them ten pounds each. Nevertheless, they met again in the afternoon, but were compelled to separate, on which they retired to Mr. Bampfield's residence, where he finished the exercises of the day. That day week he was apprehended once more, and committed to Newgate. At the next quarter sessions he and several others were placed at the bar, and the oath of allegiance tendered to them. They declined taking it, because it was understood to comprise an obligation to conform to the

[1] Ivimey, i 170.

Church of England, to which they could not bind themselves; whereupon the recorder passed sentence to this effect: "That they were out of the protection of the king's majesty; that all their goods and chattels were forfeited; and that they were to remain in jail during their lives, or during the king's pleasure." It was not "the king's pleasure" to release them. Death in jail was a common thing during the reigns of Charles II. and James II. Mr. Bampfield died in Newgate, February 16, 1684, being in the seventieth year of his age.

He was a learned man and a hard student. The titles of two of his works seem to indicate that he had embraced the views which were afterward more fully developed by Mr. Hutchinson, and are so often referred to in Parkhurst's Hebrew and Greek Lexicons. The one is—*All in One; All useful sciences and profitable arts in one book of Jehovah-Æloim, copied out, and commented upon in created Beings, comprehended and discovered in the fullness and perfection of Scripture knowledge;* 1677: folio. The other—*The House of Wisdom. The House of the Sons of the Prophets: an House of exquisite inquiry, and of deep Research; where the mind of Jehovah-Æloim in the Holy Scriptures of Truth, in the original words and phrases, and their proper significancy, is diligently studied, faithfully compared, and aptly put together for the further promoting and higher advancement of Scripture knowledge, of all useful Arts, and profitable Sciences, in one Book of Books, the Word of Christ, copied out, and commented upon in created Beings;* 1681 : folio.

HENRY D'ANVERS is best known as an author, his *Treatise on Baptism* being regarded as the most learned and complete work which at that time had been published on the subject. The full title is—*A Treatise on Baptism; wherein that of Believers and that of Infants is examined by the Scriptures, with the history of both out of Antiquity; making it appear that Infants' Baptism was not practiced for nearly four hundred years after Christ; with the fabulous traditions and erroneous grounds upon which it was, by the Pope's Canons (with Gossips, Chrysm, Exorcism, Baptizing of Bells, and other Popish Rites), founded: and that the famous Waldensian, and old British Churches, Lollards and Wicklifians and other Christians, witnessed against it: with the History of Christianity among the Ancient Britons and Waldensians.* Mr. D'Anvers had been a colonel in the Parliamentary army, and was some time governor of Stafford. While he held that office he became a Baptist. He was very strenuous for laying on of hands after baptism. He was reputed to be a Fifth-Monarchy man, and it appears evident that he expected the personal reign of the Redeemer upon earth. In 1675 he was apprehended and committed to the Tower —probably on suspicion of treasonable practices, which Venner's insurrection had led the government to connect with Fifth-Monarchy principles—but as no specific charge was brought against him, he was released on bail. It is stated by Crosby that he was one of the elders of a Baptist church, near Aldgate, London. When he was chosen to that office, does not appear. In the reign of James II. he united with some others in consultations and plans relative to the Duke of Monmouth's enterprise, and was so far compromised thereby that he was compelled to flee to Holland, where he died in 1686. The high esteem in which he was held by the principal Baptists of that period is shown by a " Vindication" of his work referred to above, to which were appended the names among others of Hanserd Knollys, William Kiffin, and Thomas Delaune. The Council of the Hanserd Knollys Society intended to republish the *Treatise on Baptism*, competently edited by a learned antiquarian of our denomination; but the inadequate support given to the Society prevented the execution of the design.

Mr. D'Anvers' complicity in the Monmouth rebellion will be differently judged of according to men's politics. That James II. was a tyrant and deserved expulsion, no one now doubts; but where the obligation to entire submission ceases, and the lawfulness of resistance begins, has not yet, I believe, been decided. We who have lived all of our days in sunshine, are but ill qualified to criticize the behavior of those who endured the peltings of the storm.

I have read with intense interest the *Records* of the Baptist Church at Broadmead, Bristol. For those Records we are indebted to Mr. EDWARD TERRILL, who was for eighteen years a ruling elder of that church. He was baptized in the year 1658, chosen to the office of elder in 1667, and died 1685. During the harassing persecutions through which the church passed, he was truly its earthly mainstay. His house was open for worship whenever it was deemed more prudent to meet in a private manner. When the pastor was in prison or compelled to be absent, he was ready to occupy the post of labor or danger. He was wise in counsel, kind-hearted to the poor, and fertile in expedients to baffle persecutors and provide for the church's spiritual wants. A Dissenter and a Baptist from conviction, he stood firm to his principles, though despoiled of his property, and not unfrequently committed to prison for maintaining them. In many instances, when tyrant-magistrates thought they might stretch their power with impunity, he checked their violence by employing the best legal advisers, and thus securing the church from unlawful oppression. In a word, he lived for the cause, and his memory is blessed.

Having acquired considerable property by his marriage, he resolved to devote it to the Lord. By a deed executed in 1678, he placed a large portion—perhaps the whole—of his estates in the hands of trustees, the income derivable therefrom to become available, as it should seem, after the death of his widow, and to be expended on the education of young men for the Christian ministry. This was done, he said, "for the glory of God, and the propagation of the gospel of our Lord Jesus Christ, and for the true love and affection he hath and beareth unto the congregation of which he is a member." With this object in view, he directed that £100 a-year should be paid to "a holy learned man, well skilled in the tongues, viz., Greek and Hebrew, and doth own and practice the truth of believers' baptism, as a pastor or teacher to the congregation." The pastor thus employed was to spend three and a half days in each week in the instruction of young men, not exceeding twelve, members of any baptized congregation in or about Bristol. Ten pounds a year were also to be paid to any four of the students whose friends might be unable to support them. These benefactions may be said to have laid the foundation of Bristol College. By them, Mr. Terrill's usefulness is perpetuated.

The history of Dr. Du Veil is extremely interesting. He was a native of France and of Jewish extraction. His parents were probably in affluent circumstances, as it is evident that he received a very liberal education. The study of the prophetical writings of the Old Testament convinced him of the Messiahship of Jesus. When he avowed that conviction and his determination to embrace Christianity, his father was so enraged that he attempted to kill him, and would have accomplished his purpose had he not been prevented by some persons present. Du Veil joined the Roman Catholic Church, and soon became an eloquent and popular preacher. He acquired considerable fame also as an author by a Commentary on the Gospels of Mark and Luke, in which he displayed much learning and controversial tact. The University of Anjou bestowed on him the degree of D.D., and he was urged to enter into the lists with the Huguenots, whose powerful defences of Protestant truths gave no small trouble to Roman ecclesiastics. He engaged in preparation for that work, but found to his astonishment that Protestantism was a purer form of Christianity than he had yet been acquainted with. Honestly following his convictions, he withdrew from France to Holland, since his life would have been in danger had he continued in the former country, and publicly abjured Popery. Shortly afterward he proceeded to England, where he was received with great respect and liberally befriended by many prelates and dignitaries of the English Church.

He was ordained to the ministry in that church. In 1679 he published *A Literal Explication of Solomon's Song*, and, in the following year, *A Literal Exposition of the Minor Prophets*. These works greatly enhanced his reputation. The bishop of London, Dr. Compton, was so pleased with them that he offered every encouragement to the learned author to continue his biblical researches, and gave him the free use of his library for that purpose. This led to another and final change. In the bishop's library he found the works of Baptist authors, and the perusal of them convinced him that the Baptists were in the right. A pious young woman, a servant in the bishop's family, introduced him to the church with which she was connected, and of which the Rev. John Gosnold was pastor. Dr. Du Veil was baptized by him, and joined the church, by that act separating himself from the rich and powerful, by whose means he would have most probably obtained ecclesiastical advancement. In 1685 his *Literal Explanation of the Acts of the Apostles* was published. This is a valuable commentary. It has been reprinted by the Hanserd Knollys Society.

I have been unable to obtain further information respecting Dr. Du Veil. Whether he preached after he became a Baptist, or confined himself to literary labor, is not recorded in any works to which I have had access. Doubtless he devoted his talents to the diffusion and defence of the truth, and it may be inferred that he was usefully employed. It is not often that we meet with such a case. There have been many in all ages who have seen the light, but failed to follow it through fear of poverty or suffering. Dr. Du Veil was not one of that class. Every change placed him lower in a worldly point of view; but that did not move him. Truth was to be embraced and conscience obeyed at all risks. Peace to his memory!

JOHN BUNYAN's fame is world-wide. He was truly a God-taught man. His "Pilgrim" tells his tale in nearly all languages, and it is listened to with rapt interest and admiration by men of every clime and of all varieties of mental culture. It is the peasant's food and the philosopher's luxury.

The history of his life is so well known that it is quite unnecessary to reproduce it here. I will only give a chronological note or two. John Bunyan was born at Elstow, Bedfordshire, in the year 1628. He was converted to God in 1653, and soon afterward began to preach. On the 13th of November, 1660, he was committed to Bedford jail for "teaching men to worship God contrary to the law." There, with no other aids than the Bible and Foxe's *Book of Martyrs*, he wrote the *Pilgrim's Progress*, and other works which have immortalized his name. He was released in December, 1672, and spent the remainder of his life in manifold labors for the cause of Christ. As pastor of the church at Bedford, to which office he was chosen December 21, 1671, while yet a prisoner, "he was instant in season, out of season," and the church greatly flourished under his ministry. When he visited London people flocked in crowds to hear him; three thousand persons were known to be assembled for that purpose at seven o'clock in the morning. Not unfrequently the learned and the great were among them. Charles II. once asked Dr. Owen how it was that he was so fond of hearing a tinker preach. "May it please your majesty," the doctor replied, "had I the tinker's abilities for preaching, I would gladly relinquish all my learning."

He had been engaged in a Christian work when he

fell under the death-stroke. A profligate son had so offended his father that he threatened to disinherit him. Bunyan affected a reconciliation. He had been to Reading on that benevolent errand, and was returning home through London, when he was attacked by fever, caused by exposure to heavy rain on his journey, and died at a friend's house after a few days' illness. This was in August, 1688, about three months before the landing of William, Prince of Orange, afterward William III. How his heart would have been gladdened could he have witnessed the nation's deliverance!

One of the last treatises which he prepared for the press was entitled *Of Antichrist and his ruin*. It expresses, in his own plain and nervous style, those sentiments respecting Popery and religious freedom which Baptists have ever maintained.

We may indulge in a pardonable pride when we boast of John Bunyan as one of ours. We have no name more honored. But I will not attempt to write his eulogy. His works praise him, and will praise him as long as the church of God abides on earth. Cowper's lines are well known:

> "O thou, whom, borne on fancy's eager wing
> Back to the season of life's happy spring,
> I pleased remember, and while memory yet
> Holds fast her office here, can ne'er forget;
> Ingenious dreamer, in whose well-told tale
> Sweet fiction and sweet truth alike prevail;
> Whose humorous vein, strong sense, and simple style
> May teach the gayest, make the gravest smile;
> Witty, and well employed, and, like the Lord,
> Speaking in parables his slighted word;

I name thee not, lest so despised a name
Should move a sneer at thy deserved fame;
Yet e'en in transitory life's late day,
That mingles all my brown with sober gray,
Revere the man whose *Pilgrim* marks the road,
And guides the *Progress* of the soul to God."

CHAPTER XII.

Biographical Notices Concluded—Thomas Grantham—Hanserd Knollys—Benjamin Keach—William Kiffin—Anecdotes.

I HAVE given some account of the principal ministers of our denomination in England who died before the glorious Revolution. The names of several others, who survived that event, will be recorded here, because their labors as public men must be chiefly referred to the period now under review.

THOMAS GRANTHAM was for many years the principal minister among the General Baptists. He was baptized at Boston, Lincolnshire, in the year 1652, and almost immediately afterward commenced his ministerial labors. In 1656 he became pastor of a church at North Elm Chapel. The petition presented to Charles II. in the early part of his reign, said to be "approved by more than 20,000," was written by him. He was several times imprisoned, and otherwise annoyed, for his principles and practices as a Baptist. So highly esteemed was he by his brethren that in 1666 he was removed from the pastoral office and appointed "messenger," in which capacity he labored many years, founding churches in Lincolnshire, Norfolk, Warwickshire, and other counties. and exercising a general superintendence over the interests of the denomination. He finally settled at Norwich, where he died, January 17, 1692.

Mr. Grantham wrote some useful works, chiefly in explanation or defence of Baptist sentiments. The largest was a folio volume, entitled "*Christianismus Primitivus*."[1]

HANSERD KNOLLYS was a native of Chalkwell, in Lincolnshire. While pursuing his studies at the University of Cambridge he experienced a change of heart, having become acquainted with "several gracious Christians, then called *Puritans*," whose conversation was blessed to him. In 1629 he was ordained by the bishop of Peterborough. At Humberstone, where he lived several years, he was accustomed to preach three, and even four, times on the Lord's Day, besides sermons on saints' days and at funerals. But scruples and doubts agitated his mind. At length he reached the conviction that his position in the Church of England was not in accordance with the New Testament, and he renounced his ordination, resolving not to preach any more till he had "received a clear call and commission from Christ to preach the gospel."

During his silence he underwent much mental distress, which was removed by the instrumentality of Mr. Wheelwright, one of the Puritan ministers. He then recommenced preaching. "I began to preach the doctrine of free grace, according to the tenor of the new and everlasting covenant, for three or four years together, whereby very many sinners were converted, and many believers were established in the faith."

The persecution was so fierce that he joined the emi-

[1] Taylor's *History of the General Baptists*, i. 308–316.

grants who were at that time flocking to New England, and arrived at Boston in the spring of 1638. He was not allowed to remain there, the ministers having unaccountably judged him to be an Antinomian, and desired the magistrates to send him away. But he found a home at Dover, on the Piscataqua, where he preached with much acceptance upwards of three years. Cotton Mather having referred to "ministers from other parts of the world" who had arrived in New England, says: "Of these there were some godly Anabaptists, as namely, Mr. Hanserd Knollys (whom one of his adversaries called *Absurd Knowless*) of Dover, and Mr. Miles of Swansley. Both of these have a respectful character in the churches of this wilderness."[1] It is observable that Mr. Knollys' arrival was in the spring of 1638. Roger Williams' baptism did not take place till the winter of that year.

Mr. Knollys returned to England about the close of 1641. He settled in London, where he gained his livelihood by teaching school. His next employment was that of chaplain in the Parliamentary army. When he left the army he established himself again in London as a schoolmaster, and preached in the churches as he found opportunity. His labors were very acceptable to the people, but were so disapproved of by the Assembly of Divines, because he preached against national churches, that he withdrew from connection with them, and opened a meeting-house in Great St. Helen Street, where he commonly had a congregation of a thousand hearers. A Baptist church was formed there, over which he was ordained pastor in 1645. He held that office till his death,

[1] *Magnalia*, book iii. p. 243 (Ed. 1855).

in 1691, though he was often prevented, by the operation of unjust laws, from fulfilling its duties. On several occasions he found it necessary to retire into the country for a while, and during the hottest period of the persecution he left England and lived two or three years in Germany and Holland. He had his share also of "bonds and imprisonments." But God graciously sustained him. His religious enjoyments abounded, and his labors were eminently successful.

"My wilderness, sea, city, and prison mercies," he observed, "afforded me very many and strong consolations. The spiritual sights of the glory of God, the divine sweetness of the spiritual and providential presence of my Lord Jesus Christ, and the joys and comforts of the holy and eternal Spirit, communicated to my soul, together with suitable and seasonable Scriptures of truth, have so often and so powerfully revived, refreshed, and strengthened my heart in the days of my pilgrimage, trials, and sufferings, that the sense, yea, the life and sweetness thereof, abides still upon my heart, and hath engaged my soul to live by faith, to walk humbly, and to desire and endeavor to excel in holiness to God's glory and the example of others. Though, I confess, many of the Lord's ministers and some of the Lord's people have excelled and outshined me, with whom God hath not been at so much cost, nor pains, as he hath been at with me. I am a very unprofitable servant, but yet by grace I am what I am."

Mr. Knollys gives the following account of his recovery from a dangerous illness. I shall copy it without comment:

"Two learned, well-practiced, and judicious doctors

of physic had daily visited me, and consulted several days together, and I was fully persuaded that they did what they possibly could to effect a cure, and knew also that God did not succeed their honest and faithful endeavors with his blessing. Although God had given a signal and singular testimony of his special blessing by each of them unto other of their patients, at least sixteen, at the same time, I resolved to take no more physic, but would apply to that holy ordinance of God, appointed by Jesus Christ, the great Physician of value, in James v. 14, 15: 'Is any sick among you? let him call for the elders of the church, and let them pray over him, anointing him with oil in the name of the Lord; and the prayer of faith shall save the sick, and the Lord shall raise him up; and if he have committed sins, they shall be forgiven him;'— and I sent for Mr. Kiffin and Mr. Vavasor Powell, who prayed over me, and anointed me with oil in the name of the Lord. The Lord did hear prayer, and heal me; for there were many godly ministers and gracious saints that prayed day and night for me (with submission to the will of God), that the Lord would spare my life, and make me more serviceable to his church, and to his saints, whose prayers God heard; and as an answer to their prayers I was perfectly healed, but remained weak long after."

As the poverty of the church prevented them from providing adequately for his support, Mr. Knollys continued in his employment as a schoolmaster almost to the close of life. His efforts were so successful that he realized considerable property. Reviewing his history some time after his wife's death—which took place in

1671—he says: "To my eldest son I had given sixty pounds per annum during life, which he enjoyed about twenty-one years ere he died. To my next son that lived to be married, I gave the full value of two hundred and fifty pounds in money, house, school, and household goods, and left him fifty scholars in the school-house. To my only daughter then living I gave, upon her marriage, above three hundred pounds in money, annuity, plate, linen, and household stuffs, and left her husband fifty scholars in the said school-house, in partnership with my said son. To my youngest son that lived to be married I gave more than three hundred pounds sterling; besides, it cost me sixty pounds in his apprenticeship, and forty pounds afterward. Thus my heavenly Father made up my former losses with his future blessings, even in outward substance, besides a good increase of grace and experience, in the space of the forty years that I and my dear faithful wife lived together. We removed several times, with our whole family; whereof, once from Lincolnshire to London, and from London to New England; once from England into Wales; twice from London into Lincolnshire; once from London to Holland, and from thence into Germany, and thence to Rotterdam, and thence to London again. In which removings I gained great experiences of God's faithfulness, goodness, and truth, in his great and precious promises; and I have gained some experience of my own heart's deceitfulness and the power of my own corruptions, and the reigning power of Christ, and his captivating and subduing my sins—making conquests of the devil, world, and sin, and then giving me the victory, and causing me to triumph, and to bless his holy name. . . . I would not want those experiences and teachings that my soul hath enjoyed for all that I ever suffered."

Among the works published by Mr. Knollys was a Grammar of the Latin, Greek, and Hebrew languages. It was written in Latin.[1]

Mr. Knollys died September 19, 1691. He was in the ninety-third year of his age. The "Hanserd Knollys Society," founded in the year 1845 for the republication of the works of early Baptist authors, was named after him.

Knollys, Keach, and Kiffin might be called "the first three" among the Baptist ministers of those days. Their talents and characters gave them influence, which appears to have been wisely exerted for the benefit of the denomination. They were honored while living, and their "memory is blessed."

BENJAMIN KEACH's sufferings have been detailed in a former section. He was twenty-four years of age when he endured the pillory. Born in 1640, he was converted in his fifteenth year, and commenced preaching, at the invitation of the church, three years afterward, though he did not undertake a pastoral charge till 1668, when he was chosen pastor of a church in the borough of Southwark, London. He remained there till his death.

An occurrence during his journey to London illustrates the state of society and the deficiency of the police arrangements in England at that time. Mr. Keach, his wife, and three children were traveling to London by the stage-coach. On their way they were attacked by a band of highwaymen, who robbed the passengers of all their money and valuables, leaving Mr. Keach, who had just

[1] Ivimey, ii. 347-359.

THE TROUBLOUS PERIOD. 441

sold his effects for the purpose of settling in London, and had the proceeds of the sale in his pocket, in a state of utter destitution. But friends relieved his immediate necessities, and assisted him in bringing an action against the county for the amount of his loss, in which he succeeded. Such a procedure would be accounted strange in these days.

Mr. Keach's labors were much blessed. For four years the church over which he presided met in private houses, often changing the place of assembly to avoid the pursuit of informers. In 1672, when Charles II. issued a "Declaration of Indulgence," a meeting-house was erected for the church. It was enlarged several times, as the congregation increased, and at length was capable of accommodating nearly a thousand persons.

Preaching was not all his work. Mr. Keach was a voluminous writer. Some of his works were "polemical," some "practical," some "poetical." The "polemical" treated of various subjects, then warmly discussed—including the laying on of hands, the lawfulness of singing in public worship, the authority of the Christian Sabbath, and baptism. On the last-mentioned theme he wrote frequently and with great earnestness. The "practical" portion of his works comprised, besides minor productions, his *Tropologia; or, Key to Open Scripture Metaphors;* his *Gospel Mysteries Unveiled; or, an Exposition of all the Parables;* and his *Travels of True Godliness,* and *Travels of Ungodliness.* The first two were bulky books, which were rather distinguished for ingenuity than just criticism. They have been reprinted several times, but, however valuable in a devotional or experimental point of view, cannot be recommended as models of sound exegesis. The two others are somewhat in Bunyan's style. They are still prized by serious readers. The most important of his "poetical compositions was *Zion in Distress; or, the Groans of the Protestant Church*, first published in 1666. This was written, as he says in the preface, because "he perceived Popery was ready to bud, and would, if God prevented not, spring up afresh in the land." After the Revolution, his prolific pen produced another poem, entitled *Distressed Sion Relieved; or, the Garment of Praise for the Spirit of Heaviness. Wherein are discovered the great causes of the Church's trouble and misery under the late doleful Dispensation: with a Complete History of, and Lamentation for, those Renowned Worthies that fell in England, by Popish rage and cruelty, from* 1680 *to* 1688; *together with an Account of the late admirable and stupendous Providence which hath wrought such a Sudden and Wonderful Deliverance for this Nation and God's Sion therein*. He also published a collection entitled *Spiritual Melody*, containing nearly three hundred hymns.

Mr. Keach's constitution was weak and his sickness frequent. In 1689 his life was despaired of; the physicians had exhausted their skill; and his relatives took leave of him, expecting his departure to be near at hand, when, as Crosby relates, "the Reverend Mr. Hanserd Knollys, seeing his friend and brother near to all appearance expiring, betook himself to prayer, and, in an earnest and very extraordinary manner, begged that God would spare him and add unto his days the time granted unto his servant Hezekiah. As soon as he ended his prayer, he said, 'Brother Keach, I shall be in heaven before you,' and quickly after left him. So remarkable was the answer of God to this good man's prayer that I cannot omit it; though it may be discredited by some, there are yet living incontestible evidence of the fact:—for Mr. Keach recovered of that illness, and lived just fifteen years afterward; and then it pleased God to visit him with that short sickness which put an end to his life." He died July 18, 1704, in the sixty-fourth year of his age.

The historian Crosby was a member of the church under Mr. Keach's pastoral care. His delineation of the character of his pastor was the result of personal and close observation. It is manifestly a picture from life, and is worthy of preservation:

"To collect every particular transaction of this worthy minister's life cannot be expected at such a distance of time; nay, even to collect all that was excellent and amiable in him is too great a task to be now undertaken. I shall only observe that he was a person of great integrity of soul—a Nathanael indeed; his conversation not frothy and vain, but serious, without being morose or sullen. He began to be religious early, and continued faithful to the last. He was not shocked by the fury of his persecutors, though he suffered so much from them for the cause of Christ. Preaching the gospel was the pleasure of his soul, and his heart was so engaged in the work of the ministry that from the time of his first appearing in public to the end of his days his life was one continued scene of labor and toil. His great study and constant preaching exhausted his animal spirits and enfeebled his strength, yet to the last he discovered a becoming zeal against the errors of the day. His soul was too great to recede from any truth that he owned, either from the powers or flatteries of the most eminent. He discharged the duties of his pastoral office with unwearied diligence, by preaching in season and out of season, visiting those under his charge, encouraging the serious, defending the great truths of the gospel, and setting them in the clearest light. How low would he stoop for the sake of peace! And how would he bear the infirmities of his weak brethren! that such as would not be wrought upon by the strength of reason might be melted by his condescension and good nature. He was prudent as well as peaceable; would forgive and forget injuries, being charitable as well as cautious. He was not addicted to utter hard censures of such as differed from him in lesser matters, but had a love for all saints, and constantly exercised himself in this, to keep a conscience void of offence toward God and toward man. He showed an unwearied endeavor to recover the decayed power of religion, for he lived what he preached, and it pleased God so to succeed his endeavors that I doubt not but some yet living may call him their father whom he hath begotten through the gospel. He affected no unusual tones nor indecent gestures in his preaching. His style was strong and masculine. He generally used notes, especially in the latter part of his life; and if his sermons had not the embellishments of language which some boast of, they had this peculiar advantage, to be full of solid divinity, which is a much better character for pulpit discourses than to say they are full of pompous eloquence and flights of wit. It was none of the least of his excellent qualifications for the ministerial work that he 'knew how to behave himself in the house of God,' in regard of the exercise of that discipline which is so necessary to a Christian Society. With patience and meekness, with gravity and prudence, with impartiality and faithfulness, did he demean himself in his congregation; and with prudence in conduct did he manage all their affairs upon all occasions."[1]

WILLIAM KIFFIN is the last of the Baptist worthies of this period. His is a truly honorable name. He was one of the merchant-princes of London, and had won his wealth by honest industry. He sought also to win souls with wisdom and earnestness answerable to the greatness of the undertaking. Like Mordecai of old, he was "accepted of the multitude of his brethren, seeking the wealth of his people, and speaking peace to all his seed."

William Kiffin was a native of London. He was born in the year 1616. When he was nine years of age he lost both his parents by the plague, which at that time raged violently in London, and was himself "left with six plague sores" upon him, so that "nothing but death was looked for" by his friends. It pleased God to restore him and to bless him with long life. His conversion took place in early youth. The instructive and powerful ministry of those times was the means of implanting conviction in his soul, and ultimately of establishing him in the faith. An extract from his autobiography may be here cited:

"At the end of the year 1632 it pleased God to bring Mr. John Goodman to London. I attended upon his ministry and found it very profitable. Delivering his judgment about the way of God's dealings in the conver-

[1] Ivimey, ii. 360-368.

sion of sinners, he showed that the terrors of the law were not of necessity to be preached to prepare the soul for Christ, because in the nature and tendency of them they drove the soul farther off from Christ; answering very many objections and Scriptures produced by other ministers to prove the contrary. This was of great use to me, so far as to satisfy me that God hath not tied himself to any such way of converting a sinner, but according to his good pleasure took several ways of bringing a soul to Jesus Christ. I had for some time seen the want of Christ, and believed that it was by him only I must expect pardon; and had also seen the worth and excellences that were in him above all other objects; so that I now felt my soul to rest upon and to trust in him."[1]

Again: "About this time [1634] I became acquainted with several young men that diligently attended the means, to whom it had pleased God to make known much of himself and his grace. These being apprentices as well as I, had no opportunities of converse but on the Lord's Days. It being our constant practice to attend the morning lecture, which began at six o'clock, both at Cornhill and Christ Church, we appointed to meet together an hour before, to spend it in prayer and communicating what experiences we had received from the Lord to each other; or else to repeat some sermon we had previously heard. After a little time, we also read some portion of Scripture, and spake from it according as it pleased God to enable us. In these exercises I found very great advantage, and by degrees did arrive to some small measure of knowledge, finding the

[1] Ivimey's *Life of Kiffin*, p. 9.

study of the Scriptures very pleasant and delightful to me; which I attended to as it pleased God to give me opportunities."[1]

The young man became an independent inquirer, prepared to follow the leadings of truth, regardless of consequences. Observing that some excellent ministers had gone into voluntary banishment rather than conform to the Church of England, he was induced to examine the points in dispute between that church and her opponents, and this issued in his joining the Nonconformists. He had been five years a member of the Independent church, then under the care of Mr. Lathrop, when, with many others, he withdrew and joined the Baptist church, the first in England of the *Particular* Baptist order, of which Mr. Spilsbury was pastor. Two years after that, in 1640, a difference of opinion respecting the propriety of allowing ministers who had not been immersed to preach to them—in which Mr. Kiffin took the negative side—occasioned a separation. Mr. Kiffin and those who agreed with him seceded, and formed another church, which met in Devonshire Square. He was chosen pastor, and held that office till his death, in 1701—one of the longest pastorates on record.

Mr. Kiffin was extensively engaged in mercantile pursuits, trading chiefly with Holland, and acquired large property. His standing in society, and his well-known integrity of character, gave him influence, and he often exerted it for the protection and relief of sufferers. It was much in his favor, too, in those changeful and stormy times, that he stood aloof from all political agitation. He never troubled himself with party disputes, nor

[1] *Life*, p. 13.

interfered in the intrigues and cabals of politicians. He was a good citizen of the Commonwealth; he submitted to the Protectorate; he honored the king. His policy was, and so he advised his brethren, to yield obedience to the existing government, in things civil, whatever might be the form of that government. Hence he was held in high esteem by all parties, and great deference was shown him.

Charles II. was always in want of money, and cared not by what means it was obtained. It is said that on one occasion he sent to Mr. Kiffin, and asked the loan of forty thousand pounds. The Baptist merchant replied that he had not then so large a sum at command, but that if his majesty would accept ten thousand pounds as a gift, he was heartily welcome. The king took the money, and Kiffin, as he was accustomed to say, saved thirty thousand pounds by his liberality; for Charles would have forgotten to pay the debt.

Several attempts were made to involve the good man in trouble. He was summoned before the Lord Mayor, during the Protectorate, for preaching against infant baptism, but the prosecution was not pressed; had it been, Cromwell would have probably quashed it. On some occasions, after the Restoration, he endured brief imprisonments, pending investigation. At one time, he was charged with uttering treasonable words in a sermon; at another, by means of a forged letter, with being privy to an insurrectionary design; at another, with having hired two men to kill the king. But his innocence was so clearly apparent that he escaped. Doubtless it was by "the good hand of God" upon him. "My Lord Arlington hath told me," he observes, " that though, in every list of disaffected persons brought him, who ought to be secured, my name was always amongst them, yet the king would never believe anything against me; my Lord Chancellor also, the earl of Clarendon, being very much my friend."[1]

In 1679, when the Conventicle Act was renewed, in a severer form, an attempt was made to bring Mr. Kiffin under its lash. "It pleased the Lord," he says, "that the laws now began to be put in execution against Dissenters; and, as I was taken at a meeting, I was prosecuted, for the purpose of recovering from me forty pounds. This sum I deposited in the hands of the officer; but, finding some errors in the proceedings, I overthrew the informers on the trial. Though the trial cost me thirty pounds, it had this advantage—that many poor men who were prosecuted upon a similar charge were by this means relieved, the informers being afraid to proceed against them."[2]

Four years after, they tried again, but with no better success. "It pleased the Lord, presently after the death of my wife, that I was again prosecuted by the informers for three hundred pounds, the penalties of fifteen meetings. They had managed this matter so secretly as to get the *record* in court for the money; but, finding there were some errors also in that record, they moved the court, Judge Jenner being on the bench, to amend the record. Some of my friends who were in court moved that I might be heard before the order was made. In this way I came to the knowledge of the prosecution, and, having employed able counsel, they pleaded that the record could

Life p. 46.   [2] *Ibid.* p. 58.

not be mended; and, after several hearings before the court, the informers let the suit fall."[1]

Had there been more Kiffins in England at that time the informers' trade would have been less gainful. Persecutors reveled in ill-gotten riches. They will at length appear before a "judgment-seat" where there will be found no "errors in the record."

A portion of Mr. Kiffin's domestic history is thus narrated:

"It pleased God to take out of the world to himself my eldest son, which was no small affliction to me and my dear wife. His obedience to his parents and forwardness in the ways of God were so conspicuous as made him very amiable in the eyes of all who knew him. The grief I felt for his loss did greatly press me down with more than ordinary sorrow; but in the midst of my great distress, it pleased the Lord to support me by that blessed word being brought powerfully to my mind (Matt. xx. 15), 'Is thine eye evil because I am good? Is it not lawful for me to do what I will with mine own?' These words did quiet my heart, so that I felt a perfect submission to his sovereign will, being well satisfied that it was for the great advantage of my dear son, and a voice to me to be more humble, and watchful over my own ways.

"My next son being but of a weak constitution, and desirous of traveling, I sent him with the captain of a ship, an acquaintance, who was bound to Aleppo. Fearing that in this voyage and travels he was in danger of being corrupted by those of the popish religion, I sent a young man, a minister, with him, to defend him from

[1] *Life*, p. 59.

anything of that kind. But I was greatly prevented; for this minister left him and the ship at Leghorn, and went to Rome; by which means I was to my sorrow disappointed. On my son's return home, when at Venice, he met with a popish priest, and, being forward to discourse with him about religion, the priest, to show his revenge, destroyed him by poison. As to the minister's name, I forbear to mention it, he being yet alive. 'I pray God that this sin may not be laid to his charge.'"[1]

Here is a fine trait of the good old Protestantism. William Kiffin would not have acted like some of the moderns, who send their children to Roman Catholic schools. So solicitous was he for his son's preservation from the insidious error that he was content to incur a double expense on his tour rather than risk his spiritual safety. All honor to him; and honored let him be for his forbearance. The name of that minister who so unaccountably deserted his charge will never be known on earth. Kiffin would not expose him to obloquy, though he richly deserved it. Kiffin was a disciple of the "meek and lowly" One.

About three years after the last-mentioned affliction the good man lost his wife, who died October 2, 1682. He records the event in his usual strain. "It pleased the Lord," he says, "to take to himself my dear and faithful wife, with whom I had lived nearly forty-four years, whose tenderness to me and faithfulness to God were such as cannot, by me, be expressed, as she constantly sympathized with me in all my afflictions. I can truly say, I never heard her utter the least discontent under all the various providences that attended either me or her; she

[1] *Life*, p. 56.

eyed the hand of God in all our sorrows, so as constantly to encourage me in the ways of God: her death was the greatest sorrow to me that ever I met with in the world."[1]

I have given a full account in a previous section of the affliction that befel Mr. Kiffin in the death of his grandsons, the Hewlings. That wound was never healed; it smarted till his dying day.

In 1687, James II. published a "Declaration of liberty of conscience," assuming for that purpose a power to dispense with the laws of the land by an exercise of the royal prerogative. Some of the Dissenters, and among them a few Baptists, were so delighted at the prospect of freedom and equality that they gratefully accepted the proffered boon, and presented addresses to the king on the occasion, expressing in strong terms their sense of obligation to him. But Mr. Kiffin and the majority of his brethren were not beguiled. They saw that the measure was wholly unconstitutional, since laws can neither be made, repealed, nor suspended, but by the united legislature; and they were convinced that James' real design was to bestow political power on the Roman Catholics, and ultimately to make popery rampant. They abstained, therefore, from any demonstration, and waited the issue of events.

When the king deprived the city of London of its charter, and displaced its magistrates, Mr. Kiffin was appointed one of the new aldermen. His account of the transaction is as follows:

"A little time after, a great temptation attended me, which was, a commission from the king to be one of the

[1] *Life*, p. 58.

aldermen of the city of London. I used all the means I could to be excused by some lords near the king; and also by Sir Nicholas Butler, and Mr. Penn, but all in vain. They said that they knew I had an interest that would serve the king; and although they knew my sufferings had been very great, by the cutting off my two grandsons, and losing their estates, yet it should be made up to me, both as to their estates, and also in what honor and advantage I could reasonably desire for myself.

"But I thank the Lord those proffers were no snare to me, being fully possessed in my judgment that the design was the total ruin of the Protestant religion, which, I hope I can say, was and is dearer to me than my life. I remained without accepting office, from the time I received the summons to take it, about six weeks, until the Lord Mayor, Sir John Peake, in court said, I ought to be sent to Newgate; and in a few days after, I understood it was intended to put me into the Crown Office, and to proceed with all severity against me. Which, when I heard, I went to the ablest counsel for advice (one that is now a chief judge in the nation), and stating my case to him, he told me my danger was every way great; for if I accepted to be an alderman, I ran the hazard of five hundred pounds [that being the penalty for taking office without first receiving the Lord's supper according to the forms of the Church of England]; and if I did not accept, as the judges then were, I might be fined by them ten, or twenty, or thirty thousand pounds, even what they pleased. So that I thought it better for me to run the lesser hazard of five hundred pounds, which was certain, than be exposed to such fines as might be the ruin of myself and family. Yet did I forbear taking the place of alderman for some time, when the alderman then sitting agreed to invite the king to dinner on the Lord Mayor's day, and laid down fifty pounds each alderman to defray the charge; which made some of them the more earnest for my holding, and they were pleased to tell me I did forbear [in order] to excuse my fifty pounds. But to prevent any such charge against me, I desired a friend to acquaint my Lord Mayor and the court that I should deposit my fifty pounds with them, yet delaying accepting the office—which I accordingly sent them. When the Lord Mayor's day came, and the dinner prepared for the king, I the next day understood that there were invited to the feast the pope's nuncio, and several other priests, that dined with them, which had I known they had been invited, I should hardly have parted with my fifty pounds toward that feast; but the next court-day I came to the court and took upon me the office of alderman. In the commission I was also a justice of the peace and one of the lieutenancy; but I never meddled with either of those places, neither in any act of power in that court, touching causes between man and man, but only such things as concerned the welfare of the city and good of the orphans, whose distressed condition called for help, although we were able to do little toward it. . . . Having been in that office about nine months, I was discharged from it, to my very great satisfaction. . . . My reason for giving this brief account of these things is, that you all may see how good the Lord hath been to prevent those designs, then in hand, to destroy both our religion and our liberties, and I heartily desire that both myself and all others concerned may acknowledge the great goodness of God therein, that he may have the glory of all our delivering mercies."

Thus wrote the Christian patriot. We see here the meek dignity of religion. I must present one more specimen. It is the concluding part of his autobiography, written in 1693, when he was in the seventy-seventh year of his age:

"I leave these few instances of the divine care to you, my children, and grandchildren, and great-grandchildren, that you may remember them with thankful hearts, as they must prove to the praise of God, on my account. I leave them also desiring the Lord to bless them to you; above all, praying for you, that you may, in an especial manner, look after the great concerns of your souls; that you may know God, and Jesus Christ, whom to know is eternal life. Endeavor to be diligent, to inquire after, and to be established in the great doctrines of the gospel, which is of absolute necessity to salvation. I must every day expect to leave this world, having lived in it much longer than I expected, being now in the seventy-seventh year of my age, and yet know not what my eyes may see before my change. The world is full of confusions; the last times are upon us; the signs of the times are very visible; iniquity abounds, and the love of many in religion waxes cold. God is, by his providence, shaking the earth under our feet; there is no sure foundation of rest and peace, but only in Jesus Christ, to whose grace I commend you."

Mr. Kiffin lived eight years after writing the above. He died December 29, 1701, in the eighty-sixth year of his age.

Although he was pastor of the church in Devonshire Square upward of sixty years, it is not probable that he devoted much of his time to its interests. His mercantile pursuits, and the numerous public duties which were imposed on him, both civil and religious, engrossed his attention, and prevented him from fulfilling the requirements of the pastoral office. This deficiency was supplied by the labors of an assistant or co-pastor. Mr. Thomas Patient was his first colleague; he had been some years pastor of a church in Ireland. On his death, in 1666, Mr. Daniel Dyke, A.M., was chosen. He was a learned man, and an excellent minister. He was one of the "Triers." He died in 1688, and was succeeded by Mr. Richard Adams, who survived Mr. Kiffin.

Mr. Kiffin was generally regarded as the chief man in our denomination. That is, his excellent character and the position which he occupied gave him influence among the brethren, and rendered his advice and co-operation desirable. His name is connected with all the public proceedings of the body for half a century. If the court wished to conciliate the Baptists, application was made to Kiffin. If country churches required aid or counsel, they seemed naturally to ask his interference, and fully confided in his discretion and integrity, knowing that he would honestly endeavor to do right.

He was an eminently good man. We cannot but admire the quiet composure and filial submission of soul with which he recorded even the most painful events of his life. "It pleased the Lord"—such was the habitual expression of his views and feelings. Whether the reference was to mercy or judgment—to manifestations of blessing—to persecuting malice—to domestic sorrow—to storms and perils—or to joyful deliverance—still, the language was the same—"It pleased the Lord." Thus he possessed his soul in patience, and "endured as seeing him who is invisible."

I might tell of other excellent men whom God raised up in the "Troublous Period," and by whom the churches were edified. There was John Gosnold, Joseph Wright, George Hammond, Samuel Taverner, Henry Forty, Benjamin Coxe, Nehemiah Coxe, D.D., William Collins, Hercules Collins, and many more. But "time would fail." I must bring this period to a close.

Our historians have preserved some interesting anecdotes, illustrative of the times. I will transcribe a few.

George Hammond was pastor of a church at Canterbury, and preached frequently in the neighboring villages. He was once overtaken by a storm, and took shelter under a tree. While there, another person joined him, who in the course of conversation said that he was an informer, and that he had heard there was to be a conventicle in the neighborhood, at which he meant to be present. "I am a man-taker also," said Mr. Hammond. "Are you so?" replied the informer; "then we will go together." They reached the house and sat some time among the people. "Here are the people," said Mr. Hammond, "but where is the minister! Unless there is a minister we cannot make a conventicle of it, and therefore either you or I must preach." The informer declined of course, and Mr. Hammond preached, much to the man's astonishment. The sermon was blessed to him, and he became a Christian.

In the early part of his ministry Nehemiah Coxe lived at Cranfield, Bedfordshire. He was committed to prison for preaching the gospel. When brought to his trial he pleaded in Greek, and on examination answered in Hebrew. The judge called for the indictment, and found him described as "Nehemiah Coxe, Cordwainer," at which he expressed his astonishment, no doubt thinking it exceedingly strange that a shoemaker should be a learned man. Mr. Coxe insisted on his right to plead in what language he chose, and as none of the lawyers could talk Greek or Hebrew the case was necessarily dismissed. "Well," said the judge to the learned counsel before him, "the cordwainer has wound you all up, gentlemen."

Jeremiah Ives, who was thirty years pastor of a church in the Old Jewry, London, was celebrated for his tact and power as a disputant. Charles II. heard of him, and invited him to court to hold a discussion with a Roman Catholic priest, who was told that his opponent was a clergyman of the Church of England. Mr. Ives was persuaded to assume that character by appearing in clerical attire In the course of the dispute he argued that notwithstanding the authorities which might be adduced in favor of Romish opinions and practices, and the plausibilities which might be urged in their defence, they could not be sustained, because they were entirely unknown in the apostolic age. That argument, the priest replied, would be of equal force against infant baptism, which was also unknown in the apostolic age. Mr. Ives admitted it, intimating that he rejected infant baptism on the same ground; whereupon the priest abruptly closed the discussion, saying that he had been cheated: he had supposed that he was disputing with a Church of England clergymen, whereas they had brought him "an Anabaptist preacher." The king and his courtiers were highly amused.

In those days, preachers were often obliged to disguise themselves that they might not be recognized by the informers. "It is said that Bunyan, to avoid discovery, went from a friend's house disguised as a carter, with his white frock, wide-awake cap, and whip in his hand, to attend a private meeting in a sheltered field or barn."

Andrew Gifford, of Bristol, adopted similar expedients, at one time appearing as an officer, at another as a gentleman. "Did you not meet me last night," he said one day to a friend, " going through Lawford's Gate? Why did you not speak to me?" "I did not see you, sir." "Did you not meet a tinker?" "Yes, sir" "That was me," said Mr. Gifford.

" It happened," says Crosby, " that the magistrates of Sevenoaks sent some officers to the congregation meeting at Brabourn, who took all the men from thence and carried them to the town, where by an order they were kept prisoners all night. On the morrow, when the justices met together, the prisoners were had before them and examined, and after some little discourse with them were dismissed. They all with one heart, full of wonder and joy, returned to the place from whence they were taken, to return thanks to God for this so unexpected a deliverance. When they came to the place, to their great surprise and inexpressible joy, *they found the women there, who had not departed from the house, but had spent that evening, the night, and morning, in prayer to God on their behalf.*"

CHAPTER XIII.

Baptists in North America—Church at Providence—Baptists in Massachusetts—Persecuting Enactment against them—The Whipping of Obadiah Holmes—First Church at Boston—Newport—Swansea—Other Churches — Roger Williams — Gregory Dexter -- Obadiah Holmes—John Miles—Elias Keach.

I NOW proceed to give some information respecting the introduction of Baptist principles into America. There were Baptists among the first emigrants to New England; but their number must have been small, as no effort was made for some time to set up separate worship. "Some few of these people," says Cotton Mather, "have been among the planters of New England from the beginning, and have been welcome to the communion of our churches, which they enjoyed, reserving their particular opinions unto themselves."[1]

Roger Williams' preaching at Salem, prior to his banishment, of which an account will be hereafter given, was distasteful to some of his hearers, because he continually testified against the assumption of power in things religious by the magistrate, and they said that he inculcated principles "tending to Anabaptism." This probably meant nothing more than that he taught the individuality

[1] *Magnalia*, book vii. chap. ii.

of religion, and laid such stress on personal piety, as essential to union with the church, as seemed inconsistent with the Pædobaptist theory of membership. It is certain that he had not then professed Baptist sentiments.

But shortly after his settlement at Providence the whole subject of baptism came under consideration and discussion. How it originated, and in what way the inquiry was carried on, we know not. The result was, however, that twelve men declared themselves Baptists in principle. Then the question arose, How were they to be baptized, since they had no minister? They might have sent to England for one; but the application might not have been successful, and it would have involved an expense which they were ill prepared to meet; beside which, a long delay would have occurred.[1] In this dilemma they adopted the only expedient that seemed to meet the case. One of their number, Thomas Holliman, was chosen to baptize Mr. Williams, who then baptized the other. This was in March, 1639. A church was immediately formed, of which Mr. Williams became pastor. But he soon vacated the office; some think after the lapse of only a few months, while others are of opinion that he resigned when he embarked for England to procure a charter for the colony, and that it was on that occasion Mr. Chad Brown was chosen his successor. On his return from England he refrained from fellowship with the church, and lived in an isolated religious condition, preaching the gospel to the Indians, as he found opportunity, but refusing to participate in the ordinances

[1] It was not perhaps known that Hanserd Knollys was then preaching at Dover, and that he was one of the "godly Anabaptists" mentioned by Cotton Mather.

He had embraced a singular notion, which is thus stated by one of his biographers: "He denied that any ministry now exists which is authorized to preach the gospel to the impenitent, or to administer the ordinances. He believed that these functions belonged to the apostolic race of ministers, which was interrupted and discontinued when the reign of Antichrist commenced, and which will not, as he thought, be restored, till the witnesses shall have been slain and raised again (Rev. xi. 11). . . . He says in his *Hireling Ministry None of Christ's*, published in 1652: 'In the poor small span of my life, I desired to have been a diligent and constant observer, and have been myself many ways engaged, in city, in country, in courts, in schools, in universities, in church, in Old and New England, and yet cannot, in the holy presence of God, bring in the result of a satisfactory discovery, that either the begetting ministry or the apostles or messengers to the nations, or the feeding or nourishing ministry of teachers, according to the first institution of the Lord Jesus, are yet restored and extant.' The only ministry which, in his opinion, now exists, is that of prophets, *i. e.* ministers who explain religious truths, and bear witness against error."[1]

The second Baptist church in Rhode Island was formed at Newport in 1644 by Dr. John Clark and eleven others. Dr. Clark became the pastor, which office he resigned in 1651, when he accompanied Roger Williams to England on business connected with the charter of the colony. He was succeeded by Obadiah Holmes, presently to be mentioned.

A second church was formed at Newport in 1656, by

[1] Knowles' *Memoir of Roger Williams*, p. 171.

twenty-one persons, who seceded from the first church on account of the use of psalmody, to which they objected—the "restraints on the liberty of prophesying"—particular redemption—and the indifference shown by the church to the laying on of hands at the admission of members—a practice regarded as essential by the seceders.

Four additional churches were organized in Rhode Island during this period, viz.: North Kingston, 1665; Seventh-day Baptists, Newport, 1671; South Kingston, 1680; Dartmouth (afterward removed to Tiverton), 1685.

Year after year, more Baptists emigrated from England to Massachusetts, and, as a matter of course, openly avowed their sentiments. "The Anabaptists," says Winthrop, "increased and spread in Massachusetts." Various methods were adopted to annoy them, which so far produced the desired effect that many of them left the country and took refuge among the Dutch in the state of New York. But others remained, who, it would seem, took no pains to conceal their views, naturally concluding that those who had fled from England to gain religious freedom would concede to their fellow-Christians what they sought for themselves. But the New Englanders were very imperfectly instructed in this matter. They still held the Establishment principle, and dreamed that the Jewish theocracy was to be perpetuated in Christian states. An act was passed for the banishment of Baptists. It was easier to banish than to convince them. Here it is:

"Forasmuch as experience hath plentifully and often proved that, since the first rising of the Anabaptists, about one hundred years since, they have been the incendiaries of commonwealths, and the infectors of persons in main matters of religion, and the troublers of churches in all places where they have been, and that they have held the baptizing of infants unlawful, have usually held other errors or heresies therewith, though they have, as other heretics used to do, concealed the same, till they spied out a fit advantage and opportunity to vent them, by way of question or scruple; and whereas divers of this kind have, since our coming into New England, appeared amongst ourselves, some whereof (as others before them) denied the ordinance of magistracy, and the lawfulness of making war, and others the lawfulness of magistrates, and their inspection into any breach of the first table [that is, the first four of the Ten Commandments]; which opinions, if they should be connived at by us, are likely to be increased amongst us, and so must necessarily bring guilt upon us, infection and trouble to the churches, and hazard to the whole commonwealth: it is ordered and agreed, that if any person or persons, within this jurisdiction, shall either openly condemn or oppose the baptizing of infants, or go about secretly to seduce others from the approbation or use thereof, or shall purposely depart the congregation at the ministration of the ordinance, or shall deny the ordinance of magistracy, or the lawful right and authority to make war, or to punish the outward breaches of the first table, and shall appear to the court willfully and obstinately to continue therein, after due time and means of conviction—every such person or persons shall be sentenced to banishment."[1]

This act was passed November 13, 1644. That same year Roger Williams had published his immortal book,

[1] *Benedict* (Ed. 1848), p. 370.

The Bloody Tenet of Persecution for Cause of Conscience Discussed. It was a bitter pill to John Cotton, the minister, and to the magistrates who were so eady to do his bidding. They gnashed their teeth at Williams, as he passed through Boston on his way from England to Rhode Island, but they durst not bite—they could not even scratch him: their claws were pared: they stood in awe of the men at home. So Williams got safe to his free colony; but "a poor man by the name of Painter" was "tied up and whipt" because he would not have his child sprinkled!

There was a pressure on the Baptists in Massachusetts. They were few and fearful. Can we wonder at it? It was no small trial to be driven beyond the bounds of civilization in those days. We hear but little of them for seven years, and then it is whipping again! William Witter, an aged Baptist, lived at Lynn. The distance, coupled with his infirmities, prevented him from enjoying Christian fellowship with his brethren of the church at Newport to which he belonged. There were other brethren in the same neighborhood. A pastoral visit was resolved on. Dr. John Clark, pastor of the church, accompanied by Obadiah Holmes, a ministering brother, and —— Crandal, repaired to Lynn for that purpose, and proposed to hold a meeting with the brethren on the Lord's Day. They were assembled, and Dr. Clark had commenced his discourse, when the constables made their appearance, charged to apprehend the intruders, and keep them safely till the next day. They obeyed their orders, and the meeting was broken up. Next day the Puritan magistrates committed them to prison, and, about a fortnight after, the Court of Assistants adjudged Dr.

Clark to pay a fine of twenty pounds, Mr. Holmes a fine of thirty pounds, and Mr. Crandal five pounds. Some friends paid Dr. Clark's fine. Mr. Crandal was released on promise to appear the next court-day. There was some talk about a disputation on baptism between Dr. Clark and the clergy of Boston, who had intimated a willingness to meet him, but it came to nothing.

Mr. Holmes' fine was the heaviest, most probably on account of the circumstances mentioned in the sentence presently to be quoted. He would not allow the fine to be paid for him, nor would he pay it himself. But he must either pay or be "well whipt." So ran the sentence. It is a curiosity, and should be preserved:

"The sentence of Obadiah Holmes, of Seaconk, the 31st of the fifth month, 1651.

"Forasmuch as you, Obadiah Holmes, being come into this jurisdiction about the 21st of the fifth month, did meet at one William Witter's house, at Lynn, and did here privately (and at other times), being an excommunicated person, did take upon you to preach and baptize upon the Lord's Day, or other days, and being taken then by the constable, and coming afterward to the assembly at Lynn, did, in disrespect to the ordinance of God and his worship, keep on your hat, the pastor being in prayer, insomuch as you would not give reverence in vailing your hat, till it was forced off your head, to the disturbance of the congregation, and professing against the institution of the church, as not being according to the gospel of Jesus Christ; and that you, the said Obadiah Holmes, did, upon the day following, meet again at the said William Witter's, in contempt to authority, you being then in the custody of the law, and did there receive the sacrament, being excommunicate, and that you did baptize such as were baptized before, and thereby did necessarily deny the baptism before administered to be baptism, the churches no churches, and also other ordinances and ministers, as if all was a nullity; and did also deny the lawfulness of baptizing of infants; and all this tends to the dishonor of God, the despising the ordinances of God among us, the peace of the churches, and seducing the subjects of this commonwealth from the truth of the gospel of Jesus Christ, and perverting the straight ways of the Lord; the court doth fine you thirty pounds, to be paid, or sufficient sureties that the said sum shall be paid by the first day of the next Court of Assistants, or else to be well whipt; and that you shall remain in prison till it be paid, or security given in for it.

"By the Court,
"INCREASE NORVEL."

The sentence was passed in July. Mr. Holmes was kept in prison till September, when he was publicly whipped, and so barbarously "that in many days, if not some weeks, he could take no rest but as he lay upon his knees and elbows, not being able to suffer any part of his body to touch the bed whereon he lay." His own account of the affair, in a letter addressed to Messrs. Spilsbury, Kiffin, and other Baptists in London, is deeply affecting, but too long for transcription here. He tells the brethren how he declined the proffered kindness of his friends, who "came to visit him, desiring him to take the refreshment of wine and other comforts," having resolved "not to drink wine nor strong drink that day, until his punishment was over," lest the world should say "that the strength and comfort of the creature had carried him through;" how he withdrew to his chamber to seek strength from the Lord, and "prayed earnestly that he would be pleased to give him a spirit of courage and boldness, a tongue to speak for him, and strength of body to suffer for his sake, and not to shrink or yield to the strokes, or shed tears, lest the adversaries of the truth should thereupon blaspheme and be hardened, and the weak and feeble-hearted discouraged;" how he attempted at the place of suffering to address the people, but was prevented by the magistrate in attendance; and how graciously he was strengthened to endure the pain. "As the man began to lay the strokes upon my back, I said to the people, 'Though my flesh should fail, and my spirit should fail, yet my God would not fail.' So it pleased the Lord to come in, and to fill my heart and tongue as a vessel full, and with an audible voice I broke forth, praying unto the Lord not to lay this sin to their charge, and telling the people that now I found he did not fail me, and therefore now I should trust him for ever, who failed me not; for in truth, as the strokes fell upon me, I had such a spiritual manifestation of God's presence, as the like thereof I never had nor felt, nor can with fleshly tongue express; and the outward pain was so removed from me that indeed I am not able to declare it to you; it was so easy to me that I could well bear it, yea, and in a manner felt it not, although it was grievous, as the spectators said, the man striking with all his strength (yea, spitting in his hands three times, as many affirmed) with a three-corded whip, giving me therewith thirty strokes. When he had loosed me from the post, having joyfulness in my heart and cheerfulness in my countenance, as the spectators observed, I told the magistrates, 'You have struck me as with roses,' and said moreover, 'Although the Lord hath made it easy to me, yet I pray God it may not be laid to your charge.'" Mr. Holmes then proceeds to state that John Hazel and John Spur, who expressed their sympathy by shaking hands with him after it was over, were sentenced "to pay forty shillings or be whipt;" and that a surgeon who dressed his wounds was inquired after as if he had committed some crime. But "it hath pleased the Father of mercies," he adds, "to dispose of the matter that my bonds and imprisonment have been no hindrance to the gospel, for before my return some submitted to the Lord and were baptized, and divers were put upon the way of inquiry. And now, being advised to make my escape by night, because it was reported there were warrants forth for me, I departed; and the next day after, while I was on my journey, the constable came to search at the house where I had lodged; so I escaped their hands, and was, by the good hand of my heavenly Father, brought home again to my near relations, my wife and eight children, the brethren of our town and Providence having taken pains to meet me four miles in the woods, where we rejoiced together in the Lord."[1]

"Bonds and imprisonment" awaited all Baptists in New England. They met for worship as they were able, and constantly testified against infant baptism, for which they were harassed by the courts without mercy. In 1665 they ventured to form themselves into a church at Charlestown, near Boston. This church was afterward removed into the city, and considered the first Boston

[1] Ivimey, ii. 208-211.

church. Its early history was one long tale of vexation and annoyance, inflicted, there is too much reason to believe, at the instigation of the ministers. Thomas Gould, the founder of the church, was ordered, with two others, after a year's imprisonment, to " depart out of the jurisdiction." This occasioned the removal of the church, for some time, to Noddle's Island, in Boston Harbor, now East Boston.

The Congregational clergy, by whom the magistrates were instigated, were proof against all influence or entreaty. Nothing softened them. When a number of persons, some of them men of high standing in the colony, petitioned for lenity to the Baptists, they were fined for petitioning. A letter of remonstrance from England, signed by Dr. Goodwin, Dr. Owen, Philip Nye, John Caryl, and other eminent divines, failed to produce any effect. Even the king's interference was in vain. A royal letter, " requiring that liberty of conscience should be allowed to all Protestants," and that " no good subjects should be subjected to fines and forfeitures for not agreeing in the Congregational way," was disregarded. When the Baptists, encouraged by this interposition, repaired for worship to a meeting-house which they had built, its doors were nailed up, and they were forbidden to open them, " at their peril." But they insisted on their rights, pleaded the king's authority, and at length were allowed to meet in peace.

Thomas Gould was the first pastor of the Boston church. Isaac Hull succeeded him, with whom John Russell was for a short time associated. John Emblem, who was sent for from England, became co-pastor with Mr. Hull in 1684.

I have given full particulars respecting the churches already mentioned, on account of the interesting circumstances connected with their early history. The remaining portion of American statistics for this period may be compressed into a small space.

In 1663, the church at Swansea, Massachusetts, was constituted by John Miles, who had just come from Swansea, Wales, with some of his brethren. The place where they ultimately settled was called after that which they had left. Meetings of the Baptists had been held there for thirteen years before, but no church had been founded. The Massachusetts government tried to strangle the church in its infancy, and actually fined all the members five pounds each for worshiping God contrary to the order established in the colony; but at last they yielded and the church lived.

A church was formed at Kittery, Maine, in 1682, but it died in its infancy. In 1683 a church was formed at Charleston, South Carolina. There were two churches in Pennsylvania—Cold Spring, founded in 1684; Pennepek, in 1688. In the same year a church was established at Middletown, New Jersey.

In 1688, the Baptist denomination in North America comprised thirteen churches only. Seven were in Rhode Island, two in Massachusetts, one in South Carolina, two in Pennsylvania, and one in New Jersey. Times have greatly changed since then! There are now upward of thirteen thousand churches! The "little one" has literally "become a thousand!"

A few biographical sketches remain to be furnished. I will begin with Roger Williams.

Very little is known of the early life of this great man.

He was a native of the Principality of Wales, and it is supposed that he was born in the year 1599. Sir Edward Coke, as tradition states, observed his attention at church, where he was accustomed to take notes of the sermons. and liberally took charge of his education, thinking that he would prove in future years an able lawyer. This was a providential interposition, for Williams' parents were poor, and had it not been for Sir Edward's generosity, he would have remained in humble life all his days. Having received a good classical education, " he commenced the study of the law, at the desire and under the guidance of his generous patron, who would naturally wish to train his pupil to the honorable and useful profession which he himself adorned. The providence of God may be seen in thus leading the mind of Mr. Williams to that acquaintance with the principles of law and government which qualified him for his duties as legislator of his little colony. But he probably soon found that the study of the law was not congenial with his taste. Theology possessed more attractions to a mind and heart like his. To this divine science he directed his attention, and received episcopal orders. It is stated that he assumed, while in England, the charge of a parish; that his preaching was highly esteemed, and his private character revered."[1]

But Roger Williams' mind was not formed for such subjection as the Church of England requires of its members. He understood Christian freedom too well to continue under the heavy yoke of an established church. Nor did he conceal his views. He had " presented his arguments from Scripture" to Messrs. Cotton and Hooker, who afterward followed him to New England, " why he

[1] Knowles *Memoir*, p. 24.

durst not join with them in the use of Common Prayer." Whether he was driven out by violence, or whether he voluntarily withdrew from the communion of the Church of England, cannot now be ascertained. This only is certain, that he left his native country in search of evangelical liberty, and landed at Boston on the 5th of February 1630, '31.

He had been but a few weeks in the colony when he was invited by the church at Salem to become assistant to their minister, Mr. Skelton. He complied, and labored there for a short time, when, in consequence of the opposition of the Boston people, he left for Plymouth, and preached there two years. Returning to Salem, and gladly received by the church in that place, he remained with them till his banishment.

Mr. Williams had been disappointed by the aspect of affairs in New England. He found that the colonists had set up a government of a theocratic kind; that none were admitted to the exercise of civil rights unless they were members of one of their churches; and that offences against religion were punishable by the magistrate. These things he abhorred, and he testified his dislike from the very commencement of his residence. There was much jangling and disputation, and no small amount of high-handed oppression on the part of the colonial authorities. At length sentence of banishment was passed upon Williams. It was thus expressed:

"Whereas, Mr. Roger Williams, one of the elders of the church at Salem, hath broached and divulged divers new and dangerous opinions against the authority of magistrates; as also writ letters of defamation, both of the magistrates and churches here, and that before any conviction, and yet maintaineth the same without any retraction; it is therefore ordered, that the said Mr. Williams shall depart out of this jurisdiction within six weeks now next ensuing, which, if he neglect to perform, it shall be lawful for the governor and two of the magistrates to send him to some place out of this jurisdiction, not to return any more without license from the court."

Such were the "tender mercies" of the New England Puritans of those days. They had resisted the magistrate at home by refusing to obey him in things ecclesiastical, and, in consequence, had gone into exile; and now they banished their ministering brother for the very offence which they had themselves been guilty of. It seemed as if their boasted love of freedom was only a love of freedom for themselves, conjoined with the assumption of power to take it away from others.

This sentence was passed November 3, 1635. Six weeks were allowed Mr. Williams for his removal. But he could not be silent. Meetings were held at his house, where he discoursed in his usual manner, much to the annoyance of the magistrates, who concluded that the only way to stop him would be to ship him off for England in a vessel then lying in the harbor. He heard of their design, and prevented its execution by flight In the month of January, 1635-6, he left his home, and for fourteen weeks wandered about, exposed to the rigors of the season—sometimes in an open boat, sometimes in the woods—"not knowing what bread or bed did mean." At last he pitched his tent at Seekonk, where he purchased land of the Indians, and began to build and plant. Yet even there the spirit of persecution followed him. The place was supposed to be within the colony of Plymouth, and the magistrates of that town were afraid of those of Boston; so they requested him to go further off. Again he sallied forth on pilgrimage, accompanied by some of his friends who had joined him. "As they approached the little cove, near Tockwotton, now Indian Point, they were saluted by a company of Indians with the friendly interrogation, '*What cheer?*'—a common English phrase, which they had learned from the colonists. At this spot they probably went on shore, but they did not long remain there. They passed round Indian Point and Fox Point, and proceeded up the river on the west side of the peninsula, to a spot near the mouth of the Moshassuck river. Tradition reports that Mr. Williams landed near a spring which remains to this day. At this spot the settlement of Rhode Island commenced—

> 'Oh, call it holy ground,
> The soil where first they trod !
> They have left unstained what there they found—
> Freedom to worship God.'

"To the town here founded Mr. Williams, with his habitual piety, and in grateful remembrance of God's merciful providence to him in his distress, gave the name of PROVIDENCE."[1]

Three years after, Mr. Williams avowed himself a Baptist, as has been already stated, and assisted in forming a Baptist church, of which he was the first pastor. The noble principles he had so fearlessly inculcated were adopted by the new colony and embodied in its constitution. The first settlers in Providence signed the following covenant:

[1] Knowles, p. 102.

"We, whose names are hereunder written, being desirous to inhabit in the town of Providence, do promise to submit ourselves, in active or passive obedience, to all such orders or agreements, as shall be made for public good of the body, in an orderly way, by the major consent of the present inhabitants, masters of families, incorporated together into a township, and such others as they shall admit into the same, *only in civil things*."

When the charter was obtained, a code of laws was prepared, of which these are the closing words: "Otherwise than thus, what is herein forbidden, all men may walk as their consciences persuade them, every one in the name of his God. AND LET THE LAMBS OF THE MOST HIGH WALK IN THIS COLONY, WITHOUT MOLESTATION, IN THE NAME OF JEHOVAH THEIR GOD, FOR EVER AND EVER."

Under the influence of the new views of religion which he had embraced, Mr. Williams did not resume his connection with the church when he returned from England, but lived apart. Yet his was no idle life. He preached the gospel among the scattered settlers; he promoted, in various ways, the temporal and spiritual welfare of the Indians; he was the adviser and friend of all the inhabitants; he took an active part in the government of the colony, of which he was repeatedly chosen President. In 1651, he visited England a second time on its behalf, and obtained a confirmation of the original charter. The uniform justice and kindness with which he treated the Indians so impressed them, that when, on occasion of "King Philip's War," they attacked the colony, in 1676, and "Mr. Williams took his staff and went to meet them," endeavoring to dissuade them from their enterprise, on the ground that the number and power of the English would prove overwhelming, one of the chiefs said: "Well, let them come—we are ready for them. But as for you, Brother Williams, you are a good man. You have been kind to us many years—not a hair of your head shall be touched."[1]

Mr. Williams, like many other true patriots, died poor. For several years before his death he was mainly dependent upon his children.

He died in the early part of the year 1683, in the 84th year of his age. No record of his last illness, and of the state of his mind at that time, has been furnished. There can be no doubt, however, that he was fully prepared for the event. In a letter addressed to Governor Bradstreet, at Boston, dated May 6, 1682, after referring to recent intelligence from England, he says: "All these are but sublunaries, temporaries, and trivials. Eternity (O Eternity!) is our business."[2] In less than a year from that time he had entered eternity. His body "was buried with all the solemnity the colony was able to show." His spirit rejoiced in perfect purity and freedom.

So little is known of Williams' successors at Providence, and of most of the other pastors of the churches founded in this period, that it is not worth while to give mere lists of names and dates. A few particulars only may be mentioned.

GREGORY DEXTER, the fourth pastor of the church at Providence, was a native of London, and by trade a printer. Mr. Callender says, in his *Century Sermon*, that Mr. Dexter "was the first who taught the art of printing in Boston, in New England. He was never

---

[1] Knowles, p. 346.   [2] *Ibid.* p. 354.

observed to laugh, and seldom to smile. So earnest was he in the ministry that he could hardly forbear preaching when he came into a house, or met a number of persons in the street."

DR. JOHN CLARKE was a native of Bedfordshire, England. He received a liberal education, and practised as a physician in London. The intolerance of the Massachusetts Congregationalists, with whom he associated on his arrival in New England, so disgusted him that he determined to seek another settlement, and united with some others in founding the colony of Rhode Island, and the town of Newport. He went to England, as has been stated, in 1651, and remained there till 1664, when he returned, and resumed his connection with the church as well as the practice of his profession. He died April 20, 1676, in the sixty-sixth year of his age. The Rev. John Callender, the historian of Rhode Island, says of him: "He was a faithful and useful minister, courteous in all the relations of life, and an ornament to his profession, and to the several offices which he sustained. His memory is deserving of lasting honor, for his efforts toward establishing the first government in the world which gave to all equal civil and religious liberty. To no man is Rhode Island more indebted than to him. He was one of the original projectors of the settlement of the island, and one of its ablest legislators. No character in New England is of purer fame than John Clarke."

OBADIAH HOLMES, whose sufferings at Boston have been described, was a native of Preston, Lancashire. He emigrated to New England in 1639, became a Baptist in 1650, succeeded Dr. Clarke in the pastorate of the first Newport church in 1652, and held that office thirty years.

JOHN MILES, founder of the church at Swansea, was rector of the parish of Ilston, Glamorganshire, whence he was ejected by the Act of Uniformity, in 1662. It is probable that he joined the Baptist church at Swansea immediately after his ejectment, and that the severity of the persecution compelled him and his friends to emigrate the following year.

The first pastor of the church at Pennepek was Elias Keach, son of the celebrated Benjamin Keach. The history of his conversion and settlement with that church is very remarkable. Rev. Morgan Edwards, in his *History of the Baptists in Pennsylvania*, writes thus: "The first minister they had was the Rev. Elias Keach. He was son of the famous Benjamin Keach, of London. He arrived in this country a wild youth, about the year 1686. On his landing, he dressed in black, and wore a band, in order to pass for a minister. The project succeeded to his wishes, and many people resorted to hear the young London divine. He performed well enough till he had advanced pretty far in the sermon; then, stopping short, he looked like a man astonished. The audience concluded he had been seized with a sudden disorder; but, on asking what the matter was, received from him a confession of the imposture, with tears in his eyes and much trembling. Great was his distress, though it ended happily; for from this time he dated his conversion. He heard of Mr. Dungan [of Coldspring]. To him he repaired, to seek counsel and comfort, and by him he was baptized and ordained. From Coldspring Mr. Keach came to Pennepek, and settled a church there, as before related; and thence traveled through Pennsylvania and the Jerseys, preaching the gospel in the wilderness with great success, insomuch that he may be considered as the chief apostle of the Baptists in these parts of America."[1] Mr. Keach returned to England in 1692, and labored several years in London with great success. He died October 27, 1699.

[1] pp. 9, 10.

THE QUIET PERIOD.

CHRONOLOGICAL NOTES.

FROM A. D. 1688 TO A. D. 1800.

1689. Episcopacy abolished in Scotland.—Toleration Act, England.
1690. Death of John Elliot, "Apostle of the Indians."
1691. Death of John Flavel, June 26th.—Death of Richard Baxter, December 8th.
1696. Death of Philip Henry, June 24th.
1698. Society for Promoting Christian Knowledge founded.
1701. Society for the Propagation of the Gospel in Foreign Parts founded.
1709. Death of John Howe, April 2d.
1714. Death of Matthew Henry, June 22d.
1721. Commencement of the Mission to Greenland.
1739. Methodist Societies formed.
1748. Death of Dr. Watts, Nov. 25th.
1749. Rise of the Swedenborgians.
1751. Death of Dr. Doddridge, October 26th.
1764. Brown University, Rhode Island, founded.
1766. First Methodist Class formed in the United States.
1770. Death of Whitefield, September 30th.
1785. American Episcopal Church founded.
1790. Death of John Howard, Jan. 20th.—Death of Benjamin Franklin, April 17th.
1791. Death of John Wesley, March 2d.
1792. Baptist Missionary Society founded, October 2d.
1793. Profession of Christianity suppressed in France.
1795. Death of W. Romaine, July 25th.—London Missionary Society founded.
1796. Scottish Missionary Society founded.
1797. Death of Parkhurst, the Lexicographer, February 21st.—Dutch Missionary Society founded.—Baptist Home Missionary Society founded.—Methodist New Connection founded.—The Sabbath abolished in France.—Death of Benjamin Beddome, September 3d.—Death of Joseph Milner, the Ecclesiastical Historian, November 15th.
1798. Death of Schwartz, the Missionary, February 13th.—The Papal Government overthrown; the Pope a prisoner in France.
1799. Death of Samuel Pearce, October 10th.—Religious Tract Society founded.

CHAPTER I.

General Character of the Period—Baptist General Assembly in London—Questions—Particular Baptist Fund—Baptist Board—The Deputies—The Widows' Fund—The Book Society—Bristol College—Dr. John Ward—Toleration Act—Schism Bill — Dissenters excluded from Office—Restrictions—Relief—Decline of the General Baptists—Communion Controversy—Effects of High Calvinism on the Particular Baptists—Commencement of Revival—Fuller and Sutcliffe—State of the Denomination in England—Foreign and Home Missions.

I HAVE named this the "Quiet Period," because it was not only a time of rest, persecution having ceased, but also a time of stillness—of slumber—of comparative inaction. The excitement had passed away. A season of exhaustion succeeded, in which there was little power or even will to engage in any religious enterprise. It seemed as if there must be an interval allowed for the gathering of strength, ere the churches could enter the field of labor which was opening before them. It is true that there had been displays—marvelous displays of moral force, that had startled and confounded the tyrants of the age, and brought to remembrance the best days of the old martyrdoms; and it might have been supposed that the power thus gained would be employed in the work of the Lord with success equally marvelous, after the obstructions were removed out of the way. But strength to endure is very different from strength to labor. If the conflict issues in death, the supernatural energy holds out to the end, and the triumph is complete. If, on the other hand, the struggle ceases, so that a calm succeeds to the storm, a reaction takes place, and it has not unfrequently happened that a state of spiritual languor has followed a time of sore trial. Other considerations might be adduced, chiefly drawn from the history of the church, tending to illustrate and confirm the remark. But whether the explanation be admitted or not, the fact in the present instance is sufficiently obvious. The Baptist interest in England fell into decline after the Revolution. Liberty did not bring life. The sunshine had for a time a withering effect. At the lapse of more than sixty years after the close of the persecution the denomination was found to have decreased! "There is no reason to doubt," says Ivimey, "that our churches were far more prosperous and numerous at the Revolution in 1688, than at this period [1753], sixty years afterward; so that prosperity had indeed slain more than the sword."[1]

A General Assembly was convened in London, at which ministers or delegates from upward of one hundred churches were present. The meetings continued nine days, from the third to the twelfth of September, 1689. The object was to unite the churches together, that by a combination of their energies certain useful purposes might be subserved, besides the benefit which might be expected to result from brotherly communications. It was particularly recommended to raise a fund,

[1] *History* iii. 279.

by "freewill offerings," and yearly, quarterly, monthly, or even weekly contributions, the proceeds of which were to be devoted to the following objects, viz. :—the assistance of such churches as were not "able to maintain their own ministry," so that their ministers might be "encouraged wholly to devote themselves to the great work of preaching the gospel;" the sending of ministers "where the gospel hath or hath not yet been preached, and to visit the churches;" and the furtherance of the wishes of "those members that shall be found in any of the aforesaid churches that are disposed for study, have an inviting gift, and are sound in fundamentals, in attaining to the knowledge and understanding of the languages, Latin, Greek, and Hebrew."

Various questions were proposed at this meeting, and the opinions and advice of the brethren sought; from which it appears that commendable care was exercised in the matter of discipline. I will furnish an extract or two:

"*Question.* Whether, when the church have agreed upon the keeping of one day, weekly or monthly, besides the first day of the week, to worship God and perform the necessary services of the church, they may not charge such persons with evil that neglect such meetings, and lay them under reproof, unless such members can show good cause for such their absence?

"*Answer.* Concluded in the affirmative (Heb. x. 25).

"*Q.* What is to be done with those persons that will not communicate to the necessary expenses of the churches whereof they are members, according to their ability?

"*A.* Resolved, that, upon clear proof, the persons so offending, as aforesaid, should be duly admonished; and if no reformation appears, the church ought to withdraw from them (Ephes. v. 3; Matt. xxv. 42; 1 John iii. 17).

"*Q.* Whether it be not necessary for the elders, ministering brethren, and messengers of the churches to take into their serious consideration those excesses that are found among their members, men and women, with respect to their apparel?

"*A.* In the affirmative :—That it is a shame for men to wear long hair, or long periwigs, and especially ministers (1 Cor. xi. 14), or strange apparel (Zeph. i. 8); that the Lord reproves the daughters of Zion, for the bravery, haughtiness, and pride of their attire, walking with stretched-out necks, wanton eyes, mincing as they go (Isa. iii. 16), as if they affected tallness, as one observes upon their stretched-out necks; though some in these times seem, by their high dresses, to outdo them in that respect. . . . We earnestly desire that men and women whose souls are committed to our charge may be watched over in this matter, and that care be taken, and all just and due means used, for a reformation herein; and that such who are guilty of this crying sin of pride, that abounds in the churches as well as in the nation, may be reproved; especially considering what time and treasure is foolishly wasted in adorning the body, which would be better spent in a careful endeavor to adorn the soul; and the charge laid out upon those superfluities, to relieve the necessities of the poor saints, and to promote the interest of Jesus Christ. And though we deny not but in some cases ornaments may be allowed, yet whatever ornaments in men or women are inconsistent with modesty, gravity, sobriety, and prove a scandal to religion, opening the mouths of the ungodly, ought to be cast off, being truly no ornaments to believers, but rather a defilement."[1]

Similar meetings were held in London for several successive years. The difficulties of transit in those days, with other considerations, led to an alteration, by which Bristol was substituted for London every alternate year. At length those general gatherings were discontinued, and associations of a smaller kind were instituted, similar to those now held; but I am inclined to think that the arrangements were not of a permanent character. The Western Association was an exception. That body has remained till the present day. The others gradually ceased to exist, and new associations were afterward organized. A large majority of those now existing were constituted or revived in the present century.

The churches in London and its vicinity were larger and wealthier than those in other parts of the kingdom. It is pleasing to observe that they were liberally disposed, and that the country churches were indebted to them for very valuable assistance. They originated the Particular Baptist Fund, which was established in 1717, and still exists. Its objects were, the relief and aid of ministers whose incomes were insufficient for their support, and the encouragement of candidates for the ministry, by helping them to purchase books or to pursue their studies. Large sums were contributed for the establishment of the fund, both by the churches and by individuals, and considerable additions have been since made by donations and legacies. The interest of the funded money constitutes the income, which is further increased by the pro-

[1] Ivimey, 1. 496.

ceeds of annual collections. In 1866 the income was £2,753 3s. 9d. (13,765.75 dollars, gold). This institution has rendered most important service to the denomination. The General Baptists established a fund of the same kind in 1726.

The ministers living in London and its vicinity formed themselves into a society, January 20, 1723-4, which has continued till now. The original purposes of the society are thus adverted to by Mr. Ivimey: "They gave their opinion and advice in any matters of difficulty in the churches that were referred to them by both parties; they received applications from the country ministers to assist them from the Baptist Fund; they sanctioned and recommended cases of building and repairing meeting-houses in the country, and to be collected for in London; they watched rigorously over the purity of the members composing the board, whether it related to charges of immoral conduct, or of erroneous principles; they received to their friendship ministers upon their being settled as pastors in the churches, and young ministers who were introduced by the pastors of the respective churches which had called them to the ministry; and they appear to have generally acted in a body in assisting destitute churches, and at the ordination of ministers—to have very strictly discouraged separations in the churches—and to have affectionately supported each other against traducers."[1] The society is now called "The Baptist Board."

Certain other organizations from which the Baptists derived benefit were composed of the various bodies of Protestant Dissenters, with whom they united on those occasions.

[1] *History*, iii. 179.

The general body of Protestant Dissenting ministers of the three Denominations was constituted in the year 1727. It consists of all approved ministers of the Presbyterian, Independent, and Baptist Denominations, resident within ten miles of the cities of London and Westminster. The objects for the promotion of which they are associated are not very strictly defined, but may be said to embrace whatever affects the welfare of the Protestant Dissenting interest, in its general or political aspects. Many advantages have resulted from this association. It is the privilege of this body to present addresses in person to the Sovereign on important occasions, such as the accession, royal marriages, deliverances from danger, great victories, restoration of peace, and the like. At such times the king or the queen is seated on the throne, attended by the great officers of state. The first opportunity of the kind was the accession of King William and Queen Mary. Mr. Ivimey has preserved in his "History" copies of the addresses presented in the period now under review, and up to the year 1820, with the royal replies.

When the general body was formed, in 1727, forty-five Baptist ministers joined it; the present number is sixty-four.

Another association, formed in 1732, has proved exceedingly useful. I refer to the body of Deputies, appointed to defend the civil rights of Dissenters. Two gentlemen are sent by each congregation of the three Denominations in and about the cities of London and Westminster. They meet annually, and at such other times as may be needful. An Executive Committee is chosen from the body once a year to manage its affairs. The objects of this combination are, the maintenance of rights and privileges, the prevention of encroachments on the same, the redress of grievances, and the removal of restrictions and burdens incompatible with eligious freedom.

The Widows' Fund, established in 1733, principally by the exertions of Dr. Chandler, a Presbyterian minister, was designed for the assistance of "the families of such ministers of the Presbyterian, Independent, and Baptist Denominations, as at their death stood accepted and approved as such by the body of ministers of the denomination to which they respectively belonged, and died so poor as not to leave their widows and children a sufficient subsistence." Large sums have been contributed for this purpose, and the utmost impartiality has been uniformly exercised in the distribution. The widows and families of Baptist ministers have been liberally aided. The amount of capital now invested is nearly £60,000, and the income is about £2,600 (13,000 dollars).

Another society in which the Baptists united with other denominations was the "Book Society," originally called "The Society for Propagating Religious Knowledge among the Poor." It was instituted in 1750. The object of the society is stated to be "the gratuitous distribution and sale of Bibles and Testaments, and other books of established excellence, and the publication of original and standard works, adapted to promote religious and moral instruction." It combines the purposes of the Bible and Tract Societies, but was formed before either of them, and continues in useful operation.

It was stated in a former chapter that Mr. Terrill had bequeathed considerable property for the purpose of providing for the education of candidates for the ministry by the pastor of Broadmead Church. Possession of the property was not obtained till some years after his death. The Rev. Caleb Jope was the first minister employed under this arrangement. He entered on his duties in 1710, but his services do not appear to have been satisfactory. He was succeeded in 1720, by the Rev. Bernard Foskett, who held the office nearly forty years. On his death, in 1758, the Rev. Hugh Evans became tutor, who was followed by his son, Dr. Caleb Evans, with whom, during the last seven years of his life, the Rev. Robert Hall was associated as assistant. Dr. Evans died in 1791, in the fifty-fourth year of his age. His father and he (and the same may be asserted of Mr. Foskett) were eminent men in all respects—as Christians, as ministers, and as theological tutors—and were held in high esteem throughout the denomination. The wishes of good Mr. Terrill were abundantly realized, and the advantages derived from his liberal bequest greatly extended, by the establishment of the Bristol Education Society, founded in 1770, chiefly by the exertions of Dr. Evans. Bristol College, as it is now called, has furnished a large number of excellent ministers and missionaries. About two hundred and fifty persons have received instruction there since its establishment.

Dr. John Ward, a learned Baptist, Fellow of the Royal Society, and professor at Gresham College, placed in trust, in the year 1754, the sum of £1,200 bank stock (6,000 dollars), the interest accruing therefrom to be yearly applied, after his decease, "to the education of two young men at a Scotch university, with a view to the ministry, preference being given to Baptists." Dr. Ward was a member of the congregation in Little Wild Street, London. He died in 1758. Some of our most celebrated men have enjoyed the benefit of his useful benefaction. It is now administered by five trustees, four of whom are Baptists.

I shall now have to call attention to the history of religious freedom during this period.

Although the sufferings of Protestant Dissenters ceased at the Revolution, their position was far from satisfactory. The Toleration Act, passed in 1689, legalized their assemblies, under certain restrictions, presently to be mentioned; but the boon was very grudgingly granted. William III. did not grudge it; he would have removed all restraints, had not the bigotry of the age prevented him. In Queen Anne's time the high Tory party attained such power and influence that measures were taken to place the iron heel once more on the Dissenters. The Schism Bill provided, "That no person in Great Britain or Wales shall keep any public or private school or seminary, or teach or instruct youth, as tutor or schoolmaster, that has not first subscribed the declaration to conform to the Church of England and has not obtained license from the respective diocesan or ordinary of the place; that under failure of so doing he may be committed to prison without bail or mainprise; and that no such license shall be granted before the party produces a certificate of his having received the sacrament according to the communion of the Church of England, in some parish church within a year before obtaining such license, and hath subscribed the oaths of allegiance and supremacy." It was further provided that if any person so licensed should "knowingly or willingly resort to any conventicle," or "teach any other Catechism than what is set forth in the Common Prayer," his license should be void, and he should suffer three months' imprisonment. This iniquitous enactment passed both houses, notwithstanding strenuous opposi .on, received the royal assent, and was to go into operation August 1, 1714. On that very day Queen Anne died, the House of Brunswick ascended the throne, ard a new policy was inaugurated. The act was never allowed to be put into execution, and in 1719 was formally repealed.

But during all this period the Dissenters were excluded by law from office and employment under the Crown and in corporations. Communion with the Church of England was a necessary pre-requisite. Several endeavors were made for the repeal of the Test and Corporation Acts, but always unsuccessfully. Presbyterians, Congregationalists, Baptists, and Methodists were considered unworthy to share in responsibilities and honors with members of the Church of England. Nay, more—the Corporation of the city of London meanly took advantage of their position to filch money from them. As no man who was not a member of the Church of England could take any office in a corporation, and, as it was well known that Dissenters would not "qualify" (as it was called) by taking the sacrament, a by-law was passed, imposing a fine of £400 on every citizen who should refuse to serve as sheriff when nominated by the Lord Mayor, or £600 when elected by his fellow-citizens. This being done, Dissenters were, from year to year, nominated or chosen, and then compelled to pay the fines, which were appropriated to the rebuilding of the Mansion House. The sum of £15,000 (60,000 dollars) had been wrung from them in this manner; it was high time to put a stop to the unjust exaction. In 1754, three Dissenters (Messrs. Stratfield, Sheafe, and Evans) were elected to the sheriff's office. The committee of Dissenters encouraged them to refuse payment of the fine on the ground of the illegality of the by-law. For this they were sued in the sheriff's court, and condemned. The judges reversed the decision, whereupon the corporation took up the cause, by writ of error, to the House of Lords, where the question was gravely and ably argued. By that time two of the defendants had died, and the death of Mr. Evans, the survivor, who was in the 82nd year of his age, was daily expected. Lord Mansfield, the Chancellor, espoused the cause of justice, and nobly vindicated the rights of Dissenters, at the same time censuring the course adopted by the corporation in terms of indignant severity. The House confirmed the action of the judges February 4, 1767; and so the oppression ceased for ever. Mr. Evans, I may add, who had persevered for thirteen years in his resistance to wrong, received the news of the successful issue as he lay on his death-bed.

It is pleasant to record that no Protestant Dissenters were implicated in the rebellions of 1715 and 1745. During the first there were riotous proceedings in various parts of the kingdom, when those who were friendly to the exiled dynasty raised the ecclesiastical war-cry that "the church was in danger," and wreaked their fury on Dissenting meeting-houses and other property. The Baptists lost two places of worship on that occasion. The breaking out of the second rebellion was the signal for loyal and patriotic demonstrations. The Dissenters took up arms in defence of their king; several of their distinguished men received commissions; and it was confessed that the vigor displayed by them tended powerfully to repress the discontented and embolden the friends of the royal house. But they had incurred the penalties of the law by presuming to serve the king without first going to church and taking the sacrament; and, ridiculous as it may appear, it was absolutely necessary to pass an act of indemnity, graciously releasing them from the penal consequences of their loyalty and zeal!

I have stated that freedom of worship was granted to Dissenters "under certain restrictions." They might worship when and where they pleased, but it was necessary to register their meeting-houses at the quarter sessions, and their ministers were required to take the oaths of allegiance and supremacy, and subscribe the *doctrinal* Articles of the Church of England (but the Baptists were not called on to subscribe the 27th article, which treats of infant baptism). The latter requisition was peculiarly offensive to them, not because they did not generally believe the doctrines enunciated in the Articles, but because they repudiated the authority of the state to demand subscription. In addition to this, Dissenting schoolmasters were still subject to penalties (notwithstanding the repeal of the Schism Bill), if they taught school without first signing a declaration of conformity to the Church of England. These grievances remained unredressed till the year 1779.

An attempt to remove them was made in the year 1772, and a bill for that purpose passed the Commons, but was rejected by the Lords. Only one bishop voted for it. Another attempt was made the next year, with a similar result. On that occasion the Archbishop of

York charged the Dissenting ministers with being "men of close ambition." "This is judging uncharitably," replied Lord Chatham, "and whoever brings such a charge without evidence defames." His lordship paused for a moment, and then added: "The Dissenting ministers are represented as men of close ambition;—they are so, my lords; and their ambition is to keep close to the college of fishermen, not of cardinals—and to the doctrines of inspired apostles, not to the decrees of interested and aspiring bishops. They contend for a scriptural and spiritual worship—we have a Calvinistic creed, a Popish liturgy, and Arminian clergy. The Reformation has laid open the Scriptures to all; let not the bishops shut them again. Laws in support of ecclesiastical power are pleaded, which it would shock humanity to execute. It is said religious sects have done great mischief when they were not kept under restraints; but history affords no proof that sects have ever been mischievous when they were not oppressed and persecuted by the ruling church."[1]

"Christian liberty!"—exclaimed Robert Robinson—"thou favorite offspring of heaven! thou first-born of Christianity! I saw the wise and pious servants of God nourish thee in their houses, and cherish thee in their bosoms! I saw them lead thee into public view; all good men hailed thee; the generous British Commons caressed and praised thee, and led thee into an upper house, and there—there didst thou expire in the holy laps of spiritual lords!"[2]

In 1774 Mr. Robinson (he was pastor of the Baptist church at Cambridge) published a work which probably

[1] Ivimey, iv. 28.   [2] *Works*, ii. 183.

influenced the public mind on this subject, and prepared the way for the repeal of the obnoxious enactments. I refer to his *Arcana, or the Principles of the late Petitioners to Parliament for Relief in the matter of Subscription.* The book was written in the form of letters, and the subjects discussed were Candor in Controversy—Uniformity in Religion—The Right of Private Judgment—Civil Magistracy—Innovation—Orthodoxy—Persecution—Sophistry. Incomparable wit sparkled in this work. No churchman could read it without being ashamed of the intolerance of his spiritual rulers.

At length even the bishops were mollified. One of their number, Dr. Ross, bishop of Exeter, in a sermon before the House of Lords on the 30th of January, 1779, expressed his wish that relief might be afforded to Dissenters. The hint was taken. A bill was speedily introduced, which passed through both houses without much difficulty, by which subscription to the Articles was abolished, and instead of it ministers were required to sign the following declaration:—"I, A. B., do solemnly declare, in the presence of Almighty God, that I am a Christian, and a Protestant, and as such that I believe that the Scriptures of the Old and New Testaments, as commonly received among Protestant churches, do contain the revealed will of God; and that I do receive the same as the rule of my faith and practice." Dissenting schoolmasters also obtained the desired relief.

I have narrated these transactions, in all which the Baptists were concerned in common with other Protestant Dissenters, in order to put my readers in possession of some facts which ought not to be lost sight of. Persecution in its violent forms existed no longer; but there were men still to be found, and the race is not yet extinct, who gladly embraced every opportunity of venting their spite against those who chose to think and act for themselves in matters of religion. Let us be thankful that this ill-conditioned tribe is dwindling away.

A sad degeneracy had taken place among the General Baptists (called *Free-will Baptists* in the United States). who, as the reader is doubtless aware, adopt Arminian views, the Particular Baptists being denominated Calvinistic. Arianism had crept in among them, and with it certain other errors. The loss of *life* followed the obscuration of *light*. Antievangelical sentiments and practices prevailed to such an alarming extent that the soundhearted of that denomination felt the necessity of withdrawment. They peaceably withdrew in the year 1770, and formed the "New Connexion of General Baptists." The blessing of God followed the movement. The new body thus constituted is now the General Baptist Denomination, the Arianized churches having for the most part fallen into Socinianism, or become extinct.

The communion controversy was revived. Nothing had been published on the subject since the time of Charles II. when Bunyan advocated free communion, and Kiffin replied to him. In 1771 Robert Robinson wrote a pamphlet entitled, *The General Doctrines of Toleration applied to Free Communion*. Messrs. Ryland, of Northampton, and Turner, of Abingdon, men of note and power, published essays, maintaining the same views. They were answered by Abraham Booth, whose *Apology for the Baptists* was the most masterly production that had yet appeared on that side of the question. No other publications on the subject were issued for many years.

I have remarked that the denomination had evidently fallen into a state of religious declension almost immediately after the restoration of freedom. The statistics prove this. To whatever other causes the condition of affairs may be ascribed, there can be little doubt that the paralyzing influence of the doctrinal sentiments entertained by many of the ministers must be regarded as mainly contributing to the result. John Brine and Dr. Gill were chief men in the denomination for nearly half a century. They were Supralapsarians, holding that God's election was irrespective of the fall of man. They taught eternal justification. Undue prominence was given in their discourses to the teachings of Scripture respecting the divine purposes. Although they themselves inculcated practical godliness, and so were not justly liable to the charge of antinomianism, there is reason to fear that numbers of those who imbibed their doctrinal views kept out of sight or but feebly urged the obligation of believers to personal holiness. And this is certain, that those eminent men, and all their followers, went far astray from the course marked out by our Lord and his apostles They were satisfied with stating men's danger, and assuring them that they were on the high road to perdition But they did not call upon them to "repent and believe the gospel." They did not entreat them to be "reconciled unto God." They did not "warn every man and teach every man in all wisdom." And the churches did not, could not, under their instruction, engage in efforts for the conversion of souls. They were so afraid of intruding on God's work that they neglected to do what he had commanded them. They seem to have supposed that *preservation* was all they should aim at; they had not heart enough to seek for *extension*. No wonder that the cause declined!

The backsliding and coldness had affected all religious communities in England. Had it not been for the merciful revival which accompanied the labors of Whitefield and the Wesleys, evangelical truth would have wellnigh died out. Those extraordinary men were raised up for a glorious purpose. The effects of their ministry were felt by all denominations. The churches began to arise and shake themselves from the dust. A new order of things may be dated from the commencement of their itinerancy, indicating a gradual return to apostolical simplicity and fervor. Christian ministers preached differently; if they uttered the same truths, there was more affection and power in the utterance. Some of them found that an addition to their creeds was necessary, to bring them into accordance with the heavenly standard, and Christian churches saw that there were duties incumbent on *them*, which they could not neglect without incurring guilt.

The restorative process did not take effect among the Baptists so soon as in some other denominations; but at length they also felt its influence, and then it was not long before improvement was discernible, as the statistical returns show. Another circumstance tended to bring it about: some excellent ministers in the central counties had long seen and lamented the prevalence of unscriptural opinions, and striven against the stream; they now saw a turn in their favor and wisely resolved to avail themselves of it. Robert Hall, of Arnsby, father of the great Robert Hall, delivered a sermon before the Northamptonshire Association, at its annual meeting in 1779, founded on Isaiah lvii. 14: "Cast ye up, prepare the way, take up the stumbling-block out of the way of my people." In compliance with the urgent request of his brethren, the discourse was shortly afterward presented to the public, in an enlarged form, under the title of *Help to Zion's Travelers; or, An Attempt to Remove various Stumbling-blocks out of the way, relating to Doctrinal, Experimental, and Practical Religion*. This instructive and useful book had a wide circulation. It corrected the religious sentiments of many, moulding them after the divine model, and was thus peculiarly serviceable to the cause of truth.

From that time we may discern religious progress. Thoughtful concern for the souls of others began to manifest itself. A monthly prayer-meeting for the revival of religion and the spread of the gospel was instituted in 1784. William Carey meditated on the state of the world, and longed to evangelize it. His *Enquiry into the Obligations of Christians to use means for the Conversion of the Heathen* was published in 1791. That paved the way for the missionary enterprise; but our fathers did not rush into it unadvisedly or in haste. They thought and prayed, and marked the leadings of the divine will, prepared to follow the light. God educated them for the work, and so, when they engaged in it, it was not so much to undertake a project as to develop a principle, trusting in the promises of him who has said of his word, "It shall not return unto me void."

Andrew Fuller and John Sutcliffe were "men that had understanding of the times, to know what Israel ought to do." When they saw that the time was come, they prepared to rouse the people. To this their discourses—delivered at a meeting of ministers at Clipstone, Northamptonshire, in 1791—mainly contributed. Fuller preached from Haggai i. 2, on "the pernicious influence of delay;" Sutcliffe from 1 Kings xix. 10, on "jealousy for the Lord of hosts." Decisive action followed shortly afterward.

On the 2nd of October, 1792, twelve ministers, deputed by the Northamptonshire Association, met in the house of Mr. Beeby Wallis, Kettering, and, after lengthened and prayerful discussion, adopted a plan of a mission, and formed a society, designated "The Particular Baptist Society for propagating the Gospel amongst the Heathen." The names of the twelve were, John Ryland, Reynold Hogg, John Sutcliff, Andrew Fuller, Abraham Greenwood, Edward Sharman, Joshua Burton, Samuel Pearce, Thomas Blundel, William Heighton, John Eayres, Joseph Timms. Their joint contributions amounted to £13 2s. 6d. sterling.

William Carey immediately offered himself as a missionary. Mr. John Thomas, who had already performed some Christian labor in Calcutta, while practicing there as a surgeon, and was then in England, joined him. They sailed from England June 13, 1793; John Fountain followed them in 1796; and in 1799 Messrs. Ward, Brunsdon, Grant, and Marshman were added to the little band. Difficulties and trials of no ordinary character oppressed the work for several years. At length the mission found a home at Serampore, under the protection of Denmark, to which country Serampore then belonged. There, on the 16th of May, 1800, the first sheet of the Bengali New Testament, translated by Carey,

THE QUIET PERIOD.

was put to press. Thus was a solid foundation laid, on which a fair and noble superstructure was afterward erected.[1]

It is observable that, five years after the institution of the Missionary Society, the claims of home began to be deeply felt. Christians saw that, if one thing was to be "done," the other was not to be "left undone." The Baptist Home Missionary Society was founded in 1797.

The denomination had been gathering strength for several years. In 1763 the number of churches was 200. In 1790 there were 326 churches in England, and 56 in Wales, besides the churches of the General Baptists, the number of which is not given.

[1] See Dr. Cox's *History of the Baptist Missionary Society*.

CHAPTER II.

Biographical Notices—Dr. John Gale—John Skepp—John Biine—Dr. Gill—John Macgowan—Robert Robinson—Robert Hall, Sen.—John Ryland—The Stennetts—Benjamin Beddome—Samuel Pearce—John Piggott—The Wallins—Dr. Andrew Gifford—Mordecai Abbott, Esq.—Thomas and John Hollis—Miss Steele—Mrs. Seward.

BEFORE proceeding to furnish information respecting the state of our body in other parts of the world, I will give a brief account of the principal ministers who flourished in England during this period.

Dr. JOHN GALE was educated at the University of Leyden, where he obtained the degree of Doctor in Philosophy at the early age of nineteen. Proceeding thence to Amsterdam, he studied theology under Limborch, author of the *History of the Inquisition*, and other works. On his return to England, in 1705, he became assistant to Mr. Allen, then pastor of the church in the Barbican, London, and afterward to his successor, Mr. Joseph Burroughs. He died in 1721, in the 41st year of his age.

Dr. Gale is best known by his answer to Dr. Wall, in a volume entitled, *Reflections on Dr. Wall's History of Infant Baptism*. This is a standard work in the Baptist controversy. The author's various learning is advan tageously employed, and in a very effective manner. Even those who differed from him acknowledged the great merit of his work. It is reprinted, I observe, in the Oxford edition of *Wall's History*. This evinces remarkable fairness and impartiality.

I am sorry to be compelled to say that Dr. Gale's religious sentiments were lamentably defective on some points. He inculcated the morals of Christianity rather than its evangelical truths.

JOHN SKEPP, who was some time pastor of the church in Paul's Alley, Cripplegate, London, and was a self-taught, learned man, published a volume entitled *Divine Energy; or, the Operations of the Spirit of God upon the Soul of Man, in his effectual Calling and Conversion, stated, proved, and vindicated*. In assigning his reasons for the publication, he said, "that he had heard and read of much contempt thrown upon the doctrine and preaching of the Spirit's work, as if it was not necessary to make the gospel ministry effectual for illumination, conviction, and conversion, and for carrying on the work of faith with power." Doubtless this was true; for it was a day of declension: yet it must be confessed that, though Mr. Skepp's book contained much important truth, the opinions he held on one subject disqualified him for the work of revival. He refused to address the invitations of the gospel to the unconverted: he would declare — proclaim — announce to men their sin and danger; but he would not call upon them to return to the Lord. That would be interfering with God's work! So serious a mistake could not but affect his ministry and mar his usefulness. Mr. Skepp died in 1721.

JOHN BRINE became pastor of the same church in 1730.

and labored there thirty-five years. His views harmonized with Mr. Skepp's. They were placed before the public in numerous books, sermons, and tracts, and probably influenced the minds of many of his brethren in the ministry; the more so, as from his character, talents, and high standing in the denomination, he was likely to be consulted and followed. Messrs. Skepp and Brine were eminently pious men, who contended earnestly for the faith, and stated with great clearness and force the distinguishing doctrines of the gospel. It was much to be deplored that their minds were warped on the subject before alluded to, as the results were certainly injurious to a great extent. But I turn with pleasure to the record of Mr. Brine's last hours. It is said that, "not long before his decease, he expressed the state of his mind by saying, 'I think I am of sinners the chief, of saints the least: I know that I am nothing; but, by the grace of God, I am what I am;' which words he ordered should be inscribed on his tombstone."[1] His wish was complied with. He was buried in Bunhill Fields. Perhaps some have read the words on his tombstone, and received them as a message from God to their souls.

Mr. Brine died February 21, 1765. A great man, with whom he had long co-operated in Christian labor, followed him to the grave little more than six years afterward. I refer to Dr. Gill, who was, in some respects, the most learned man that had yet appeared in our denomination. Nor, indeed, have any equalled him to the present day, in acquaintance with Hebrew and the Rabbinic literature.

JOHN GILL was born at Kettering, Northamptonshire,

[1] Ivimey, iii. 371.

November 23, 1697. He was educated in the grammar-school of that town, but was taken from it at the age of eleven, in consequence of the unreasonable conduct of the master, who insisted on the attendance of the scholars at prayers in the parish church on week-days. To this, those of the parents who were Dissenters would not submit, and therefore removed their children from the school. Young Gill had made such extraordinary progress in Latin and Greek that his friends endeavored to procure assistance with a view to the prosecution of his studies at one of the universities; but they were unsuccessful. This did not damp his ardor. Part of his time was necessarily spent in attendance on his father's business (he was engaged in the woolen trade); every minute of the remainder was employed in gathering knowledge. He improved himself in Latin and Greek; he studied logic, rhetoric, and natural and moral philosophy; he acquired a knowledge of the Hebrew, in which language " he took great delight;" he read a large number of Latin treatises on various subjects, but especially on theology. All this was accomplished by his own unaided exertions.

In 1716 he was baptized, on confession of faith, and immediately afterward commenced preaching. His labors were very acceptable, and the church at Kettering would have gladly detained him among them; but that was not his destined sphere. In compliance with the request of the church at Horselydown, Southwark—over which the celebrated Benjamin Keach formerly presided, who was succeeded by his son-in-law, Mr. Benjamin Stinton, then lately deceased—he visited them; and after preaching several months, was chosen pastor. The ordination took place March 22, 1720.

More than fifty years of unremitting toil succeeded that transaction. Mr. Gill's life was emphatically a laborious one. His duties as pastor were punctually and faithfully discharged. Besides attending to these, he constantly enlarged his acquaintance with all learning. He watched the movements of the enemies of truth, and held himself in readiness to repel assaults. His pen was never idle.

The great work of his life was the *Commentary on the Scriptures*. It was originally given to his people from the pulpit, in the form of expository discourses. He began with Solomon's Song, on which he preached one hundred and twenty-two sermons. *The Exposition* was published in 1728, in a folio volume. Three folios more were occupied with the New Testament, the third of which appeared in 1748. In that year the author received from Marischal College, Aberdeen, the degree of Doctor in Divinity. In the diploma special mention was made of Dr. Gill's proficiency in sacred literature, in the Oriental languages, and in Jewish antiquities. *The Exposition on the Prophets*, in two folios, was issued in 1757, 1758. The remaining volumes appeared in 1763, 1764, 1765, and 1766. Truly it was a gigantic undertaking!

The particular excellence of this work lies in its plain, strong sense, its perspicuous style, the care with which every sentence and almost every word is explained—and especially, the light thrown upon many passages by extracts from Jewish authors. Dr. Gill was a profound Rabbinical scholar. He was familiar with the whole circle of Jewish literature. None could compete with him on this his own ground.

A judicious reader may derive much benefit from the

use of Dr. Gill's *Exposition*. He will know how to supply his deficiencies, and he will abstain from following him in the interpretation of allegorical passages. For the results of modern criticism he must repair, of course, to other sources. But this *Exposition* will ever be a mine which will repay the labors of the discreet explorer.

In addition to the *Exposition*, Dr. Gill published a *Body of Divinity*, in three quarto volumes, which, like the *Exposition*, was first preached to his congregation:— *The Cause of God and Truth*, being an examination of all the passages of Scripture usually adduced in the Arminian Controversy;—and *Sermons and Tracts* (including a learned *Dissertation on the Antiquity of the Hebrew Language*), in three volumes, 4to.

Dr. Gill's preaching was rather solid than attractive. Like Messrs. Skepp and Brine, he abstained from personal addresses to sinners by inviting them to the Saviour, and satisfied himself with declaring their guilt and doom, and the necessity of a change of heart. It is not surprising that the congregation declined under such a ministry. His steady refusal to have an assistant or co-pastor operated also injuriously on the welfare of the church.

He preached but once on the Lord's Day during the last two years of his life. Yet he labored on in his study till within a fortnight of his death. A short time before that event he said to his nephew, the Rev. John Gill, of St. Alban's, "I depend wholly and alone upon the free, sovereign, eternal, unchangeable love of God, the firm and everlasting covenant of grace, and my interest in the Persons of the Trinity, for my whole salvation; and not upon any righteousness of my own, nor on anything in me, nor done by me under the influences of the Holy Spirit; not upon any services of mine, which I have been assisted to perform for the good of the church; but upon my interest in the Persons of the Trinity, the free grace of God, and the blessings of grace streaming to me through the blood and righteousness of Christ, as the ground of my hope. These are no new things to me, but what I have been long acquainted with—*what I can live and die by.*"[1]

Dr. Gill died October 14, 1771, in the 74th year of his age, having been fifty-one years pastor of the church.

Robert Hall "did not like Dr. Gill as an author. When Mr. Christmas Evans was in Bristol, he was talking to Mr. Hall about the Welsh language, which he said was very copious and expressive. 'How I wish, Mr. Hall, that Dr. Gill's works had been written in Welsh.' —'I wish they had, sir; I wish they had, with all my heart, for then I should never have read them. They are a continent of mud, sir.'"[2]

This was a severe verdict. But it was the language of an eccentric though wonderfully great man, whose elegant taste was shocked by what he deemed the uncouth bluntness of Dr. Gill's style; probably, also, he was repelled by the sternness or the obscurity of some of his opinions.

Mr. Walter Wilson, a Pædobaptist, author of *The History and Antiquities of the Dissenting Churches in London*, gives a different decision. He says, "Such were the life and death of Dr. Gill, who, for the value

---

[1] Rippon's *Memoir of Dr. Gill*, p. 134.
[2] *Works*, vi. 125. London Edition, 8vo.

and extent of his writings, will be considered by future generations as one of the fathers of the church."

The Rev. Augustus Toplady, an Episcopalian clergyman, writes as follows: "If any one man can be supposed to have trod the whole circle of human learning, it was Dr. Gill. His attainments, both in abstruse and polite literature, were (what is very uncommon) equally extensive and profound. Providence had to this end endued him with a firmness of constitution and an unremitting vigor of mind which rarely fall to the lot of the sedentary and learned. It would, perhaps, try the constitutions of half the *literati* in England only to read, with care and attention, the whole of what he wrote.

"The doctor considered not any subject superficially, or by halves. As deeply as human sagacity enlightened by grace could penetrate, he went to the bottom of everything he engaged in. With a solidity of judgment and with an acuteness of discernment peculiar to few, he exhausted, as it were, the very soul and substance of most arguments he undertook. His style, too, resembles himself; it is manly, nervous, plain; conscious, if I may so speak, of the unutterable dignity, value, and importance of the freight it conveys, it drives directly and perspicuously to the point in view, regardless of affected cadence, and superior to the little niceties of professed refinement.

* * * * *

"His learning and labors, if exceedable, were exceeded only by the invariable sanctity of his life and conversation. From his childhood to his entrance on the ministry, and from his entrance on the ministry to the moment of his dissolution, not one of his most inveterate opposers was ever able to charge him with the least shadow of immorality. Himself, no less than his writings, demonstrated that the doctrine of grace does not lead to licentiousness.

* * * * *

"His doctrinal and practical writings will live and be admired, and be a standing blessing to posterity, when their opposers are forgotten, or only remembered by the reputation he has given them. While true religion and sound learning have a single friend remaining in the British empire, the works and name of Gill will be precious and preserved."[1]

I will close this account with an anecdote of Dr. Gill. A weekly lecture was established at Lime Street, London, in 1730, for the purpose of counteracting certain infidel and erroneous sentiments then beginning to prevail. Nine lecturers were appointed, seven of whom were Independents and two Baptists, viz., Dr. Gill and Mr. Samuel Wilson. Dr. Abraham Taylor, who delivered two of the lectures, took occasion to animadvert, in severe terms, on Calvinistic tenets, upon which a controversy arose between him and Dr. Gill. "When Dr. Gill first wrote against Dr. Abraham Taylor, some of the friends of the latter called on Dr. Gill to dissuade him from proceeding, telling him that he would lose the esteem and the subscription of some wealthy persons who were Dr. Taylor's friends. '*Don't tell me of losing,*' replied Dr. Gill; '*I value nothing in comparison with gospel truths; I am not afraid to be poor.*'"[2]

JOHN MACGOWAN, who was fifteen years pastor of the

---

[1] Rippon, pp. 137-140. [2] Ivimey, iii. 203.

church in Devonshire Square, London, has acquired considerable celebrity among authors, by his *Dialogues of Devils*, in which he satirizes the follies, vices, and inconsistencies of men, especially of professing Christians, in a masterly manner. Some affect to be greatly shocked at the dramatic style of the work, and the language ascribed to the interlocutors in the dialogues; but, for my part, I cannot help thinking that there is a marvellous vein of naturalness in the supposed reports of the conferences of the diabolical preachers; and I am disposed to believe that the devil has more to do with much that occurs in human history than is commonly imagined. If the existence and operations of good and evil spirits were more thoroughly realized by Christians generally, it might be useful to them.

In another publication by Mr. Macgowan, entitled, *The Shaver, or Priestcraft defended; a Sermon occasioned by the Expulsion of Six Young Gentlemen from the University of Oxford, for praying, reading, and expounding the Scriptures*—he inflicted a well-merited rebuke on the university authorities, and held them up to ridicule for their antireligious propensities, and the folly of their endeavor to stop the progress of the revival, to which, by God's blessing, even the Church of England has been largely indebted.

Mr. Macgowan died November 25, 1780, in the fifty-fifth year of his age.

I wish it were possible to give a pleasing and favorable portraiture of the celebrated ROBERT ROBINSON. Gifted with remarkable talents—of sprightly genius—vigorous in imagination—capable of writing in an easy, clear, and flowing style—and well-informed on all subjects—

he might have rendered eminent service to the **cause of** truth had truth really obtained a lodgment in his heart.

Mr. Robinson professed to be converted under the ministry of Mr. Whitefield. He began to preach almost immediately after his baptism. He took charge of a small church at Cambridge, with which he continued all his life. As a preacher he was deservedly popular with all classes. The educated admired his discourses; the illiterate could understand them. As a writer, he attracted great attention. His *Village Discourses* are models of exquisite tact in the adaptation of style and manner to special circumstances. To his translation of Claude's *Essay on the Composition of a Sermon*, he appended voluminous notes, curious and instructive, containing plans of sermons, illustrative of the advice given by the author, together with pertinent and pithy observations. His Tracts on Nonconformity were like " sharp arrows of the mighty with coals of juniper." The *History of Baptism* exhausts the subject; all writers on the controversy, on our side of the question, make use of the work. When he compiled his *Ecclesiastical Researches* he had renounced the Trinity and other truths connected with it. The effects of his change of sentiments appear in every part of the volume. There is a constant endeavor to *write down* the Orthodox or Trinitarian party, while all excellence is ascribed to Arianism and other *isms* of a lower kind. But, being a posthumous work, it is less open to criticism, as it did not receive a final revision from the author; I will only add, therefore, that the statements in the text should be always carefully compared with the authorities cited in the notes, and that the originals should be consulted, whenever practicable.

Mr. Robinson died at Birmingham, June 9, 1790, in the fifty-fifth year of his age. He had preached in Dr. Priestley's meeting-house on the preceding Lord's Day. "His discourse," said Dr. P., "was unconnected and desultory, and his manner of treating the Trinity savored rather of burlesque than serious reasoning. He attacked orthodoxy more pointedly and sarcastically than I ever did in my life."[1] On the following Tuesday morning he was found dead in his bed. What a difference between his beautiful hymn, "Mighty God, while angels bless thee," etc., and that last sermon!

ROBERT HALL, of Arnsby, has been mentioned as the author of the valuable and useful book, *Help to Zion's Travelers*. He also wrote several of the Circular Letters of the Northamptonshire Association, which were in fact brief treatises on doctrinal and practical subjects. Mr. Hall died March 13, 1791.

JOHN COLLETT RYLAND, A.M., was, in some respects, an extraordinary man, though now reckoned among the forgotten ones. His *Contemplations on Religious Subjects* (in three volumes, 8vo.) were received by the public with considerable favor. His address at the grave of Dr. Andrew Gifford, entitled *The First and Second Coming of Christ Contrasted*, was a rare specimen of sublime eloquence. He was an enthusiast in education, and his influence over the young was peculiarly powerful. After a successful ministry at Northampton, where he labored twenty-six years, he resigned his charge into the hands of his son, afterward Dr. Ryland, of Bristol, and spent the remainder of his life at Enfield, Middlesex. There he presided over a large and flourishing school, in

[1] Dyer's *Memoir of Robinson*, p. 397.

which many were trained for future usefulness. The late Dr. Newman, of Stepney College, was for some time his assistant. Mr. Ryland died July 24, 1792. "Well do I remember," said Dr. Newman, more than forty years afterward, "the awful stillness of that evening. I felt as if all the world were dead! . . . When a large allowance has been made for his eccentricities, we shall find much to admire in his quick apprehension—his lively imagination—his tenacious memory. To use an expression of his own, 'All his brains were fish-hooks.' Who that ever knew him did not express astonishment at his insatiable thirst for knowledge; his unwearied zeal in the instruction of the rising generation; his aptness to teach; his tongue of fire? Surely there are some still living that can never forget his love of country; his ardor in the cause of civil and religious freedom; his childlike, unsuspecting simplicity; his noble disinterestedness, and uniform devotedness to the cause of God and truth; the unimpeachable integrity and purity of his life, from the period of his conversion to his death; his affection for all good men; and especially the condescending encouragement he gave to the young, the poor, and the weak, among his brethren in the ministry."[1]

The Baptist denomination is under deep obligations to the STENNETT family. EDWARD STENNETT was some time pastor of the church at Pinner's Hall, London, where he was succeeded by his son Joseph, in the year 1690, who presided over the church till his death, in 1713. Both were Sabbatarians. Distinguished among his brethren for the extent and variety of his literary acquirements, his earnestness of soul, his profound and practical

[1] Pritchard's *Memoir of Dr. Newman*, p. 51.

wisdom, and his unswerving integrity, Mr. JOSEPH STEN-
NETT was held in high esteem by all religious parties.
If he would have conformed to the Church of England
he might have attained an exalted position; but he was
proof against temptation, though liberal offers were made
him. His influence was known to be powerful, and
strenuous efforts were employed by the court, in the latter
end of Queen Anne's reign, to gain him over to the Tory
policy, in the hope that other Dissenters might be induced
to follow him. Mr. Stennett understood the principles
of freedom too well to be caught in such a trap. His
firmness had a happy effect on others. Numerous treatises on religious subjects and a considerable number of
poetical compositions were published by Mr. Stennett.
A collected edition of his works was issued after his
death. He is most advantageously known among Baptists by his *Answer to Russen*, a learned and elaborate
work on baptism, to which succeeding writers have been
much indebted.

His son and grandson were also "shining lights."
DR. JOSEPH STENNETT, who died February 7, 1758,
was upward of twenty years pastor of the church in
Little Wild Street, London. He distinguished himself
for loyalty and patriotism during the rebellion in 1745.
He enjoyed the esteem of the king, George II., and was
on terms of friendship with some of the great ones of the
day. Adverting to an interview with the then bishop of
London, Dr. Gibson, he said in a letter to a friend, " I
told his lordship that I more than ever saw the usefulness of the Book of Common Prayer; for, considering
how little the Scriptures are read by the common people,
and how little the gospel preached by the clergy, if it

were not for what is said of Christ in the prayer book, multitudes would forget there was any such Person. He heartily joined in my observation, and told me he had lately heard a sermon by an eminent preacher, who seemed to labor to keep the name of Christ out of it. 'For my part,' added he, 'my time is now short, and therefore my charge to all my clergy is short too.' I say to all of them that come to me, 'See to it that you preach Jesus Christ; don't preach Seneca, nor Plato, but preach Jesus Christ.'"[1]

Dr. SAMUEL STENNETT, son of the above, succeeded his father at Little Wild Street, and held the pastorate till his death. He had been assistant-pastor for ten years previously. Few men have risen so high in general estimation. His learning—his discretion—his benevolence —his earnest zeal—his holy and uniformly consistent conduct, secured for him an amount and power of influence rarely enjoyed. His pulpit labors were highly appreciated; his writings were acceptable and much valued. Besides two treatises on the baptismal controversy, he published three volumes of discourses, *On Personal Religion, On Domestic Duties,* and *On the Parable of the Sower.*

The celebrated John Howard honored Dr. Stennett with his friendship, and was accustomed to attend his ministry when he visited London. In a letter addressed to him from Smyrna, dated August 11, 1786, he says: "With unabated pleasure I have attended your ministry; no man ever entered more into my religious sentiments, or more happily expressed them. It was some little disappointment when any one occupied your pulpit. Oh

[1] Ivimey, iii. 581.

sir, how many Sabbaths have I ardently longed to spend in Wild Street: on those days I generally rest, or, if at sea, keep retired in my little cabin. It is you that preach, and I bless God I attend with renewed pleasure. God in Christ is my rock, the portion of my soul. I have little more to add—but accept my renewed thanks. I bless God for your ministry; I pray God reward you a thousand-fold."[1] Dr. Stennett died August 24, 1795.

BENJAMIN BEDDOME, A.M., who ministered to the church at Bourton on the Water more than fifty-four years, was one of those whose "memory is blessed." We are indebted to him for many excellent hymns, in the use of which the churches praise God, and will probably continue to praise him for many ages yet to come. He was accustomed for a long time to compose a hymn to be sung after his sermon on the Lord's Day morning; these were afterward collected into a volume. It was somewhat remarkable that, having preached on Lord's Day, January 4, 1778, from Psalm xxxi. 15: "My times are in thy hand," and read at the close of the discourse that most appropriate hymn, "My times of sorrow and of joy," etc., he received intelligence next morning of the sudden death of his son, a young physician of great promise. God had graciously prepared him for the stroke by the spiritual exercises connected with the sermon and hymn.

A writer in the *Baptist Register*, probably Dr. Rippon, gives the following account of Mr. Beddome's preaching:

"The labors of this good man among his charge were unremitted and evangelical. He fed them with the finest

---

[1] *Baptist Magazine*, 1843, p. 142.

of the wheat. No man in all his connections wrote more sermons, nor composed them with greater care; and this was true of him to the last weeks of his life. In most of his discourses the appreciation of a student and the ability of a divine were visible. He frequently differed from the generality of preachers by somewhat striking either in his text or in his method. If the passage were peculiar or abstruse, simplicity of illustration and familiarity in discussion characterized the sermon; or if his text were of the most familiar class, he distributed it with novelty, discussed it with genius, and seldom delivered a hackneyed discourse. Indeed, sermonizing was so much his forte that at length, when knowledge had received maturity from years, and composition was familiarized by habit, he has been known, with a wonderful facility of the moment, to sketch his picture at the foot of the pulpit stairs, to color it as he was ascending, and, without turning his eyes from the canvas, in the same hour to give it all the finish of a master. One instance of this will long be remembered, which happened at a ministers' meeting at Fairford, in Gloucestershire. After public service began, his natural timidity, it seems, overcame his recollections. His text and his discourse, for he did not preach by notes, had left him; and in the way from the pew to the pulpit he leaned his head over the shoulder of the Rev. Mr. Davis, pastor of the place, and said, 'Brother Davis, what must I preach from?' Mr. Davis, thinking he could not be at a loss, answered, 'Ask no foolish questions.' This afforded him considerable relief. He turned immediately to Titus iii. 9, 'Avoid foolish questions;' and he preached a remarkably methodical, correct, and useful discourse on it."

Mr. Beddome died September 3, 1797, in the seventy-fifth year of his age. Three volumes of his sermons were published after his death, and extensively circulated.

SAMUEL PEARCE, pastor of the church in Cannon Street, Birmingham, died October 10, 1799. He was greatly beloved by his brethren, and justly so; for his character was an embodiment of Christian loveliness. Born at Plymouth, July 20, 1766, converted at the age of sixteen, called to the ministry by the church in 1786, he studied at Bristol College, under Dr. Caleb Evans, and was ordained at Birmingham in 1790. His ministry in that town was eminently successful, because it was evangelical to the core, and because it was recommended and supplemented by his seraphic and consistent piety. Three hundred and thirty-five persons were added to the church during his pastorate.

Mr. Pearce was extremely desirous of joining Dr. Carey in missionary labors, but yielded to the advice of his friends and brethren, who judged that he could not be spared from England. They were compelled to give him up, however, for his Lord summoned him to the palace above.

During a protracted and painful illness he exemplified Christian character in some of its sublimest aspects. "Of all the ways of dying," he observed, a short time before his departure, "that which I most dreaded was by a consumption, in which it is now highly probable my disorder will issue. But, O my dear Lord, *if* by *this death* I can most *glorify thee*, I prefer it to all others, and thank thee that, by this means, thou art hastening my fuller enjoyment of thee in a purer world." Surely, that was heroism.

"We have seen men," said Mr. Fuller, "rise high in contemplation, who have abounded but little in action. We have seen zeal mingled with bitterness, and candor degenerate into indifference; experimental religion mixed with a large portion of enthusiasm; and what is called rational religion void of everything that interests the heart of man. We have seen splendid talents tarnished with insufferable pride; seriousness with melancholy; cheerfulness with levity; and great attainments in religion with uncharitable censoriousness toward men of low degree;—but we have not seen these things in our brother Pearce."[1]

A few more names may be more briefly referred to. JOHN PIGGOTT was several years pastor of the church in Little Wild Street. He was a powerful and popular preacher, and a leading man in the denomination. Preaching at the first meeting of an Association of Baptist churches in London in 1704, he said, "We have work of the highest importance on our hands; let us not waste the little time we have to do it in. It was a cutting reproof which the mariners gave the philosopher, who would have entertained them with an impertinent harangue in the midst of a storm—'We perish while thou triflest.' All our warm disputes about indifferent things are but laborious trifling."[2] Mr. Piggott died in March, 1713.

EDWARD WALLIN (died in 1753) and his son, BENJAMIN WALLIN (died in 1782), were pastors of the church in Maze Pond, London; the first for twenty years, the

[1] *Memoirs of the Rev. Samuel Pearce, M. A.* Works. (American Edition), iii. 430.
[2] Ivimey, ii. 452.

second for forty years. They were exceedingly beloved and revered.

Samuel Wilson, upward of twenty years pastor of the church in Prescot Street, London—of whom Dr. Gill said, "He came forth, even at first, with clear evangelical light, with great warmth, zeal, and fervency of spirit, and, like another Apollos, with a torrent of eloquence, being mighty in the Scriptures"—died in 1750, in the forty-eighth year of his age. His *Scripture Manual, or a Plain Representation of the Ordinance of Baptism*, is a useful tract, and by it his memory will be perpetuated.

Dr. Andrew Gifford, whose father and grandfather had been pastors of the Pithay Church, Bristol, presided over the church in Eagle Street, London, nearly fifty years. His ministry was remarkably successful. He was a thoroughly learned man, and possessed excellent taste and judgment in regard to coins, manuscripts, and other relics of antiquity. In 1757 he was appointed Assistant Librarian to the British Museum, which situation he held till his death. The following anecdote is worthy of preservation: "Some gentlemen were inspecting the Museum, under the Doctor's guidance, amongst whom was a profane youth, who hardly uttered a sentence without taking the name of the Lord in vain. The Doctor, who had kept his eye upon him, was at length asked by him, 'Whether they had not a very ancient manuscript of the Bible there?' On coming to it, the Doctor asked the youth if he could read it. Being answered in the affirmative, the Doctor wished him to read a paragraph which he pointed out. It was, 'Thou shalt not take the name of the Lord thy God in vain.'

The irreverent youth read, and blushed; the countenances of his companions seemed to acknowledge the justness of the reproof, and the polite and Christian manner in which it was administered."[1]

Dr. Gifford died July 19, 1784, in the eighty-fourth year of his age, and was buried in Bunhill Fields, at an early hour in the morning, in compliance with his own wish, "to testify his faith in the resurrection of Christ, who arose early on the first day of the week, and likewise his hope of the resurrection morning at the last day."

Honorable mention should be made of some other Baptists, not in the ministry, who lived during this period.

MORDECAI ABBOTT, Esq., after filling other offices under government, became Receiver-General of the Customs. But he held fast his nonconformity, and refused to qualify for office, as the Test Act required, by receiving the Lord's supper in the Church of England. His high reputation, and the esteem with which he was regarded by the king, William III., saved him from persecution. Mr. Abbott remained a consistent Dissenter and a Baptist, under circumstances of great trial and difficulty. He died February 29, 1699-1700, in the forty-fourth year of his age.

THOMAS HOLLIS, Esq., was more than sixty years a member of the same church, Pinner's Hall. He vied with Mr. Abbott in liberality and zeal. Both of them "lavished gold out of the bag" for the support of education and religion. Mr. Hollis, in particular, "denied himself and lived frugal, that he might more extensively

[1] *Funeral Sermon* by Dr. Rippon, p. 41.

express his goodness." He died September 12, 1718. He was blind many years before his death.

His two sons, THOMAS and JOHN HOLLIS, were also members of the same church. Thomas joined the church in the year 1680, and was fifty years a member; he died January 13, 1730, in the seventy-second year of his age. His name has been handed down to posterity as one of the most liberal benefactors to Harvard College, Massachusetts. "In 1720, Mr. Hollis sent over so much money as to found a professorship of theology in Harvard College, with a salary of eighty pounds a year to the professor, and ten pounds per annum to ten scholars of good character, four of whom should be Baptists, if any such were there; also ten pounds a year to the college treasurer for his trouble, and ten pounds more to supply accidental losses or to increase the number of students. And in 1726 he founded in that college a professorship of the mathematics and experimental philosophy, with a salary of eighty pounds a year to the professor; and he sent over an apparatus for the purpose, which cost about one hundred and fifty pounds sterling, besides additions to the college library. No man had ever been so liberal to it before as was this Baptist gentleman."[1] But the theological sentiments held by Mr. Hollis are not now taught in Harvard University.

Joseph Lovering, Esq., A.M., is now "Hollis Professor of Mathematics and Natural Philosophy." There is no "Hollis Professor of Divinity" at present. One of the halls of the college is called "Hollis Hall."

John Hollis did not attain the renown of his brother Thomas; yet he too was a generous upholder of useful

[1] Backus' *History of the Baptists in New England*, chap. vii.

institutions, and annually contributed large sums toward their support. He bequeathed eleven hundred pounds sterling, the interest of which was to be yearly distributed among the poor of several Baptist churches.

Many excellent hymns sung by us in public worship bear the name of " Steele." The writer was a lady—Miss ANNE STEELE, daughter of a Baptist minister in Hampshire. She " discovered in early life her love of the Muses, and often entertained her friends with the truly poetical and pious productions of her pen." Two volumes were published during her lifetime, and a third appeared in 1780, after her death. The profits of her works were appropriated to benevolent objects.

Another lady, MRS. ELIZABETH SEWARD, widow of Benjamin Seward, Esq., of Evesham, Worcestershire, bequeathed the sum of four thousand five hundred and fifty pounds, the interest whereof was directed to be annually distributed amongst the ministers or the poor of several Baptist churches named in the will, in the proportions therein specified. England abounds in voluntary endowments of that kind, among all denominations.

CHAPTER III.

Progress of the Denomination in North America—Sufferings in New England—Mrs. Elizabeth Backus—Mrs. Kimball—Virginia—Whitefield's Preaching—The "New Lights"—First Churches in Different States—Philadelphia Association—Other Associations—Correspondence with London Ministers—Great Revivals—Brown University—Nova Scotia—New Brunswick—Canada.

AT the commencement of this period there were but thirteen Baptist churches in North America. In the year 1740, the number of churches was thirty-seven, with less than 3000 members. But in 1790 there were 872 churches, containing 64,975 members. Twenty-four new churches were formed in the first half of the period; in the second half, no fewer than 835 churches. This is surely a wonderful increase.

Our Baptist forefathers had a hard struggle in the New England States. The Congregationalists were the "Standing Order," and the support of their ministers was provided for by law, in the shape of a tax levied on all the inhabitants. They had fled from one establishment, and they set up another! A backward movement had taken place in the introduction of the "half-way covenant," which filled the churches with men who were strangers to godliness.[1] The assessment for ministers' salaries was rigorously enforced. It was in vain that the Baptists pleaded their conscientious dissent from the "Standing Order," and the obligation under which they lay to support their own ministers. Their oppressors would not listen, nor abate one jot of their demands. The scourge was in their hands, and they applied it without mercy.

"From the year 1692 to the year 1728, the Baptists were everywhere, except in Boston and some few other towns, taxed for the support of Congregational ministers. The fact of their maintaining worship by themselves was not allowed to be a sufficient reason for exempting them from rates to sustain a ministry which in point of conscience they could not hear. For their refusal to pay such rates, we are told that they 'oftentimes had their bodies seized upon, and thrown into the common jail, as malefactors, and their cattle, swine, horses, household furniture, and implements of husbandry forcibly distrained from them, and shamefully sold, many times at not one-quarter part of the first value.' And it is added 'that the heavy pressures and afflictions occasioned by these distraints, imprisonments, and the losses consequent thereupon, made many of the Baptists bend, almost ruined some of our people, and disheartened others to such a degree that they removed, with the remaining effects they had left, out of the province.'"[2]

[1] Persons who had been baptized in infancy, and were not scandalous in life, were admitted to membership, though there was no proof of personal religion. If one of the parents of a child belonged to the church, the child might be baptized, and ultimately become a member. Thus infant baptism produced church degeneration.

[2] Dr. Hovey's *Life and Times of Isaac Backus*, p. 167.

In the year 1728 an act was passed by the General Court of Massachusetts, exempting Baptists from the tax; but as it relieved the *persons* only, but left the *property* still liable, it was of little service. Other acts were afterward passed, to be in force for short periods, professedly to give relief; but they were clogged with so many difficulties and obnoxious conditions, that the Baptists continued to suffer in many places and for many years. The following letters from Christian females furnish painful illustrations of these statements.

Elizabeth Backus, mother of the Rev. Isaac Backus, writes thus to her son:

"NORWICH, Nov. 4, 1752.

"MY DEAR SON: I have heard something of the trials amongst you of late, and I was grieved, till I had strength to give up the case to God and leave my burden there. And now I would tell you something of our trials. Your brother Samuel lay in prison twenty days. October 15th the collectors came to our house, and took me away to prison about nine o'clock, in a dark, rainy night. Brothers Hill and Sabins were brought there the next night. We lay in prison thirteen days, and were then set at liberty, by what means I know not. Whilst I was there a great many people came to see me, and some said one thing and some said another. Oh, the innumerable snares and temptations that beset me! more than I ever thought of before. But oh, the condescension of Heaven! though I was bound when I was cast into this furnace, yet I was loosed and found Jesus in the midst of a furnace with me. Oh, then I could give up my name, estate, family, life and breath, freely to God. Now the prison looked like a palace to me. I could bless God for all the laughs and scoffs made at me. Oh, the love that flowed out to all mankind! then I could forgive as I would desire to be forgiven, and love my neighbor as myself. Deacon Griswold was put in prison the 8th of October; and yesterday old Brother Grover; and they are in pursuit of others, all which calls for humiliation. The church has appointed the 13th of November to be spent in prayer and fasting on that account. I do remember my love to you and your wife, and the dear children of God with you, begging your prayers for us in such a day of trial. We are all in tolerable health, expecting to see you. These from your loving mother,

"ELIZABETH BACKUS."

"MR. BACKUS: I understand that you are collecting materials for a Baptist History, in which you propose to let the public know how the Baptists have been oppressed in Massachusetts Bay. This is to let you know that in the year 1768, in a very cold night in winter, about nine or ten o'clock in the evening, I was taken prisoner, and carried by the collector in the town where I live from my family, consisting of three small children, in order to be put into jail. It being a severe cold night, I concluded by advice, while I was detained at a tavern in the way to jail some hours, to pay the sum of 4-8 L. M. [*i. e.* legal money], for which I was made a prisoner, it being for the ministerial rate. The reason why I refused paying it before was because I was a Baptist, and belonged to the Baptist Society, in Haverhill, and had carried in a certificate to the assessors, as I suppose, according to law. Thus they dealt with a poor widow-woman in Bradford, the relict of Solomon Kimball, late of the said town; at whose house the Rev. Hezekiah Smith was shamefully treated by many of the people in Bradford, who came headed by the sheriff, Amos Mulliken, at a time when Mr. Smith was to preach a sermon in our house, at the request of my husband, and warmly contended with him, and threatened him if he did preach. Mr. Smith went to begin service by singing, notwithstanding the noise, clamor, and threats of the people. But one of their number snatched the chair behind which Mr. Smith stood from before him. Upon which my husband desired Mr. Smith to tarry a little till he had quelled the tumult; but all his endeavors to silence them were in vain. Upon which my husband desired Mr. Smith to begin public service; which accordingly he did, and went through then without further molestation.

"Martha Kimball.
"Bradford, Sept. 2, 1774.

"N. B. The above I can attest to. It may be observed that the tavern whither they took me is about two miles from my house. After I had paid what they demanded, then I had to return to my poor fatherless children, through the snow on foot, in the dead of the night, exposed to the severity of the cold."[1]

In the other New England states, Rhode Island excepted, the Baptists met with similar treatment. The Rev. Mr. Marshall, for instance, who labored in Connecticut, was put in the stocks for preaching in another minister's parish, and afterward sent to jail for "*preaching the gospel contrary to law.*" The tongue of slander was busy against them, and they were "everywhere

[1] Hovey, pp. 28, 184.

spoken against." Unrighteously taxed, unlawfully imprisoned, the butts of all men's ridicule, they quailed not, nor did they slacken in zeal or effort; and God wonderfully blessed them.

Their success was great also in Virginia. After the revival under Whitefield and his associates, many Baptist ministers itinerated in that state, and so preached that multitudes believed and were converted. Persecution soon broke out. Several of the ministers were arrested. "May it please your worship," said the lawyer, "these men are great disturbers of the peace; they cannot meet a man on the road but they ram a text of Scripture down his throat." As they would not promise to desist from preaching, they were committed to prison, to which they went cheerfully, singing as they walked through the street Dr. Watts' hymn, "Broad is the road that leads to death." This was in the county of Spottsylvania, in the year 1768. The same course was pursued by the magistrates in other parts of the state. About thirty ministers, besides many exhorters and others who manifested Christian earnestness for the salvation of souls, were imprisoned, some of them repeatedly.[1]

"The magistrates, in all parts of the Commonwealth, impelled and directed by the State clergy and their more zealous friends, commenced a relentless annoyance of the people and a heartless persecution of the ministers of our churches. Attempts were made to set aside the Toleration Act, and old and obsolete laws were hunted up, and essays were made to enforce their provisions. Assessments were prosecuted with new vigilance; fines imposed and collected; meetings were disturbed and

[1] Benedict's *History of the Baptists*, p. 654.

violently dispersed; and pastors and other ministers were arrested, dragged before the courts, browbeaten, and ignominiously punished. All this, and more, is acknowledged by the ministers and historians of the 'State Church' themselves. Dr. Hawks, for example, says, 'No Dissenters in Virginia experienced for a time harsher treatment than did the Baptists. They were beaten and imprisoned, and cruelty taxed its ingenuity to devise new modes of punishment and annoyance. The usual consequences followed. Persecution made friends for its victims; and the men who were not permitted to speak in public found willing auditors in the sympathizing crowds who gathered round the prisons to hear them preach from the grated windows. It is not improbable that this very opposition imparted strength in another mode, inasmuch as it at least furnished the Baptists with a common ground on which to make resistance.'"[1]

"In all the prisons where our brethren were incarcerated, they preached daily from the windows to the crowds who there assembled to hear them."[2]

Irritated beyond measure at this boldness, their enemies resorted to various expedients to check it. "In some cases," says Benedict, "drums were beaten in the time of service; high enclosures were erected before the prison windows; matches and other suffocating materials were burnt outside the prison doors." But all was in vain. The servants of God *would* preach, and the people were equally determined to hear. Converts were multiplied; new churches sprang up all over the state: "so mightily grew the word of God, and prevailed."

[1] *History of the Protestant Episcopal Church in Virginia*, p. 121.
[2] Howell's *Early Baptists of Virginia*, p. 39.

The persecuted have sometimes become persecutors when the power has come into their own hands. In the fourth century the Orthodox banished the Arians; but when an Arian emperor occupied the throne the Arians banished the Orthodox. There is no proof, however, of the adoption of a persecuting policy by Baptists. John Holmes was a Baptist magistrate in Philadelphia in 1691, when the "Keithian Baptists" appeared in that city, and created trouble among the Quakers, some of whom were desirous of suppressing them by force. Mr. Holmes refused to act, observing "that it was a religious dispute, and therefore not fit for a civil court."[1] Thirty years afterward a bill was brought into the House of Assembly of New Jersey, "to punish such as denied the doctrine of the Trinity, the divinity of Christ," etc. The Rev. Nathaniel Jenkins, pastor of the Baptist church at Cape May, who was a member of the house, opposed the bill with great earnestness and warmth. "I believe the doctrines in question," he said, "as firmly as the promoters of that ill-designed bill; but will never consent to oppose the opposers with law, or with any other weapon save that of argument." His sturdy resistance prevailed, and the bill was quashed.[2]

The great increase of our denomination took place after the year 1740. In the fall of that year Whitefield landed at Newport, Rhode Island, and commenced that course of evangelical labor in the United States which was productive, under the divine blessing, of such remarkable results. The revival at Northampton, Massachusetts, in 1734, had already prepared the minds of the people,

[1] Morgan Edwards' *History of the Baptists of Pennsylvania*, p. 56.
[2] Edwards' *History of the Baptists of New Jrsey*, p. 41.

in some measure, for a general outpouring of the Spirit. It was graciously vouchsafed, and so glorious was the manifestation that "in the term of two or three years thirty or forty thousand souls were born into the family of heaven in New England."[1] Some of the converts joined the existing churches, but a large number formed separate churches, requiring satisfactory evidence that the candidates for communion were the subjects of regeneration. This New Testament rule had been departed from by the "Standing Order," and the *New Lights*, as they were called, determined to reinstate primitive principles in their proper place. The natural effect was that many of them became Baptists.

The new converts were "fervent in spirit." They thirsted for the salvation of souls. Unexampled efforts were immediately employed for the spread of the gospel. Some went from house to house in their respective neighborhoods, "warning every man and teaching every man," and exhorting all to turn to the Lord. Pious ministers were stirred up to unusual exertion, and old Christians renewed their youth. "The Lord gave the word; great was the company of them that published it." They were not all suitably qualified for the work, as we should now judge; mistakes were committed, and measures of doubtful propriety adopted, in some places; but such things might be expected in times of great spiritual excitement. It cannot be denied that the laborers were generally men of God, "full of the Holy Ghost and of faith." They had deep convictions of the evil of sin and the peril of a rebellious state. The love of God in Christ overpowered their souls. Their views of the solemn realities of an-

[1] Trumbull's *History of Connecticut*, quoted by Dr. Hovey, p. 35.

other world were vivid and heart-affecting. They "set the Lord always before" them, and walked as in the sight of the judgment-seat. Their earnest appeals made the stout-hearted tremble, awed many a reprobate into silence, and wrung tears from daring and hardened offenders. Tens of thousands bowed before the majesty of truth.

Some of the most powerful preachers emigrated to other states, and wherever they went the floods of blessing poured over the land. Virginia was remarkably indebted to their labors. In 1768 there were but ten Baptist churches in that state; in 1790 there were two hundred and ten. The Carolinas and other states in the South were also visited by the New Lights, and marvelous effects followed.

It will be interesting to note the dates of the establishment of the first churches in the several states.

DELAWARE.—This state originally formed part of Pennsylvania, and did not acquire an independent existence till 1776. The first Baptist church in the district which is now the state of Delaware was formed at *Welsh Tract*, in 1703. Sixteen persons, all Baptists, emigrated in a body from Wales in 1701. They settled first at Pennepek, and in the year above mentioned removed to Welsh Tract. Thomas Griffith, one of the original emigrants, became pastor of the church. He died in 1725.

CONNECTICUT.—Baptist principles were introduced into this state from Rhode Island. Mr. Valentine Wightman planted a church at *Groton* in 1705. Other ministers followed, and when the "New Light Stir" took place, the cause advanced encouragingly, in spite of the persecutions urged by the "Standing Order."

VIRGINIA.—There were Baptists in this state at the

commencement of the eighteenth century. In 1714, Robert Nordin, an ordained minister, arrived from England, and gathered a church at *Burleigh*, Isle of Wight county. Other Baptists entered from Maryland. About the middle of the century Shubael Stearns and other New England itinerants traversed a considerable part of the state, and kindled a flame that will not be quenched.

NEW YORK.—Some of the persecuted Baptists sought refuge among the Dutch settlers in New York during the seventeenth century, but it does not appear that any church was formed. William Wickenden, of Providence, Rhode Island, preached frequently in New York, and had the honor to be imprisoned four months for it. Valentine Wightman preached two years in the city, and baptized a number of converts. This was in 1714. Nicholas Eyres, one of the baptized, became their minister. They erected a place of worship on *Golden Hill* in 1728. The exact date of the formation of the church is not known. It was probably soon after the baptism.

NORTH CAROLINA.—There were scattered Baptists in this state from the latter end of the seventeenth century. The first church was constituted about 1727, by Paul Palmer, at *Perquimans*. But to the labors of Shubael Stearns and his companions, from the year 1754, must be attributed, under God, the extensive spread of Baptist views and practices, and the remarkable revival of religion by which the eighteenth century was distinguished.

MARYLAND.—At *Chestnut Ridge*, was founded in 1742, the first Baptist church in this state. It originated with Henry Sator, an Englishman who emigrated in 1709 He invited Baptist ministers to preach in his house. Conversions followed, and the church was formed.

NEW HAMPSHIRE.—Mrs. Scammon, a Christian woman, who removed from Rehoboth, Massachusetts, into New Hampshire in 1720, was the means of introducing the Baptist denomination into this state, though the first church was not established till after her death. By conversation with her neighbors she endeavored to lead them to Christ; and when they became Christians she distributed among them copies of *Norcott on Baptism* (first published in England, about the year 1660, and extensively circulated), with a view to guide them into the paths of New Testament observances. A church was formed at *Newtown* in 1755.

MAINE.—The formation of the church at Kittery in 1682 has been mentioned. It did not live long. Benedict says: "As the result of a long-cherished and well-organized intolerance, venting itself in vehement and impassioned persecution, these humble Christians became disheartened and overcome. In less than one year from its organization the church was dissolved and the members scattered 'like sheep upon the mountains!'"[1] In 1764, eighty-one years after the dissolution of the church at Kittery, another church was formed at *Berwick*, Joshua Emery being the first pastor. About twenty years after, Isaac Case, another devoted man, itinerated through the state, and was greatly blessed.

VERMONT.—The first settlers in this state were mostly Congregationalists. A number of them embraced Baptist sentiments, and many Baptist ministers removed into the state from time to time, by whose unwearied efforts the cause of truth and holiness was furthered. The first church was formed at *Shaftesbury* in 1768.

[1] *History*, p. 507.

GEORGIA.—There were many Baptists in various parts of Georgia for many years before any organization took place. Georgia was chiefly indebted to the New Lights, Daniel Marshall and others, who were abundant in labors and astonishingly successful. The first church was formed at Kiokee in 1772.

TENNESSEE.—Two churches were formed in Eastern Tennessee about the year 1765, but they were scattered in the Indian war in 1774. The first permanent church was established at *Buffalo Ridge* in 1780.

KENTUCKY.—The early settlers in Kentucky encountered great difficulties and dangers; pioneering was hard work in a country without roads, and where hostile attacks from Indians might be expected any day and any hour. But they persevered and succeeded. Among them were many Baptists from Virginia. In 1781 the first church was organized at *Nolinn*. That church "is supposed to have been the first Protestant religious society organized in the Great West." [1]

---

[1] The following notices refer to periods not embraced in this history:

ARKANSAS.—1800? Fouche à Thomas.
MISSISSIPPI.—1800? Natchez.
INDIANA.—1802. On the Whitewater.
MISSOURI.—1804. Tyawappity.
ALABAMA.—1810. Clarke co.
LOUISIANA.—1812. Calvary.
MICHIGAN.—1822. Pontiac.
IOWA.—1836. Big Creek.
TEXAS.—1836?
WISCONSIN.—1837. Rochester.
CALIFORNIA.—1847. San Francisco.
MINNESOTA.—1849. St. Paul.
OREGON.—1846. Astoria.

OHIO.—A company of settlers located themselves in the summer of 1789 at the mouth of the Little Miami river. Some of them were Baptists, who immediately commenced holding religious meetings, each taking his turn, as he was able, in carrying on the service. The Rev. S. Gano, of Providence, Rhode Island, visited the settlement in 1790, and formed the *Miami* church.

ILLINOIS.—"The Baptists," says J. M. Peck, D. D., "were the first Protestants to enter this region." They held meetings and edified one another as well as they could for some time. The Rev. James Smith, a Kentucky Baptist minister, visited the Illinois settlements three times, and labored with great acceptance among the people. He was once captured by the Indians, who did not release him till his brethren had raised one hundred and seventy dollars (a large sum in those times) for his ransom. The first church was formed at *New Design* in 1796.

* As soon as the Baptist churches became sufficiently numerous, they proceeded to combine in Associations, which arrangement has proved eminently conducive to the prosperity of the body. Carefully guarding against the assumption of ecclesiastical power, and avoiding all interference with the affairs of individual churches, the ministers and delegates who assembled from time to time exercised a brotherly supervision over the Baptist cause, and often "devised liberal things" on its behalf. Personal edification was promoted by the religious services; Christian friendship was renewed and extended; important questions of doctrine and practice were discussed, and advice given in difficult cases; weak and destitute churches were assisted; and plans for the wider diffusion

of gospel truth were originated. Almost all our denominational enterprises may be referred to the influence of these associational gatherings.

The Philadelphia Association was the first of the kind. It was formed in the year 1707. "This Association," says Dr. Samuel Jones, in his *Century Sermon*, "originated in what they called General, and sometimes Yearly meetings. These meetings were instituted as early as 1688, and met alternately in May and September, at Lower Dublin, Philadelphia, Salem, Cohansey, Chester, and Burlington, at which places there were members, though no church or churches were constituted, except Lower Dublin and Cohansey. At these meetings their labors were chiefly confined to the ministry of the word and the administration of gospel ordinances. But in the year 1707 they seemed to have taken more properly the form of an Association; for then they had delegates from several churches, and attended to their general concerns. We therefore date our beginning as an Association from that time, though we might, with but little impropriety, extend it back some years. They were at this time but a feeble band, though a band of faithful brothers, consisting of but five churches, viz., those of Lower Dublin, Piscataway, Middletown, Cohansey, and Welsh Tract. There were at that time but these five in North America, except in Massachusetts and Rhode Island."[1]

This Association is still a large and flourishing body, notwithstanding the numerous offshoots which it has given out. In October, 1868, it was composed of 66 churches and a membership of 14,474. There are seventeen other Associations in the state.

[1] Benedict's *History*, p. 605.

The list below gives the name of the first Association formed in each state within this period, with the date of the formation:

1751. Charleston Association, S. Carolina.
1758. Sandy Creek Association, N. Carolina.
1766. Ketockton Association, Virginia.
1767. Warren Association, Rhode Island.
1772. Stonington Association, Connecticut.
1780. Shaftesbury Association, Vermont.
1782. Salisbury Association, Maryland.
1784. Georgia Association.
1785. New Hampshire Association.
1785. Elkhorn, S. Kentucky, and Salem Associations, Kentucky.
1786. Holston Association, Tennessee.
1791. New York Association.
1797. Miami Association, Ohio.[1]

A few years after the establishment of the Philadelphia Association, a correspondence was opened with the Bap-

---

[1] The following Associations were formed subsequent to the period embraced in this history:

1807. Illinois Association.
1807. Mississippi Association.
1809. Whitewater Association, Indiana.
1814. Flint River Association, Alabama.
1816. Bethel Association, Missouri.
1821. Louisiana Association.
1827. Michigan Association.
1829. Spring River Association, Arkansas.
1838. Wisconsin Association.
1838. Desmoines Association, Iowa.
1840. Union Association, Texas.
1842. Florida Association.
1848. Willamette, Oregon.
1851. San Francisco Association, California.
1856. Mound City Association, Kansas.
1858. Nebraska Association, Nebraska.

tist ministers of London. In a letter dated August 12, 1714, Abel Morgan says, "We are now nine churches. . . . . In these churches there are about five hundred members, but who are greatly scattered on this main land. Our ministers are necessitated to labor with their hands. We hope, if it please God to supply us with more help, we shall be more churches in a little time. Most churches administer the sacrament once a month. These ministers are all sound in the faith, and we practice most things like the British churches." Another letter, written the following year, contained a request for assistance in books, etc., "for the preservation and further promoting of the truth in those parts." Two gentlemen responded to the request. "Mr. Thomas Hollis and Mr. John Taylor gave a supply of books; Mr. Hollis sent twelve copies of Mr. Burkitt's *Annotations on the New Testament*, directing that each minister in those parts might have a copy; and Mr. John Taylor gave twenty pounds' worth of old books, and several copies of the Baptist Catechism." Acknowledging the gift, the church at Philadelphia wrote as follows: "Your letter was read in our meetings in town and country. We concluded that the books might be disposed of as intended: the family-books for the benefit of well-disposed folks; the *Annotations* to be for particular qualified persons. The other books for the public use, for our leading brethren to resort to, are lodged here in the city, to be lent and returned again; whereby the rising-generation may have the benefit of them as well as the present. The contents of the letters and a catalogue of the books are recorded in our church-books, to prevent all mistakes." An acknowledgment was also forwarded by the Association at its annual meeting, held September, 1717. An extract from their letter will show the nature of the struggle which the Baptists in Pennsylvania had at that time to maintain: "We think that the very minds of the people in common here are tainted with Arminianism, Socinianism, and what not. The common notion of religion among them is like a leprous house: it is not to be mended by patching, but must be pulled down, and rebuilt upon the right foundation—the covenant of grace. This we labor to do, and therefore go against the current of the times, that others who succeed us may see no cause to lament our having gone before them; and this we will still do, God permitting."[1] They did it, and that right well. None of their successors have lamented "their having gone before them."

I have adverted to the remarkable increase of our denomination in the latter half of the period now under notice. It was the fruit of a series of revivals. The ministers of those times were not satisfied with discharging the duties of their pastorates. They undertook long journeys, preaching as they went, often with no preconceived or definite plan, but traveling and laboring as they believed themselves to be directed from above. Mighty effects followed, "the Lord working with them, and confirming the word," not indeed by "signs following," such as apostolic churches saw, but by still greater displays of power and mercy—by the conversion of souls. These manifestations were not confined to any particular part of the country; they were everywhere enjoyed. Rhode Island experienced a rich blessing in 1774. The churches in the northern parts of New England were more than

[1] Ivimey, iii. 127, 131, 133.

doubled in number in the ten years preceding 1792. Many thousands were added in Virginia and other Southern states. In 1791 there was an extensive revival in Massachusetts, which reached far into the state of New York. Two hundred and ninety-three members were added to the churches of Saratoga and Stillwater in that year.[1]

We need not be surprised at some oddities. All society was in a ferment; strange things bubbled up to the surface now and then, and were gazed upon, or smiled at, or it may be wept over, till they sank into oblivion. If the churches composing the Sandy Creek Association in North Carolina were tenacious of the kiss of charity, the laying on of hands upon members, the appointment of elderesses, and such things; if a large Baptist body in Virginia were so mistaken as to choose, in the year 1774, three of their number, and designate them " apostles," investing them with a power of general superintendence; and if, in some respects, the fervency of New Light feelings got the better of discretion and decorum, we must bear in mind the peculiarities of the times. After a long season of cold and drought, the Lord " poured water upon him that was thirsty, and floods upon the dry ground;" the spiritual vegetation sprang up thick and strong, requiring skillful cultivators; and some detriment was experienced for want of care in pruning and training. In the course of a few years these wants were supplied, and suitable arrangements constituted. Surely we ought to prefer a revival of religion, though dashed with some irregularities, to the death-like coldness of mere orthodoxy and form.

[1] Hovey, p. 258.

The year 1764 was memorable for the founding of Rhode Island College, now called "Brown University." This institution originated with the Philadelphia Association. The desirableness of the measure had been long felt. The Rev. Morgan Edwards was the principal mover in the undertaking, and his views were zealously forwarded by the Pennsylvania Baptists. They chose Rhode Island as the seat of the proposed college, because it was supposed that the preponderance of the Baptists in that state would secure the bestowment of a suitable charter of incorporation. The Rev. James Manning, then of Philadelphia, being at Newport, R. I., in 1763, on his way to Halifax, Nova Scotia, called a meeting of the chief Baptists, and laid the subject before them. The result was that a plan was formed, preliminary measures taken, and application immediately made to the legislature for a charter. Some difficulties arose, from the dishonest dealing of a Presbyterian minister whose assistance had been asked in the preparation of the charter, and who actually drew it up in such a manner that the Presbyterians would have had the control. His design was defeated, and the original promoters of the object obtained their wishes. The college was founded on the following plan:

"That into this liberal and catholic institution shall never be admitted any religious tests; but, on the contrary, all the members thereof shall for ever enjoy full, free, absolute, uninterrupted liberty of conscience; and that the places of professors, tutors, and all other officers, the president alone excepted, shall be free and open for all denominations of Protestants; and that youth of all religious denominations shall and may be freely admitted

THE QUIET PERIOD. 547

to the equal advantages, emoluments, and honors of the college or university, and shall receive a like fair, generous and equal treatment during their residence therein, they conducting themselves peaceably and conforming to the laws and statutes thereof; and that the public teaching shall in general respect the sciences; and that the sectarian differences of opinions shall not make any part of the public and classical instruction.

"The government of the college is vested in a Board of Fellows, consisting of twelve members, of whom eight, including the president, must be Baptists; and a Board of Trustees, consisting of thirty-six members, of whom twenty-two must be Baptists, five Friends or Quakers, four Congregationalists, and five Episcopalians. These represent the different denominations existing in the state when the charter was obtained. The instruction and immediate government of the college rests in the president and Board of Fellows."[1]

Mr. Manning, afterward Dr. Manning, was chosen president. He commenced his labors at Warren in 1766, and was soon encouraged by the resort of students to him for instruction. The erection of a college building became necessary, and Providence was chosen as the site, that city having offered the largest contribution toward the object. The work was accomplished in 1770. On the breaking out of the American war the institution was suspended for six years, and the building was used for barrack and hospital purposes by the army. Dr. Manning died in 1791, and was succeeded by Dr. Maxcy, who resigned his office in 1802, when Dr. Messer became president. He was followed in 1826 by Dr. Wayland,

[1] Hovey, p. 151.

who resigned, "full of honors," in 1856. The University was next under the presidency of Dr. Barnas Sears, who resigned in 1867, in order to superintend educational arrangements in the South, founded by the munificent liberality of George Peabody, Esq. Dr. Alexis Caswell is now the president.

This venerable institution is now a hundred years old. About two thousand students have graduated there, upward of five hundred of whom have become ministers of the gospel.[1]

Valuable aid was received from England, both in money and books, chiefly on the application of Morgan Edwards, who went to that country for the purpose, and was very successful, "considering," as he said, "how angry the mother country then was with the colonies for opposing the Stamp Act."

Rhode Island College was named " Brown University" in 1804, in honor of Nicholas Brown, Esq., to whose liberality it has been largely indebted. In the year above mentioned he founded a Professorship in Rhetoric and Belles Lettres. He afterward erected "Hope Hall," a spacious structure, designed to afford the increased accommodation required for the students, which cost thirty thousand dollars. "Manning Hall," more recently built by the same generous benefactor, has the library on the ground floor, and the upper part was used for a chapel. The library contains between thirty and forty thousand volumes.

The importance of providing means of instruction for those who intended to enter the ministry was early felt

---

[1] The *History of Brown University*, by R. A. Guild, the librarian, published in 1867, is a very interesting volume.

by the Baptists of America. A considerable sum was raised for the assistance of such persons by the Philadelphia Association. Private seminaries of education were established in different parts of the country, which were attended by many who afterward became ministers of the gospel. The first academy of the kind was opened by the Rev. Isaac Eaton, at Hopewell, New Jersey, in 1756. Dr. Samuel Jones established another, at Lower Dublin, Pennsylvania, in 1766; and a third was founded at Wrentham, Massachusetts, in 1776, by Rev. W. Williams, one of the first graduates of Rhode Island College. These were useful efforts. They were the germs of the noble undertakings which have characterized the present age.

The introduction of Baptist principles and practices into that part of the American continent which is now called "British North America" remains to be recorded.

In 1760, Shubael Dimock and family, with other persons, emigrated from Connecticut and settled in Newport, Nova Scotia. The vexations they had endured in their own country in being taxed for the support of the ministers of the "Standing Order" (Congregational) led to their removal. The Rev. John Sutton, a Baptist minister, accompanied them. He remained about a year in the province, baptized Mr. Dimock's son Daniel and many more, and then returned. The Dimocks, father and son, preached the gospel in the district where they had settled, and many were converted and baptized, but no church was formed.

The Rev. Ebenezer Moulton, of Massachusetts, visited the same province in 1761, and preached chiefly at Yarmouth. The same results followed as at Newport. He also returned.

In 1763, the Rev. Nathan Mason removed from Swansea, Massachusetts, to Sackville, which was then in Nova Scotia, but is now in New Brunswick, the separation into two provinces having taken place in 1784. A church had been formed, of which Mr. Mason was chosen pastor before he left. The whole church emigrated. They remained at Sackville about eight years, during which time they had increased to sixty members. The original emigrants then returned, and the church died out. Another church was formed in the same place in 1799.

The first Baptist church formed in the province was at Horton. Ten persons were constituted a church October 19, 1778, and the Rev. Nicholas Pearson, who had been preaching there some time, was chosen their pastor. His labors were so successful that fifty-two persons were added to the church in 1779 and 1780. In the latter year the church adopted open communion, by admitting Congregationalists to their fellowship. The other churches which were established during the century adopted the same policy.

The ministers to whose labors the denomination was chiefly indebted for its maintenance and extension in Nova Scotia were, Thomas Handly Chipman, Joseph Dimock, John Burton, James Manning, Theodore Seth Harding, Harris Harding, Edward Manning, Enoch Towner, and Joseph Crandal.

Thomas Handly Chipman was baptized at Horton in 1778. He became pastor of the church at Annapolis and Upper Granville, and died Oct. 11, 1830.

Joseph Dimock was baptized at Horton in 1787. He was ordained at Chester, April 10, 1793, and was **pastor of that** church till his death, June 29, 1846.

THE QUIET PERIOD.

Theodore Seth Harding was baptized in 1795, ordained at Horton, July 31, 1796, and died there June 8, 1855.

James Manning was baptized in 1796, ordained in Lower Granville, September 10, 1798, and died May 27, 1818.

John Burton was ordained in 1794, and became pastor of the church at Halifax in 1795. He died February 6, 1838.

Edward Manning was ordained in 1795 over the church in Cornwallis, at that time in the Congregational order. He was baptized in 1707, and remained in Cornwallis (the church becoming a Baptist church), where he died January 12, 1851.

Harris Harding began to preach in 1784. He was baptized in 1799, and died at Yarmouth, where he had spent fifty-seven years of his ministry, March 7, 1854.

Enoch Towner was ordained at Digby in 1799. He died January 12, 1851.

Joseph Crandal was ordained at Sackville in 1799. His labors were chiefly confined to New Brunswick. He died February 20, 1858.

All these were eminent men in their time. Uneducated, in the common meaning of the word, they were well versed in Bible theology, and they were powerful preachers. They did not confine themselves to the neighborhoods in which they lived, but itinerated through the province, proclaiming the glad tidings wherever they could gain access to the people, and turning many "from the power of Satan unto God." Their names are held in high honor in Nova Scotia.

Mixed fellowship prevailed in all the churches, that at

Halifax excepted, which was the only Baptist church, properly so called, in Nova Scotia at the close of the eighteenth century. But all the pastors were Baptists, and the converts were invariably baptized. Strict communion became the practice of the churches in 1809.

The first association in British North America was formed in Lower Granville, Nova Scotia, June 23, 1800. It consisted of nine churches, viz.: Annapolis and Upper Granville, Digby, Lower Granville, Horton, Newport, Cornwallis, Chester, Yarmouth, and Sackville, N. B.

A Baptist church was formed in the township of Hallowell, Prince Edward county, Canada West, about the year 1795. The Rev. Joseph Winn was pastor, and probably exercised a general oversight over other Baptist communities which were subsequently founded in that part of Canada. The Rev. Reuben Crandell was also an active and successful minister in the same province.

CHAPTER IV.

Biographical Notices—Shubael Stearns—Daniel Marshall — Samuel Harris—John Gano—Lewis Lunsford—John Waller—Isaac Backus, A.M.—Morgan Edwards—D. Thomas—E. Kinnersley—Oliver Hart —Drs. Mercer, Smith, Manning, Foster, and Stillman.

I WILL bring this brief account of the American Baptists to a close by furnishing a notice of the more prominent ministers of the period.

SHUBAEL STEARNS was a New Light preacher in Connecticut. He became a Baptist 1751. Three years afterward, under the influence of an impression that he was called of God to a great work in a distant land, he left New England, accompanied by a number of his friends, and, after a short residence in Virginia, settled at Sandy Creek, North Carolina, in 1755. A Baptist church, consisting of sixteen members, was immediately formed, and active operations were commenced, much to the surprise of the neighborhood.

"The inhabitants about this little colony of Baptists," says Benedict, "although brought up in the Christian religion, were grossly ignorant of its essential principles. Having the form of godliness, they knew nothing of its power. Stearns and his party, of course, brought strange things to their ears. To be born again, appeared to them as it did to the Jewish doctor, when he asked if he must enter the second time into his mother's womb and be born. Having always supposed that religion consisted in nothing more than the practice of its outward duties, they could not comprehend how it should be necessary to feel conviction and conversion; and to be able to ascertain the time and place of one's conversion was, in their estimation, wonderful indeed. These points were all strenuously contended for by the new preachers; but their manner of preaching was, if possible, much more novel than their doctrines. The Separates in New England had acquired a very warm and pathetic address, accompanied by strong gestures and a singular tone of voice. Being often deeply affected themselves when preaching, correspondent affections were felt by their pious hearers, which were frequently expressed by tears, trembling, screams, and exclamations of grief and joy. All these they brought with them into their new habitation, at which the people were greatly astonished, having never seen things on this wise before. Many mocked, but, the power of God attending them, many also trembled. In process of time, some of the inhabitants became converts, and bowed obedience to the Redeemer's sceptre. These uniting their labors with the others, a powerful and extensive work commenced, and Sandy Creek church soon swelled from sixteen to six hundred and six members."[1]

Mr. Stearns was pastor of the church. Daniel Marshall, his brother-in-law, full of zeal and love, went from place to place preaching the gospel, and soon formed another church, **thirty** miles from Sandy Creek. Many of the new converts became preachers, and plunged into

[1] *History of the Baptists*, ii. 38. Ed. 1813.

the work without any human preparation, borne away by the love of Christ and compassion for perishing souls. County after county received the truth from them, and churches were rapidly organized, Mr. Stearns being generally engaged on such occasions. "He seems to have possessed the talent of arranging the materials when collected, and well understood discipline and church-government." Some of the preachers traveled southward, and evangelized South Carolina and Georgia. Others went northward, into Virginia. "Sandy Creek," said Morgan Edwards, "is the mother of all the Separate Baptists. From this Zion went forth the word, and great was the company of them that published it. This church, in seventeen years, has spread her branches westward as far as the great river Mississippi; southward as far as Georgia; eastward to the sea and Chesapeake Bay; and northward to the waters of the Potomac: it, in seventeen years, is become mother, grandmother, and great-grandmother to forty-two churches, from which sprang one hundred and twenty-five ministers, many of which are ordained, and support the sacred character as well as any set of clergy in America." This was written in 1775.

Thus Shubael Stearns' impression was realized. He was really called to do a great work; and he toiled on to the end, becoming at length a patriarch among the churches. It is said of him, that "his voice was musical and strong, which he managed in such a manner as one while to make soft impressions in the heart, and fetch tears from the eyes; and anon, to shake the very nerves, and throw the animal system into tumults and perturbations;"—that "in his eyes was something very penetrating, which seemed to have a meaning in every glance;"—and that "many stories have been told respecting the enchantments of his eyes and voice." Whatever may be thought of such statements as these, it is indisputable that God greatly blessed the good man's labors.

Shubael Stearns died at Sandy Creek, November 20, 1771.

DANIEL MARSHALL was a native of Windsor, Connecticut. He was born in the year 1706. Converted in his twentieth year, he joined the Presbyterians, and was a useful member of their society till the year 1744, when the preaching of Mr. Whitefield, who was at that time on a visit to the New England states, so powerfully affected him and many more that they literally "left all," and went forth to labor for God, whithersoever they might be guided. "Firmly believing," says his son, "in the near approach of the latter-day glory, when the Jews, with the fullness of the Gentiles, shall hail their Redeemer and bow to his gentle sceptre, a number of worthy characters ran to and fro through the Eastern states, warmly exhorting to the prompt adoption of every measure tending to hasten that blissful period. Others sold, gave away, or left their possessions, as the powerful impulse of the moment determined, and, without scrip or purse, rushed up to the head of the Susquehanna to convert the heathens, and settled in a town called Onnaquaggy, among the Mohawk Indians. One, and not the least sanguine, of these pious missionaries, was my venerable father. Great must have been his faith, great his zeal, when, without the least prospect of a temporal reward, with a much-beloved wife and three children, he exchanged his commodious buildings for a miserable hut; his fruitful and loaded orchards for barren deserts; the luxuries of a well-furnished table for coarse and scanty fare; and numerous civil friends for rude savages!"[1] He remained among the Indians about eighteen months, and was beginning to reap the fruit of his endeavors—several of them being converted—when, on the breaking out of a war among their tribes, he removed into Pennsylvania. Thence, after a short residence, he proceeded to Opeckon, in Virginia. There he became acquainted with some Baptists, and, after a careful examination of their sentiments and practice, was convinced of their agreement with Scripture. He and his wife were baptized in the year 1754. He was immediately licensed as a preacher, and engaged in the work with great ardor. Removing to North Carolina, in connection with Shubael Stearns, he itinerated very extensively, and was everywhere blessed as the instrument of turning men to God. He was ordained pastor of Abbot's Creek church in 1758. Soon after, he baptized Samuel Harris, with whom he "made several tours, and preached and planted the gospel in several places, as far as James River." His next station was Beaver Creek, South Carolina, where a large church was the reward of his labors, and where, also, the whole surrounding district was evangelized by him. A similar blessing attended him at Horse Creek. As this place was on the borders of Georgia, he soon began a series of missionary journeys in that state; and in 1771 he settled at Kiokee. There, too, surprising effects followed. A church was formed in 1772, which, in the course of a few years, became the

[1] Benedict, ii. 351.

mother of many other churches. There Mr. Marshall continued till his death. He was spared to a good old age. On the 2d of November, 1784, he "went home." "I have been praying," he said, "that I may go home to-night. . . . God has shown me that he is my God, that I am his son, and that an eternal weight of glory is mine."

SAMUEL HARRIS, a native of Hanover county, Virginia, born in 1724, was one of the most useful men of his day. He held a higher position in society than most of those who joined our denomination at that time. He was "churchwarden, sheriff, a justice of the peace, burgess for the county, colonel of the militia, captain of Mayo Fort, and commissary for the fort and army." He became "serious and melancholy without knowing why," till at length, "by reading and conversation, he discovered that he was a hopeless sinner, and that a sense of his guilt was the true cause of his gloom of mind." While on one of his military tours of inspection, he "ventured to attend Baptist preaching," and obtained relief by faith in the Saviour. Daniel Marshall baptized him. From that time his life was one act of devotedness and zeal. Practicing rigid economy in his house, he employed his whole surplus income in advancing the cause of religion. At the time of his conversion he was engaged in erecting a large mansion for the accommodation of his family, in a style suited to his rank and station; it was turned into a meeting-house, and he continued to reside in the old building. Immediately after his baptism he commenced preaching, and traveled far and wide, proclaiming the great salvation. There was scarcely any place in Virginia where he did not sow the gospel seed. In the course of his ministry he met with many rebuffs and some injurious treatment, but nothing diverted him from his object. He was "bold as a lion" for Christ. Benedict says that "his excellency lay chiefly in addressing the heart, and perhaps even Whitefield did not surpass him in this. When animated himself he seldom failed to animate his auditory. Some have described him, when exhorting at great meetings, as pouring forth streams of celestial lightning from his eyes, which, whithersoever he turned his face, would strike down hundreds at once. Hence he is often called 'Boanerges.'" In common with the New Light preachers of these times, he was extremely impulsive. "If he began to preach, and did not feel some liberty of utterance, he would tell his audience he could not preach without the Lord, and then sit down."

So highly esteemed was he by his brethren that at associations and other public assemblies he always occupied a prominent place, and was usually requested to preside. The universal confidence reposed in him was shown in a singular manner in the year 1774, when the association, having come to the conclusion that all the offices mentioned by the apostle Paul in Ephesians ii. 20 should be kept up in the church, resolved to appoint an "apostle." The lot fell on Samuel Harris, and he was ordained to the office; "the hands of every ordained minister were laid upon him." The work assigned him was to visit the churches, "for the purpose of performing, or at least of superintending, the work of ordination, and to set in order the things that were wanting." The success of the experiment was not sufficiently encouraging, so that the operation of the new arrangement soon ceased.

The good brethren evidently mistook the New Testament meaning of the word "apostle." The phraseology employed by them—"Messenger or Apostle"—indicated that their design was to establish a general superintendency, in fact, a kind of modified episcopacy. But Baptist democracy would not endure it.

And yet Samuel Harris was truly "the apostle of Virginia," in the sense in which that word is not unfrequently used, since, as has been stated, he preached the gospel "throughout all that region." He died in 1794.

These three, Shubael Stearns, Daniel Marshall, and Samuel Harris, were the principal founders of the Baptist interest in the South. They were "the first three;" and their names should be held in everlasting remembrance.

JOHN GANO, born at Hopewell, New Jersey, in 1727, and ordained to the ministry in 1754, had the privilege of spending half a century in his heavenly Master's service. At the request of the Philadelphia Association he undertook a missionary tour in Virginia and the Carolinas, which issued, shortly afterward, in his removal to Jersey Settlement, North Carolina, where his labors were abundantly blessed. In the year 1762 he became pastor of the first Baptist church, New York, over which he presided, with much acceptableness, till 1787, the period of the American war excepted, during which many churches were scattered abroad, that at New York among the number. Mr. Gano was one of the chaplains in the army, in which capacity he was respected and useful. At the close of the war he resumed his pastorate. The fragments of the dispersed church were gathered together, and in a very powerful revival, which shortly afterward took place, forty persons were added at one communion season.

In 1787, Mr Gano removed to Kentucky, in which state the remainder of his life was passed. A paralytic affection partially disabled him; but he recovered sufficiently to preach, during "the great revival" in 1802, "in an astonishing manner."

"As a minister of Christ," said Dr. Furman, "he shone like a star of the first magnitude in the American churches, and moved in a widely-extended sphere of action. For this office God had endowed him with a large portion of grace and with excellent gifts. 'He *believed*, and therefore *spake*.' Having discerned the excellence of the gospel truths, and the importance of eternal realities, he felt their power on his own soul, and accordingly he inculcated and *urged* them on the minds of his hearers with persuasive eloquence and force. He was not deficient in doctrinal discussion, or what rhetoricians style the demonstrative character of a discussion; but he excelled in the pathetic, in pungent, forcible addresses to the heart and conscience."

Mr. Gano was prompt at reply and retort, and evinced admirable tact in adapting remarks to circumstances. I will give an instance or two:

"While in the army, Mr. Gano had frequent opportunities of administering reproof in his skillful and forcible manner. One morning, as he was going to pray with the regiment, he passed by a group of officers, one of whom, who had his back toward him, was uttering his profane expressions in a most rapid manner. The officers, one after another, gave him the usual salutation. 'Good morning, Doctor,' said the swearing lieutenant. 'Good-morning, sir,' replied the chaplain; 'you pray early this morning.' 'I beg your pardon, sir.' 'Oh, I cannot pardon you: carry your case to your God.'"

"In one of his journeys he was informed that there had been a revival of religion at a certain place which lay in his route. He arrived there in the night, and called at a house of which he had no previous knowledge. A woman came to the door, whom he addressed as follows: 'I have understood, madam, that my Father has some children in this place; I wish to inquire where they live, that I may find lodgings here to-night.' 'I hope,' replied the woman, 'I am one of your Father's children; come in, dear sir, and lodge here.'"[1]

LEWIS LUNSFORD began to preach when he was so young that he was called "The wonderful boy." He possessed good natural talents, which he improved by assiduous study, and became a public speaker of the first order. In 1774 he engaged in a mission in the lower counties of Virginia, and was astonishingly blessed. Great numbers were converted in many places. Attempts were made to stop him; on one of those occasions, the constable who was sent to apprehend him waited till he had done preaching, and then declared that "he would not serve a warrant against so good a man."

Mr. Lunsford became pastor of a church in 1772. His stated labors were as successful as his itinerancy. There were two revivals under his ministry, during which he "preached incessantly." "Certain it is," says the author to whom I am indebted for the materials of these notices, and whose description in this case savors somewhat of the rhapsodical, "that during several of the last years of his

[1] Benedict, ii. 319, 320.

life, he was more caressed, and his preaching more valued, than any other man's that ever resided in Virginia. Lunsford was a sure preacher, and seldom failed to rise pretty high. In his best strains he was more like an angel than a man. His countenance, lighted up by an inward flame, seemed to shed beams of light wherever he turned. His voice, always harmonious, now seemed to be tuned by descending seraphs. . . . So highly was he estimated among his own people that there were but few preachers that visited them to whom they would willingly listen, even for once, in preference to their beloved pastor."[1]

So earnest was he in his work that sometimes, after having retired to his chamber on account of being too ill to preach, he would rise from the bed, repair to the place of meeting, and pour out his soul in impressive exhortations and appeals.

The flame was too powerful to last long. He blazed out. At the age of forty he was called to his rest, in the year 1793.

"Swearing JACK WALLER" was a native of Spottsylvania, Virginia, and served Satan faithfully for many years. It was said "that there could be no deviltry among the people unless 'Swearing Jack' was at the head of it." They called him "the devil's adjutant." To debauchery, gambling, and other vices he added intense hatred of the Baptists. He was a member of the grand jury which presented Louis Craig, a Baptist minister, for preaching the gospel. Mr. Craig's meek and serious address to the grand jury sank into Mr Waller's heart, and produced deep conviction of sin,

[1] Benedict, ii. 343.

which drove him to the brink of despair. He was seven or eight months in that state, and for some time after he obtained peace he walked in much fear and trembling. At length he followed Christ in baptism, and then entered on a career of zealous and very successful labor A church was constituted in his neighborhood, of which he became pastor. He preached the gospel in all the adjacent counties, journeying often and extensively for that purpose. The enemies of religion raged against him, being the more infuriated on account of his defection from their ranks. He was four times imprisoned, and suffered much for the cause in various other ways. But the Lord strengthened him, so that he rejoiced in tribulation.

For a few years his usefulness was diminished in consequence of his embracing Arminian sentiments, and separating from his brethren as " an Independent Baptist preacher." During that time he established camp meetings and drew immense multitudes together, but it does not appear that much good resulted from these experiments.

In 1787 Mr Waller resumed his former station. A great revival commenced almost immediately, and lasted several years, embracing the whole district in which he labored. He baptized "many hundreds" during that time, and his church or churches (for he presided over five churches) increased to thirteen hundred members. He died July 4, 1802, in the 61st year of his age.

I would have given a lengthened account of ISAAC BACKUS, A.M., the historian of the Baptists of New England, to whose indefatigable diligence and zeal the denomination was indebted for the suppression of the intolerance under which it had long groaned, and who was deservedly loved and honored by his brethren in every part of the Union; but this is rendered unnecessary by the publication of Dr. Hovey's very interesting volume, entitled *The Life and Times of the Rev. Isaac Backus, A.M.*, which ought to be in the hands of every Baptist. I will only state that Mr. Backus was born January 9, 1724, born again 1741, ordained pastor of a Congregational church 1748, baptized 1751, installed pastor of a Baptist church 1756, and that he died November 20, 1806. It is to be hoped that the Backus Historical Society will soon accomplish their purpose to publish a new edition of his *Ecclesiastical History of New England*.

A few other names may be briefly recorded.

MORGAN EDWARDS was born in Wales, received his education at the Baptist Seminary, Bristol (now "Bristol College"), labored several years in England and in Ireland, and after a short pastorate at Rye, Sussex, settled in America. He was eleven years pastor of the First Baptist Church, Philadelphia. In the latter years of his life he read "lectures in divinity" in several places. He rendered valuable service to the denomination by his efforts on behalf of Rhode Island College, by useful publications—among which his *Materials toward a History of the Baptists in Pennsylvania and New Jersey* may be particularly mentioned—and in other ways. He died in 1795, in the 73d year of his age.

DAVID THOMAS labored many years in Virginia, with much success. He was educated at Hopewell, New Jersey, under the Rev. Isaac Eaton, and was deemed worthy of the degree of M. A. bestowed on him by the authorities of Brown University. His qualifications for the ministry, religious as well as intellectual, were of a high order, and God greatly blessed him. Men hated him for it, and Satan stirred up his servants to unusual manifestations of malignity. Mr. Thomas was reviled and slandered, and sometimes roughly assaulted. One man attempted his life, but was prevented from executing his purpose. The servant of God was "immortal till his work was done," and that was not till he had reached an advanced age.[1]

EBENEZER KINNERSLEY, A. M. He was a native of Gloucester, England. His father was a Baptist minister, who emigrated to America in 1714, and became pastor of the church at Pennepek, Pennsylvania. His son was called to the ministry by the same church, 1743, and received ordination, but did not undertake the pastoral office. Literary and scientific pursuits engaged his attention. In 1755 he was appointed one of the professors in the college of Philadelphia, which office he held till 1772, when failing health compelled him to resign. He died July 4, 1778, in the sixty-eighth year of his age.

Horatio Gates Jones, Esq., of Philadelphia, observes, in a letter to Dr. Sprague: "It is impossible now to ascertain for how long a time, or to what extent, Mr. Kinnersley labored as a minister of the gospel, though it is known that he retained his connection with the Baptist Church till the close of his life. It is certain, however, that he acquired his chief renown, not in the exercise of his ministry, but in his scientific pursuits and discoveries. .... I cannot withhold the opinion that, owing to various circumstances, posterity has done him but very meagre

[1] Taylor's *Lives of Virginia Baptist Ministers.*

justice. That he was intimately associated with Dr. Franklin in some of his most splendid discoveries, and that Franklin himself more than once gratefully acknowledged his aid; that he attracted the attention of many of the most eminent philosophers of his day on both sides of the Atlantic; that he delivered lectures in Philadelphia, New York, Boston, and Newport, on the great subjects that were then engrossing the attention of the philosophical world, and that these lectures excited great interest, especially among the more intelligent classes, —are proved by evidence the most incontrovertible."[1]

OLIVER HART, A. M., enjoyed in early life the advantages of the ministry of Whitefield, the Tennents, and other eminent men, and was converted to God in his eighteenth year. He became pastor of the church in Charleston, S. C., in 1750, and held the office thirty years. In 1780 he removed to Hopewell, N. J., where he died, December 31, 1795, in the seventy-third year of his age. Dr. Furman said of him, in a sermon preached on occasion of his death, that he was "not only *truly* but *eminently* religious;" that "his sermons were peculiarly serious, containing a happy assemblage of doctrinal and practical truths, set in an engaging light, and enforced with convincing arguments;" and that "for the discussion of doctrinal truths he was more especially eminent, to which also he was prepared by an intimate acquaintance with the sacred Scriptures, and an extensive reading of the most valuable, both of ancient and modern authors."

SILAS MERCER, born of Church of England parents n 1745, in North Carolina, became a Baptist in 1775,

[1] Sprague's *Annals of the American Pulpit*, vi. 45-47.

after a long and anxious mental struggle. He was immediately called to the ministry. During the American war he labored in his native state: so diligent was he in his work that he preached two thousand sermons in six years. At the close of the war he settled at Kiokee, Georgia, and "was the means of planting a number of churches in different parts of the country. He was justly esteemed one of the most exemplary and useful ministers in the Southern states."[1] He died in 1796, in the fifty-second year of his age. The late Dr. Jesse Mercer was his son.

HEZEKIAH SMITH, D. D. This excellent man was born on Long Island, N. Y., in 1737. He was converted in early life. His classical education was received at the academy at Hopewell, N. J., whence he proceeded to Princeton College, where he graduated in 1762. While traveling for his health in South Carolina, he formed an acquaintance with many of the Baptists of that state, and was ordained to the Christian ministry. In 1765 he became pastor of the church at Haverhill, Massachusetts, over which he presided with distinguished ability and success till January 22, 1805, when "God took him." During the war he was appointed one of the chaplains of the army, in which capacity he served four years. "He became the intimate friend of Washington, and possessed the confidence and esteem of the officers and men of the whole army. Repeatedly did he expose his life in battle, and ever was he among the foremost in encouraging the soldiers and in soothing the sorrows of the wounded and dying."[2]

---

[1] *History of the Georgia Baptist Association*, p. 390.
[2] Dr. S. F. Smith, in Sprague's *Annals*.

Dr. Smith was an instructive and powerful preacher, an active home missionary, and a wise and affectionate pastor.

JAMES MANNING, D. D., a native of New Jersey, was associated with Hezekiah Smith, both at Mr. Eaton's academy and at Princeton. They graduated at the same time. Mr. Manning undertook the pastoral charge of the church at Warren, R. I., and established an academy there. That academy may be regarded as the germ of Rhode Island College, now Brown University, of which he became the first president in 1770. He occupied the station with great efficiency till July 24, 1791, when, at the comparatively early age of fifty-three, he was summoned to his rest. His usefulness was not confined to the college: he aided his country in the session of 1787 as a member of Congress; and he served the First Baptist Church of Providence as its pastor nearly the whole time of his presidency.[1]

BENJAMIN FOSTER, D. D., born at Danvers, Massachusetts, received his education at Yale College. His parents were Congregationalists. While at Yale, the subject of infant baptism was selected for discussion, and he was appointed to defend it, but instead of doing so he avowed himself a convert to believers' baptism, having seen reason to change his sentiments while prosecuting the necessary researches for the debate. He pursued theological studies under Dr. Stillman, of Boston, and was ordained pastor of the Baptist church at Leicester, Massachusetts, in 1776. Nine years afterward he re-

[1] See *The Life, Times, and Correspondence of James Manning*, by Reuben Aldridge Guild — a valuable addition to our biographical literature.

moved to Newport, R. I., and in 1788 to New York. He was pastor of the First Baptist Church in that city till his death, August 26, 1798, in the forty-ninth year of his age. Dr. Foster was a learned man and a sound divine.

SAMUEL STILLMAN, D. D., was forty-two years pastor of the First Baptist Church, Boston, and enjoyed the affectionate confidence of its members, who loved him as a fellow-Christian and revered him as a faithful minister of the Lord Jesus. He was converted under the ministry of the Rev. Oliver Hart, at Charleston, S. C., and set apart to the Christian ministry, by ordination, in 1759. After two brief pastorates in other places, he formed a happy connection with the Boston church—a connection which was mutually conducive to comfort and usefulness. But the beneficial effects of that influence were by no means confined to the church. Dr. Stillman was an active, wise, and large-hearted philanthropist, and a patriot of the Christian stamp. To the public institutions of Boston he gave the benefit of his powerful advocacy, and not unfrequently of personal effort; and the interests of Brown University constantly shared his practical sympathy. He pleaded with effect in the pulpit for the benevolent enterprises of the day. He instructed his people and the public, through the press, by the numerous discourses with which he favored them. The cause of God prospered under his instrumentality, as repeated revivals testified.

Dr. Stillman had recently completed his seventieth year when the death-stroke came. Dr. Baldwin visited him in his last illness, and expressed his sorrow in the prospect of their approaching separation. "God's government," replied the dying saint, "is infinitely perfect"—

a pregnant saying, and a fitting close of the earthly ministry. His death took place March 12, 1807.

Many other names might be mentioned; but "time would fail," and want of space forbids.

By "wonderful works" of grace God had been preparing the Baptists of the United States, in the latter half of the eighteenth century, for still more striking manifestations, and for extensive missionary enterprise, at home and abroad.[1]

[1] The reader may be referred to Dr. Sprague's *American Baptist Pulpit* for full information respecting Baptist ministers in the United States.

STATISTICS AND REFLECTIONS

CHAPTER I.

Effects of the Mission Enterprise—Revivals—Extension of the Denomination—Statistical Table—Societies—Diversity and Adaptation of Talent—Baptist Agency now employed—Peculiarities of the Present Period—Duties of Baptists.

THE formation of the Baptist Missionary Society in England was an era in the history of our denomination. Enlarged views took the place of the selfish and narrow-minded notions which had so long prevailed. When the nature and extent of Christian obligation in reference to the diffusion of the gospel were understood, and corresponding action resulted, a healthy religious condition was soon experienced. The new vigor demanded scope. Other enterprises besides foreign missions were undertaken, and they were carried on with persevering ardor, characteristic of the altered state of feeling.

Domestic missions engaged the attention of the Baptist churches in England as early as 1797, and have been ever since prosecuted with judicious activity. On the North American continent extensive itinerancies were the ordinary modes of home effort. The rapidly increasing population could be evangelized in no other way. These exertions are now directed by the Home Mission Society, or by the respective state conventions.

In 1813 the Baptist churches of the United States were awakened to a sense of their indebtedness to the world by the gracious interposition which brought Judson and Rice among them. Then their missionary career commenced. It has been prosperous in an unexampled degree.

The astonishing revival of religion which occurred throughout the United States at the beginning of this century was an educational process, tending to prepare the servants of God for the adoption of a widely aggressive policy. Sanctified talent was developed eager for employment in the Lord's cause. The spirit of consecration rested powerfully on the churches. Dr. Carey's terse saying, " Expect great things, attempt great things," became the watchword of the large-hearted. Holy activity was the fruit; increased power was evolved to be expended on new exertions; and the old promise was fulfilled, " I will bless thee, and make thy name great, and thou shalt be a blessing" (Gen. xii. 2).

And now, let us look around and abroad, and exclaim, " What hath God wrought!"

At the close of the "Quiet Period" the number of Baptist churches in Great Britain and Ireland somewhat exceeded four hundred, containing probably about twenty thousand members. There are now upward of two thousand four hundred churches, and the number of members is estimated at two hundred and eighty thousand. Besides this, our principles have taken root in the colonies and dependencies of the empire, and are spreading rapidly. Baptist churches have been planted in the West Indian

Islands, in Australia, in Van Diemen's Land, in Africa, in various parts of India, and plenteously in British North America, where, seventy years ago, there were but two churches of our denomination in existence.

On the continent of Europe, the labors of our beloved Brother Oncken and his energetic coadjutors have been remarkably blessed. Churches of the primitive faith and order exist in Hanover, in Prussia, in several of the German states, in France, in Switzerland, in Denmark, and in Sweden.

But it is in the United States that the most marvelous progress has been witnessed. Several causes have contributed to it. One is the immense tide of emigration annually conveying to that country many tens of thousands from all parts of Europe, Great Britain, and Ireland, and among them numerous Baptists. Another is the congeniality of the mode of government and the state of society with the freedom of Baptist principles. The adaptation of the Baptist ministry, generally, to the condition and habits of the people is not to be overlooked. These, however, are but secondary considerations, although due weight must be allowed them. Doubtless Baptist churches have shared largely in those outpourings of the Spirit which have peculiarly distinguished Christian effort in that part of the world, and which, it may be believed, are ever specially connected with plain, faithful preaching and scrupulous adherence to the laws of the "King of kings." In the year 1790 there were in the United States 872 churches, containing 64,975 members. There are now, of Regular Baptists, leaving out the Freewill, the Anti-mission, Six-principle, and Seventh-day Baptists, the "Church of God," the Disciples (or

Campbellites), the Tunkers, and the Mennonites, 13,355 churches, with 1,109,926 members.

Gathering up the statistics into one sum, the following table exhibits an approximation to the present strength of the denomination:

	Churches.	Members.
United States	13,355	1,109,926
Great Britain and Ireland	2,411	280,000
British North America	567	41,000
West Indies	205	36,000
Burmah, Assam, and Siam	375	17,000
Continent of Europe	292	23,494
India	70	3,000
Total	17,275	1,500,420

It is an approximation only. China, Africa, and Australasia are left out of the account, the returns not being sufficiently clear and full to warrant a definite statement. With the exception of the United States, Europe, and British North America, all the items in the foregoing list are *estimates*, founded on official reports. I believe that they are below the actual amounts; but it was better to err on that side, if entire accuracy could not be attained.

There is another view of the subject. This is the age of societies. Designs which would be otherwise impracticable can be carried into effect by combination of effort and division of labor. We have joined Christians of other names in founding and sustaining institutions of general utility, and have borne our full share of the burdens of philanthropy. But there are some departments of Christian enterprise in which we must be content to labor alone. Among our own benevolent organizations are the following:

STATISTICS AND REFLECTIONS.

A.D.
- 1797. English Baptist Home Missionary Society.
- 1814. Baptist Irish Society.
- 1816. Baptist Highland Mission.
- " Society for Aged or Infirm Baptist Ministers.
- 1824. Baptist Building Fund—London.
- " American Baptist Publication Society.
- 1832. American Baptist Home Mission Society.
- 1838. American and Foreign Bible Society.
- 1840. Bible Translation Society—London.
- 1841. Baptist Tract Society—London.
- 1845. Southern Baptist Convention (Home Missions and Bible).
- 1850. American Bible Union.
- 1853. American Baptist Historical Society.

In the Foreign Mission Department we have—

- 1792. Baptist Missionary Society—London.
- 1814. American Baptist Missionary Union, formerly the "Baptist General Convention."
- 1816. General Baptist Missionary Society—London.
- 1843. American Baptist Free Mission Society.
- 1845. Southern Baptist Convention (Foreign Missions).

In supporting these institutions we are enabled, by the blessing of God, to expend at least $750,000 annually, besides sustaining extensive educational operations, and defraying all the expenses connected with public worship and the maintenance of the Christian ministry.

Let me further call to mind the character of the agencies by which the great work entrusted to us has been hitherto accomplished. It has been often remarked that when God is about to execute some great purpose he prepares beforehand the appropriate agency; and providential interferences of a surprising kind, in order to bring about the appointed issue, have been not unfrequently noticed. Let us think for a moment of the men

God has given us for the work of the last threescore years. Think of the immortal three at Serampore—Carey, Marshman, and Ward. Think of other missionaries, that have now ceased from their labors, who were admirably qualified for the positions they were called to occupy—Adoniram Judson, with his incomparable wives, and George Dana Boardman, in Burmah; Comstock, in Arracan; Chamberlain and Yates, in India; Coultart, Knibb, and Burchell, in Jamaica; with many yet living whose names are familiar to the friends of missions. Think of the writers by whose powerful pens our principles have been explained and defended. Think of the men of eloquence and the men of counsel who have swayed and guided public opinion, preserved from discouragement, or prevented mistakes. Think of the men of wealth, whose hearts were moved by the grace of God to " devise liberal things," and whose examples have so stimulated others that the treasury of Christian benevolence has seemed to be, like the widow's " barrel of meal" and " cruse of oil," inexhaustible. " This also cometh forth from the Lord of hosts, who is wonderful in counsel and excellent in working" (Isa. xxviii. 29).

There is yet another fact which must not be lost sight of. I refer to the intellectual machinery now in operation for the benefit of mankind under Baptist superintendence or as the result of Baptist labor. Our brethren have aken the palm among translators. Their versions of the Scriptures will be read by the nations of the East from generation to generation. The swarming multitudes of India are mainly indebted to Carey and Yates for the word of God, and even Brahmins receive that word in their own venerated Sanscrit from Baptist hands. The natives of Burmah, Assam, and Siam owe to Judson and his associates their acquaintance with the divine oracles. In those Eastern countries, too, and wherever else our missionaries have planted the heavenly standard, the education of the young has been regarded as a matter of prime importance. By the institutions they have established, or assisted in establishing, a foundation has been laid on which the temple of knowledge will be reared in coming times.

In England, with the exception of theological institutions—which each denomination must necessarily found for itself—Baptists avail themselves of those facilities for the acquisition of learning and science which are abundantly provided for all classes of the community. But in the United States they have manifested, at the same time, enlightened patriotism and denominational zeal. Colleges and seminaries of the first order, amply endowed and well furnished with instructors, supply the wants of their own families, and offer inducements to others to participate in the advantages. By this means a salutary influence is exerted on the community at large. The following are the educational statistics of the denomination:

GREAT BRITAIN.

LOCATION.	PRESIDENTS.	FOUNDED.
Bristol College	Rev. F. W. Gotch, LL.D.	1770
Chillwell College	Rev. W. Underwood, D.D.	1797
Rawdon College	Rev. S. G. Green, B.A.	1804
Pontypool College, Wales	Rev. Thos. Thomas, D.D.	1807
Regent's Park College	Rev. Joseph Angus, D.D.	1810
Haverfordwest College	Rev. Thos. Davies, D.D.	1839
Glasgow	Rev. James Paterson, D.D.	1856
Pastor's College	Rev. C. H. Spurgeon	1861
North Wales	Rev. Hugh Jones, M.A.	1862
Chamber Hall	Rev. H. Dowson	1866

BAPTIST HISTORY.

DOMINION OF CANADA.

NAME.	LOCATION.	PRESIDENTS.	FOUNDED
Acadia College	Wolfville, Nova Scotia	J. M. Cramp, D D.	1838
Horton Collegiate Academy	Wolfville, Nova Scotia	T. A. Higgins, A.M.	1828
Baptist Seminary	Fredericton, N. Brunswick	J. E. Hopper, B.A.	1834
Canadian Literary Institute	Woodstock, Ontario	R. A. Fyfe, D.D.	

THE UNITED STATES.

NAME.	LOCATION.	PRESIDENT.	FOUNDED.
Brown University	Providence, R. I.	Alexis Caswell, D.D., LL.D.	1764
Madison University	Hamilton, N. Y.	Ebenezer Dodge, D.D.	1814
Colby University	Waterville, Me.	J. T. Champlin, D.D.	1820
Columbian College	Washington, D. C.	G. W. Samson, D.D.	1821
Georgetown College	Georgetown, Ky.	N. M. Crawford, D.D.	1829
Richmond College	Richmond, Va.	T. G. Jones, D.D.	1832
Denison University	Granville, Ohio	Samson Talbot, D.D.	1832
Mercer University	Penfield, Ga.	H. H. Tucker, D.D.	1833
Shurtleff College	Upper Alton, Ill.	Daniel Read, LL.D.	1835
Wake Forest College	Wake Forest, N. C.	W. M. Wingate, D.D.	1838
Howard College	Marion, Ala.	E. L. Thornton, A.M.	1841
Baylor University	Independence, Texas	William Carey Crane, D.D.	1845
University at Lewisburg	Lewisburg, Pa.	J. R. Loomis, LL.D.	1849
William Jewell College	Liberty, Mo.	Thomas Rambaut, LL.D.	1849
University of Rochester	Rochester, N. Y.	M. B. Anderson, LL.D.	1850
Union University	Murfreesboro', Tenn.	D. H. Selph.	1840
Furman University	Greenville, S. C.	James C. Furman, D.D.	1851
Mississippi College	Clinton, Miss.	Walter Hillman, A.M.	1851
Mount Lebanon University	Mt. Lebanon, La.		1853
Kalamazoo College	Kalamazoo, Mich.	Kendall Brooks, D.D.	1855
Chicago University	Chicago, Ill.	J. C. Burroughs, D.D.	1859
Bethel College	Russellville, Ky.	N. K. Davis, A.M.	1860
Waco University	Waco, Texas	Rufus C. Burleson, D.D.	1861
Petaluma College	Petaluma, Cal.	Mark Baily, A.M.	1866

BAPTIST THEOLOGICAL INSTITUTIONS IN THE UNITED STATES.

NAME.	LOCATION.	SENIOR PROFESSORS.	FOUNDED.
Theol. Dep. Madison University	Hamilton, N. Y.	Geo. W. Eaton, D.D.LL.D.	1820
New Hampton Theol. Seminary	Fairfax, Vt.		1825
Newton Theological Institution	Newton Centre, Mass.	Alvah Hovey, D.D.	1826
Western Bap. Theol. Institution	Georgetown, Ky.	C. Lewis, A.M.	1840

STATISTICS AND REFLECTIONS. 583

NAME.	LOCATION.	SENIOR PROFESSORS.	FOUNDED.
Kalamazoo Theological Seminary.	Kalamazoo, Mich	Silas Bailey, D.D	1846
Rochester Theological Seminary...	Rochester, N. Y.	E. G. Robinson, D.D	1850
Southern Baptist Theol. Seminary	Greenville, S. C.	J. P. Boyce, D.D.	1858
Theological Dep. Shurtleff College	Upper Alton, Ill.	Daniel Read, LL.D.	1863
Chicago Theological Seminary	Chicago, Ill.	G. W. Northrup, D.D.	1867
Crozer Theological Seminary	Chester, Pa.	H. G. Weston, D.D.	1868

The Baptist periodicals published in Great Britain are —*The Freeman*, weekly, edited by the Rev. Dr. Angus, and other gentlemen; *The Baptist Magazine*, monthly, established in 1809, and now edited by the Rev. W. G. Lewis; *The General Baptist Magazine; The Sword and the Trowel*, monthly, edited by the Rev. C. H. Spurgeon; *The Primitive Church Magazine, The Gospel Herald, The Church, The Baptist Messenger, The Christian Dial*, and *The Voice of Truth*,—all monthly. There are also eight Welsh Periodicals, for the use of the Baptists of the Principality.

BAPTIST PERIODICALS IN THE UNITED STATES.

NAMES.	ISSUED.	WHERE PUBLISHED.
Christian Herald	Weekly.	Tuscumbia.....Ala.
Evangel	"	San Francisco, Cal.
Christian Secretary	"	Hartford......Conn.
Christian Index and S. W. Baptist	"	Atlanta..........Ga.
Standard	"	Chicago..........Ill.
Western Recorder	"	Louisville......Ky.
Louisiana Baptist	"	Mt. Lebanon...La.
Watchman and Reflector	"	Boston.........Mass.
Christian Era	"	Boston.........Mass.
Zion's Advocate	"	Portland.........Me.
Baptist Tidings	"	Mason......... Mich.
Central Baptist	"	St. Louis.......Mo
Examiner and Chronicle	"	New York.....N.Y
American Baptist	"	New York.....N.Y
Journal and Messenger	"	Cincinnati.......O.
Biblical Recorder	"	Raleigh..........N.C.
National Baptist	"	Philadelphia...Pa.

NAMES.	ISSUED.	WHERE PUBLISHED.
South Carolina Baptist	Weekly.	Anderson........S.C.
Baptist	"	Memphis......Tenn.
Texas Baptist Herald	"	Houston.....Texas.
Religious Herald	"	Richmond...... Va.
Cottage Visitor	"	Hendersonville,N.C
Arkansas Baptist	"	Little Rock...Ark.
Baptist Missionary Magazine	Monthly.	Boston.........Mass.
Baptist Visitor	"	Newtown........Md.
Macedonian and Record	"	{ New York.....N.Y. { Boston.........Mass.
Der Muntere Saemann, (German)	"	Cincinnati.........O.
Young Reaper	"	Philadelphia...Pa.
Der Sendbote (German)	"	Cincinnati......... O.
Seren Orllewinol (Welsh)	"	Pottsville........Pa.
Kind Words	"	Memphis.....Tenn.
Child's Delight	"	Macon............Ga
Sunday School Banner	"	Atlanta...........Ga
Bible Advocate	Quarterly.	New York.....N.Y.
Baptist Quarterly	"	Philadelphia...Pa.

BAPTIST PERIODICALS IN THE DOMINION OF CANADA.

NAMES.	ISSUED.	WHERE PUBLISHED.
Canadian Baptist	Weekly.	Toronto....Can. W.
Le Moniteur	"	Granby....Can. E.
Christian Messenger	"	Halifax........N.S.
The Christian Visitor	"	St. John.......N.B.

God has assigned us an honorable position. It remains that we prove ourselves worthy of it.

The principles of the Reformation of the sixteenth century are undergoing expansion. Men are busily engaged in examining the foundations and tracing all things to their origin. The claims of prescription and custom are disallowed. In religion, the stand taken by the old Reformers is fully recognized: nothing is to be admitted which cannot be sustained "by Scripture and necessary reason." With such views, inquirers conduct their investigations fearlessly, and push them on in every direction. Abandoning the traditionary, they ask for a system of truth and practice which will abide the test of searching criticism. They desire to clear away all rubbish and to find " the old paths."

We profess to be walking in them and to carry out the Reformation to its legitimate issues. It is not unreasonable to suppose that, as independent inquiry proceeds, scrutinizing all forms of religious profession, our sentiments and practices will be extensively embraced, as presenting the nearest resemblance to primitive Christianity. The observance of infant baptism is dying away among our Pædobaptist brethren. We may fairly infer that large accessions to our ranks will follow.

What, then, are the duties especially incumbent on us under such circumstances? To this question, it may be briefly replied: That, if we would maintain our position, we must, in the first place, cultivate with growing earnestness intelligent and warm-hearted piety; we must adopt measures for the exposition and diffusion of our sentiments on those points in which we differ from other religious denominations; we must extend our Christian influence by home-missionary efforts, conducted on a liberal scale; we must foster rising talent, and give to all the Lord's servants opportunities of being employed in his cause, according to their respective gifts; we must cherish an enthusiastic zeal for education; we must effectually engage the sympathies of the young; we must be ever ready to promote social improvements and o forward philanthropic designs; and we must exemplify, in the whole, unbroken union, devotedness to the Saviour, and believing reliance on divine aid.

It would be easy to enlarge on each of these topics.

I will confine myself, however, to the most important—personal piety.

Baptists should be a pre-eminently devoted people. Our profession and practice are peculiar. We deem it our special mission to plead for personal obedience to the will of the Lord. For this we have always contended. We reject hereditary membership, holding that men are not born Christians, but that they become Christians when they are born again, and that, until then, they have no right to Christian ordinances, because they cannot enjoy Christian blessings. We deny sacramental power, maintaining that the soul is renewed and sanctified, not by any outward act performed upon us or by us, but by the truth of the gospel and the grace of the Holy Spirit. We gather from the teachings of the apostles that a man should *be* a Christian before he avows himself to be one; and, in full accordance, as we believe, with the instructions of the New Testament, we admit none to our fellowship without a profession of repentance toward God and faith in our Lord Jesus Christ. Their baptism is at the same time a declaration of their sole reliance on the Saviour, and a symbol of their union with him in his death and his resurrection—a spiritual, vital union. Our churches, so constituted, profess to be societies of believers, congregations of saints.

Membership in Baptist churches, therefore, implies piety. The object of our union is to nurture godliness in each other, and to diffuse it abroad to the greatest extent possible. Abjuring all attempts at mere outward attraction, our efforts tend exclusively to the advancement of personal religion. We invite men to the faith and holiness of the primitive churches. Our desire is first to call them to God, and then to train them for heaven by a course of spiritual education. All this cannot be accomplished but by a truly spiritual community, nor can such efforts be long sustained unless there be a continued spiritual progress. Orthodoxy is necessary, and order is necessary; but neither orthodoxy nor order will ensure prosperity without a living likeness to Christ. How earnestly should we aspire after that blessing! How diligently should we labor to obtain it, and in increasing measure! With what ardor should we adopt all scriptural means to promote communion with the Redeemer, and to enkindle sympathy and love among his servants! The extent and saving efficacy of our influence must depend on the amount of our spiritual attainments. There are sects which can prosper without those attainments, because of the worldliness that is inherent in their constitutions, and the connection of church privileges with natural descent; but the Baptists depend altogether for success and enlargement on the prevalence of true godliness among their members. Our churches will be fit asylums for those who shall escape from the perils of cold and torpid formality only as they shall exemplify the "work of faith, and labor of love, and patience of hope," by which the early followers of the Lord were distinguished. If these be wanting or notably deficient, inquirers will go where there is more power, though the form and order may be less agreeable to the apostolic pattern, and our "future" will be darkened by clouds of disgrace and failure.

With what eagerness, then, should we engage in all endeavors by which earnest Christian piety and zeal may be promoted among us! How closely should we cling to evangelical truth, watching against all tendency to lower the standard or to substitute the elegant essay for biblical teaching and fervent appeal! How carefully should the spirit of the gospel be cherished! How diligently should all opportunities for furthering mutual progress in piety be improved! How numerous and well sustained should be the efforts of benevolence and zeal, thus establishing the connection between Christian activity and spiritual-mindedness, and "proving what is that good, and acceptable, and perfect will of God." And with what vigilant observance should the laws of discipline be honored, so that, the purity of the churches being maintained, their members may be "epistles of Christ, known and read of all men." If by these methods a vigorous and fruitful godliness becomes characteristic of our denomination, the force of the attraction will be felt by all around us; union with our churches will be regarded as not merely a duty, but a privilege, and thousands will say, "We will go with you, for we have heard that God is with you." Men will perceive that our profession of adherence to primitive simplicity and purity is warranted by fact—that our devotedness to the Saviour's cause is not impulsive, but habitual—and that in joining our ranks they will not only obey the dictates of scriptural conscientiousness, but also secure a large measure of Christian enjoyment, and a fuller unfolding of the Christian life.

"There is a future for the Baptists," and it is our duty to prepare for it. Thousands of souls, just looking out of obscurity and "feeling after God," ask our guidance in the search for truth and life. Freedom, outraged and down-trodden by earthly tyrants, calls upon us to assert the rights of conscience and its entire immunity from human control; and, while it beckons us to the holy war, reminds us that it is our glory—a glory in which most Protestant communities have no share—to wield the sword of the Spirit with hands that have never been reddened by a brother's blood. Our martyrs—burnt, beheaded, strangled, or drowned, in every European country at the era of the Reformation, and as yet unknown to fame, although their Christian heroism was right noble —expect us, in the diffusion and defence of the truths for which they suffered, to display a zeal befitting the privileges we enjoy. A great work is before us, both at home and abroad, demanding ardent love, enterprising boldness, and indomitable perseverance.

INDEX.

ABBOTT, Archbishop, 299.
Abbott, Mordecai, 524.
Act of Uniformity, 324, 330, 419, 479.
Alberic, Cardinal, 133.
Albigenses, 99, 116.
Aldegonde, Saint, counselor of the Prince of Orange, 263.
Algerius burned, 157.
Alva, Duke of, 270.
Alzey, Martyrdoms at, 168.
Anne, of Bohemia, befriends Wycliffe, 122.
Apostles appointed in Virginia, 545.
Apostolic Fathers, 20.
Arefastus, his treachery, 83.
Arnaldistae, 100.
Arnold of Brescia, 97, 135; banished, 136; St. Bernard's testimony to, *Ib.*; martyrdom at Rome, 137; opinions on, *Ib.*
Arras, heretics at, 83; reject baptism, 84.
Arthur Prince, immersed, 148.
Askew, Anne, 235.
Assembly of Divines, 313.
Association formed, 540; date of, in different states, 542.
Augustine, St., favors infant baptism, 44.
Augustine, the monk, his course in England, 63.
Aurelius, Marcus, 22.
Austin, Abraham, anecdote of, 58.
Aylesbury, Baptists in, 332.

BACKUS, Isaac, A.M. 564.

Backus, Mrs. Elizth., 529.
Bair, Johannes, letter of, 173.
Bampfield, Francis, 422; died in prison, 425.
Baptism, defined, 15; administered to believers only, *Ib.*; at first administered as soon as person believed, 43; where administered, 49; by immersion, 19; progress of error respecting, 26; Justin Martyr's account of, 22; additions to ordinance in third century, 28.
Baptismal controversy, publications on in seventeenth century, 266.
Baptismal regeneration, one of the earliest corruptions of Christianity, 47; its demoralizing effects, *Ib.*
Baptismal service, in earliest writings only for catechumens, 43.
Baptist Board, English, 488.
Baptists, act of banishment of, 463; a future for, 588; books burned, 205; books by, 299; duties of, 585-588; excepted from general acts of pardon, 234; expelled from Moravia, 194, 266; do. from Switzerland, 269; first witness for God during Reformation age in Germany, 161; hard names applied to, 156; in America, 460; in England, 231; in Moravia. 188; in Netherlands, 195; in Switzerland, 179; no sympathy from Reformers, 152; persecuted by all sects in England, 261; persecutions in America, 127-523; principles

and practices of in England, 379-390; spread of, 164, 169; statistics of, 471, 503, 527, 576-578; testimony of Bullinger and Meshovius to, 179; under the Commonwealth, 317; use of press by, 291; vanguard of Protestants in England, 242.

Baxter, Richard, on liberty of religion, 308; on immersion, 314.
Beddome, Benjamin, A.M., 519-21.
Bede, quoted, 64, note.
Berengar, of Tours, his fame as a teacher, 125; writings on baptism and the Lord's supper, 126; death of, 127; followers of, *Ib.*
Bernard of Clairvaux, 133.
Bernard, St., opposes Arnold, 136.
Bernkop, Leonhard, burned, 173.
Bestevaer, martyr, 200.
Betrayer, a, his fearful end, 209.
Bible translation, 580.
Blackwood, Christopher, the "oracle of Anabaptists in Ireland," 399.
Blietel, Hans, minister, martyr, 229.
"Bloody Tenet of persecution," 465.
Bocking, England, arrest of Baptists at, 241.
Bockleson, Jan, introduces polygamy at Munster, 253.
Bogaert, Peter, 262.
Bohemia, spread of gospel in, 122, 144.
Boniface, puzzled by sponsorship, 57.
Boni Homines, 139.
Bonner, Bishop, zeal against Baptists, 242.
Book Society, English, 490.
Bosch, Jan, or Jan Durps, 227.
Boucher, Joan, why burned, 155, 235, 236.
Bouwens, Leonard, baptized 10,000 persons, 156.
Bradford, 244, 245.
Brand-Hueber, Wolfgang, put to death, 166.
Breal, Hans, imprisoned, 175; death, 176.
Brewer, Thomas, imprisonment of, 302.
Brine, John, 499, 505.

Bristol College, 491.
British North America, first Baptists in, 549; first church in, 550; prominent ministers in, 550; first association in, 552.
Broadmead Church, Bristol, founded, 345; persecutors of, 346, 427.
Brown, Chad, 461.
Brown, Nicholas, Esq., 548.
Brown University, 546-548.
Brownists, 286.
Bucer, 170.
Bullinger, testimony to Baptists, 179.
Bunsen, Baron, on Tertullian's opp. to baptism of young, 30; on baptism and inf. baptism in early church, 41, 42.
Bunyan, John, 325, 431; death of, 432; Cowper's lines on, 432; 439.
Busher, Leonard, writings of, 291.

CALCUITH, England, synod at, forbids pouring, 87.
Canne, John, 411; his writings, 412.
Carcassone, papal atrocities at, 114.
Carey, William, 502, 576.
Caswell, Dr. Alexis, 548.
Catechumens, 42.
Cathari, 99, 104, 105.
Catholic and orthodox defined, 52.
Chalmers, Dr., 18.
Charles I., unremitting persecution, 301.
Charles II., promises liberty of conscience, 322; promise broken, *Ib.*; persecution of Baptists on his return, 324, 329, 359.
Charles V., cruelty to women, 152; bitter against Baptists, 167; further edicts, 170, 195; introduces Inquisition into Netherlands, 198.
Charlemagne, capitulary of, decrees infant baptism, 88.
Charlestown, Baptist church formed in, 469.
Chase, Dr. Ira, 24, note; 32, note.
Cheare, Abraham, 418.
Chedsey, Dr., against Baptists, 245.
Cheshire, early Baptist church in, 232.
Chipman, T. H., 550.

INDEX. 593

"City Remonstrance," of London against toleration, 310.
Claeson, Jan, martyr, 200
Clapham, Enoch, 286.
Clark, Dr. John, 462, 478.
Claudia, 37.
Colleges, Baptist, 581.
Collins, William and Hercules, 457.
Confession of Faith of London churches, 1644, 306; 358.
Colporteurs, early, 106, 205.
Congregational clergy persecute Baptists, 470.
Connecticut, Baptists in, 536.
Consolamentum, 139.
Constance, Council of, condemns Wycliffe, 120.
Constantine defers baptism, 44; expected to govern the church, 51.
Constantine, of Mananalis, conversion, labors, and martyrdom, 72, 73.
Constantine, Pogonatus, 73.
Conventicle Act, 338; its results, 339.
Cornwell, Francis, 397; his work on baptism, 398.
Cortenbosch, J., 262.
Councils, no decrees of, against heretics till eleventh century, 85; at Carthage, 33; Constance, 120, 122; Third Lateran, 113; Lombers, 139; London, 142; Mileyi, 62; Oxford, 143.
Coverdale signs sentence of Van Pare, 239.
Coxe, Benjamin, and Nehemiah, D. D., 457.
Cranmer, 235, 236.
Cromwell and the Baptists, 317-320.
Crusades, results, 92
Cyprian, 33.
Cyril of Jerusalem, 48.

D'ANVERS, HENRY, 425.
Darkest time for Dissenters, 375.
Deaths in prison, 34, 272; 356; of eight thousand persons, 364; 425.
Declaration of Indulgence, 357; not favored by Dissenters, *Ib.*; 377, 452.
Declension, in England, 498, 499.

"De Hæretico Comburendo," statute, 122.
Delaune, Thomas, 360: his Plea for Nonconformists, 361; dies in prison in consequence, 364, 427.
Delaware, Baptists in, 536.
Denne, Henry, 327, 393; answers ' The Dippers Dipt," 399; labors, 396, 397.
Deoduin, testimony to Berengar and Bruno, 126.
Deputies, body of, 489.
Diet of Spires, edict of, 168, 170.
Dimock, Joseph, 550; Shubael, 549.
"Dippers Dipt," by Dr. Featley, 305.
Dirks, Clement, martyr, 205, 226.
Discipline of English churches, 381-385, 485-487.
Dissenters, trick on, 493.
Dominic, 114.
Dominicans, founded, 112.
Donatists, 55, 59; rebaptizers, 60; said to reject infant baptism, 60.
Dutch Baptists, 270-282.
Du Veil, Dr., 429.
Dyke, Daniel, 319.

EATON, REV. ISAAC, 549.
Eckbert, sermons on heretics, 139.
Education of ministers, 358, 428, 491, 548.
Education Society, Bristol, 491.
Edward VI., immersed, 148.
Edwards, Rev. Morgan, 479, 565.
Elders, 385.
Elizabeth, Princess, immersed, 148.
Elizabeth, Queen, 245; orders Baptists out of England, 247.
Emblem, John, 470.
Emperors, German, persecutors, 113.
Ephrem of Edessa, 46.
Erasmus, 181.
Essex, Baptists in, 241.
Eugenius, Pope, 133.
Eusebius, 21.
Evans, Rev. Hugh and Dr. Caleb, 491.
Evervinus, 138.
Ewins, Thomas, of Broadmead, 345.
Exeter, Synod of, prescribes immersion of infants, 148.

INDEX.

FEATLY, DR, his book against the Baptists, 305.
Felbinger, Claes, martyr, 228.
Fenstanton Church, 382.
Ferdinand of Hungary, edict against Baptists, 167.
Fidus, writes to Cyprian, 33.
Five-Mile Act, 339; cruelly enforced by Archbishop Sheldon and his clergy, 341.
Fonts for immersing of adults, 50; of children, 148.
Foreign Missions, beginning of, in England, 502; an era in history, 575; in United States, 576.
Forty, Henry, 457.
Foster, Benj., D. D., 569.
Fownes, George, pastor of Broadmead Church, 351; dies in prison, 356.
Fox, John, his letter of intercession, 273.
Franc, Sebastian, 168.
Franciscans, founded, 112.
Frederic II., Emperor, edict against heretics, 138.
Free communion, 498.
Free Will Baptists, 498.
Fuller, Andrew, 501, 502.
Fuller, Thomas, on the ashes of Wycliffe, 120.

GALE, DR. JOHN, 504.
Gano, John, 560-562.
Garden-brethren, 166.
Gardiner, Bishop, 234, 243.
Gaunt, Elizabeth, 373.
General Assembly in London, 484, 487.
General Baptists, 498.
Genesius, 74.
Georgia, Baptists in, 539.
Germany, heretics burned in, 113.
Gibbon on Constantine's delay of baptism, 47; 69, 80.
Giesler on spread of infant baptism, 45.
Gifford, Dr. Andrew, 523.
Gill, John, D. D., 499, 506.
Gosnold, John, 457.
Gould, Thos., first pastor of Boston Church, 470.

Grantham, Thomas, 434.
Gregory IX. establishes Inquisition, 124.
Gregory Nazianzen, 46.
Gregory the Great, 49.
Gretser the Jesuit, character of the Anabaptists, 109.
Grovenstein, Count of, 177.
Guitmund, testimony to Berengar, 127.

HAGENBACH on infant baptism, 17; on Irenæus, 24.
"Half-way Covenant," 527.
Hall, Robert, 491, 510.
Hall, Robert, of Arnsby, 500, 515.
Hammond, George, 457.
Hampton Court Conference, 285.
Hardcastle, Thomas, pastor of Broadmead Church, 347.
Harding, Theodore S. and Harris, 550, 551.
Harris, Samuel, 558-560.
Harrison, Major-General, 399; letter to Cromwell, 401.
Hart, Oliver, A. M., 567.
Hase-poot, Gerrit, martyr, 204
Hawks, Dr., on Baptists in Virginia, 533.
Helwys, Thos., 287, 391, 392.
Henry of Lausanne, 98; labors of, 131; imprisoned, 132; dies in prison, 134.
Henry VIII., 231.
Heresy, recipe for suppression of, 88.
Heretics defined, 52; activity of, cause of complaint, 103.
Hetzer, Louis, martyr, 187.
Hewlings, grandsons of Wm. Kiffin, their death, 365-373.
Heynes, Richt, martyr, 201.
Hildebert, bishop of Mans, 134.
Hildebrand, in his age light begins to spread, 91.
Holliman, Thos., baptizes Roger Williams, 461.
Hollis, Thos., Esq., 524.
Hollis, Thos. and John, 525.
Holmes, Obadiah, 465; fined, 466, whipped, 467-469.
Hombourg, Diet of, against Baptists, 169.
Hooper, his difficulties, 236-238.

INDEX. 595

Hopewell, New Jersey, academy at, 549.
Howard, John, 518.
Howe, Samuel, his burial in the highway, 304.
Hubmeyer, Balthazar, martyr, 182-186.
Hull, Isaac, 470.
"Humble Supplication," 297.
Humiliati, 100.
Huss, John, 122.
Hutter, Jacob, leader of Baptists in Moravia, 188; noble letter of, 189-194.
Hutchinson, Colonel, 402; becomes a Baptist, 403.
Hyde, Chief-Justice, 335.

IGNATIUS, 22.
Illinois, Baptists in, 540.
Immersion, 18, 19, 48, 49, 87, 148.
Ina, king of West Saxons, law of, compelling infant baptism, 86.
Infant baptism by immersion, 87, 88, 148; enjoined by law, 53, 88; origin of, 32-34; protested against for five centuries, 147; rejected by Reformers in twelfth century, 124; religious declension, the cause and effect of, 37; rests on two pillars, 54; slow progress, 45; unknown to Tertullian, 29.
Infant communion, 35.
Innocent III., crusade against heretics, 114.
Inquisition established, 114.
Inzabatati, 100.
Ireland, early Baptist churches in, 320.
Itinerancy in America, 575.
Ives, Jeremiah, 458.

JACOBI, PROFESSOR, 16.
James I., his intolerance, 285; sufferings of Baptists under, 296.
James, John, shameful cruelty to, 328.
Jerome, 48.
Jessey, Henry, 319, 406; his large charities, 403; knowledge of Scripture, 410.
Jewel, Bishop, letter about Baptists, 247.
Jones, Samuel, 549.
Judaism, 13.
Judson, Dr. Adoniram, 576.

Justinian ignores rights of conscience, 53
Justin Martyr, 23.
Justus stones Constantine, 73; betrays Simeon, 74.

KAYE, BISHOP, on Tertullian, 28.
Keach, Benjamin, his "Child's Instructor," 333; indicted for it, 334; in the pillory, 336; 440; works, 441; 479.
Keach, Elias, 479.
Kemels, Christian, his death in prison 273.
Kent, Baptists in, 241, 325.
Kentucky, Baptists in, 539.
Kiffin, William, 302, 327, 333, 378, 427 440; sketch of life, 445-457.
Kimball, Mrs. Martha, 530.
Kinnersley, Ebenezer, A. M., 566.
Kittery, church at, 471.
Klampherer, Julius, 177.
Knipperdolling at Munster, 253.
Knollys, Hanserd, 328, 427, 435-440; 461, note.
Koch, Hans, put to death, 161.

LABBE THE JESUIT, on Peter of Bruys, 131.
Landis, John, minister, martyr, 269.
Langedul, Andries, martyr, 207.
Langedul, Christian, martyr, letter of, 209.
Languedoc, slaughters in, 114.
Latimer, Bishop, on the Baptists, 232 235.
Laying on of hands after baptism, 388.
Leander, bishop of Seville, letter of Gregory to, 49.
Legate, Bartholomew, burned in Smithfield, 289.
Legislation in the church, sin of, 53.
Leo the Great, 49.
Lewes, in Sussex, Baptists fined in, 343
Lichtenstein, Prince, 145.
Lingard on mode of baptism, 87.
Lollards, 104, 121, 143.
Lombers, Baptists at, 139.
Long imprisonments of ministers, 390.
Lucius, King, 37.

Lucius, Pope, proscribes Arnoldists, 138, 139.
Lunsford, Lewis, 562, 563.
Luther, 151; burns pope's bull, 160.

MACGOWAN, JOHN, 512.
Maine, Baptists in, 538.
Manes, his system, 67.
Manichæans, their system a compound of Oriental philosophy and Christianity, 67; common to call all opponents by this name, 68.
Mannings, the, Dr. James, 546, 569; Edward and James, 551.
Mantz, Felix, martyr, 180-182.
Martin V., Pope, orders Wycliffe's bones to be burned, 120; views of, 142.
Mass, origin of word, 43.
Matthys, Jan, at Munster, 250; killed, 251.
Marshall, Daniel, 554, 556-558.
Marshall, Rev. Mr., 531.
Maryland, Baptists in, 537.
Mason, Rev. Nathan, 550.
Massachusetts, Baptists in, 463-475; 529-531.
Maxcy, Dr., 547.
Mendicant orders, 118, 119.
Menno, 156, 199, 211; life of, 212-221; works of, 221-224.
Mercer, Silas, 567; Dr. Jesse, 568.
Meshovius, testimony to Baptists, 179.
Messer, Dr., 547.
Meyster, Leonard, put to death, 161.
Middleton, Humphrey, burned, 242.
Miles, John, of Swansea, 479.
Milton, John, lines on intolerance, 311.
Missions, Baptist, Foreign, beginning of in England, 502; an era in history, 575; beginning in United States, 576; Home, beginning of, in England, 503; do., in United States, 576.
Missionaries, Baptist, 580.
Monmouth's Rebellion, 364.
Monthly concert, 501.
Moravia, Baptists expelled from, 266.
Moulton Ebenezer, 549.

Munster, madmen cf, 249-256; disowned by Baptists of their day, 256.
Munzer, Thomas, 161-163.

NEANDER on infant baptism, 17.
Neglecting worship, censure for, 346, 483.
Netherlands, Baptist martyrs in, 195-211.
New Hampshire, Baptists in, 538.
New Lights, 535.
New York, Baptists in, 537.
Nice, Council at, in regard to heretical books, 88.
Nidermair, Hans, put to death, 166.
"Noble Lesson, the," Waldensian book, 106.
Nonconformists, 331, 332.
North British Review on infant baptism, 16.
North Carolina, Baptists in, 537.
Nova Scotia, Baptists in, 549-551.
Novatian, his imperfect baptism, 36, 55; his history, 56.
Novatians, 55; the Puritans of the early church, 56; first Anabaptists, 57.

OATES, SAMUEL, indicted for murder, for baptizing, 314.
Ohio, Baptists in, 540.
Orchard's " History of Baptists," mistakes in, 69.
Origen, 30-32.
Orleans, ten heretical canons at, 82.
Otto of Frisingen on Arnold, 137.

PARKER, ARCHBISHOP, 248.
Parkhurst, Bishop, winks at Baptists, 247.
Particular Baptist Church, first one in England, 302.
Particular Baptist fund, 487.
Patient, Thos., letter to Cromwell by, 320.
Paulicians, origin, 71; martyrdom of, 76; take up arms, 77; seek aid of Saracens, 77; doctrines and practices, 77-81; enter Europe, 85; in Italy, 97.
Pearce, Samuel. 521.

INDEX.

Pearson, Nicholas, 550.
Peasant war, 163, 164.
Peckham, Archbishop, in London, 116.
Pelagianism, 62.
Pelagius, his teachings, 62.
Periodicals, Baptist, 583.
"Persecution Judged and Condemned," 294.
Persecution, origin of, 53.
Peter of Bruys, 98, 122; labors of, 127; martyrdom, 131; Mr. Walls on, 134.
Peter the Venerable on progress of reform, 130.
Phil. Association, 541; corresponds with London ministers, 542; books sent to, Ib.; letter from, to London, 544.
Philip II., edict against Baptists, 198.
Philpot, Archdeacon, harsh opinion of Joan Boucher, 236; 244.
Photius writes against the Paulicians, 72.
Petrus Siculus, writes against the Paulicians, 72.
Pichner, Hans, tortured, 174.
Pieters, Jan, burned in Smithfield, 278.
Piggott, John, 522.
Plurality of elders, 385.
Polycarp, 22.
Poor men of Lyons, 98.
Powell, Vavasor, 328; the "Whitefield of Wales," 412; death in prison, 416.
Prayer answered, 437, 459.
Preaching, success of, 111; papacy adopts, 112.
Presbyterians of seventeenth century abhorred toleration, 308-317; objections to the English Establishment, 323.
Puritans, 285.

REFORMERS, spread of, 116.
Reinerus Saccho, anecdote of one of the Cathari, 104; against Waldenses, 106.
'Religion's Peace," 292.
Reynerson, Tjaert, martyr, 199.
Rhode Island, Baptists in, 475-478.
Rhode Island College, 546-548.
Richardson, Samuel, pamphlet on toleration, 312.
Ridley persecutes Baptists, 234, 236

Robinson, Robert, 496, 498, 513-515.
Rogers, John, martyr, 236.
Russell, John, 470.
Ryland, John C., 515.

SALZBURG, martyrdoms at, 166.
Samson, singular notion of, 87.
Sandys, bishop of London, 270; his sermon before Parliament, 272.
Satler, Michael, martyr, 165.
Savoy Conference, 323.
Scammon, Mrs., her zeal, 538.
Schism Bill, 492.
Schlaffer, Hans, beheaded, 165.
Schnabet, George, disputes with Bucer, 170.
Schoener, Leonard, martyrdom, 165.
Scholastic philosophy, 94.
Scholastic theology, Hallam's account of, 93.
Schoolmen, 95; names and titles, Ib.
Scriptures, translations pleaded for, 101.
Sears, Dr. Barnas, 548.
Segerson, Jeronimus and Lysken, martyrs, 202.
Semisch on Justin Martyr, 22.
Serampore Mission, 502.
Sergius, an eminent Paulician, 75; his conversion, labors, and martyrdom, 76.
Seward, Mrs., 526.
Simeon, a Paulician convert, 73.
Simons, Joriaen, martyr, colporteur, 205, 226.
Simplician, bishop of Milan, consulted, 60.
Singing in worship, 387, 463.
Siricius, bishop of Rome, consulted, 60.
Skepp, John, 505.
Smith, Hezekiah, D.D., 568.
Smithfield, burnings in, 233.
Smyth, John, confession of faith of church in Amsterdam, 287-289.
Snyder, Leopold, beheaded, 166.
Societies, Baptist, 579.
Socinianism, 152.
Speronistæ, 100.
"Standing Order" in New England, 528
Spilsbury, John, 303 392.

Stearns, Shubael, 553-556.
Steele, Miss Anne, 526.
Steinborn, cruelty at, 171.
Stennells, the, 516-519.
Stephen II., Pope, sanctions infant baptism with wine, 87.
Stillman, Samuel, D.D., 570.
Strict communion, 386.
Stuart, Moses, on infant baptism, 17.
Sturgion, John, his "Plea for Toleration," 327.
Support of church, refusing to contribute toward worthy of discipline, 486.
Sutcliffe, John, 501.
Swansea, church at, 471; 479.
Swarte, Jan de, martyrdom with wife and children, 208, 209, 228.
Switzerland, Baptists in, 178-188, 268.

TAVERNER, SAMUEL, 457.
Tennessee, Baptists in, 539.
Terrill, Edward, 627.
Tertullian, 27-30.
Terwoort, Hendrick, his martyrdom in Smithfield, 278.
Texerants, 100.
Theodora, Empress, puts to death one hundred thousand Paulicians, 76.
Theological institutions, Baptist, 582.
Thomas, David, 565.
Toleration Act, 1689, 492.
Tombes, John, B.D., 319, 421; his works, 422.
"Triers, The," 319.
Trine immersion, 49.

UNIVERSITIES, foundations of, 96.
University of Paris, 96.
Utrecht, Union of, its provisions, 264; gives rest to churches, Ib.

VAN BYLER, GERRIT, his firmness, 272.
Van den Houte, Soetgen, 158.
Van der Sach, Franciscus, martyr, 177, 228.
Van Pare, George, martyr, 239.

Van Straten, Hans, 282.
Vaser, Juriaen, minister, martyr, 229.
Vaughan, Dr., on views of Wycliffe, 142
Venner's Rebellion, 325; Baptists protest against, 326.
Verbeek, Joos, martyr, minister, 207.
Vermont, Baptists in, 538.
Vienna, police of, capture Baptists, 171.
Virginia, Baptists in, 532, 536.

WADDINGTON on Novatian, 57.
Waldenses, 98; were Baptists, 146, 147
Waldo, Peter, 98, 144, 145.
Waller, John, 563, 564.
Wallin, Benjamin, 522.
Wallin, Edward, 522.
Walls, Mr., statement of, 134.
Ward, Dr. John, fund for ministers' education, 491.
Wayland, Dr. Francis, 547.
Whitgift, his invectives against the Baptists, 280, 281.
Widows' Fund, English, 490.
Wightman, Edward, burned at Lichfield, 290.
William of Newbury, 139.
William, Prince of Orange, aided by Baptists, 262; respected rights of conscience, 263; favors Baptists of Holland, Ib.; noble answer of, 264; 492.
Williams, Roger, 460, 464; sketch of, 471-477.
Wilson, Samuel, 523.
Wippe, Joris, martyr, 206.
Worship of English churches, 535.
Wright, Joseph, 457.
Wycliffe opposes mendicants, 119; retires to Lutterworth, Ib.; translates Bible, 120; books and bones ordered to be burned, 120.

ZACHARY, POPE, says immersion necessary to baptism, 86.
Zwingli, nearly became a Baptist, 178.
Zurich, Baptists drowned at, 181.

THE BAPTIST STANDARD BEARER, INC.
A non-profit, tax-exempt corporation
committed to the Publication & Preservation
of The Baptist Heritage.

SAMPLE TITLES FOR PUBLICATIONS AVAILABLE IN OUR VARIOUS SERIES:

THE BAPTIST *COMMENTARY* SERIES
Sample of authors/works in or near republication:
John Gill - *Exposition of the Old & New Testaments (9 & 18 Vol. Sets)*
 (Volumes from the 18 vol. set can be purchased individually)

THE BAPTIST *FAITH* SERIES:
Sample of authors/works in or near republication:
Abraham Booth - *The Reign of Grace*
Abraham Booth - *Paedobaptism Examined (3 Vols.)*
John Gill - *A Complete Body of Doctrinal Divinity*

THE BAPTIST *HISTORY* SERIES:
Sample of authors/works in or near republication:
Thomas Armitage - *A History of the Baptists (2 Vols.)*
Isaac Backus - *History of the New England Baptists (2 Vols.)*
William Cathcart - *The Baptist Encyclopaedia (3 Vols.)*
J. M. Cramp - *Baptist History*

THE BAPTIST *DISTINCTIVES* SERIES:
Sample of authors/works in or near republication:
Alexander Carson - *Ecclesiastical Polity of the New Testament Churches*
E.C. Dargan - *Ecclesiology: A Study of the Churches*
J. M. Frost - *Paedobaptism: Is It From Heaven?*
R. B. C. Howell - *The Evils of Infant Baptism*

THE *DISSENT & NONCONFORMITY* SERIES:
Sample of authors/works in or near republication:
Champlin Burrage - *The Early English Dissenters (2 Vols.)*
Franklin H. Littell - *The Anabaptist View of the Church*
Albert H. Newman - *History of Anti-Paedobaptism*
Walter Wilson - *History & Antiquities of the Dissenting Churches (4 Vols.)*

For a complete list of current authors/titles, visit our internet site at
www.standardbearer.com or write us at:

The Baptist Standard Bearer, Inc.
No. 1 Iron Oaks Drive • Paris, Arkansas 72855

Telephone: (501) 963-3831   Fax: (501) 963-8083
E-mail: baptist@arkansas.net
Internet: http://www.standardbearer.com

www.ingramcontent.com/pod-product-compliance
Lightning Source LLC
Chambersburg PA
CBHW022005300426
44117CB00005B/38